Origami Tessellations *for Everyone* 2

29+ Original Designs by Ilan Garibi

Hand-Drawn Diagrams by Franziska Schwarz

Origami Tessellations for Everyone 2

How to find me:

Internet Site: www.garibiorigami.com

E-mail: garibiilan@gmail.com

Facebook: Ilan Garibi

Instagram: garibiilan

Designer: Elina Gor

Cover image: verso view of Mystery tessellation (page 140) from chamois elephant hide paper.

ISBN: 978-965-92700-4-0

To my mother, who bought me my first origami book, and started a chain reaction, in which a flip of pages in my childhood changed completely my life, 30 years after.

Acknowledgments

It took ten years to make volume one, and only two for the second. The collection of models here is based on the same time span, the last 12 years, with just a few designs coming to light after the first volume was out.

The level of models in this book is higher than volume 1. That is why I strongly recommend you to go through the first volume, or at least download the free sample from Origami-shop.com. There you have the full version of chapter 1, which explains all the basic tools and knowledge in detail. Here chapter 1 is brief and short.

The projects here are more demanding and the complexity is higher. The molecules are more acrobatic and flexible. With small changes in their parameters, you can achieve a big change in the outcome. And this is exactly what makes it into a huge playground you can explore and enjoy.

The models are divided into families, and like in real life, some are more closed and connected, and others are less attached. The circular models are a family by marriage only, while the Zipper one is made from first-relation kins.

This book is a natural development from the first volume and benefits from the same structure and graphic design thanks to the hand-drawn diagrams of Franziska W. Schwarz, and the touches of Elina Gor, my graphic designer.

My group of test folders and proofreaders—Maria Sinayskaya, Inbar and Alona Duani, my professional mini team, Kathleen Sheridan, and Wojtek Burczyk—showed me friendship and support, making this book a better one!

—Ilan Garibi

I started Origami at the age of 6 ...and until now I never ran out of paper...

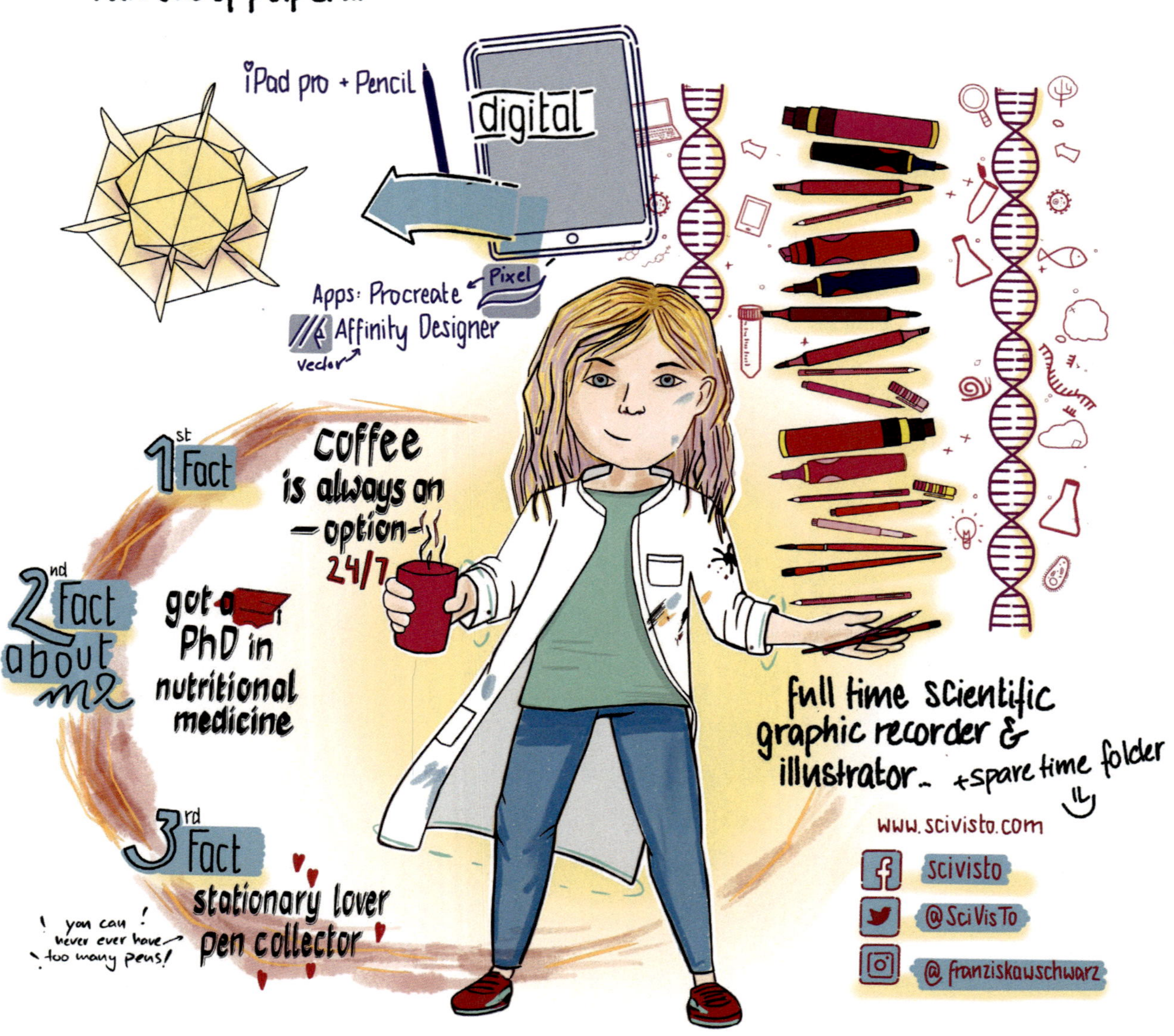

—*Franziska Schwarz*

Contents

Introduction

What Is an Origami Tessellation?

Tessellation is a mosaic. In other words, it is a covering of an infinite geometric plane with repetitive geometric shapes, without gaps or overlaps. In origami, it is the name we give geometric origami folded with a single sheet of paper. There are many categories and subcategories—corrugations, curved tessellations, and self-similarity folds, to name a few.

The core property of origami tessellations is the use of a single sheet of paper. A fold (or a group of folds) is repeated again and again and in all directions. In this book, this grouping is called a **molecule**.

Some tessellations are based on a square grid while others use a grid made of equilateral triangles that form hexagons.

Why Does It Work?

The molecule must have two main properties.

First, each molecule must be fully rotationally symmetric, which means it looks the same if rotated by 90° or 180°; it should be a design that has every two parallel edges identical. The common case is to have the same pattern of folds on all of its four sides.

Second, the edge of the single-molecule is the edge of the original sheet of paper it was folded from. This doesn't just apply to a single molecule; it also applies to a field of molecules. As long as the edges of the molecules lie on the edges of the paper, the rule is satisfied.

If a molecule edge is fully symmetrical, you can add the next one just by shifting the molecule to the side. For some asymmetric design, you have to mirror every two adjacent molecules.

How to Make a Tessellation: the Three Basic Steps

Step 1—Make a grid.

The grid serves two purposes: it provides reference points for all the pre-creases and it almost always plays a role in the molecule structure.

Step 2—Add all pre-creases.

This step includes all the creases beside the grid that are needed to enable a collapse. Most of them are made before you start to collapse. Some, quite rarely, will be added during or after the collapse. Putting in the pre-creases is usually the longest part.

Step 3—Collapse.

The process of executing the folds to form a three-dimensional state is the most challenging and satisfying step. However, the phase in which part of the paper is still flat while another part is already folded may create a tension that isn't always easy to handle. Just saying.

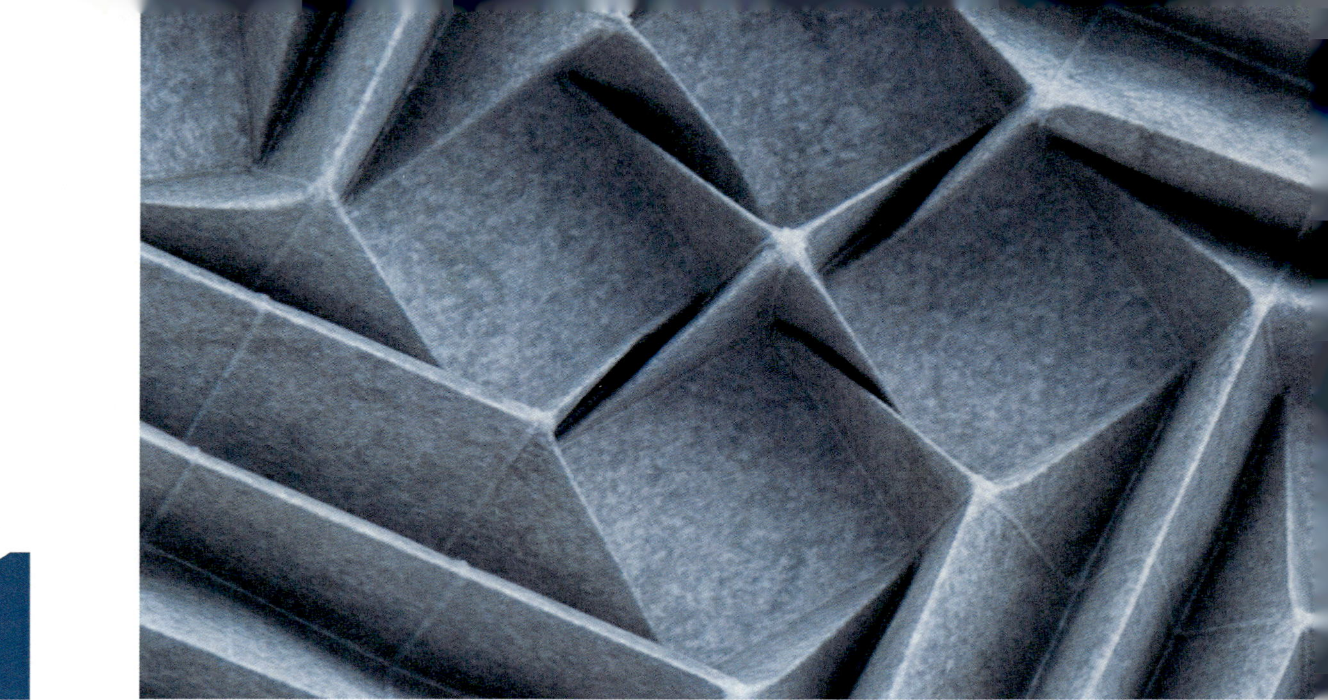

1 How to Use This Book

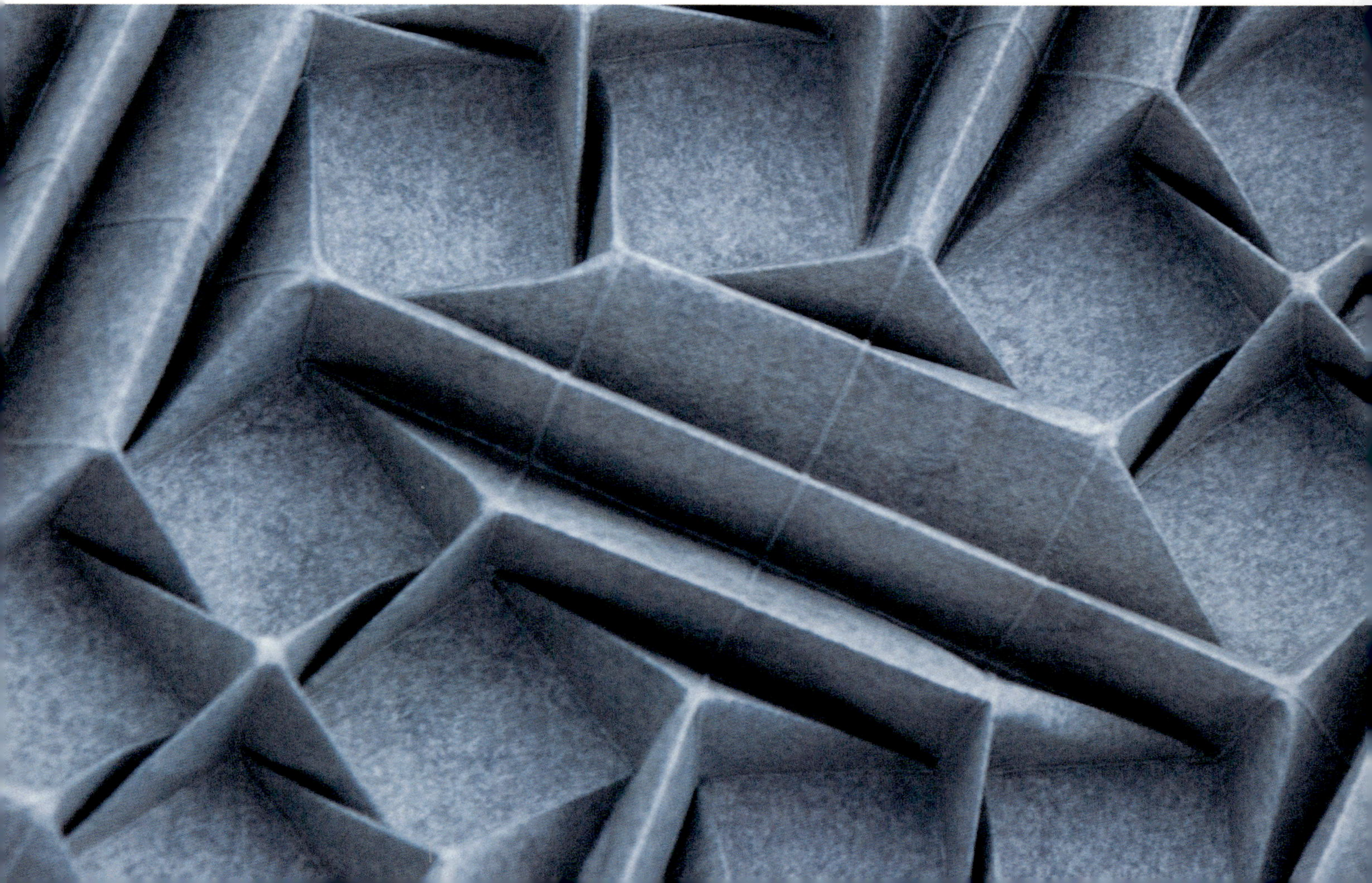

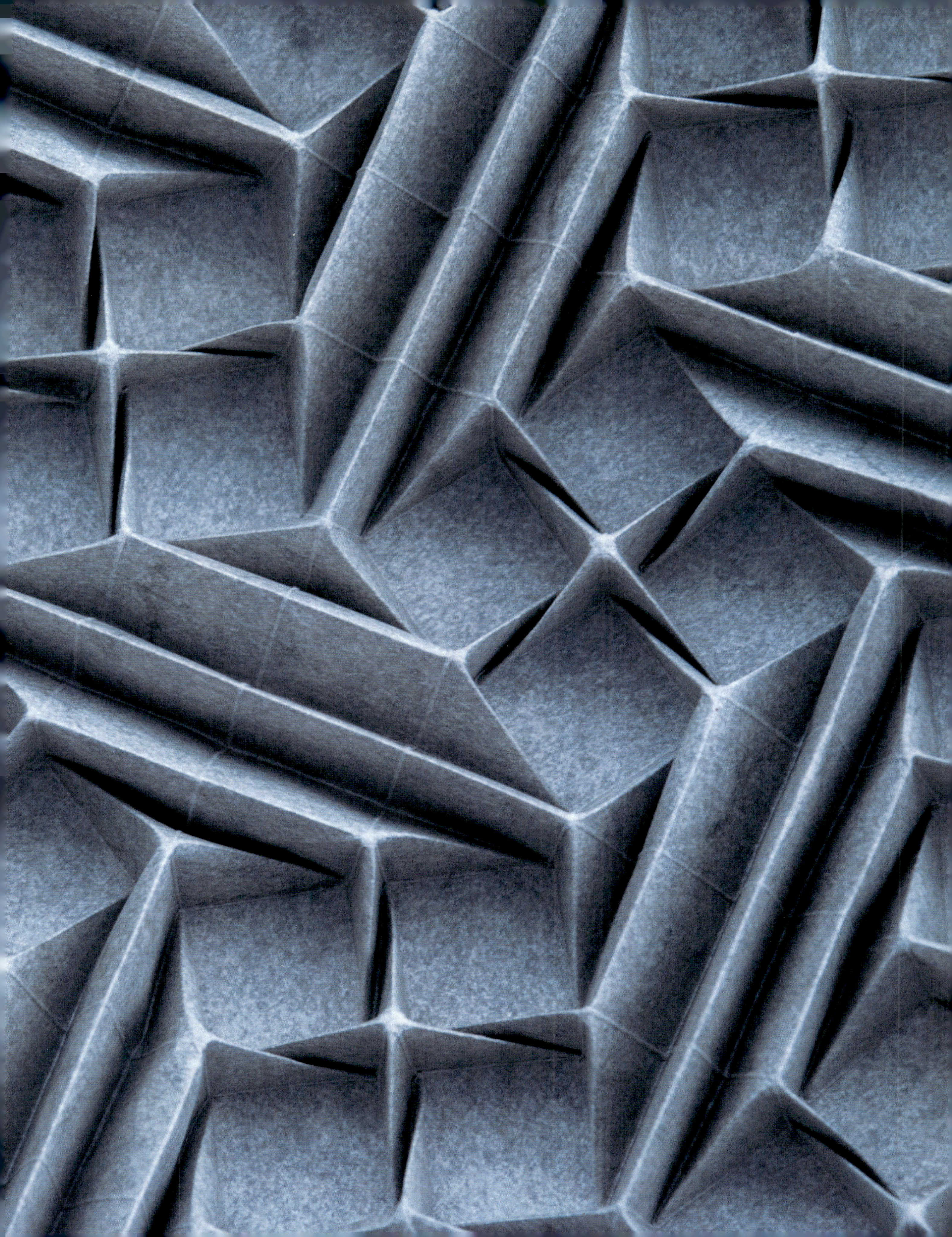

1 1 The Structure of the Book

This book is divided into families of tessellations. Most of the families are based on a certain principle, which is presented in the first (easiest) model.

From there I explore some variations on that principle. Every model is presented in three (or more) stages.

The first stage is always the simplest—*the single molecule*. Learning how to form the single unit will help the folder understand the logic of the molecule and how it collapses.

To keep the diagrams easy to understand, I may not clutter things up by showing all the crease lines that align with the grid. However, they will still be used during the collapse and shown on the complete *crease pattern (CP)* later on.

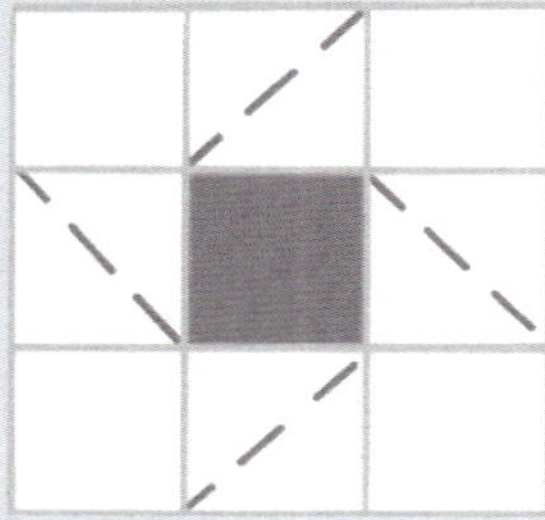

Single molecule, precreases only and no added edges.

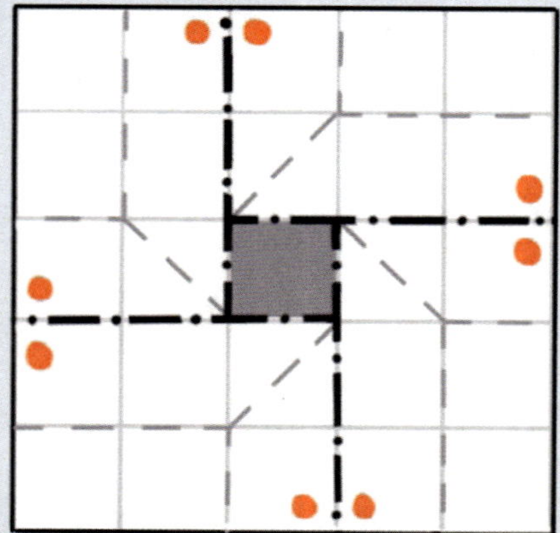

The complete CP (with edges).

While folding a tessellation, it is usually easier to handle it if there's a little extra paper around the edge of the project. A border one square wide goes around the molecule, providing something to hold onto or a place to pinch the sides of the molecules. This extra space is presented on the step-by-step instructions of the single-molecule as well as on the larger projects if needed.

Here I also present how much the molecule shrinks in comparison to the original size of the paper. For example, a shrinkage rate of 5:3 means that the starting size of a molecule was 5 by 5 squares, while the size of the collapsed molecule is 3 by 3 squares.

Next is a *2 by 2 molecule project*. A CP is presented with all pre-creases needed, as well as a 3D isometric projection of the final projects.

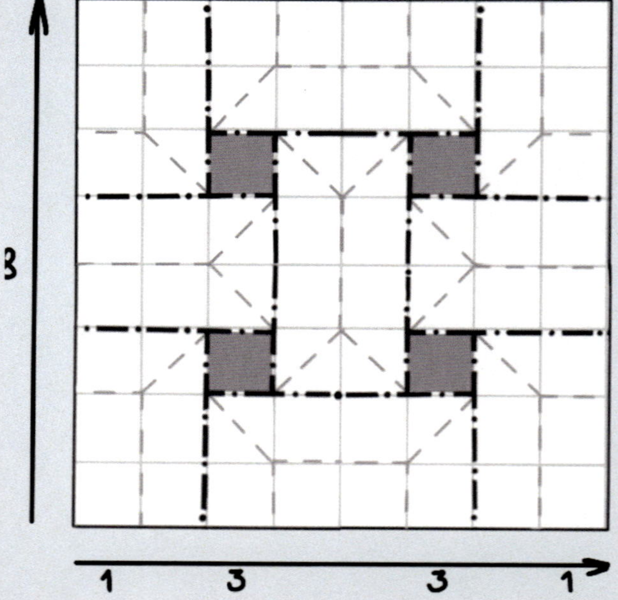

A crease pattern for a 2 by 2 project.

Be aware that the 2 by 2 and 4 by 4 CPs do **not** show all the fold lines. I emitted some of the folds that are aligned with the grid to reduce the intensity of the diagrams and keep them clear. This does not mean those lines are not needed, of course. Follow the instructions of the single-molecule to see the complete picture.

One exception to this rule is the lines that are going from the outer molecules to the raw edges of the paper. I found it helpful for the first steps in the collapse. I always include some general tips and advice at this stage, but each model has its own tricks and I present these as well.

Next is the *4 by 4 project*, complete with step-by-step instructions, a full CP, and my recommended shortcuts, special techniques to make the process as efficient as possible.

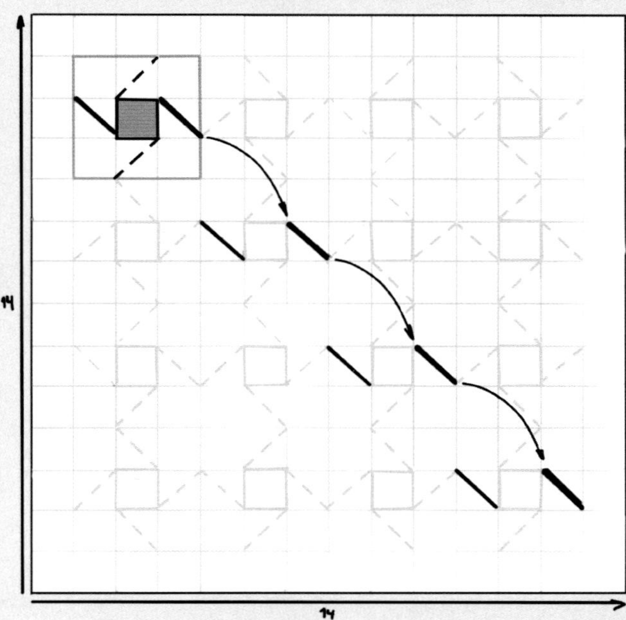

This crease pattern shows the placement of many molecules and my recommendation for folding shortcuts.

For full projects, I suggest having a wider frame, with two and even three, extra columns and rows.

Images at the beginning present the 4 by 4 project from both sides and can help you to understand the mechanics of the collapse. In relevant cases, there is an image of the model with back-light.

Another important feature of the 4 by 4 CP is the ***grid size***. The vertical axis represents the total number of rows, while the horizontal axis is divided into columns with a numerical sequence. For example, the Mexico tessellation has a grid sequence expressed like this: [2 + 4 × 5 + 2 = 24]. This tells you that you need a grid 24 squares tall and 24 squares wide, or more simply a grid of 24.

For each specific project, I show the size of the collapsed project, including the extra rows and columns.

Here I present the final size (in squares) of the resulting model.

Last, ***Above and Beyond*** shows the potential of the molecule, either by showing a large-scale model or a special use for the design, like a pendant or wall tiles.

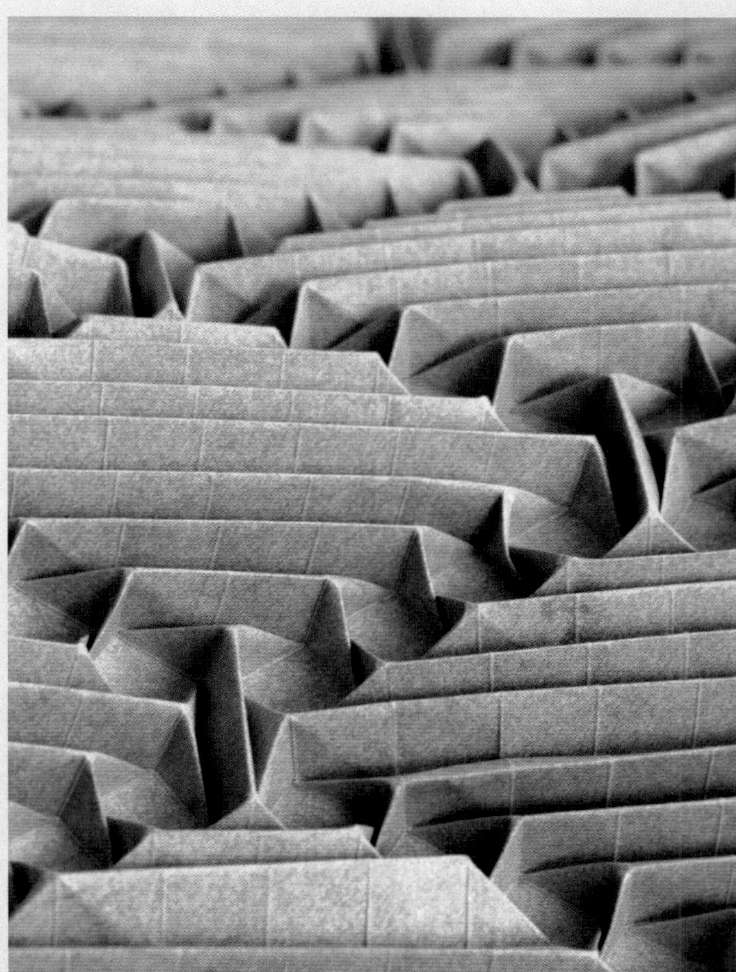

1 2 How to Read the Diagrams

Unlike traditional origami diagrams with arrows and fold-as-you-go instructions, the diagrams here show the slow transformation of a flat sheet of paper into an object with dimensionality. But there are still some symbols that you must learn in order to make the right folds and execute the collapse properly.

Symbols

In some models, I use the traditional symbol system:

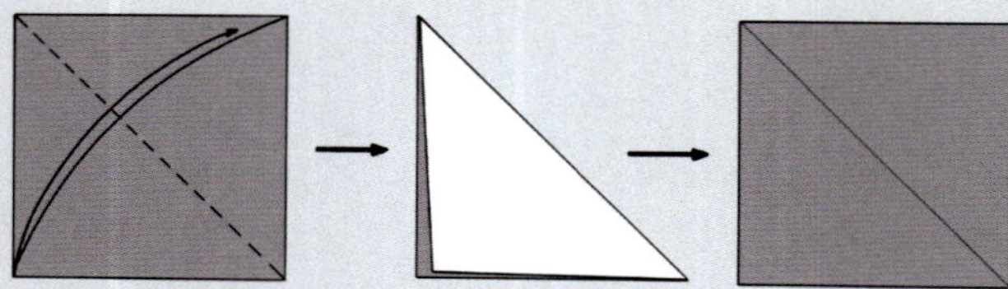

A *valley fold* is marked with a dashed line. In traditional diagrams, an arrow will accompany it. The paper is always folded forward from the tail of the arrow to its head. *Fold and unfold* is shown using a double-headed arrow, back and forth. Note that after the paper is unfolded, a thin crease line appears. The grid creases are always shown with these thin lines.

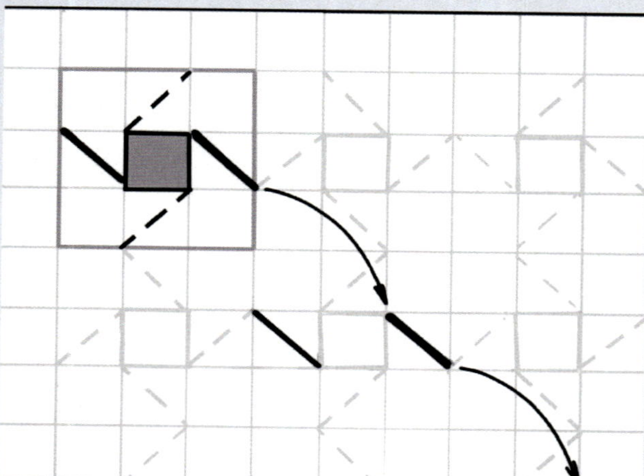

I also use *arrows* to indicate the workflow of my recommended shortcuts. In this figure, the bold lines indicate where to put the valley folds and the arrows indicate where to skip to next on the same diagonal. Here the arrow tells you to skip diagonally across two squares to find the next valley to fold. This is true of all the valleys on the CP.

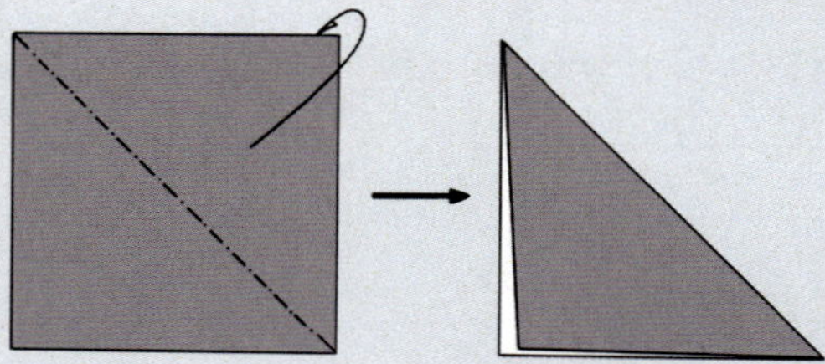

A *mountain fold* is marked with a broken dashed line. In a traditional diagram, a hollow arrow head will accompany it, indicating that you should fold behind. I do not use it in this book.

Turn over—a spiraled arrow tells you to flip the paper over to the other side.

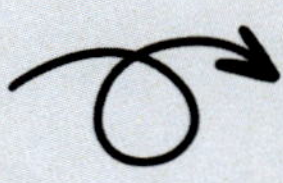

Repeat arrow—an arrow with a notch on its tail asks you to repeat the last command here.

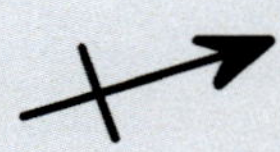

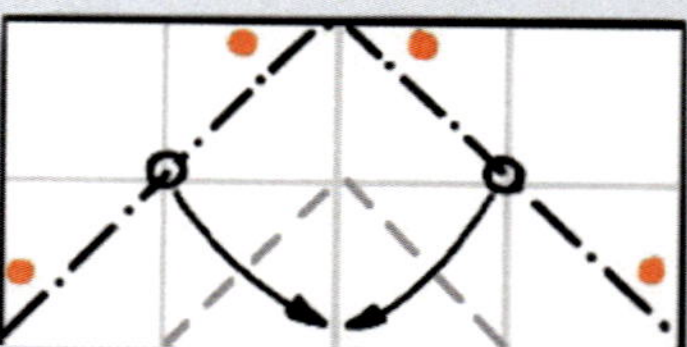

Areas of interest are shown with white circles around them. Red dots are used to show where to *pinch or hold* the paper.

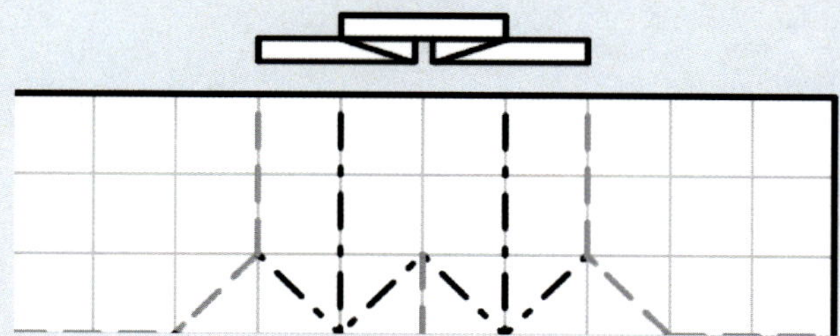

Pleated edges—a zigzag line above or to the side of the model shows how the edges of the paper are folded. This helps you understand how the edges of the molecule are formed.

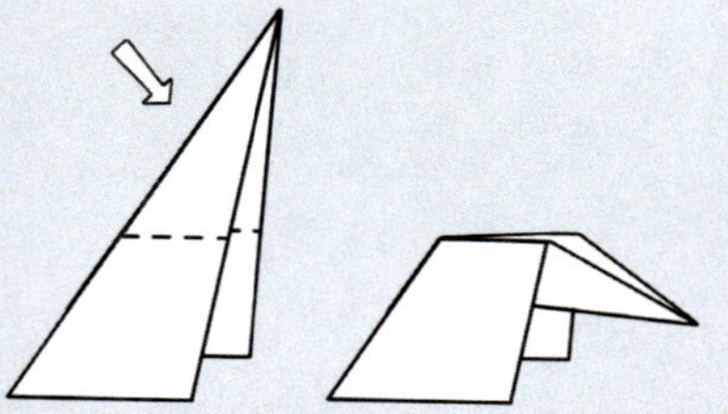

Inside Reverse Fold—a fold line is reversed to switch its orientation. The command is presented by a wide white arrow. Here the upper part of the mountain crease is reversed to be a valley by collapsing inward (hence the name).

1 3 How to Read a Crease Pattern (CP)

A CP holds a lot of information: the size of the grid, the structure of the molecule, and the number of the molecules included in the project. All of this can be found in one handy diagram. Valley and mountain fold lines show where to mark the pre-creases and indicate the orientation of the folds when you are ready to execute the collapse.

As I mentioned earlier, in many tessellations there are ways to make the pre-creasing process much more efficient than molecule by molecule. The idea is to combine creases that are on the same diagonal or straight line in order to minimize the number of times you move or rotate the paper.

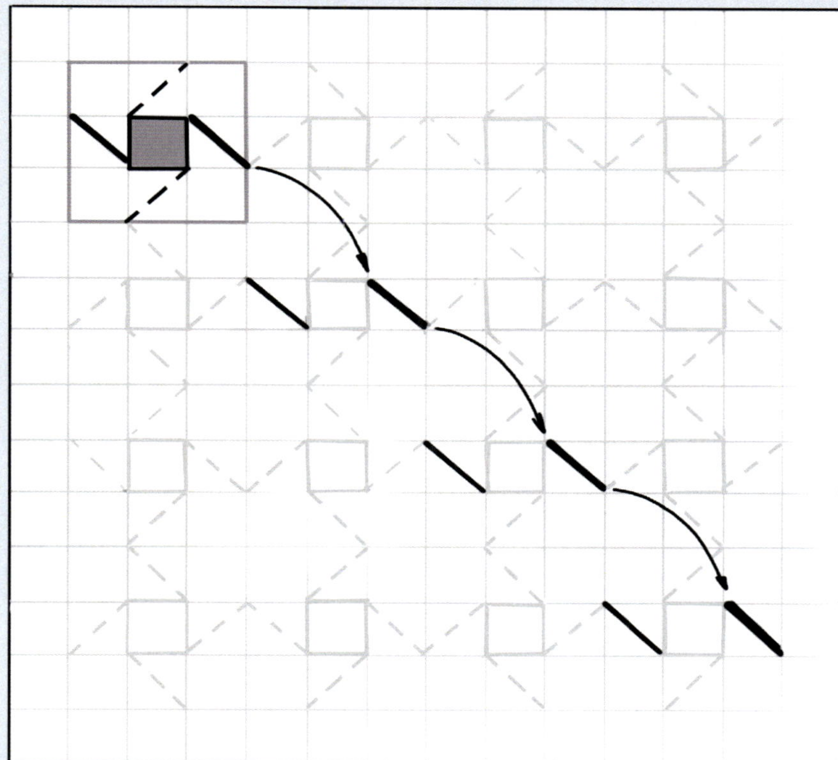

These shortcuts are presented in a workflow or pattern that points out which single-square diagonals to fold and which to skip while your hand is moving along the imaginary line that connects them.

I can't stress enough that you must fold **one square at a time** or your accuracy will be compromised. The lines to be folded are bolded and arrows show which ones to skip.

1 4 Deciding on the Paper Size

As you will notice, I don't provide the paper size in the diagrams; I leave that for the folder to decide.

All you really need to decide on is the size of the molecule, and from there you can determine the grid size (see later on).

A grid made of 2-cm (¾") squares is a good size for beginners. One-cm (⅜") squares would be more of a challenge. Try your hand at any 2 by 2 project, folding molecules of various sizes, before you determine which suits you best.

1 5 Deciding on the Grid Size

All my CPs show the breakdown of the grid width on the horizontal axis.

Most of the tessellations in this book call for a border around the molecules. This border is usually an extra row and column on all sides. This border has two important uses—it is easier to fold the edge molecule with something to hold onto or clip together, and it brings a nice frame to the finished model. Some models will benefit from a wider border, 2 or 3-square wide.

To determine the grid size, you have to calculate the sum of this equation: the width of borders plus [the width of a molecule × the number of molecules]. For example, in the CP on the previous page, there are four molecules and each is three squares wide. Therefore, the total number of squares needed for the molecules alone is 3 × 4, or 12. If we add a row to the left and right, two extra squares need to be counted, for a width of 14 squares. This can be expressed as 1 + 4 × 3 + 1 = 14.

1 6 How to Make a Grid

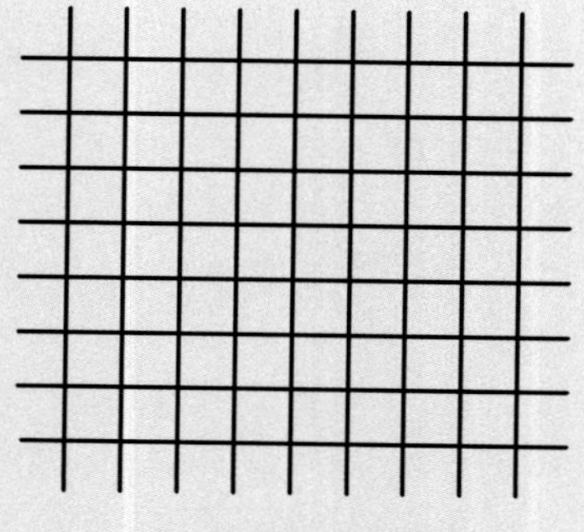

Square grid

Diamond grid

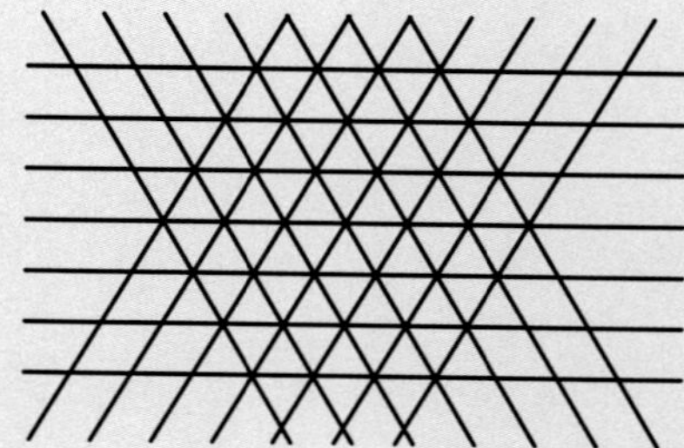

Triangle/Hexagon grid

Tessellations are usually made from grids. A grid can be made from squares or from equilateral triangles that form hexagons (which is why these grids are usually referred to as hexagon grids). Each unit (square, triangle, etc.) is also called a tile.

Grid size is determined by the number of tiles. For a square grid, two numbers are given: for 16 by 16, or for short, grid 16. For a hexagon grid, three numbers are given, one for each pair of parallel edges.

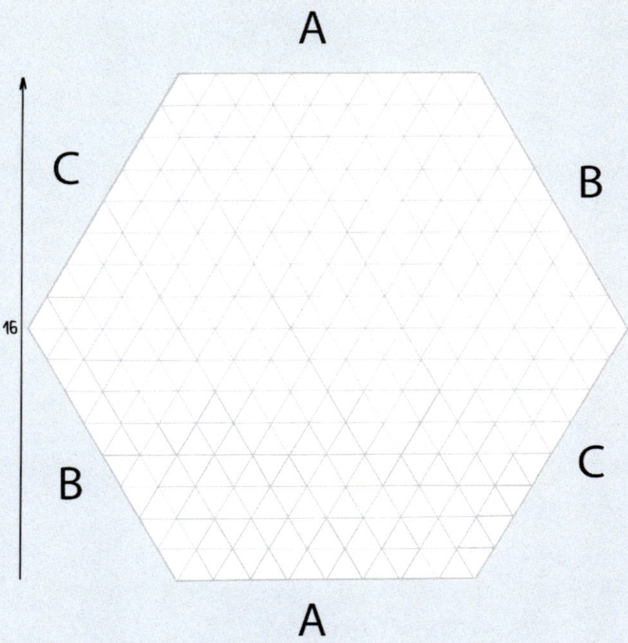

This CP shows 16 rows (15 divisions) between every pair of edges; AA, BB, and CC, so the grid size would be 16 by 16 by 16.

Folding a Grid

To divide an 8 grid to 16, fold crease line to crease line.

The diagram below shows how to get from a grid of four to a grid of eight. In order to get the 3/8 crease, pinch the 1/4 line and fold the edge to the 1/2 line. To get the 23/64 line, pinch the 22nd line to the nearest crease.

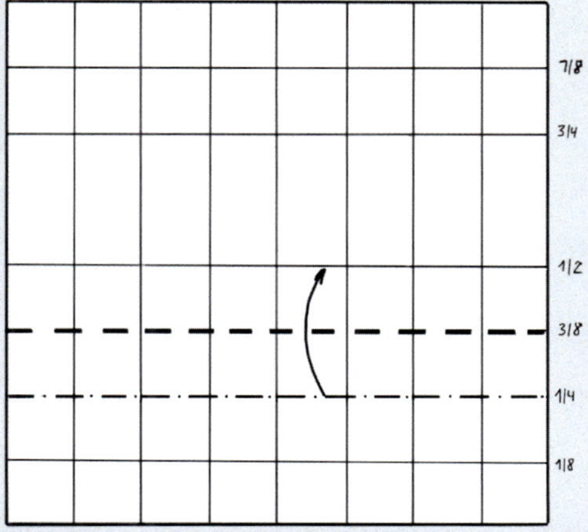

Tips

- I always make my creases bidirectional, meaning, I reverse all of them.
- Rotate the paper 90° after every division.
- Make only mountain folds. If you are asked to make a valley, turn the paper over and fold a mountain.

1 7 How to Precrease

This is the most time-consuming phase. The most basic molecule in this book needs four creases; usually, there are many more.

Luckily, there are shortcuts to this process. Many creases will align and can be folded in one stroke, with or without skipping some squares. The text and diagrams for the 4 by 4 projects include all the shortcuts I found.

Tips

- Long diagonal creases need to be folded one square at a time.

- Mistakes are inevitable. Mark the center of each of the molecules with a pencil or bit of Blu Tack to keep you oriented.
- Remember not to make a pre-crease in the first and last row or column!
- For the pre-ceases, use the side of the paper on which the creases are more evident.

18 How to Collapse

With a square grid, you start at the upper left corner and complete one molecule. Then add another one to the right, working one molecule at a time to complete a row. When you work on a row, make sure all the folds go all the way to the edges of the paper (see image below).

The second molecule of the second row is where the difficulties lie. It is surrounded on two sides with folded molecules and the other two sides are flat paper. If you can manage to fold that second molecule, you can do the rest!

With some tessellations, it is good to partially collapse all molecules in a row, before collapsing each completely, one by one. This saves a bit of work by unfolding creases that will be in your way for the next row.

For a hexagon tessellation, I recommend that you start from the center, making one molecule that has the others clustered around it.

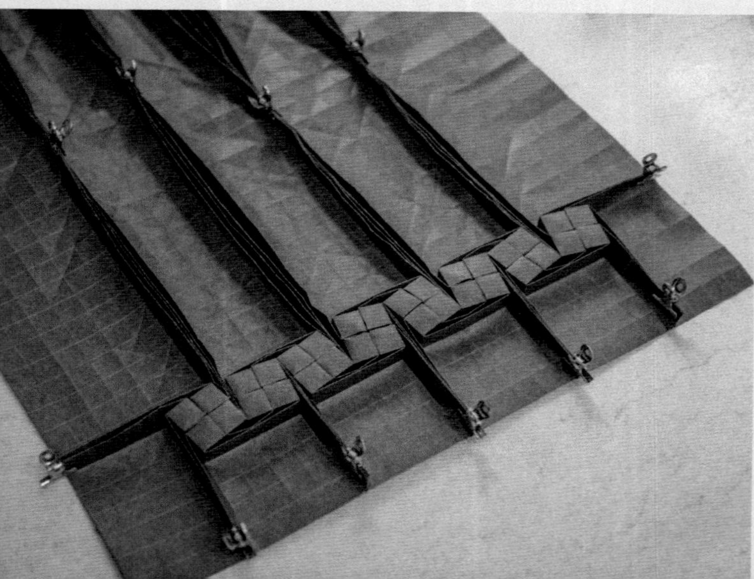

Then you make a ring around the center with six molecules. The last one (and sometimes even the fifth one) may give you some trouble, as it connects with the first one and involves unfolding some pleats made earlier to allow you to work on the paper. When opening the paper, you need to be careful not to unfold the adjoining molecules too much, but some unfolding will be necessary to complete that final molecule. If this proves too difficult, try to fold the fifth and sixth together instead! The folding continues in this fashion, building rings around the center.

Tips

- Take heart! Do not give up! The folder is stronger than the paper.
- Use clips (see the next section) to hold folds and edges in place, if needed.
- There is literally always another side with an origami tessellation. Many times it is easier to work the collapse from both sides of the model. The structure might be more visible to you from the other side and so even easier to handle. Give it a try.
- When folding a tessellation, sometimes you work out that there is a special rhythm or pattern of work that makes things easier. Write it down the moment you realize that sequence. It will help you tremendously the next time you try to fold it.

1 9 The Right Tools for the Job

Clips

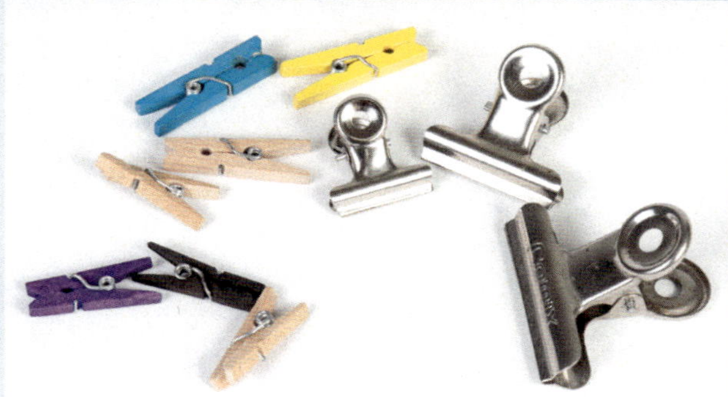

Metal and wooden clips.

Clips, either metal or wood, are a must! The wood ones won't mark your paper, but they are usually not as strong as the metal ones. The metal ones can be too strong, though, and leave unsightly marks on the paper.

Bone Folders

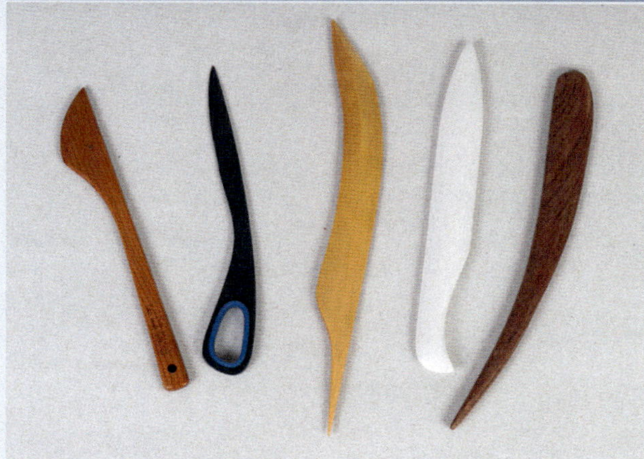

Various types of bone folders.

A bone folder can be used to press the paper into nice, sharp creases. In the long run, it will help you keep your hands healthy. My favorite is the middle one, bought from Origami-Shop (www.origami-shop.com).

Reusable Adhesive Putty

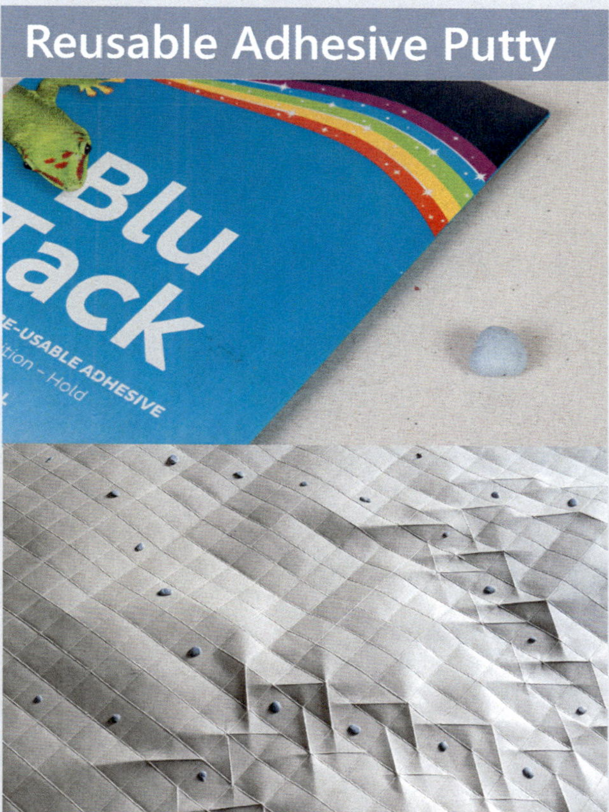

Blu Tack can be used to mark tiles.

I use this to help me keep track of where I am during the long pre-creasing process. I like to use tiny bits to mark the centers of molecules or help me block off the border rows and columns. You could always use light pencil marks, but the putty is easier to see. It can easily be removed without any residue and will help you stay oriented through the entire project.

Cotton Swabs

Cotton swabs are helpful to puff and stretch paper molecules that include a pocket, or a rounded face, without tearing it. Any swab with a soft tip works well.

1 10 Papers Used in the Book

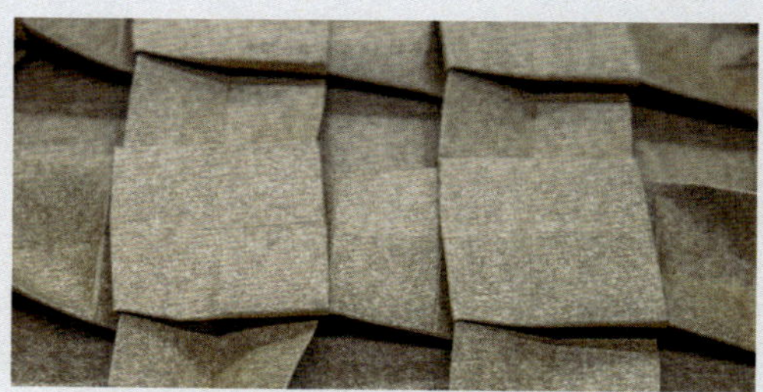

Elephant hide (110 GSM) is probably the best paper for tessellations. It has the best mix of properties that makes folding tessellations from it a joy! The color palette, though, is dull, unless you can find in shops the rare colors that were out of production around 2010!!

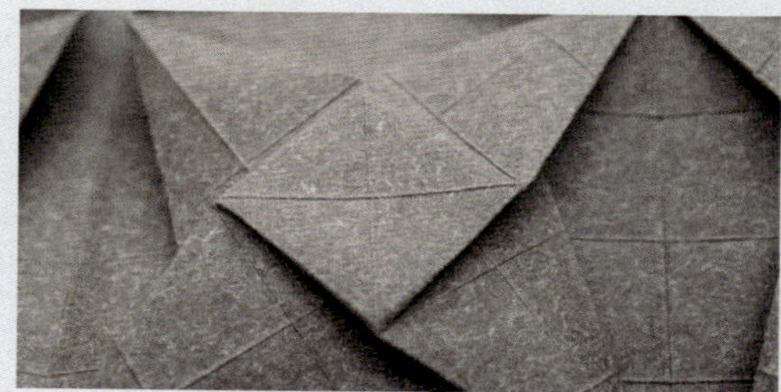

Khepera (120 GSM), is a thick paper, but the texture is so beautiful and interesting, that I just fell in love with it. It is not good for small projects, but it is strong and firm, and the result is beautiful. It may be hard to find it though. The color choices are much better than Elephant hide, and the shades are unique.

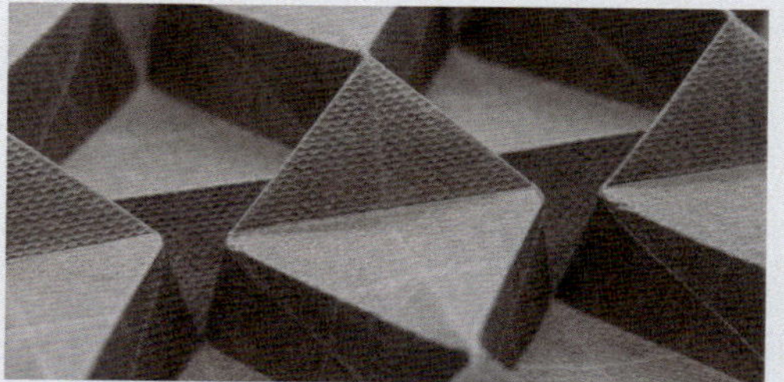

Efalin (120 GSM) is just as thick as Khepera. It comes in a few versions, and the one that I like is embossed. The embossing can be problematic, especially when the crease lines almost align to it. Color choices are the basic set, like blue, green, and red. The colors are bright and solid.

1 11 How to Keep a Tessellation Flat

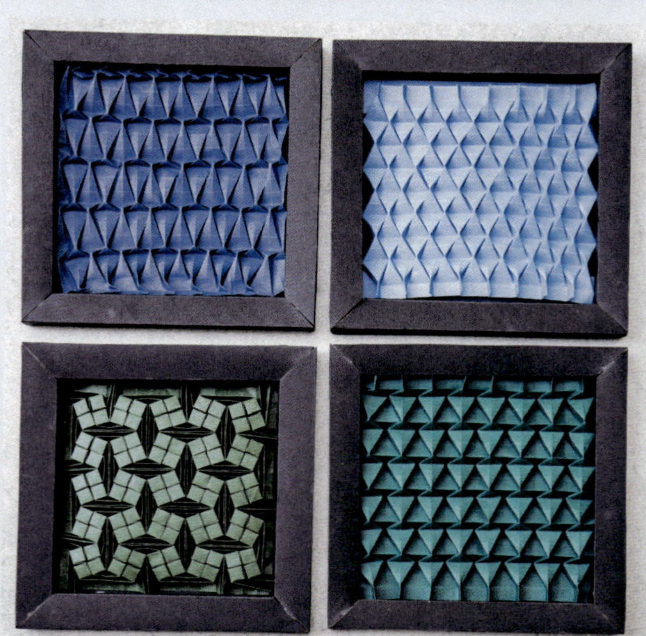

There are several ways to keep your work flat.

On a small scale, I make frames from thick paper, and I fit the model perfectly.

Another way is to spray it with water and let it dry under a heavy plate. After two, sometimes three, cycles, it will hold nicely without the heavy weight.

Option three is to glue the double layers that reach the edges.

Another good piece of advice is to have a wide frame around the model. A bigger frame makes it easier to glue. With most of the models here it is wise to use 2 or 3 squares for the frame, even 4 or 5!

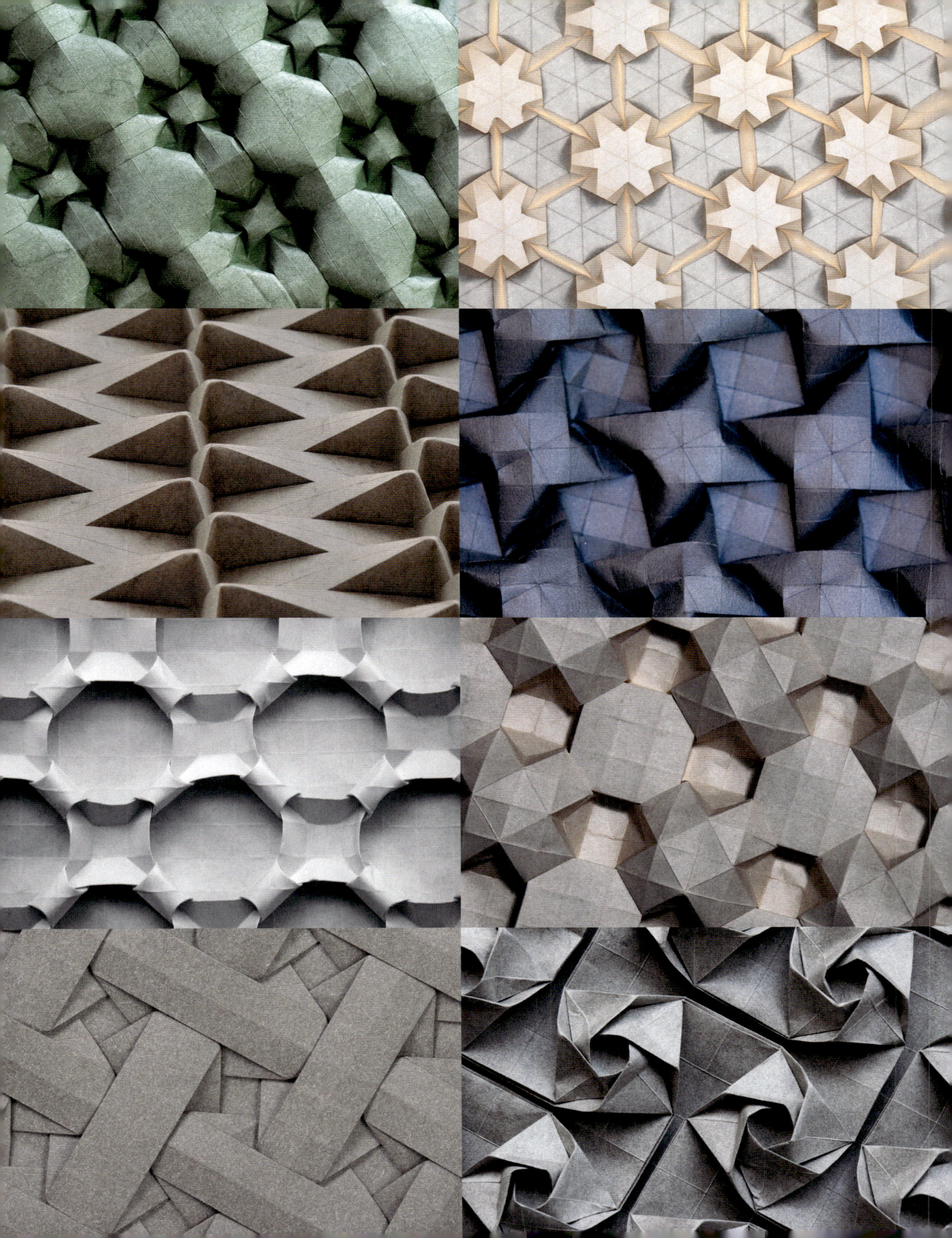

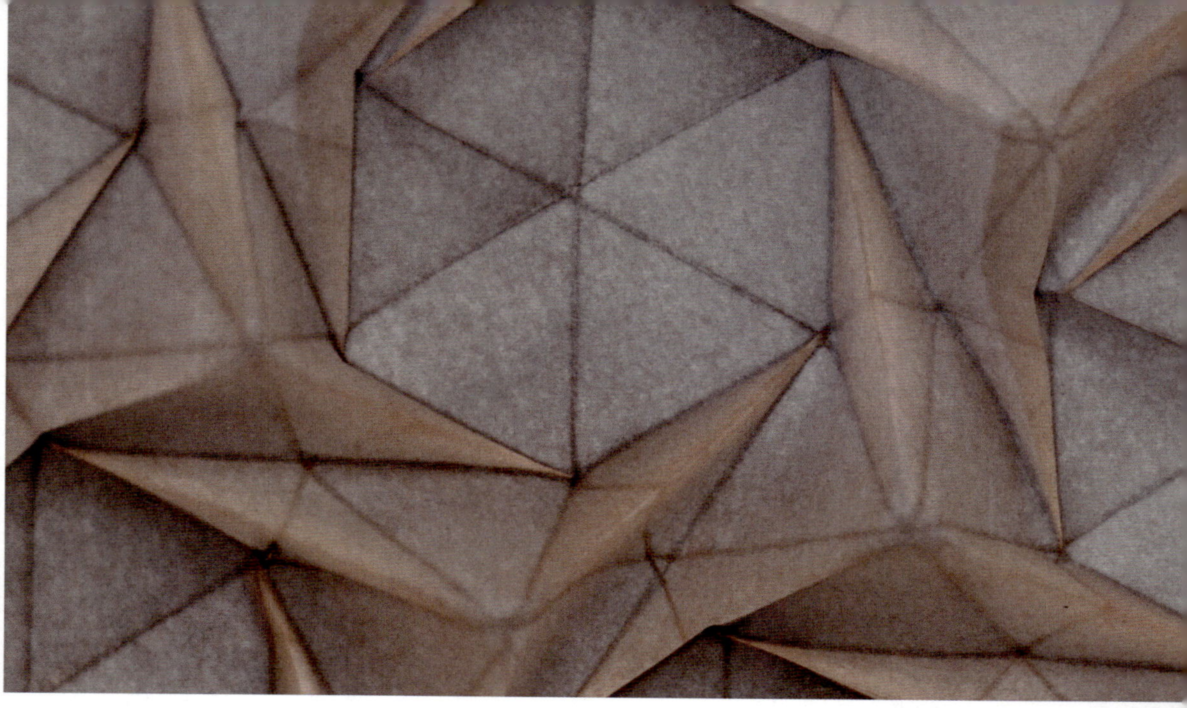

2
The Advanced Cube Family

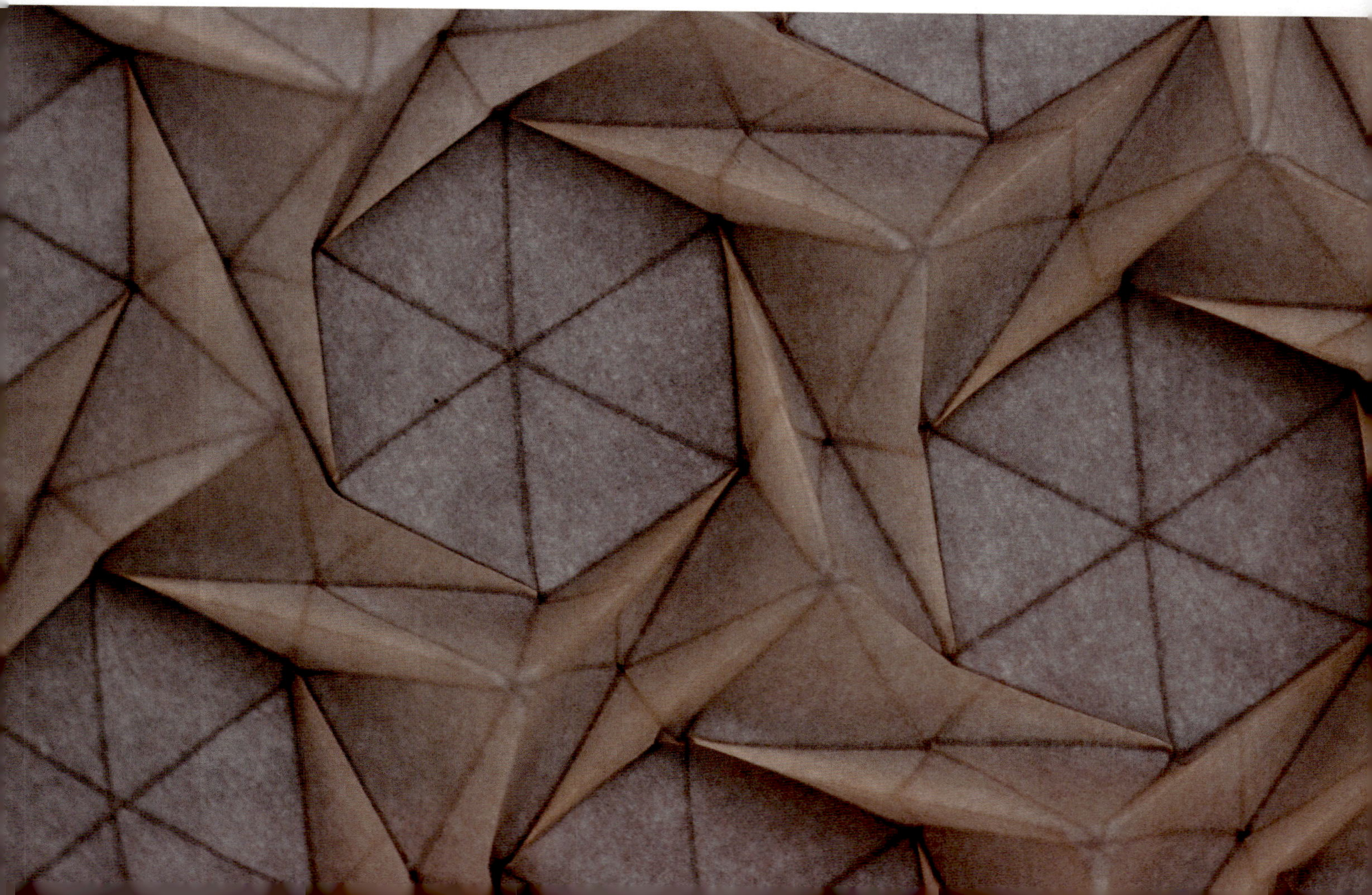

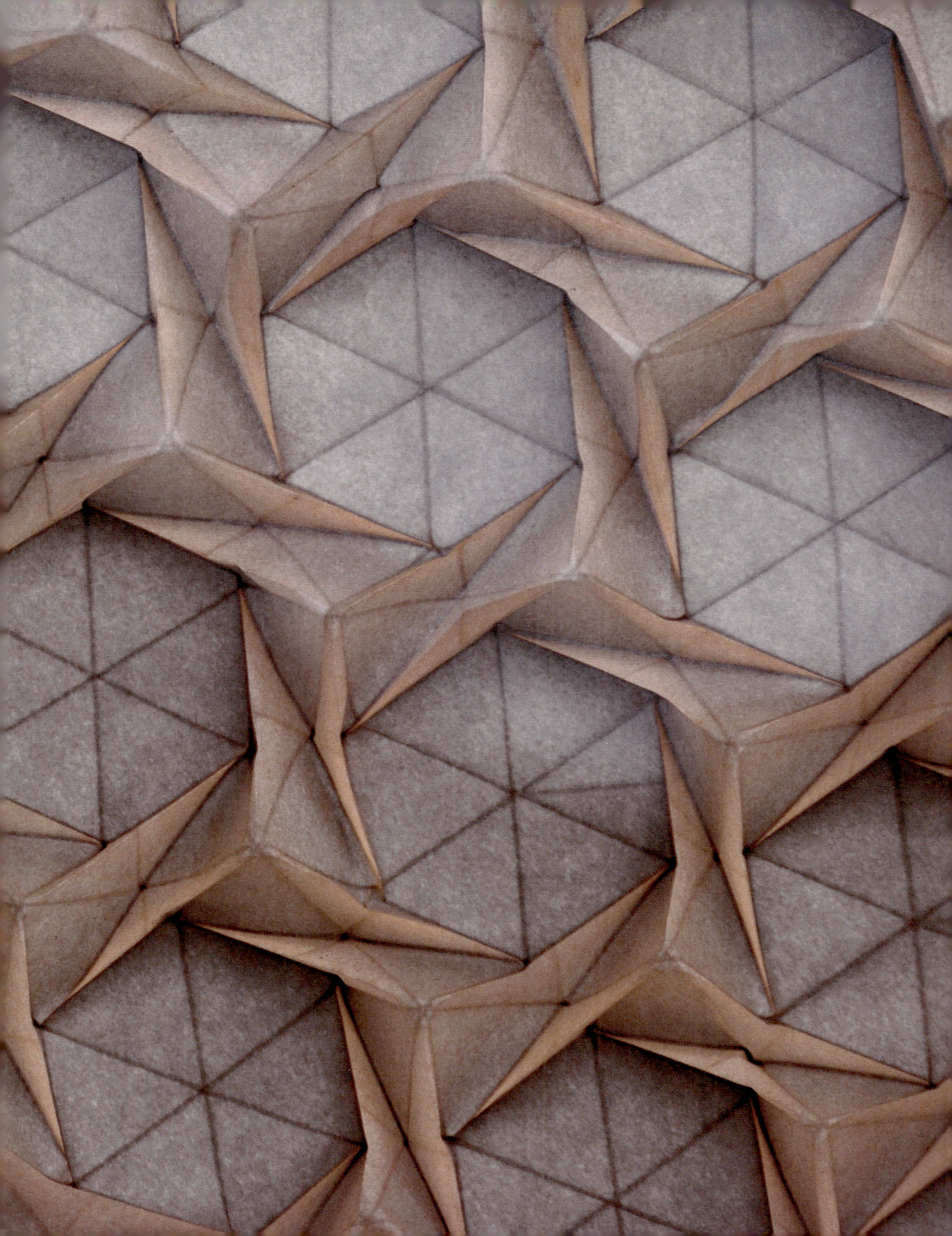

Introduction

The Cube tessellation family is based on a 3D molecule with a simple structure. It uses a grid of 3 by 3 squares with only four additional creases. From this simple starting point, there are many ways to make variations. The main ones are presented in my first book, *"Origami Tessellations for Everyone"*.

In this chapter, we have more variations on this theme. For example, the Waterbomb tessellation is transformed into a molecule, or the core of the molecule is transformed from a square to a hexagon.

In all cases, the collapse is accomplished by rotating the middle square. It's like a twist fold, that creates volume.

2 1 Cube and Waterbomb

Cube

The Single Molecule

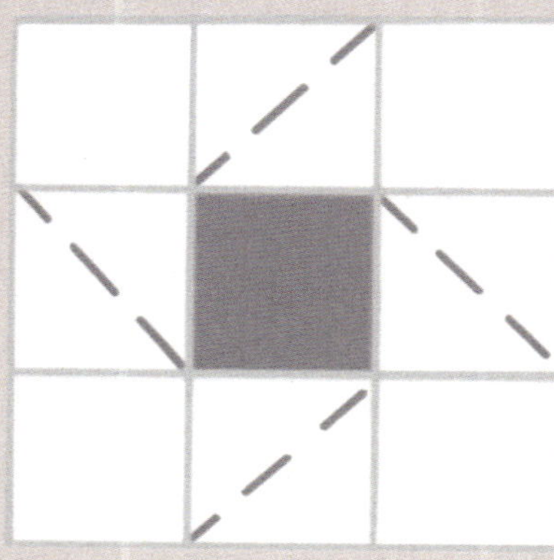

The simplest molecule in this family is a cube made of a 3 by 3 grid.

While the cube is formed, the central square (in gray) is rotated by 90°, counterclockwise.

Molecules are tessellated by mirroring, which means that every two adjacent molecules are mirror images of each other.

The shrinkage ratio is 3:1.

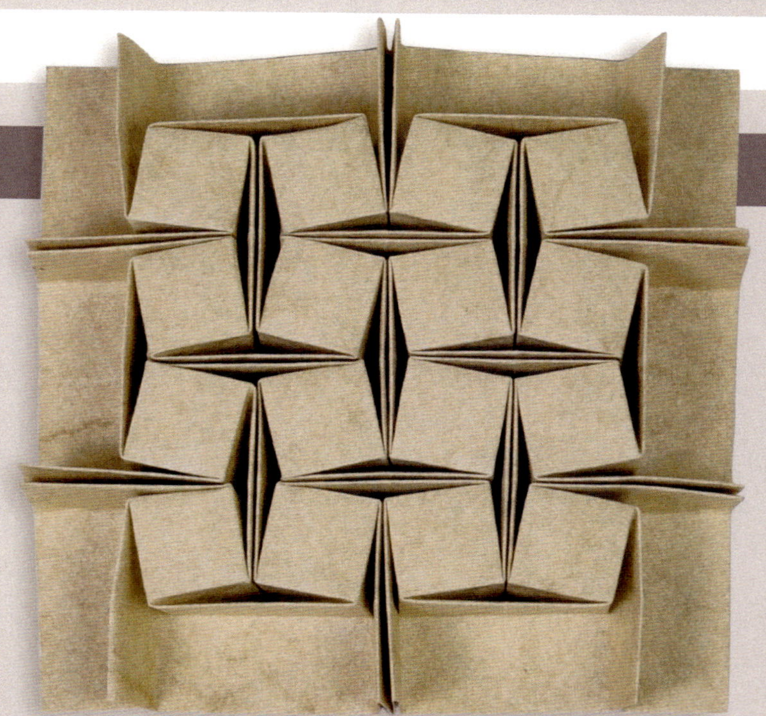

Recto view of a 4 by 4–molecule Cubes tessellation.

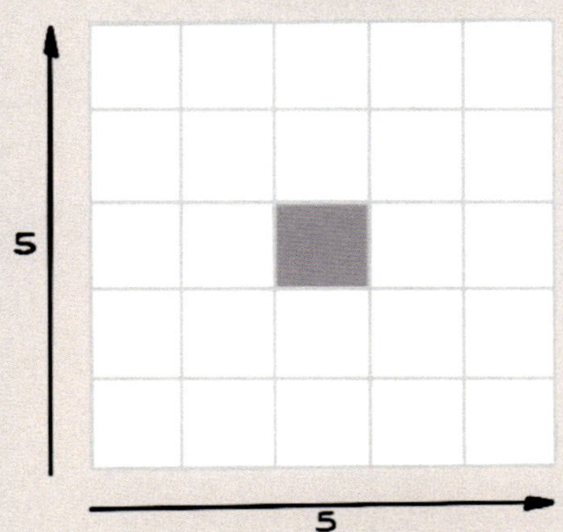

Start with a 5 by 5 grid, mountain side up. Mark the central square.

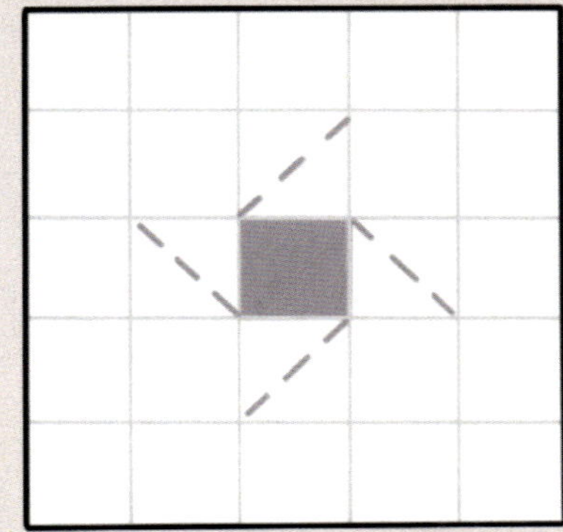

Valley fold the four diagonals.

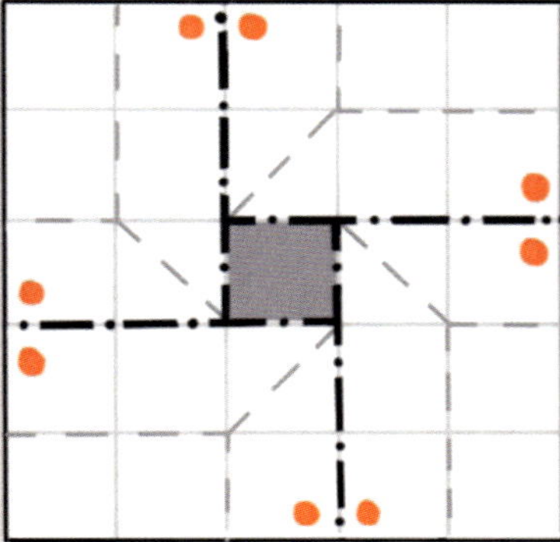

Put in remaining creases as shown. Pinch at the dots to collapse, forming mountain folds that extend from the central square to the edges.

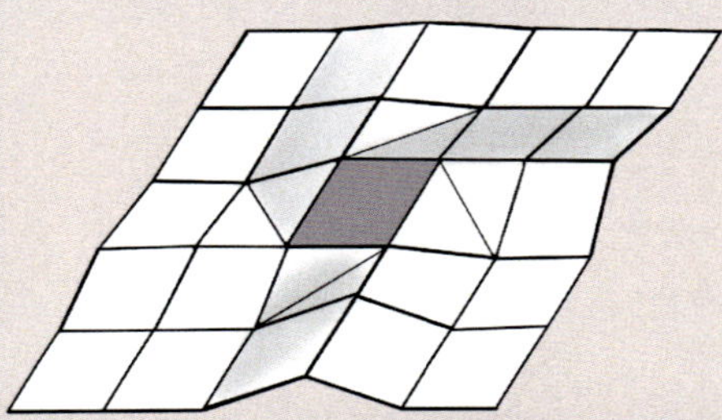

Pinch the mountain folds. The central square should be raised.

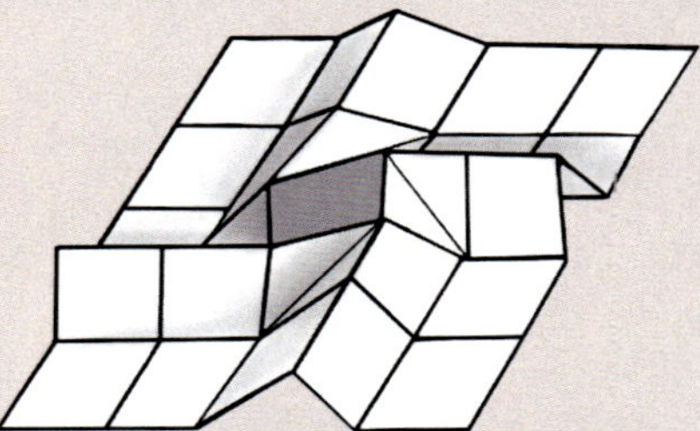

In process. The central square rotates counter-clockwise, and is pushed up.

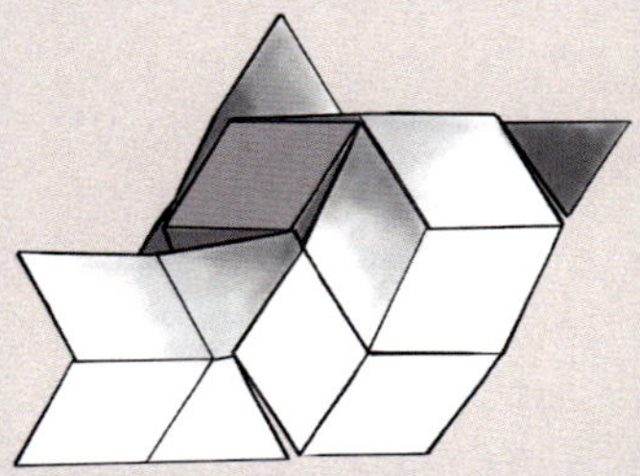

Fully collapsed, the middle square is one square-length above the table level. It was rotated by 90°.

2 by 2 Molecules

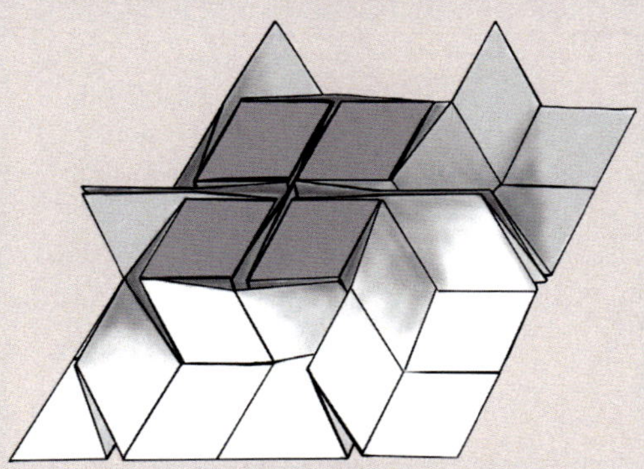

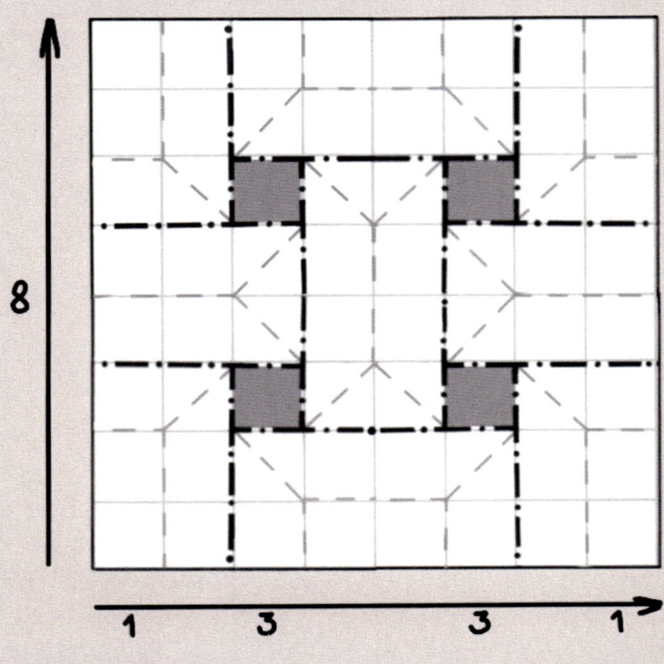

Use a grid of 8 by 8. Add all precreases.

First collapse only the top left molecule, and take all the mountain folds to the edges.

Now collapse the top right molecule.

While collapsing the next row of molecules, rotate both into place at the same time.

4 by 4 Molecules

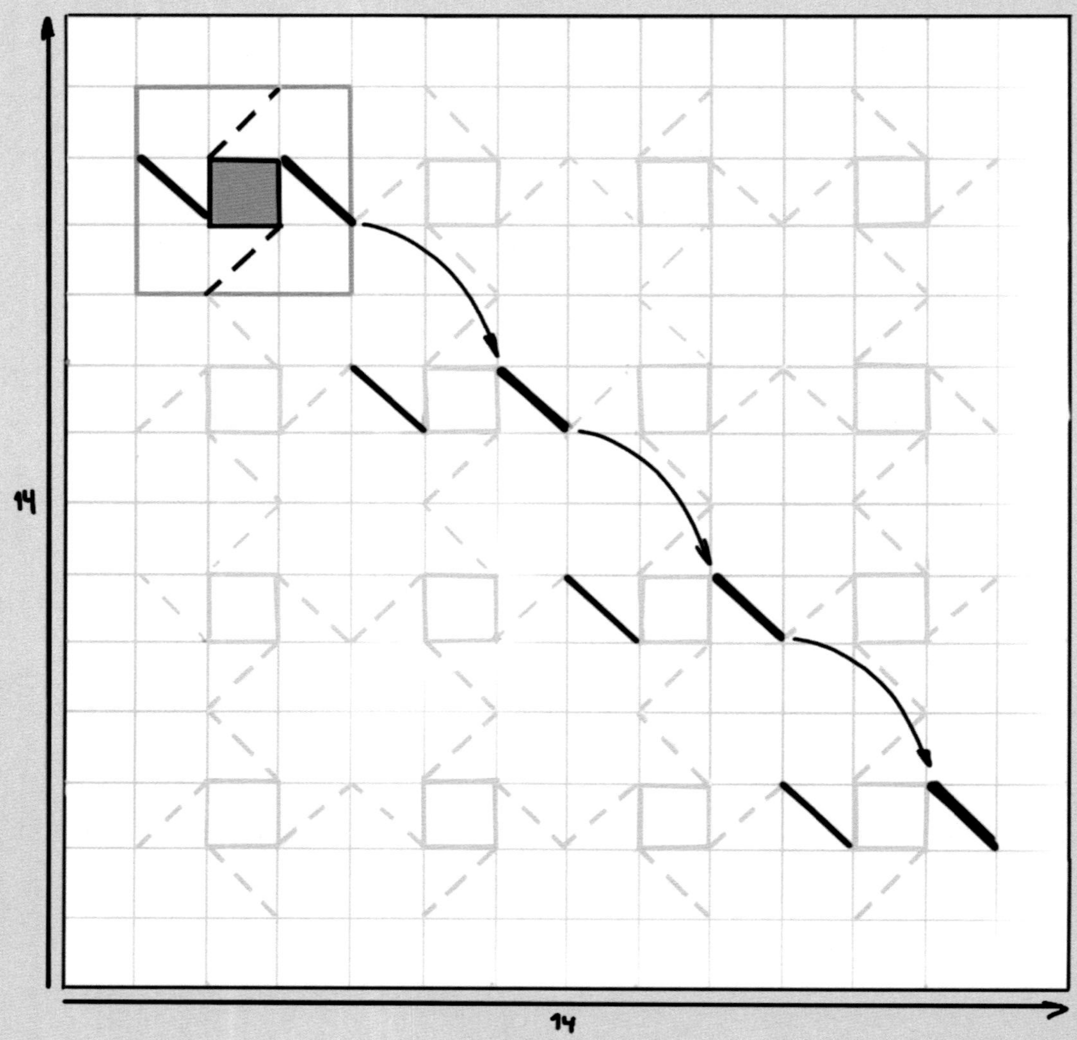

For a 4 by 4–molecule project, start with a 14 by 14 grid: 1 + 4 × 3 + 1 = 14.

The final result will be six squares wide.

Make all the precreases marked above. Note the pattern of the precreases. If you start with the top left molecule, it is easier and faster if you continue making all the creases that are on the same diagonal line.

Fold the first diagonal to bisect a square, then skip two squares to fold the next diagonal in line (see arrows). You can repeat this action on the parallel diagonals opposite as you come back from the bottom right molecule.

When finished with the first set of diagonals, complete the creases of the top left molecule. Move on to the next molecule, and follow the "fold one, skip two" shortcut again.

Repeat the process, until all the precreases are made.

Follow the collapse process outlined in the 2 by 2 project. Start at the top corner and collapse row by row.

Use clips to hold the folded edges in place as you proceed with the collapse.

Mirroring (Cube) and Shifting (Waterbomb)

Look at the single-molecule - its four edges are identical. Let us focus on the right-hand edge of the first molecule. The vertical part is not located on the center of the edge, but on the upper third. This is why the adjacent molecule must be mirrored. If we add another molecule the vertical parts won't meet, and there will be no continuity.

If we do want to join two molecules that are the same, we have to shift the second molecule one square higher.

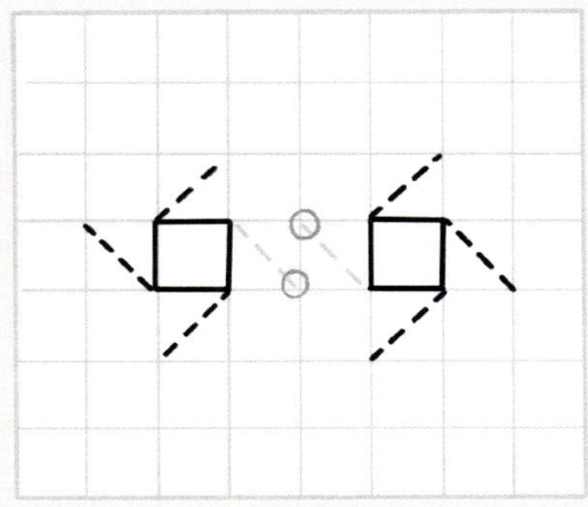

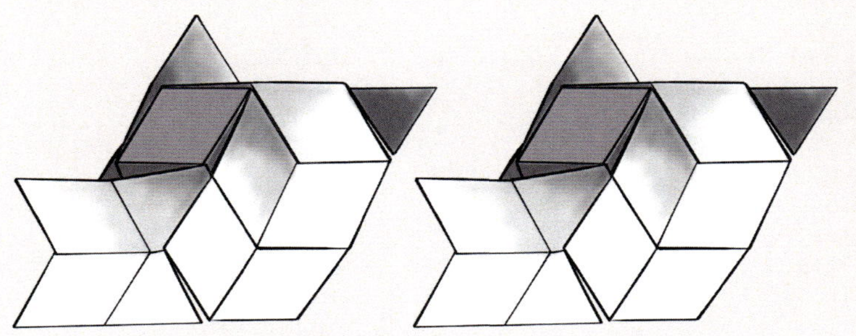

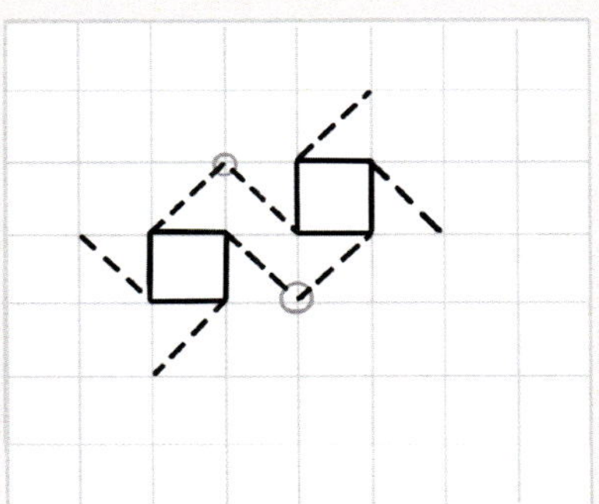

Waterbomb

The molecule is identical to the Cubes tessellation molecule. The difference is in the way the molecules are grouped together. This is why we skip the presentation of the single molecule and go straight to the project of 2 by 2 molecules.

This model was designed by Ron Resch.

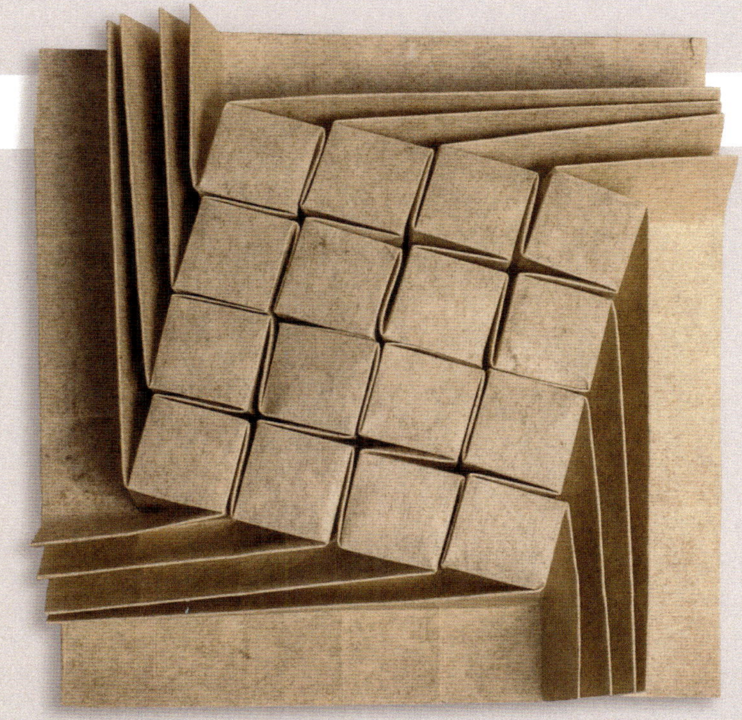

Recto view of a 4 by 4–molecule Waterbomb tessellation.

2 by 2 Molecules

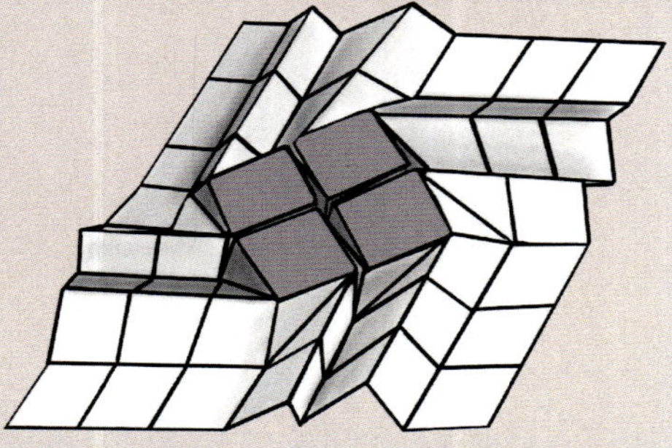

Here the molecules are not mirrored. Instead, the central square of the next molecule is shifted in a Chess Knight move.

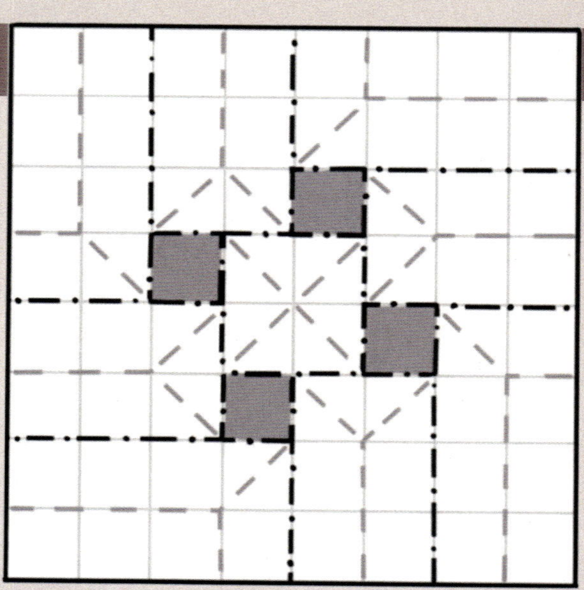

In this grouping of the four molecules the four diagonals join together to form a Waterbomb base in the middle.

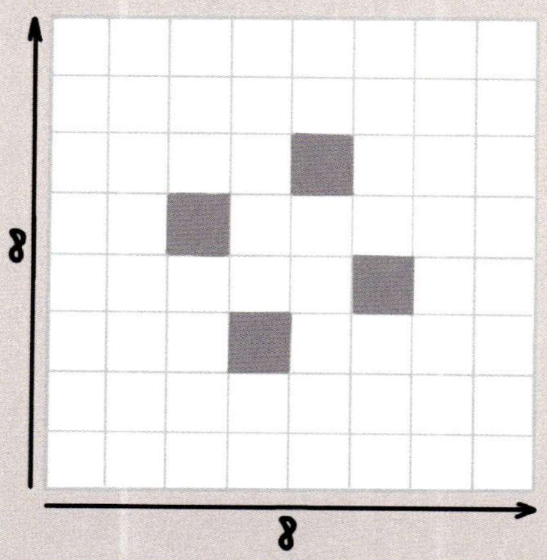

8

8

Start with an 8 by 8 grid and mark off the central squares.

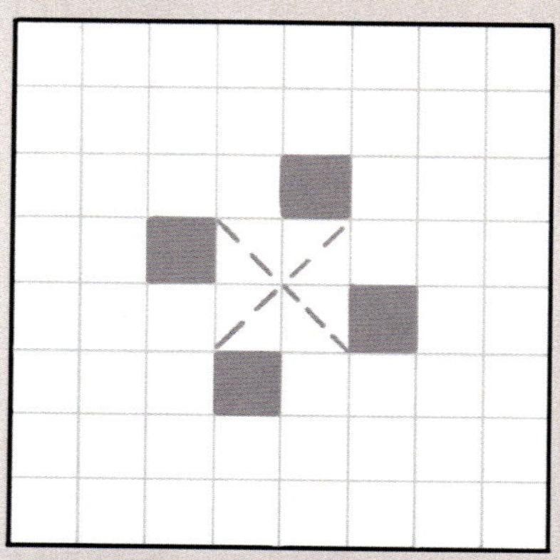

Crease the X between the four squares.

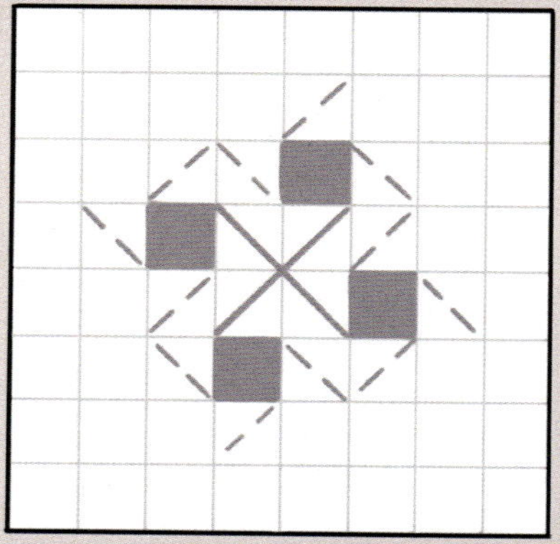

Surround each square with the other three valleys needed.

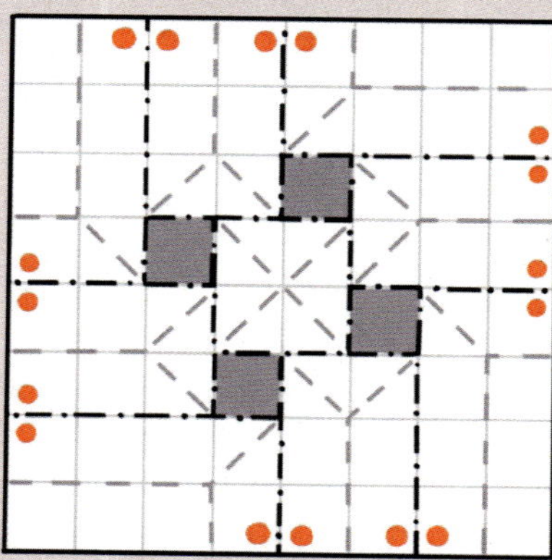

Add the remaining creases as shown.

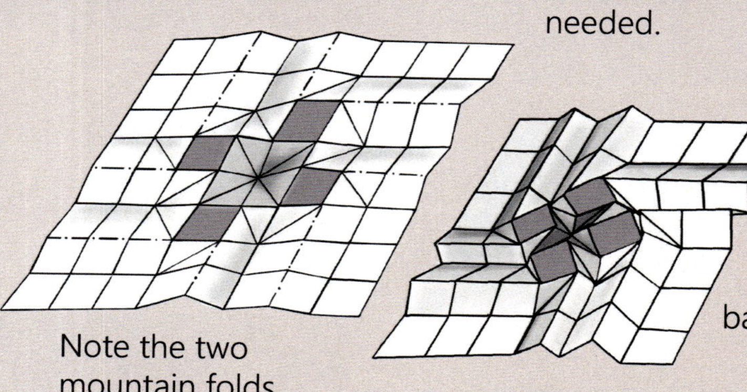

Note the two mountain folds extending out to each edge. Begin the collapse there. Form all the mountain lines from the squares to the edges in pairs.

In process. Note the Waterbomb base is forming in the center.

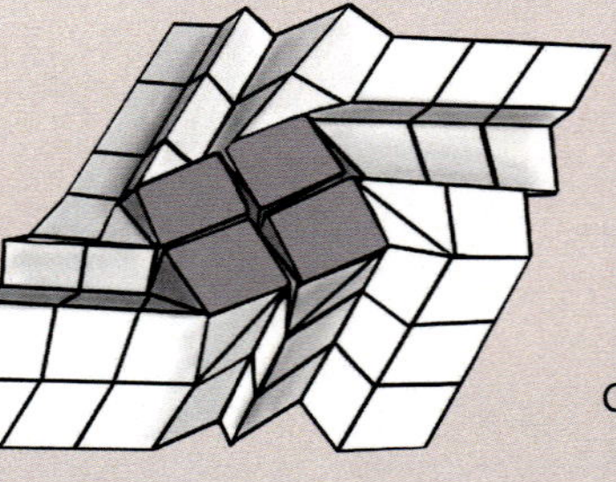

Close the Waterbomb base in the center to complete the move.

4 by 4 Molecules

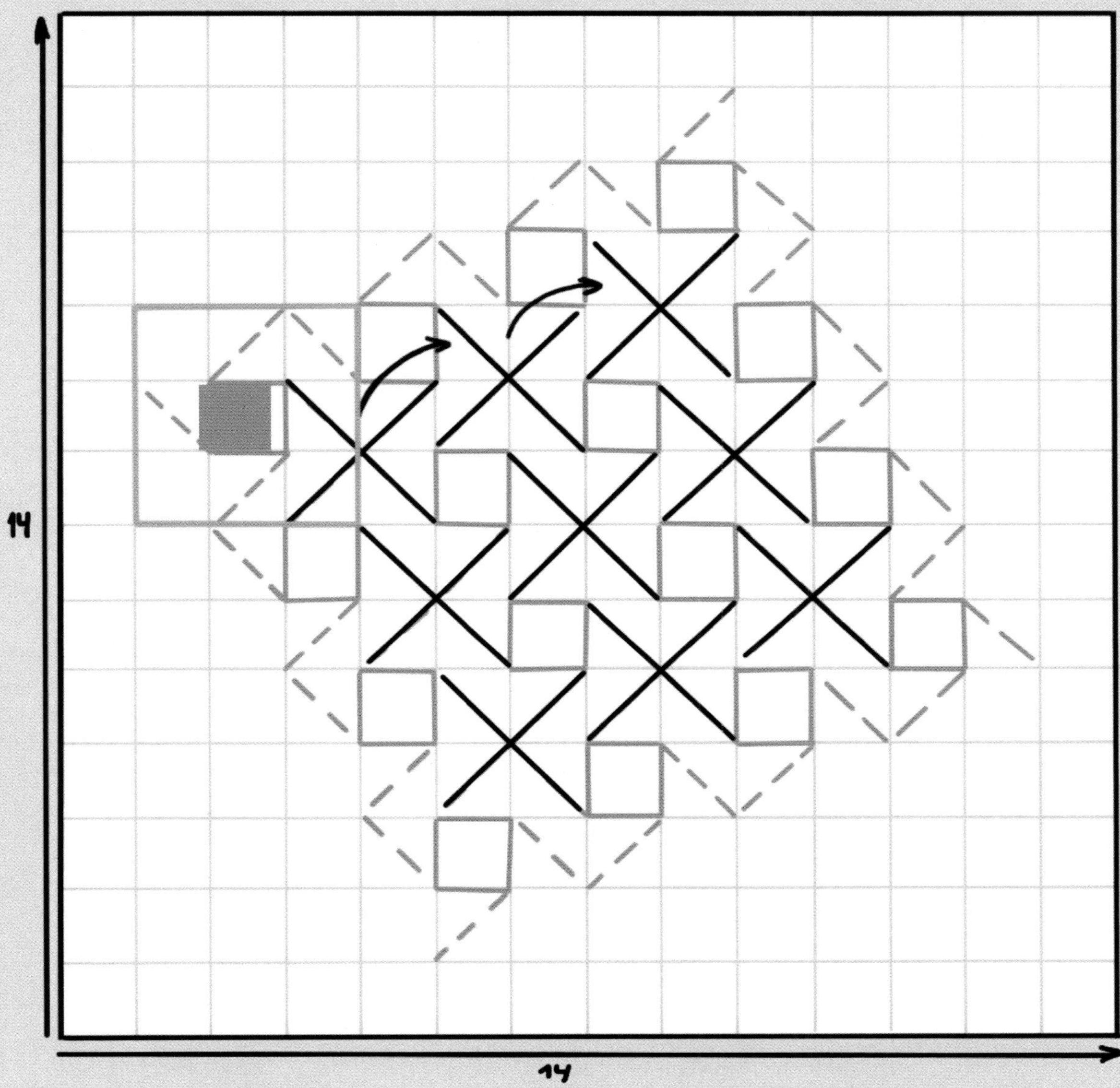

Start with a 14 by 14 grid. The fact that the molecules are shifted (and not mirrored as with the **Cube** tessellation), doesn't change the way to calculate the final sheet size. The grid used is exactly the same size as for a 4 by 4-Cube project.

If you mark a diagonal line from the left-most molecule to the right-most one, you can see why—every molecule needs a 3 by 3 space, and there are four molecules on this line.

The final result will be six squares wide.

There is no best order for the precreases, since none are aligned with any others, but it is easier if you put in all the Xs first.

The collapse is done around the waterbombs (the Xs). Make the first one on the outer rim and continue along the edge (following the arrows).

Complete the model by following this process on the next rows of Xs.

2 2 2 by 2 Cube

The Single Molecule

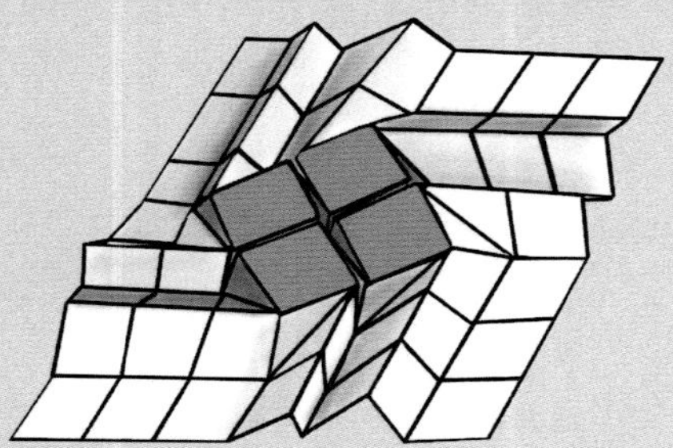

The molecule is a 2 by 2 **Waterbomb** tessellation (page 29). Like all the other **Cube** tessellations, its four sides are identical, and the edge of the paper is the edge of the molecule, hence it can be tessellated.

Molecules are spread by mirroring.

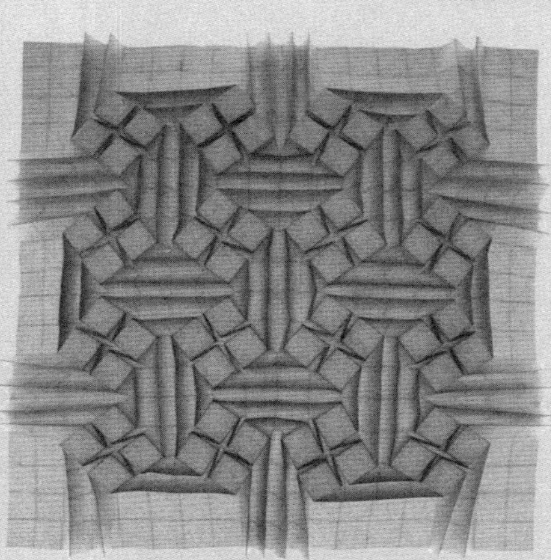

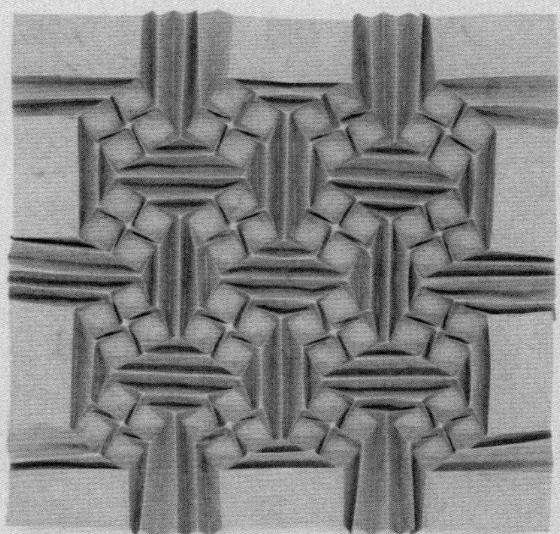

Top: recto view of a 4 by 4–molecule 2 by 2 Cube tessellation.
Bottom right: verso view of a 4 by 4–molecule 2 by 2 Cube tessellation.
Bottom left: recto view with back-light.

2 by 2 Molecules

Use a grid of 14 by 14.

The molecules are mirrored.

The shrinkage ratio is 3:1.

Collapse every group of four cubes together. Do not hold the made molecules tightly, because it will interfere with the collapse of the rest. Look for the big Xs as a guide, and form the four cubes around each one.

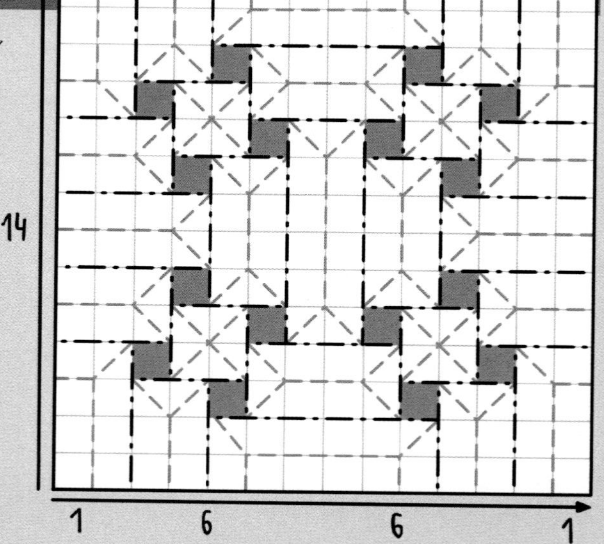

4 by 4 Molecules

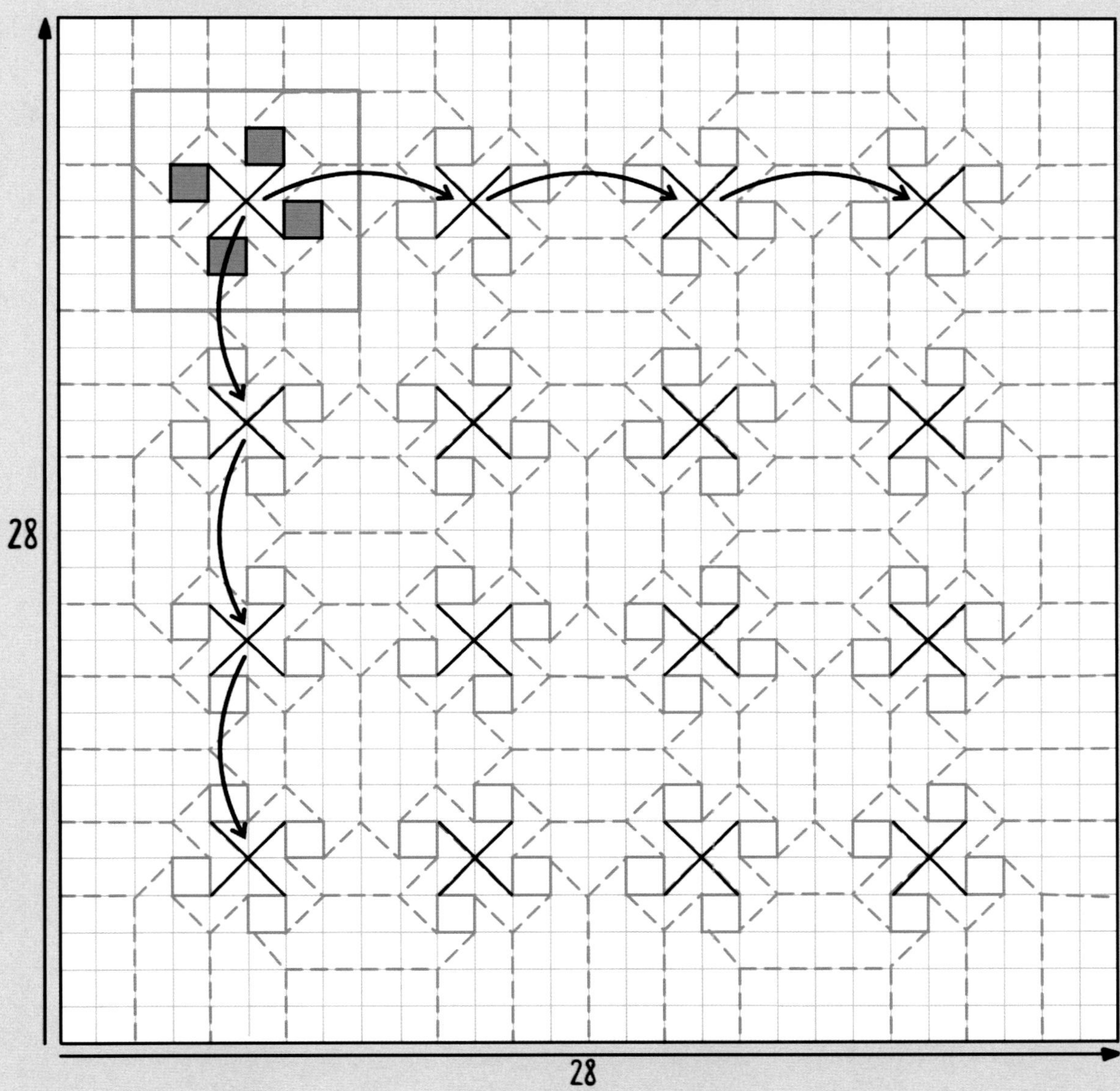

For a 4 by 4–molecule project, start with a 28 by 28 grid: 2 + 4 × 6 + 2 = 28.

The final result will be 10 squares wide.

This is a confusing pattern, so mark **all** the central squares before you start to fold them. Now fold all the Xs, where each X-center is 6 squares aside from the previous one.

Then surround every square center with the missing fold lines.

Collapse by focusing on the Xs, creating in each a small Waterbomb base. First collapse only the top left molecule, trying to collapse all four cubes at once. To complete a row of molecules, make sure that before you collapse a molecule, the next one is arranged for collapse as well, meaning all its central squares are raised (pushed up from below).

Continue to add rows, one by one.

Above and Beyond—A 5 by 5 Project

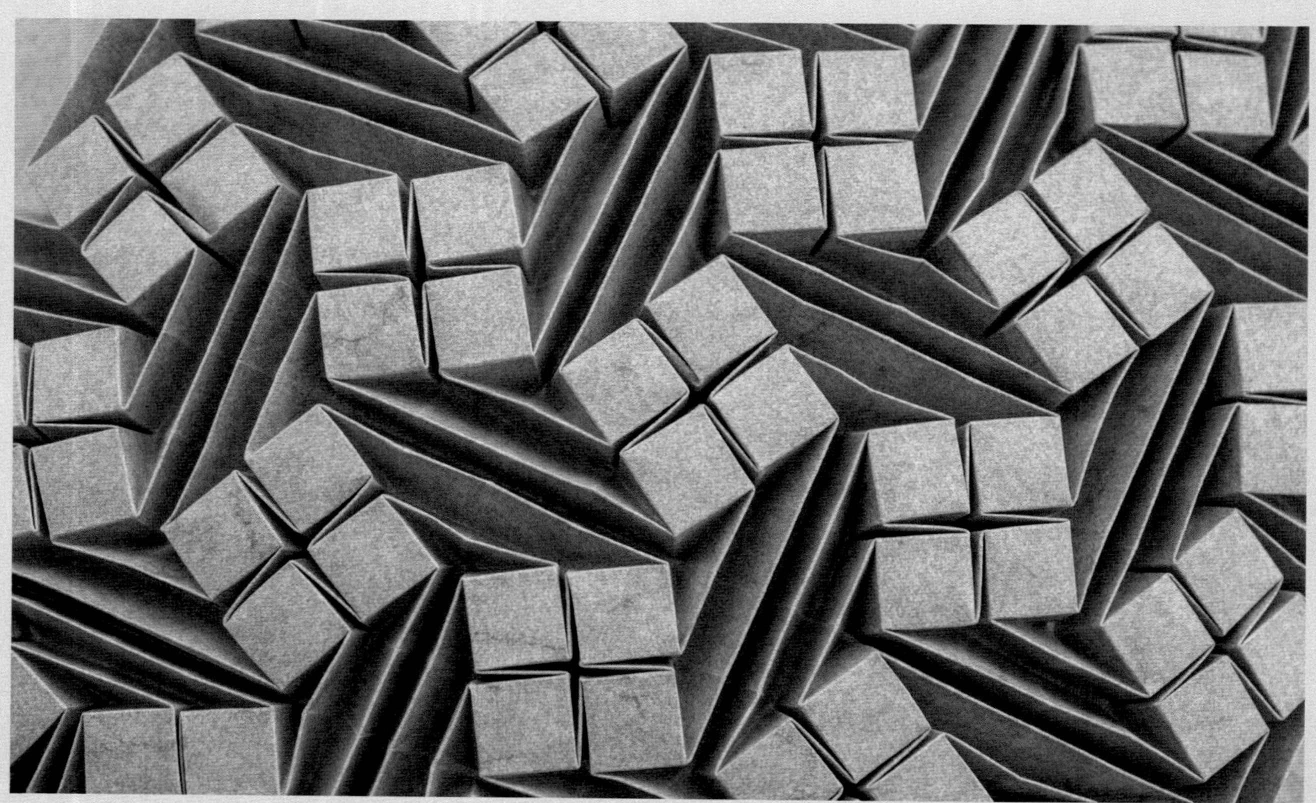

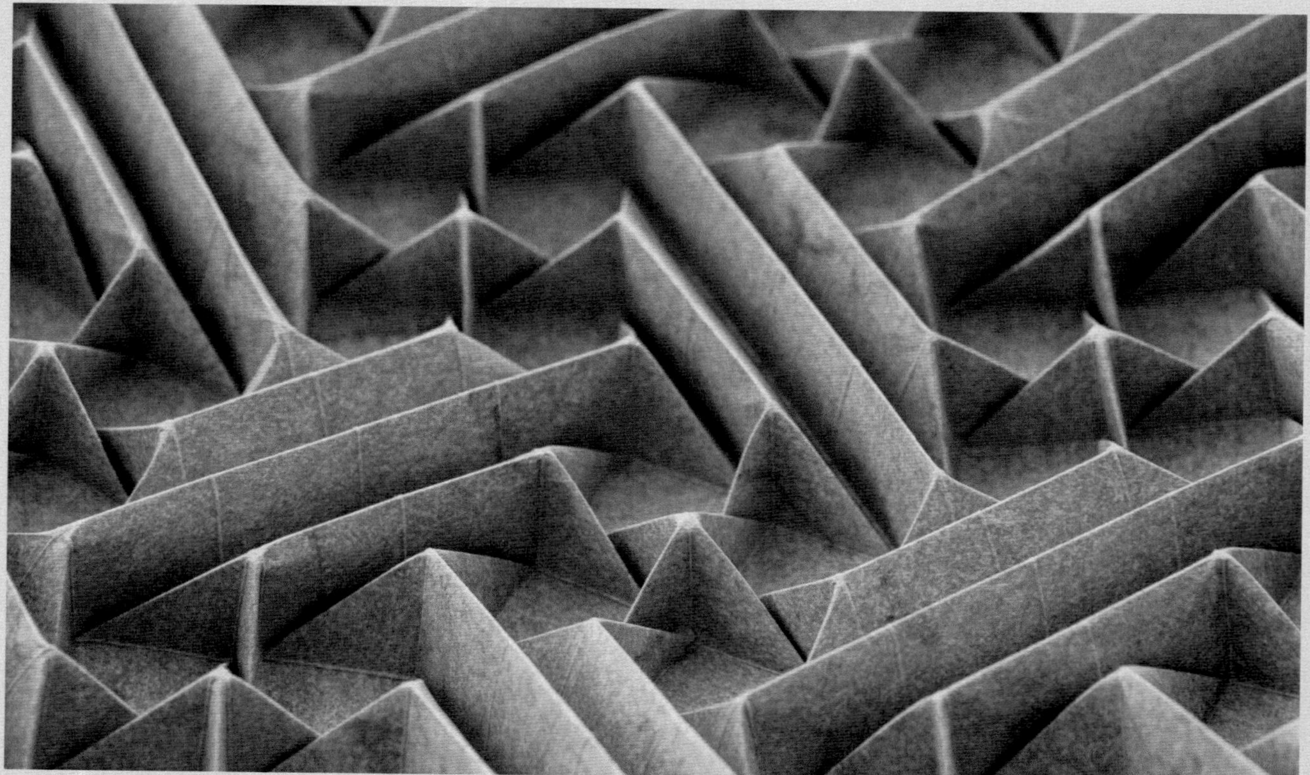

2 3 3 by 3 Cube

The Single Molecule

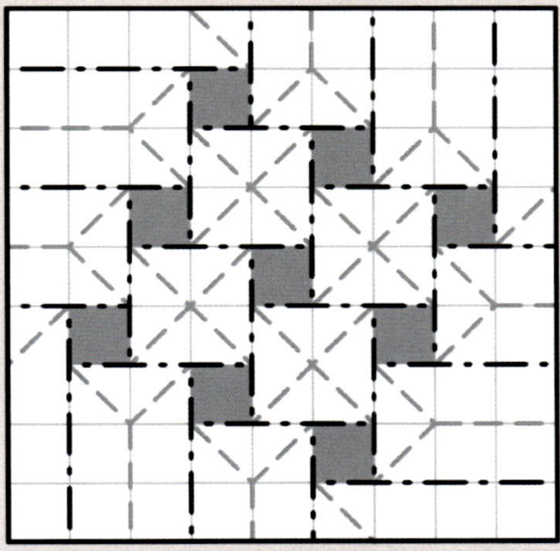

The molecule is a the 3 by 3 **Waterbomb** tessellation (page 29). It is the natural development of the previous model.

Molecules are spread by mirroring.

The shrinkage ratio is 3:1.

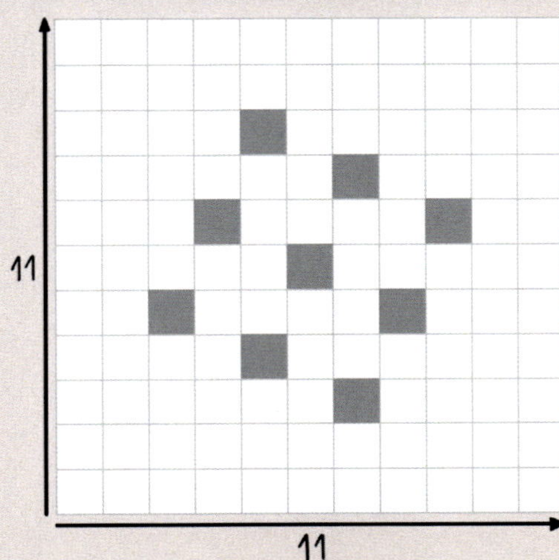

Start with an 11 by 11 grid and mark off the central squares.

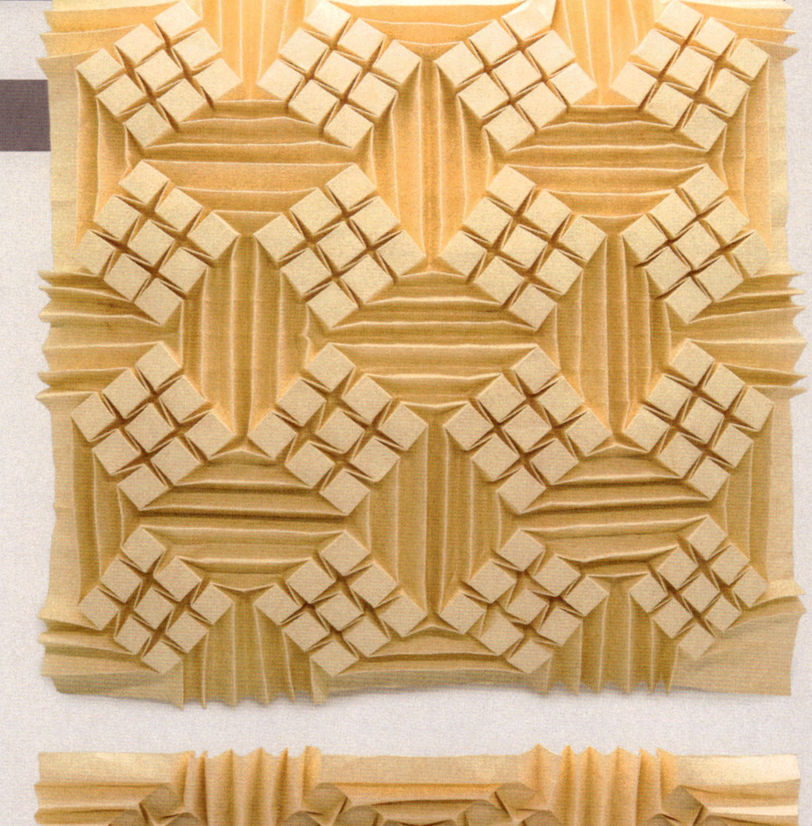

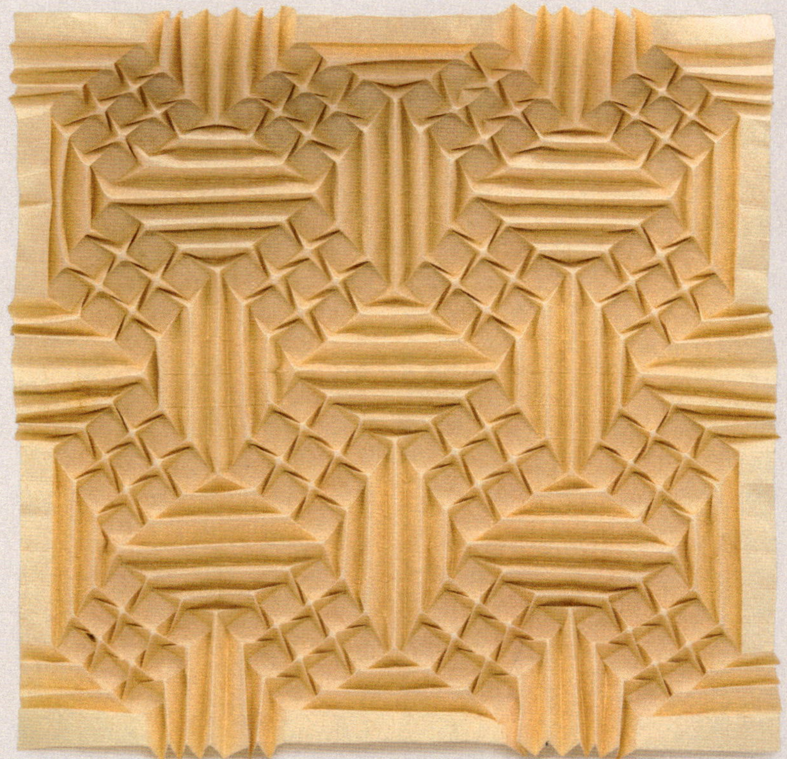

Top: recto view of a 4 by 4–molecule 3 by 3 Cube tessellation.

Bottom: verso view of a 4 by 4–molecule 3 by 3 Cube tessellation.

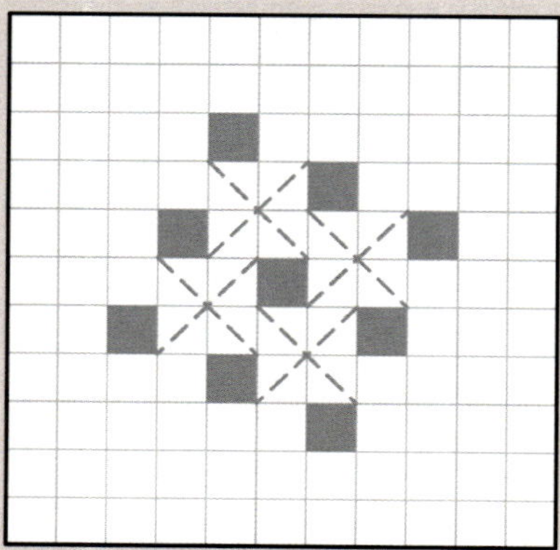

Crease the Xs between every set of four squares. There are four such Xs.

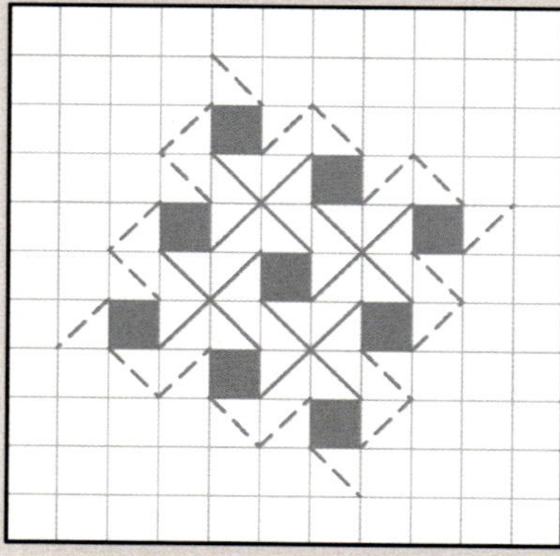

Surround each square with the other three valleys needed.

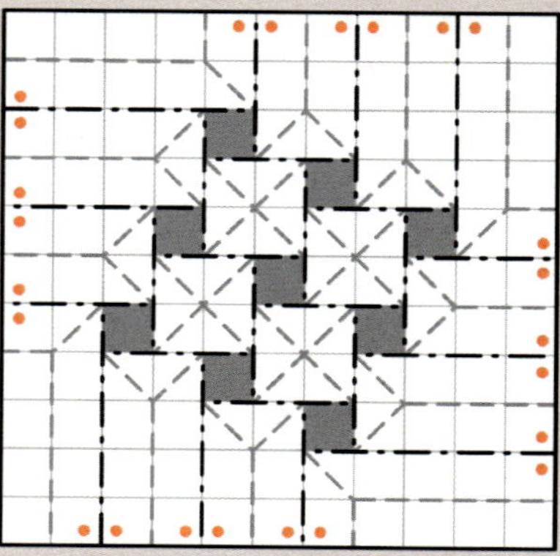

Add the remaining creases as shown. Collapse by pinching the orange dots, and forcing a waterbomb out of every X.

2 by 2 Molecules

Use a grid of 20 by 20.

The molecules are mirrored.

The shrinkage ratio is 3:1.

Collapse every group of nine cubes together. Do not hold the completed molecules tightly, because it will interfere with the collapse of the rest. Look for the four Xs as guides, and arrange around each their four cubes. Complete a molecule with all of its nine cubes and move on to the next one.

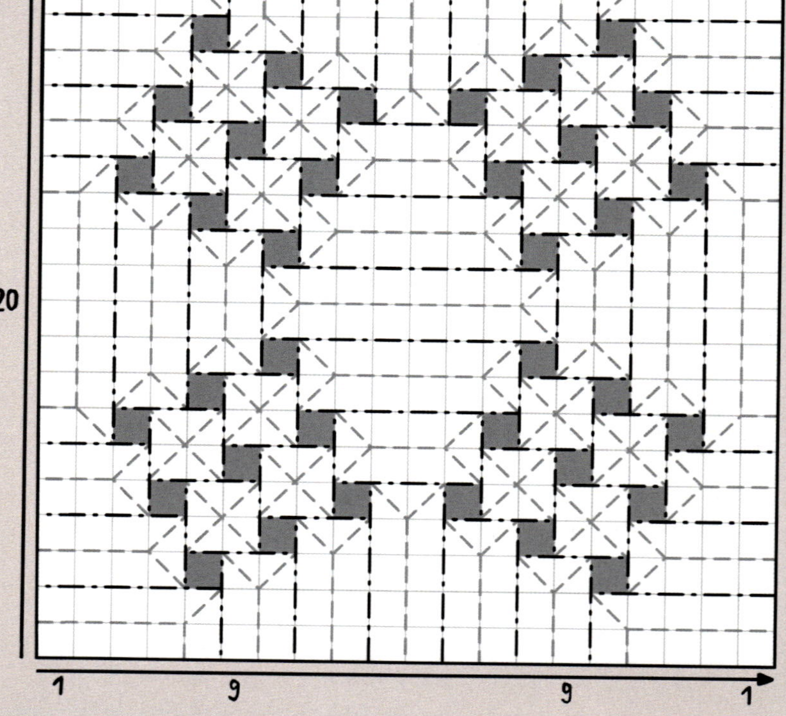

4 by 4 Molecules

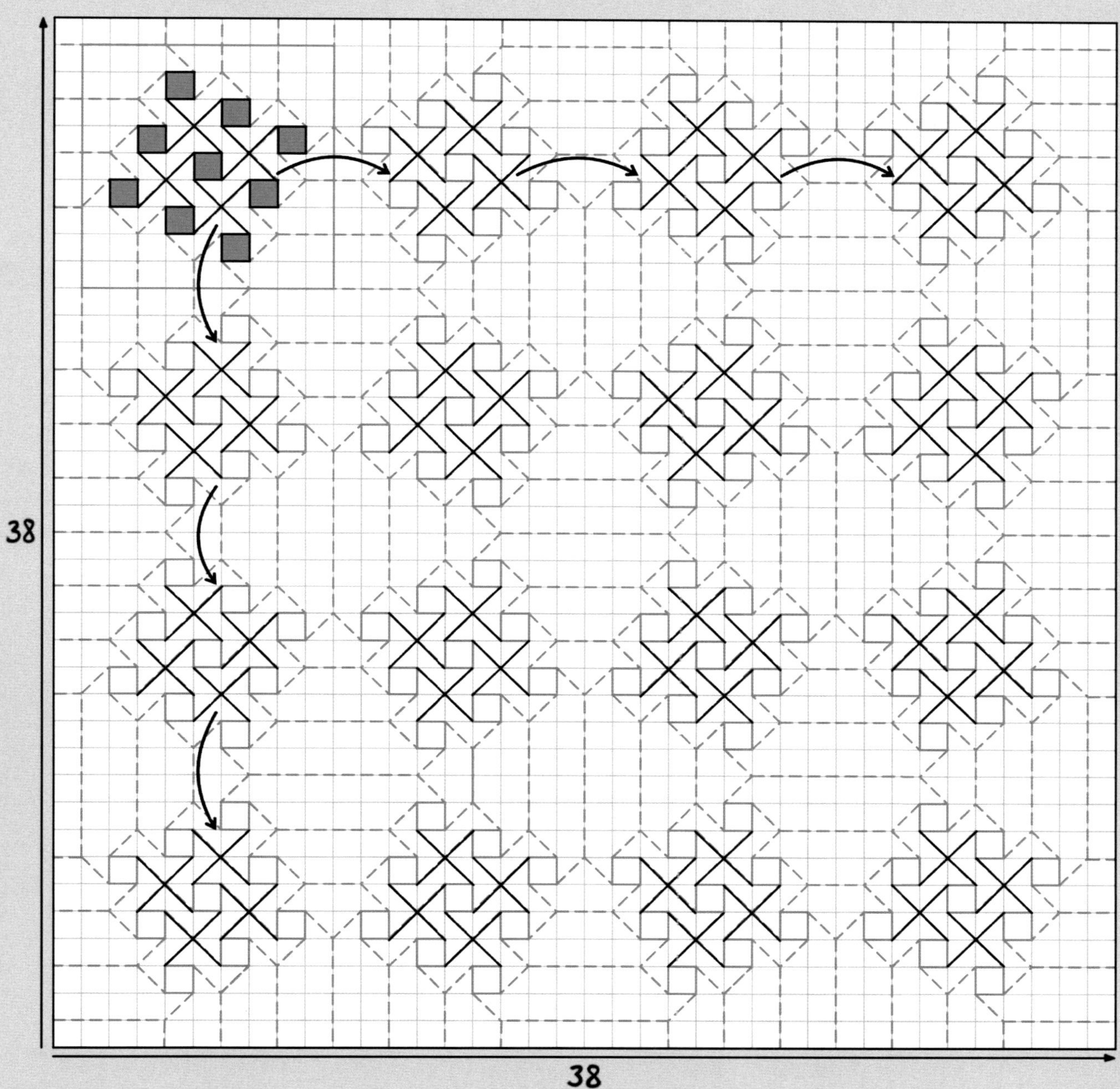

For a 4 by 4–molecule project, start with a 38 by 38 grid: 1 + 4 × 9 + 1 = 38. (You can also try a border of two rows and columns, hence starting with a grid of 40).

The final result will be 10 squares wide.

Mark all the central squares, and even mark (with a pencil or BluTack) all the Xs, before you start to fold them.

Fold all the Xs first, and then surround every square with the missing fold lines.

Collapse by focusing on the Xs, creating in each a small Waterbomb base.

2 4 1 by 4 Cube

The Single Molecule

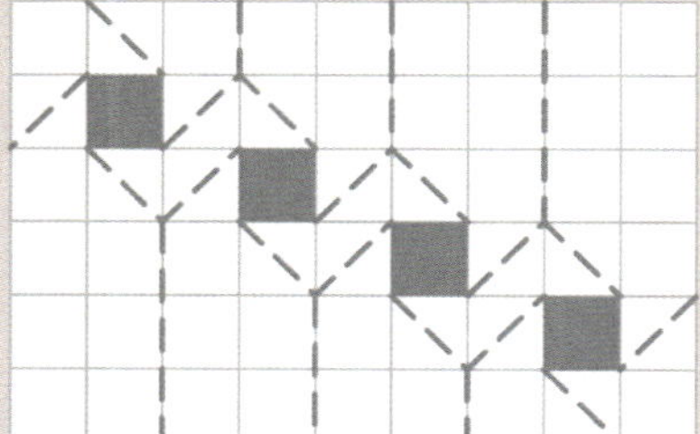

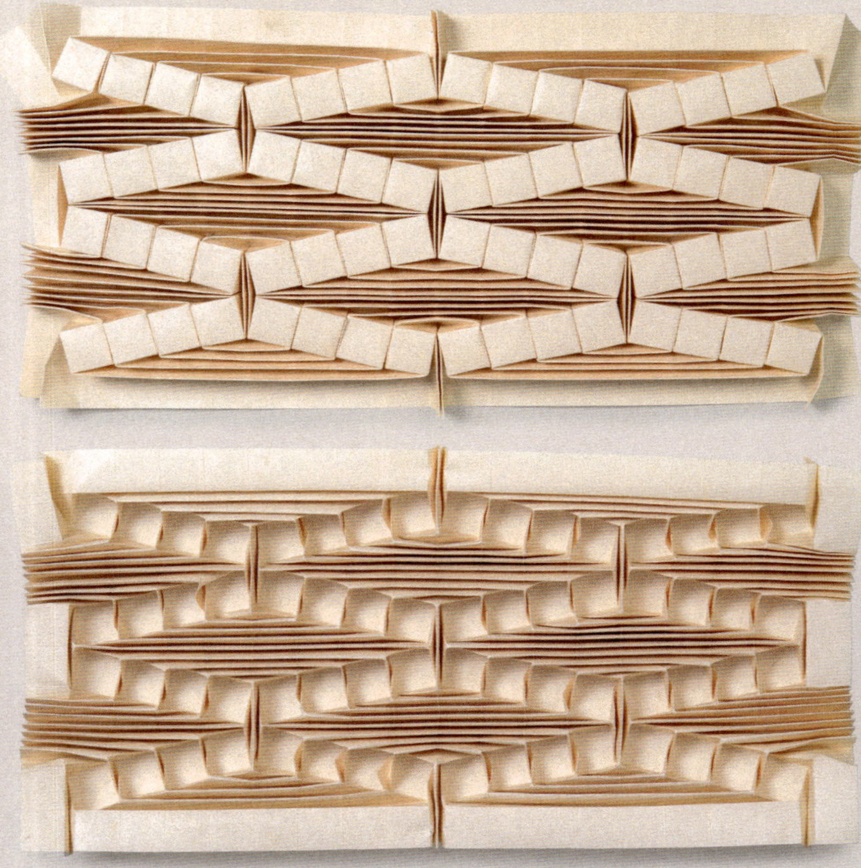

Top: recto view of a 4 by 4–molecule 1 by 4 Cube tessellation.

Bottom: verso view of a 4 by 4–molecule 1 by 4 Cube tessellation.

The molecule is a unique 1 by 4 **Waterbomb** tessellation (page 29). It introduces the fact that the molecule does not have to be a square. Here, it is a narrow rectangle. Every two opposite edges of the molecule are the same, and this is enough for the molecule to be tessellatable.

By understanding this, you can design any size you want to a molecule - 2 by 3, 4 by 2, and even 6 by 10.

Molecules are spread by mirroring.

Shrinkage ratio is 9:1 horizontally and 3:2 vertically.

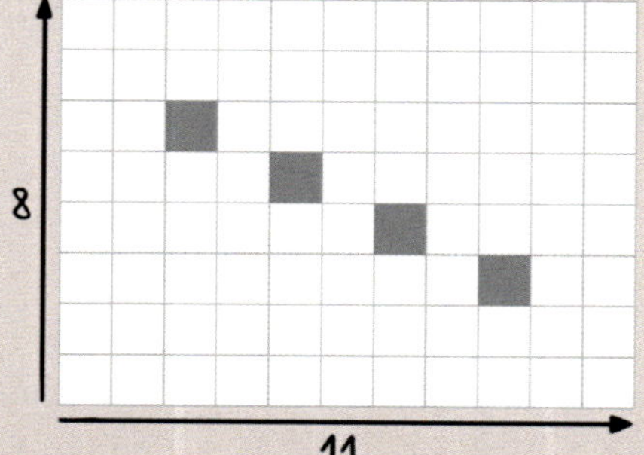

Start with a grid of 8 by 11 and mark off the central squares.

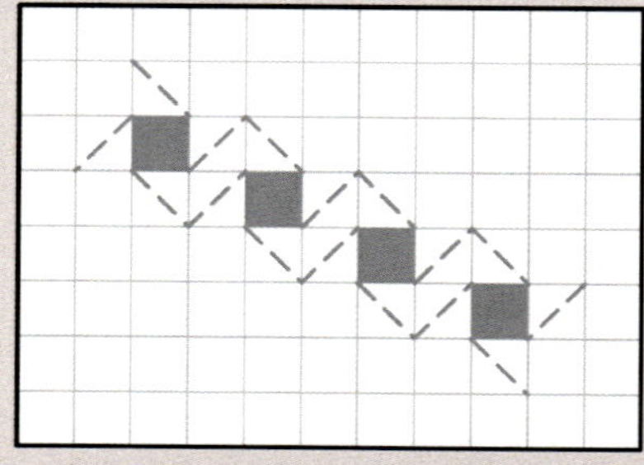

Surround each with the four diagonal creases.

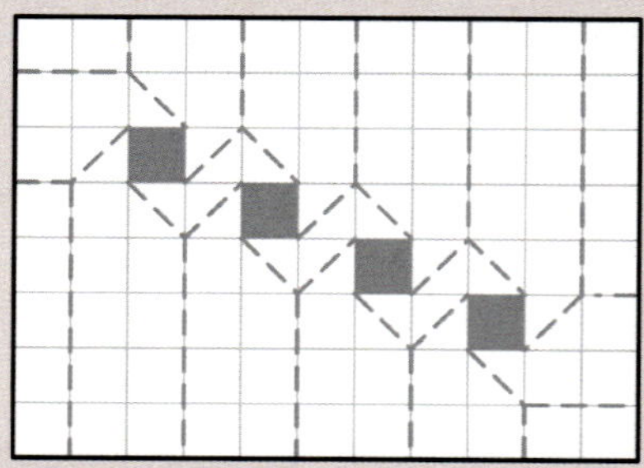

Add the needed valleys on top of the grid lines.

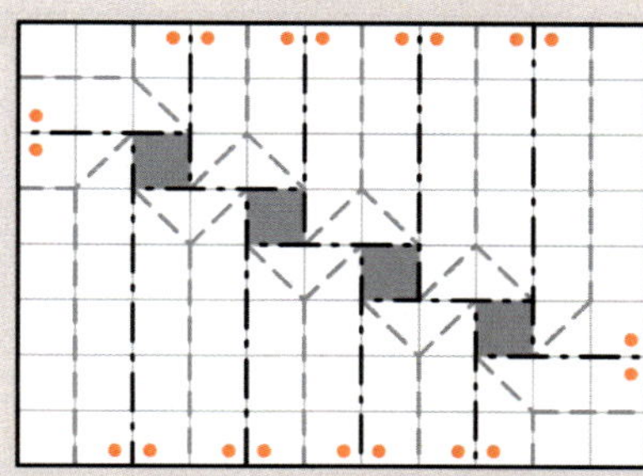

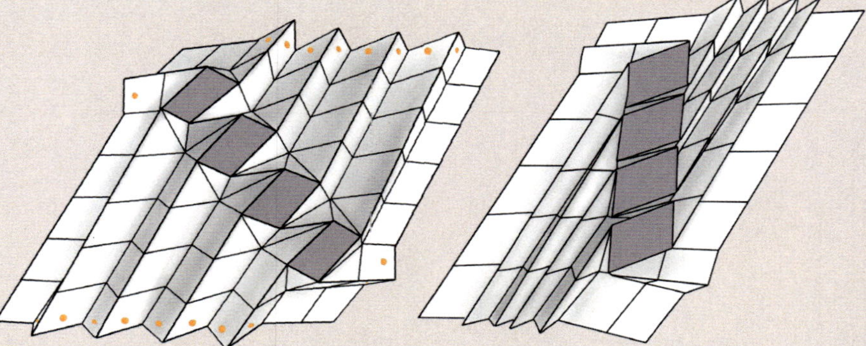

Add the remaining creases as shown. Collapse by pinching the orange dots.

Notice how all the mountains above and below are gathering together.

Fully collapsed.

Note that the result is a vertical line of cubes, although the CP (wrongly) hints it should be a horizontal one.

2 by 2 Molecules

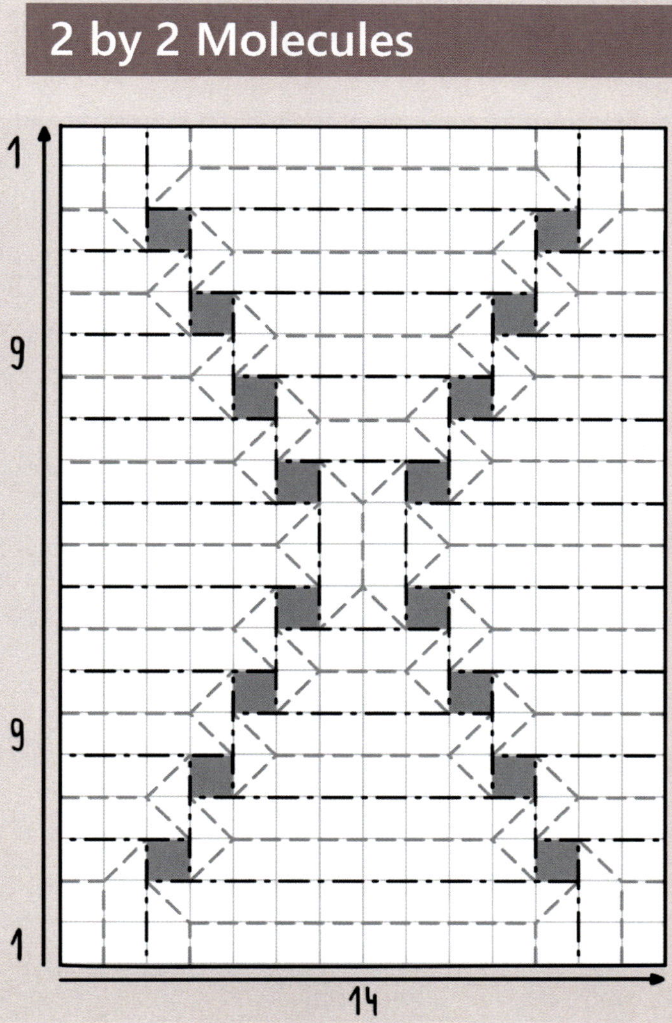

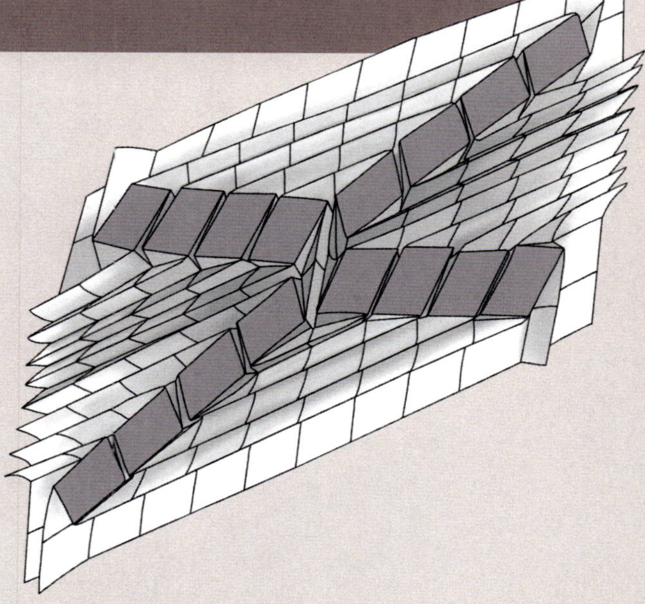

Use a grid of 14 by 20.

The molecules are mirrored.

Collapse every group of four cubes together. Do not hold the completed molecules tightly, because it will interfere with the collapse of the rest. The Xs are not here anymore, so follow the rows of four cubes, and complete molecule by molecule.

4 by 4 Molecules

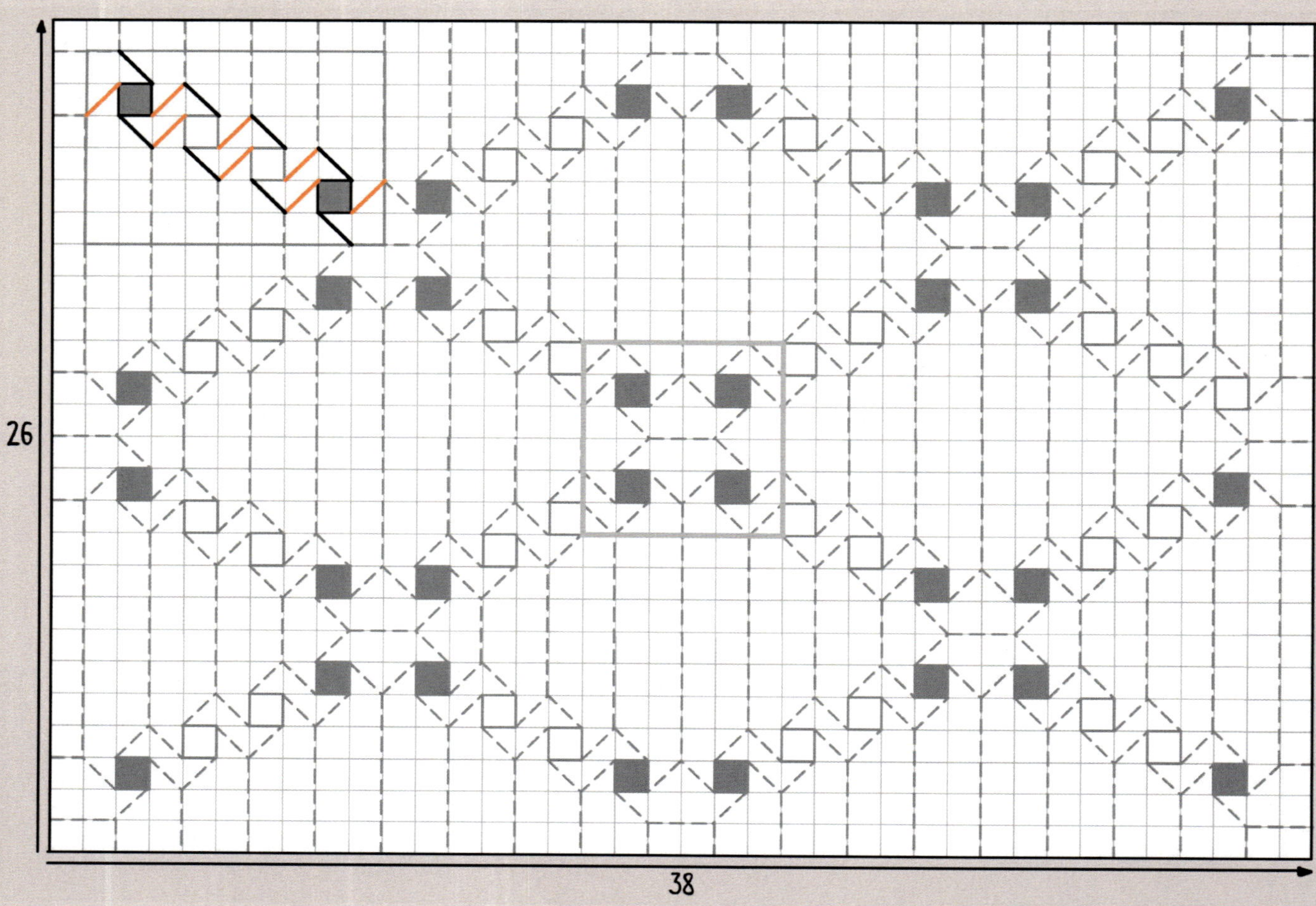

Make a 26 by 38 grid.

The formula for the height is 1 + 4 × 6 + 1 = 26.
For the width it is
1 + 4 × 9 + 1 = 38.

The final result will be 18 squares high and 6 squares wide.

Since all the single cubes in a molecules are the same orientation, it is best to crease all top and bottom creases of a molecule, and then all the left and right. Finish a molecule and move to the next.

You must be careful while making the precreases, since it is very confusing! It is wise to mark the four central squares of each molecule.

For the collapse, I strongly advice to go slowly, and hold every four tabs (of each molecule) separately. For example, on the bottom edge, while collapsing the two left molecules, the accumulated number of tabs to hold is eight (four for each molecule).

Hold each group of four together with a clip. Do not use a single clip to hold all the eight at once.

Please note the area where every four molecules meet (marked in the center of the CP). This area is exactly like the **Cube** tessellation (page 26), so it can help you get orientated when you collapse the model.

Above and Beyond—A 6 by 6 Project

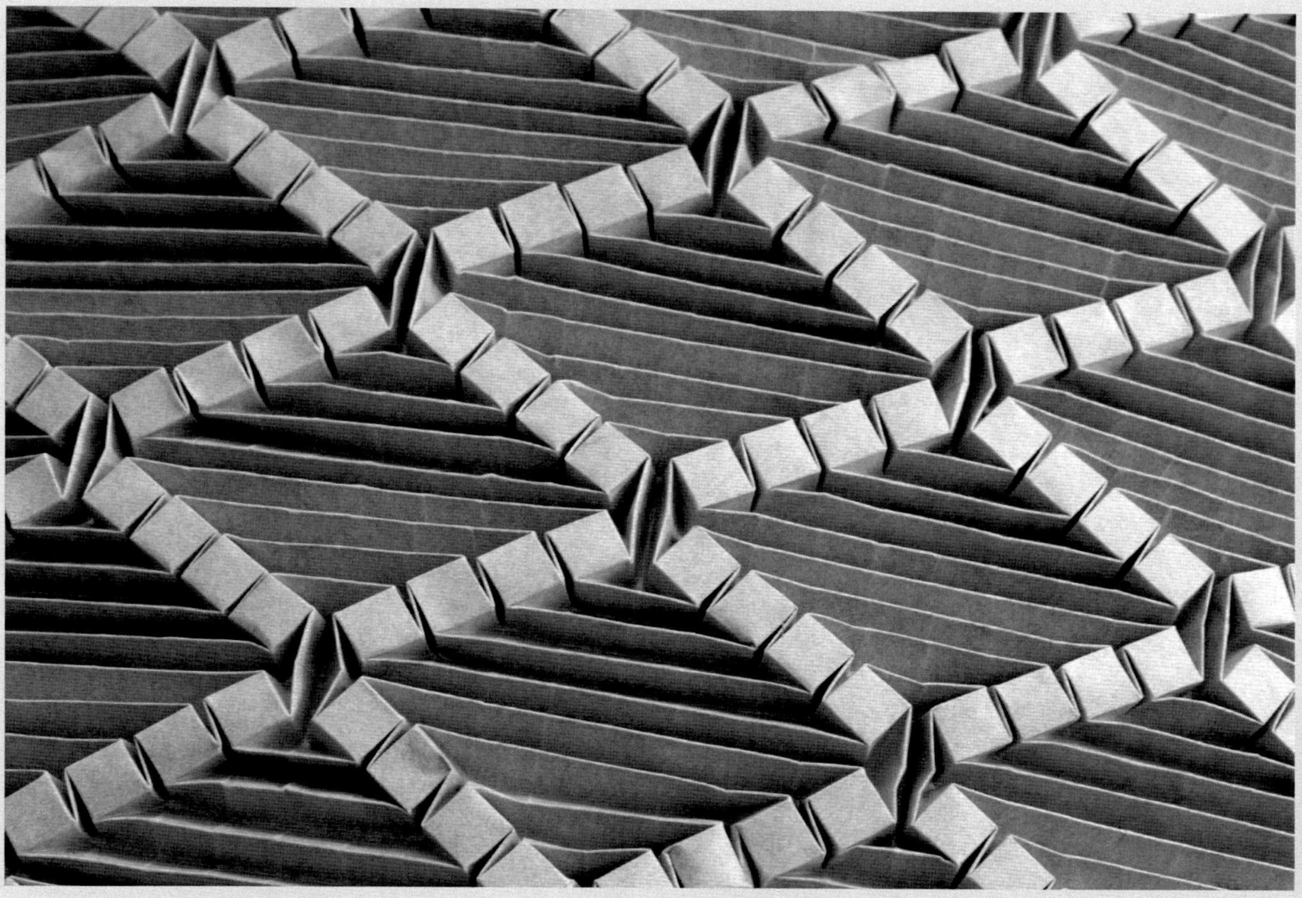

It is better to let the model open up, and not to squeeze it tight.

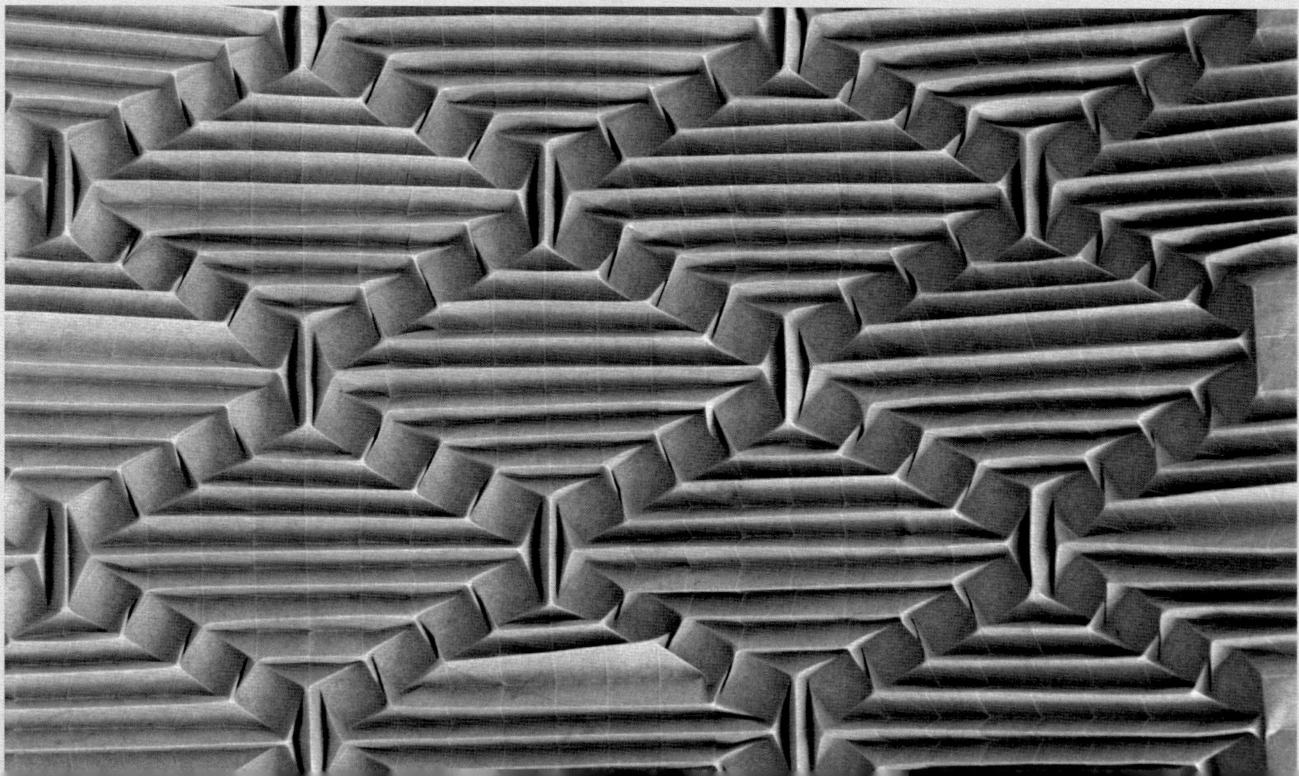

2 5 Wall of Bricks

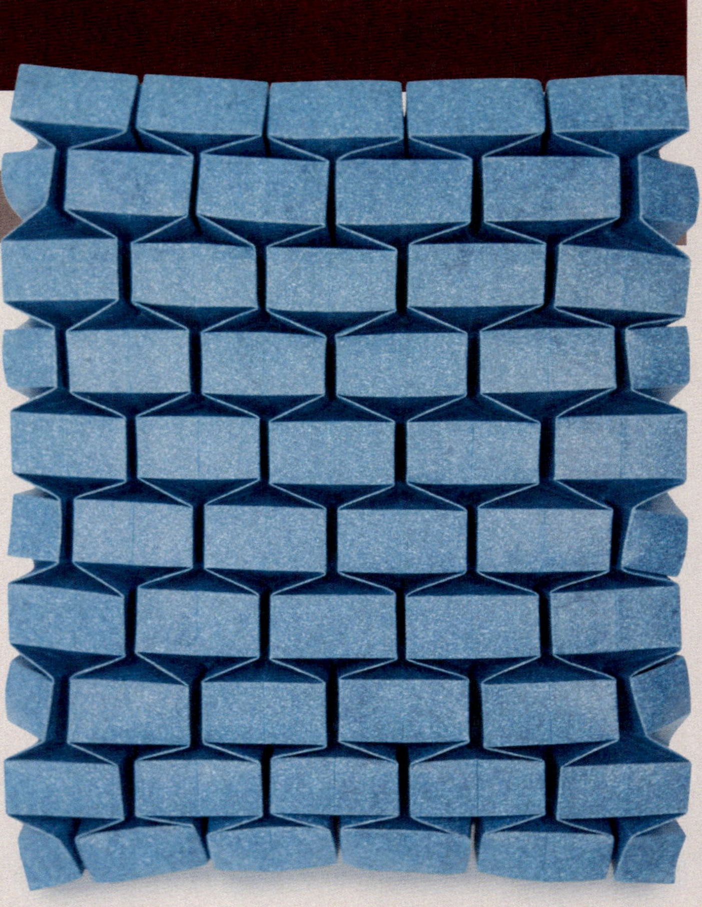

The Single Molecule

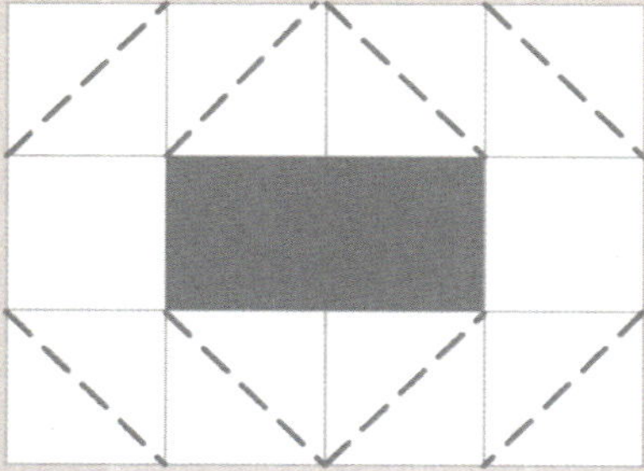

The single molecule is based on a rectangle of 1 by 2.

The molecule size is 3 by 4.

The molecules are shifted and raised.

The shrinkage ratio is 2:1.

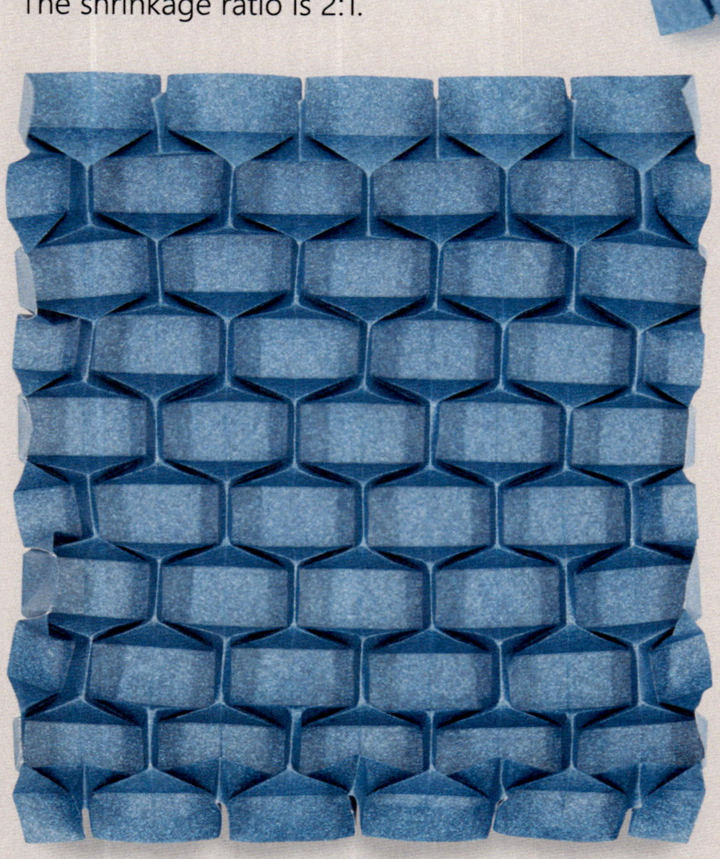

Above: recto view of a 5 by 8–molecule Wall of Bricks tessellation.

Left: verso view of a 5 by 8–molecule Wall of Bricks tessellation.

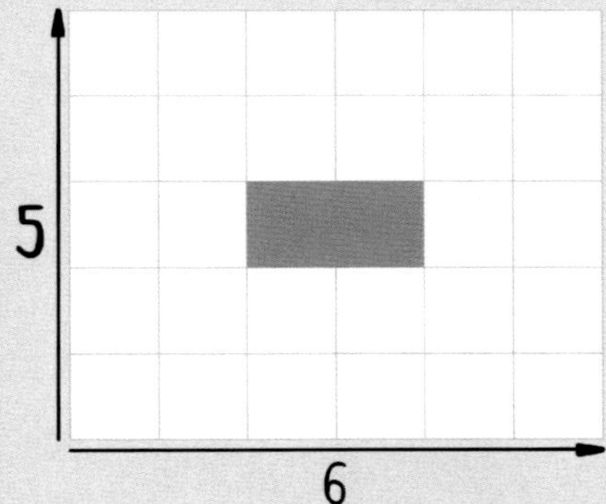

Start with a 5 by 6 grid. Mark the center rectangle.

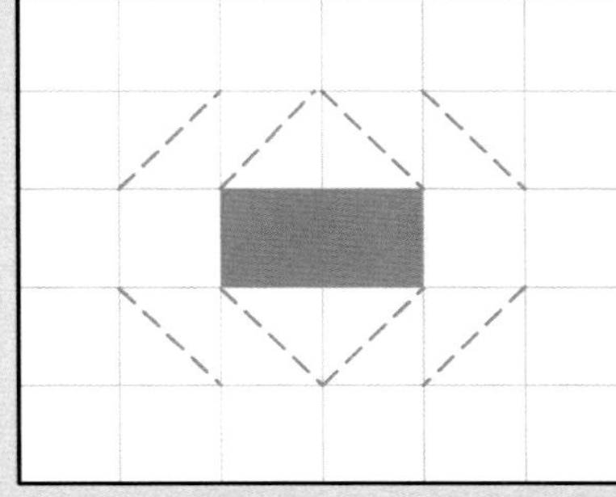

Add the needed valley creases.

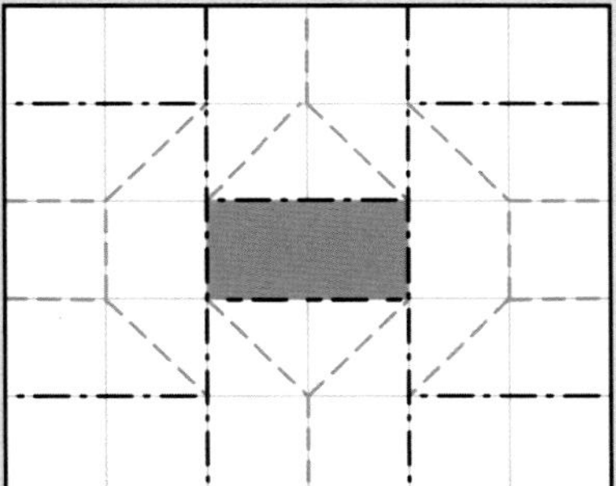

Force all the mountain creases as shown on the grid.

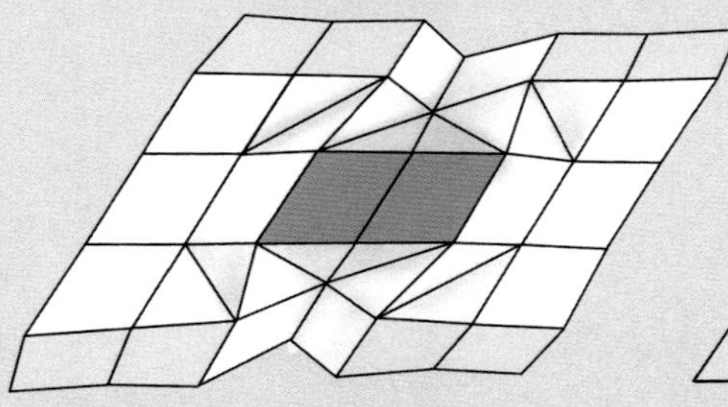

Start the collapse by raising the central rectangle, and lowering the valleys that run through the center of the molecule.

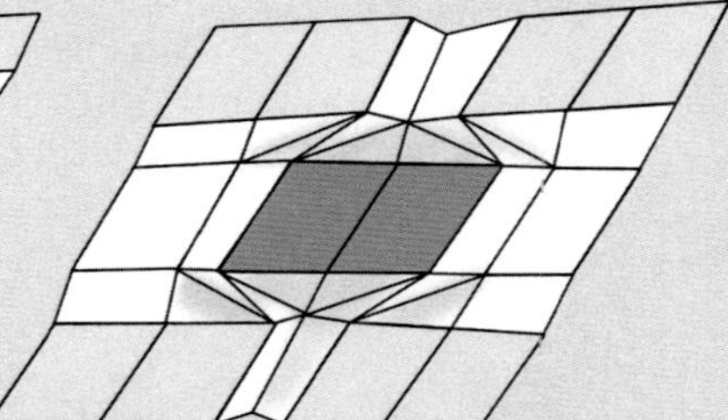

In process. See that all four corners also rising...

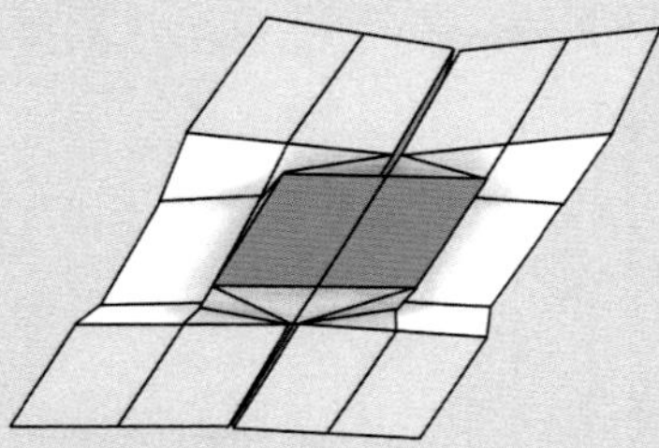

...until they close the gaps between them.

The molecule is fully collapsed!

2 by 2 Molecules

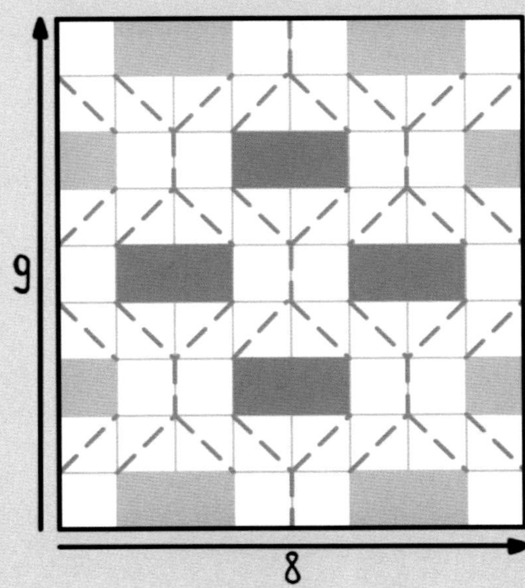

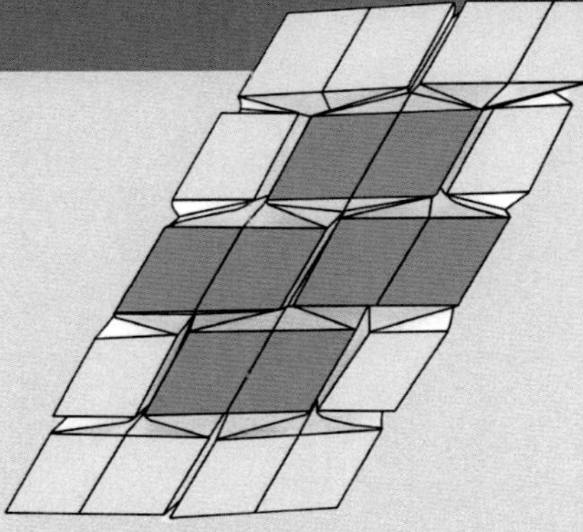

Use a grid of 8 by 9.

As with all the Cube family, look for the headless stick-men. It may be easier to pinch them from the backside.

Make sure the rectangles are raised. Use the rectangles that are on the edges, they are easy to hold and position.

5 by 8 Molecules

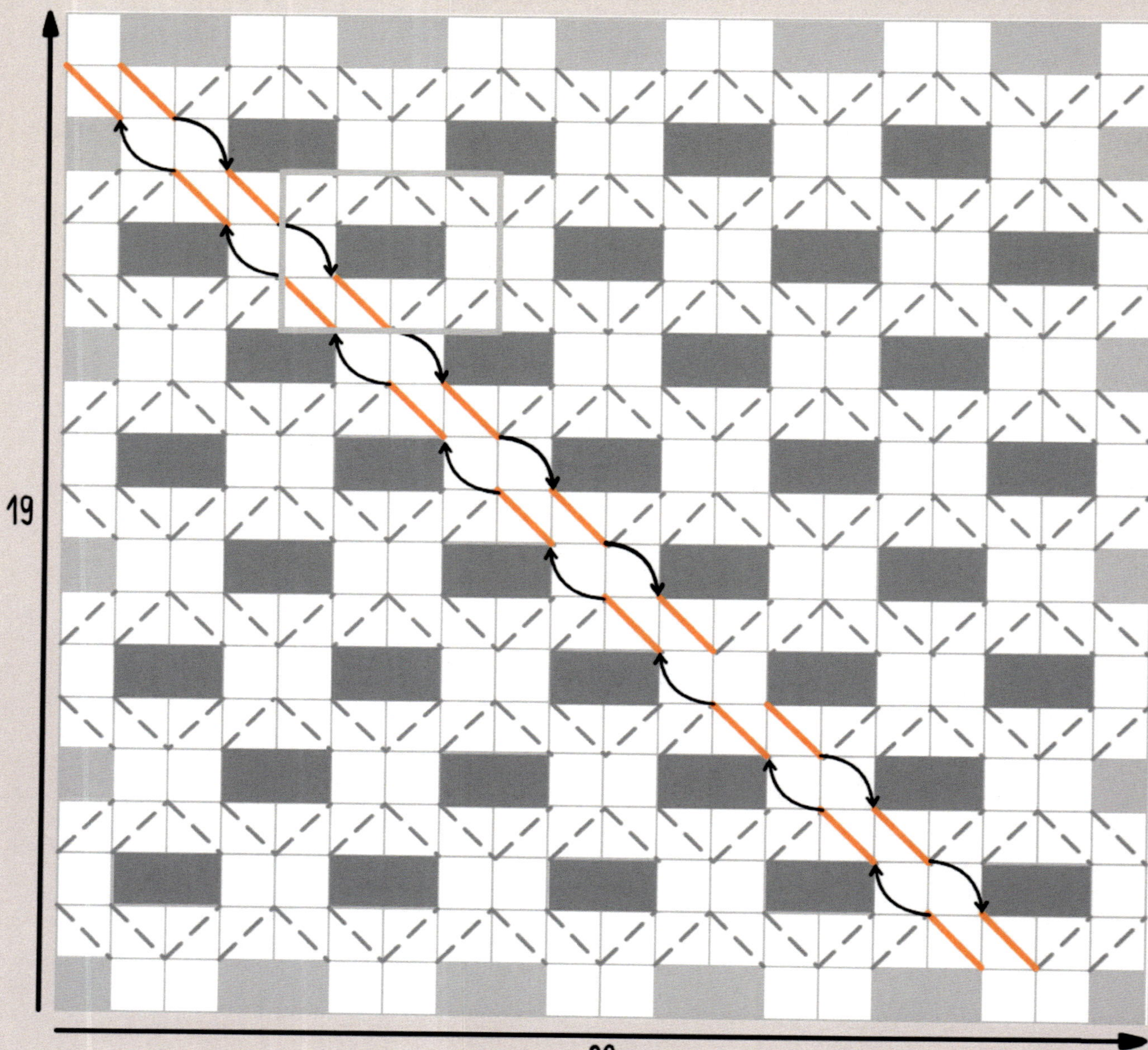

Make a 19 by 20 grid.

A rim around the model will have to include partial molecules (marked in light gray).

Since the molecules are horizontal you need to have more rows than columns to have a square-ish result.

The formula for the height is 1 + 1 + 8 × 2 + 1 = 19.

(1 + 8 × 2) is the result of a gap between every two grey rectangles.

On top of that, we add a row at the bottom and top, to frame the work.

For the width it is

5 × 4 = 20.

The final result will be 10 squares in height and 10 squares wide.

Note the pattern of the pre-creases - all follow the fold 1-skip 1 pattern.

For the collapse, follow the spread Waterbomb bases.

Variation A
Fat Molecules
2 by 2 Project

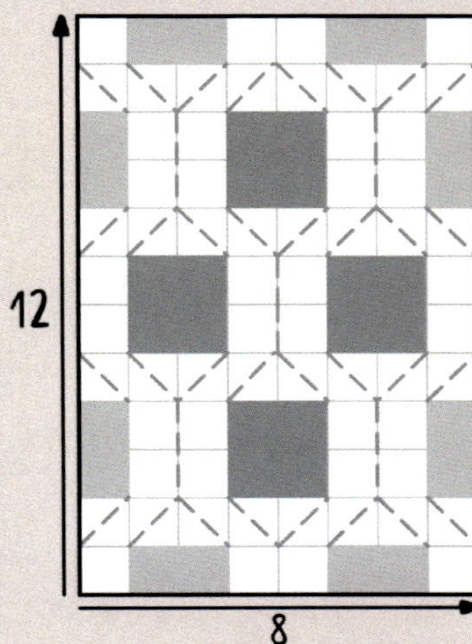

Every molecule has doubled, and instead of being a rectangle of 1 by 2, it is now a square of 2 by 2.

Variation B
Long Molecules
2 by 2 Project

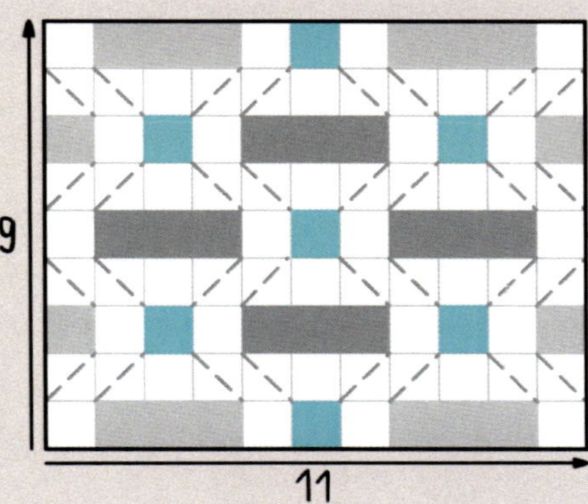

Every molecule is longer, and instead of being a rectangle of 1 by 2, it is now a rectangle of 1 by 3.

The blue areas are new cubes that emerge from the extra length of the molecule.

Variation C
Fat and Long Molecules
2 by 2 Project

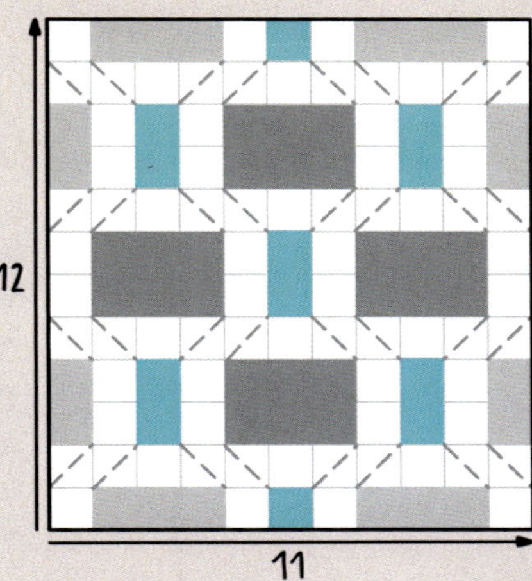

This combines the two previous variations. Every molecule is longer and fatter. Instead of being a rectangle of 1 by 2, it is now a rectangle of 2 by 3.

Overlapping Molecules

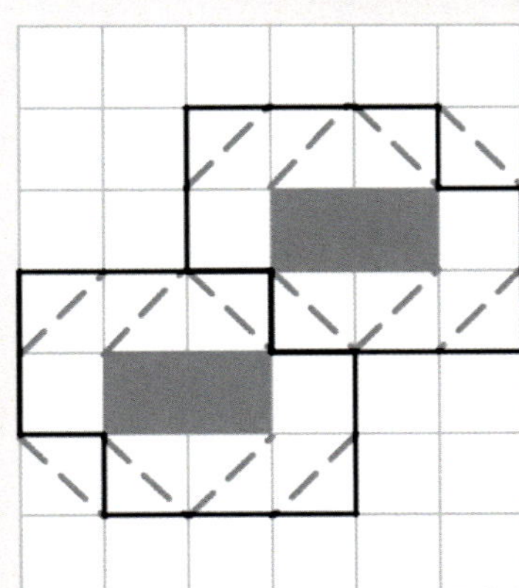

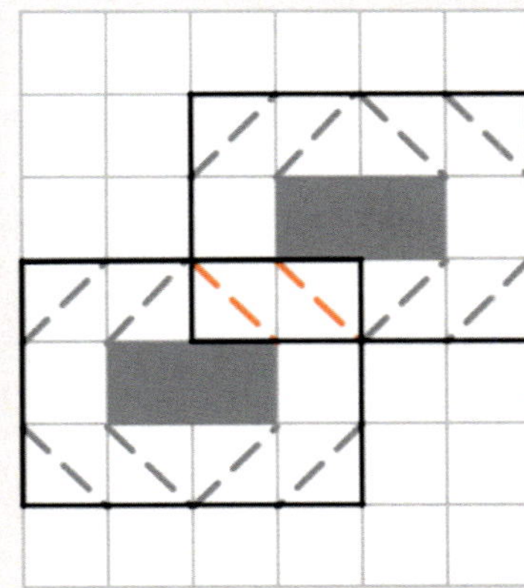

Overlapping molecules are caused when a molecule does not fit into a rectangle or a square but rather into a polygon.

On the left, the molecules are marked correctly. If we want to force the molecule into a rectangle we need to introduce overlapping molecules, where certain tiles (with the orange diagonals) participate in both molecules.

26 Zig-Zag Cubes

Designed by Hagay Golan

The Single Molecule

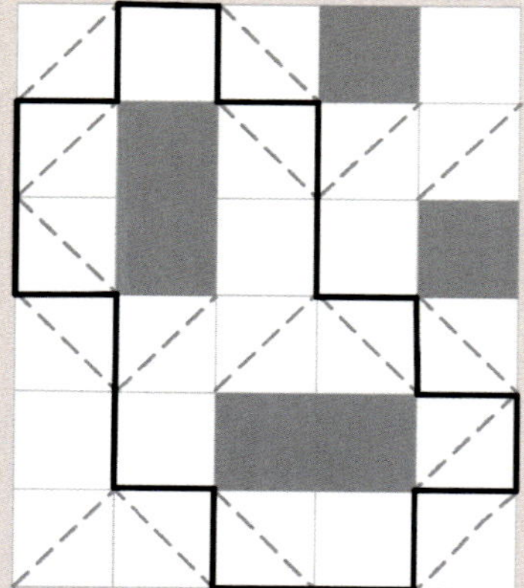

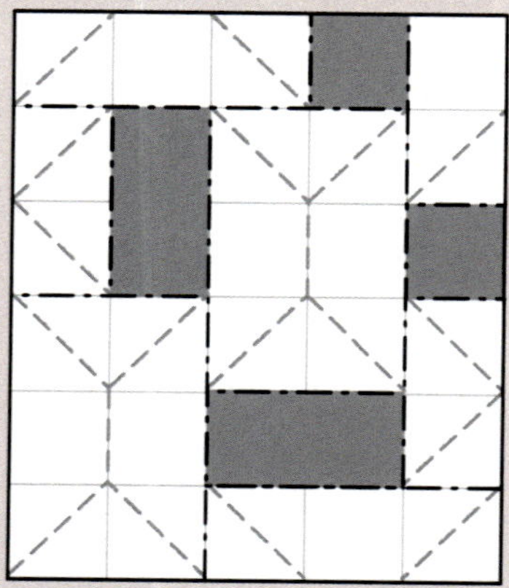

I tried to design this combination of zig-zagged rectangles for a week and failed. So I challenged Hagay, a friend and colleague, to do it for me. He came up with the solution the next day.

I relate the combination of a vertical rectangle with the horizontal one as the molecule (the upper CP).

This molecule has an irregular shape that cannot be bound by a square or a rectangle. Notice the molecule includes all the squares that are attached to any of the two grey rectangles, and only to them! The lower CP shows the molecule we are going to fold.

The molecules are shifted and raised.

The shrinkage ratio is 3:1.

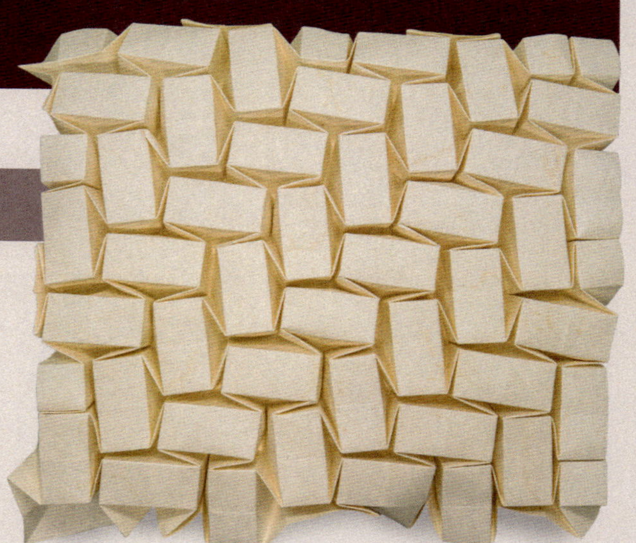

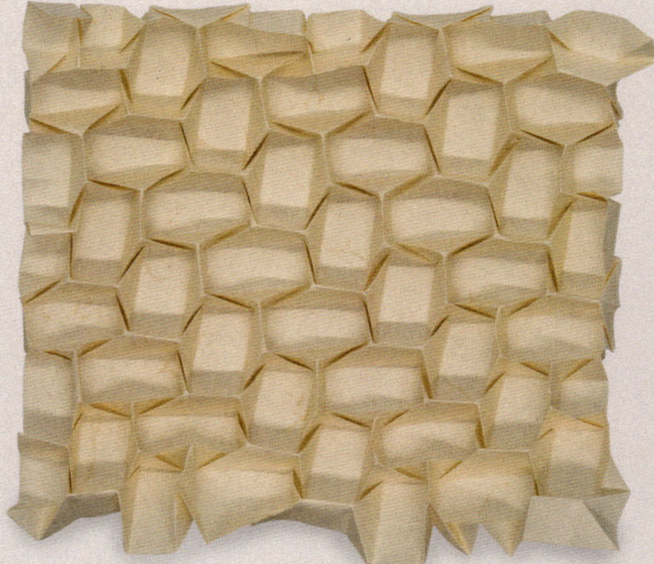

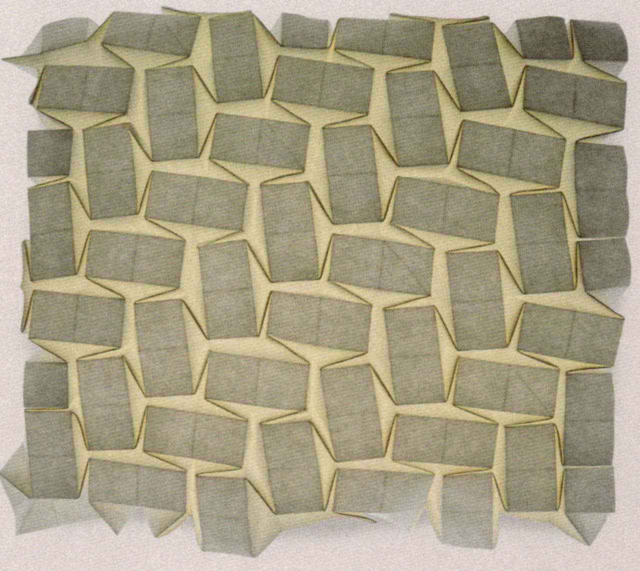

Top: recto view of a 18–molecule Zig-Zag Cubes tessellation.

Center: verso view of a 18–molecule Zig-Zag Cubes tessellation.

Bottom: recto view with back-light.

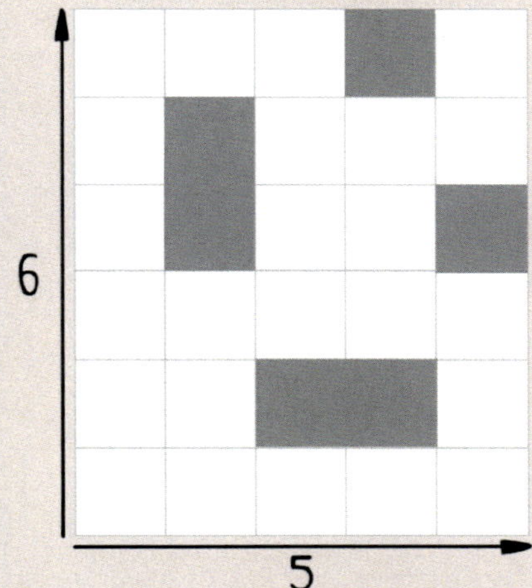

Start with a 6 by 5 grid and mark off the central rectangles.

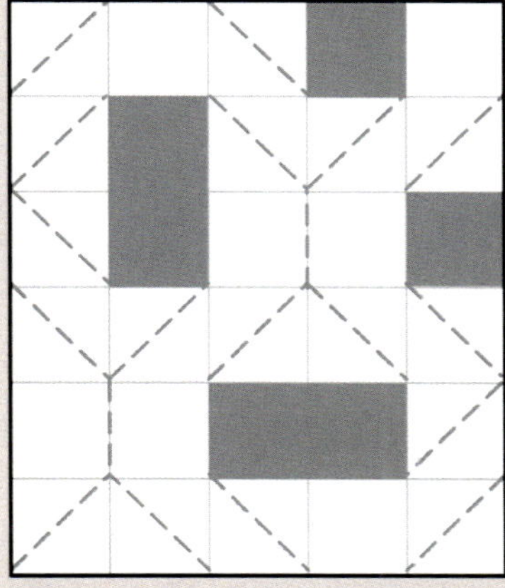

Crease all the valley folds, as marked. Follow the "headless raising-hands spreading-legs stick-man" shape (the spread Waterbomb base).

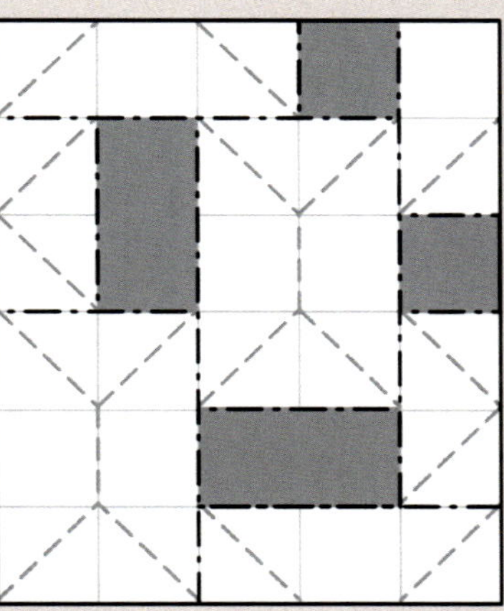

Add the remaining mountain creases as shown.
Collapse by forcing the spread Waterbomb base inward.

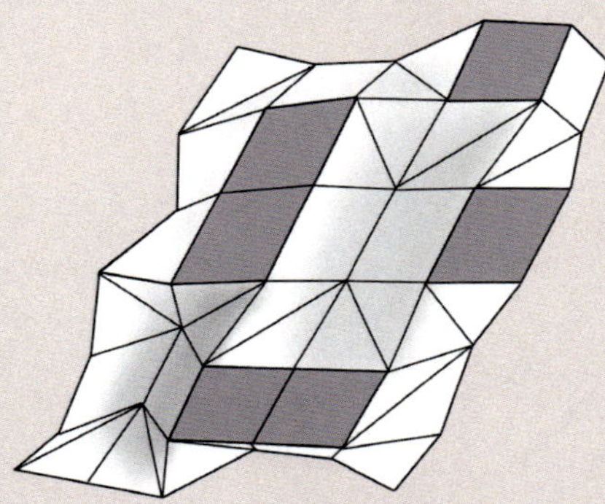

In process.

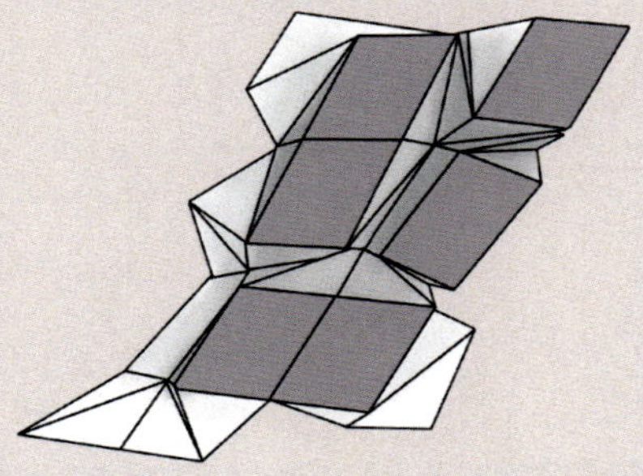

Fully collapsed.

Now you have a vertical rectangle by a horizontal one, and two rectangle-halves of the next molecule (on the right edge).

Simple Project

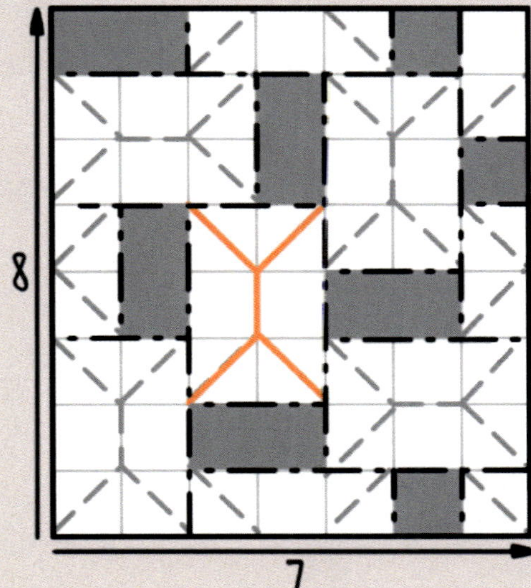

Use a grid of 8 by 7.

Although this looks quite similar to the Single Molecule project, we have two copies of the combination of vertical and horizontal rectangles.

The molecules are shifted.

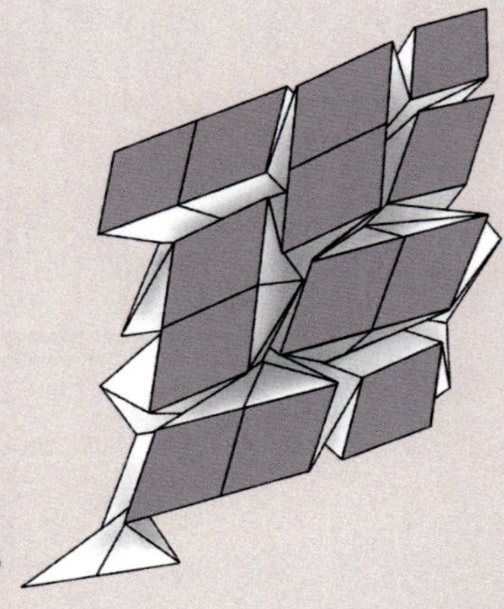

Follow the spread Waterbomb base, shown in orange! Sink them, while making sure the grey rectangles stay flat and high. It may be easier to check the other side and squeeze them from there.

Advanced Project

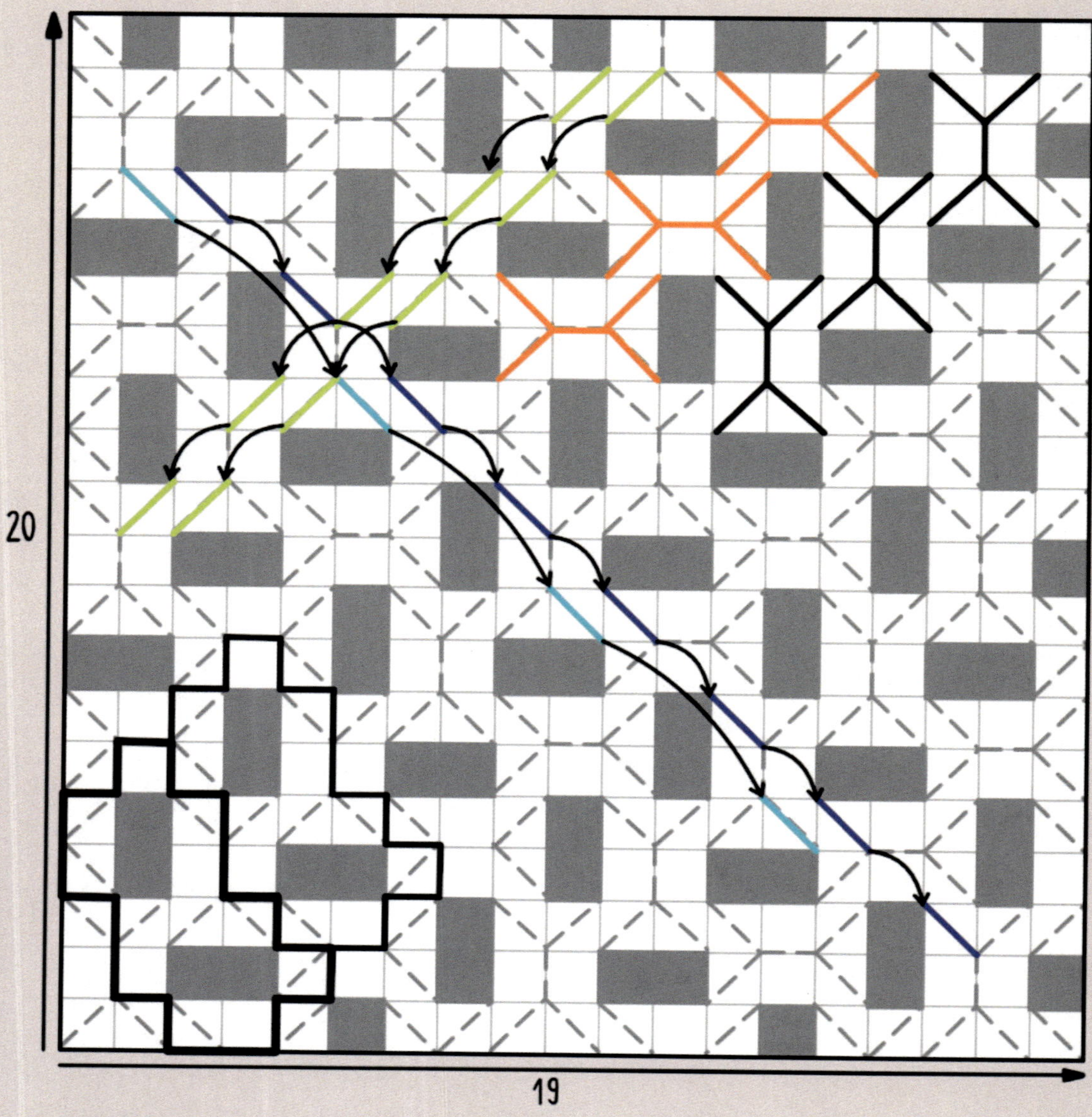

Make a 20 by 19 grid.

There is no simple formula for this model. You can choose any size, and copy the pattern to see how many molecules will feet.

There are some shortcuts for the precreases, but be careful while using them.

The blue lines follow a fold 1-skip 1 pattern. The light blue lines are fold 1, skip 3.

From the top right to bottom left you have pairs of green lines, both are fold 1-skip 1 pattern.

Alternatively, you can follow the orange and black spread Waterbomb bases. This will require more rotation of the paper, but it will make sure you will set all the precreases in place.

In both cases, it is wise to mark the rectangles of each molecule.

For the collapse, follow the spread Waterbomb bases.

Note the shape of the molecule on the bottom left, and how it covers the grid.

27 Hexa Cube

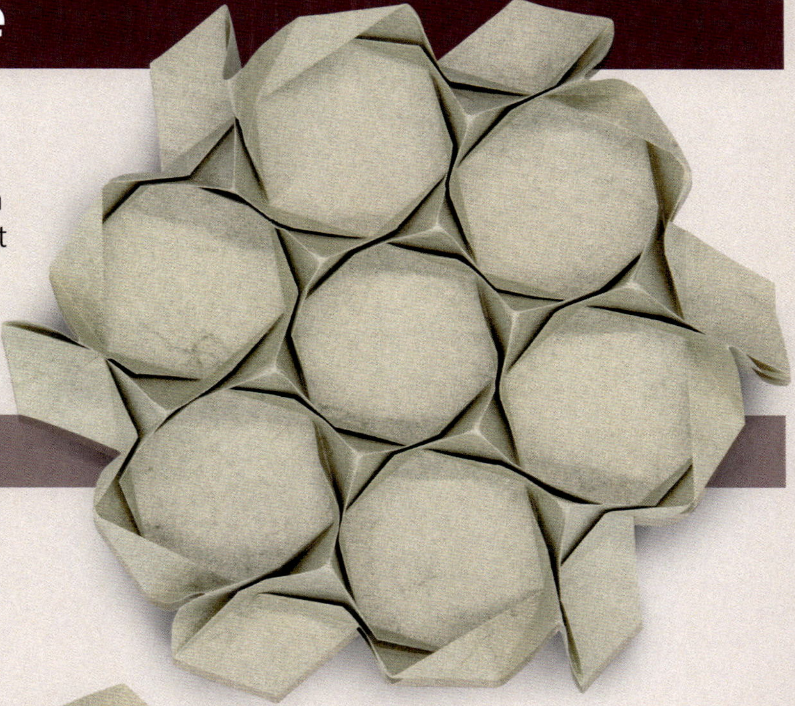

One of the obvious variations is to change the center from a square to a hexagon. The diagonals here connect two opposite corners of a rhombus, and the center will rotate when collapsed.

The Single Molecule

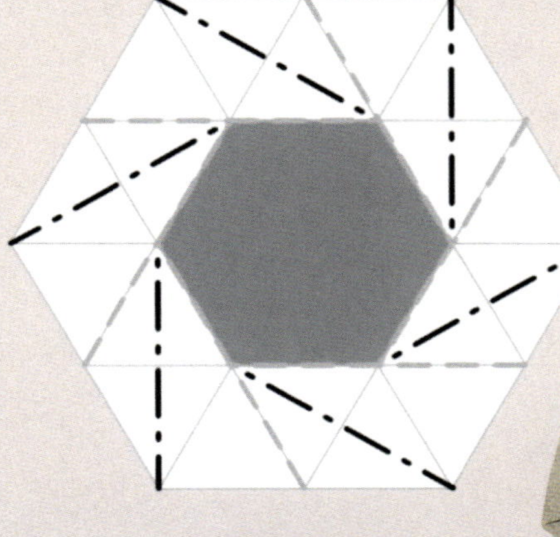

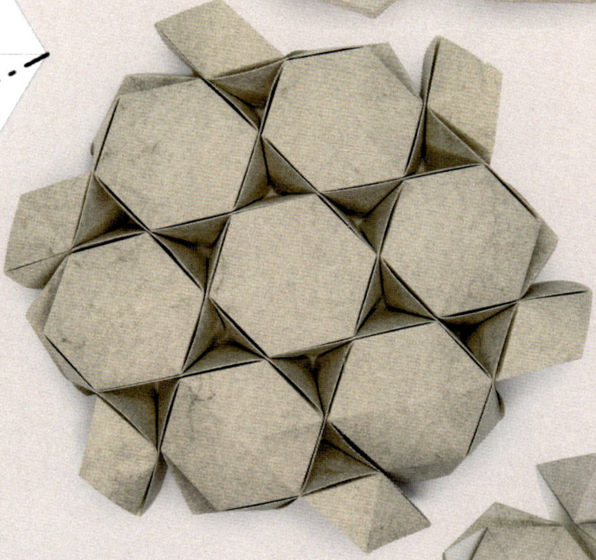

The molecule size is a grid of 4 by 4 by 4.

The molecules are rotated 60° and raised.

The shrinkage ratio is 2:1.

Please note that in this model the gray area in the center will stay flat on the table.

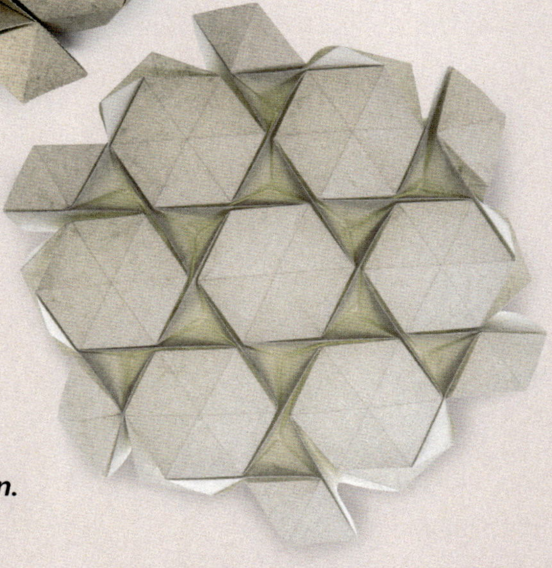

Top: recto view of a 7-molecule Hexa Cube tessellation.

Center: verso view of a 7-molecule Hexa Cube tessellation.

Bottom: recto view with back-light.

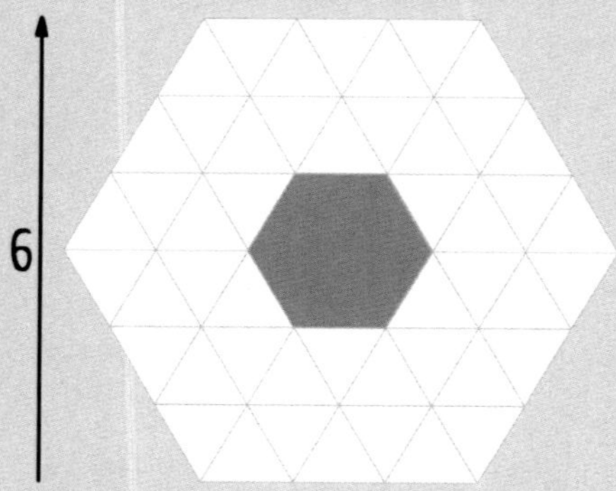

Start with a grid of 6 by 6 by 6.

Mark the center hexagon.

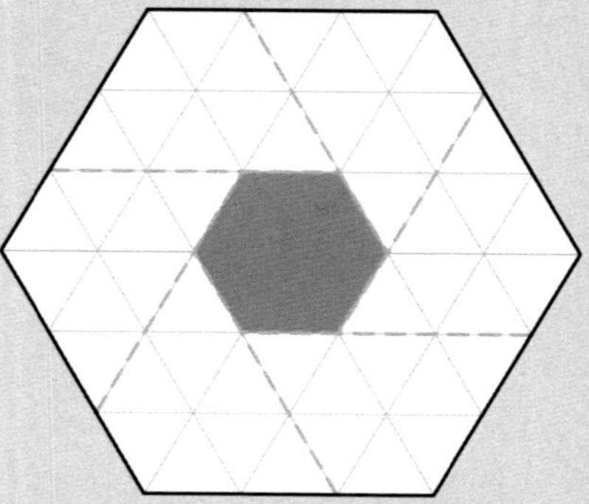

Mark the valleys.

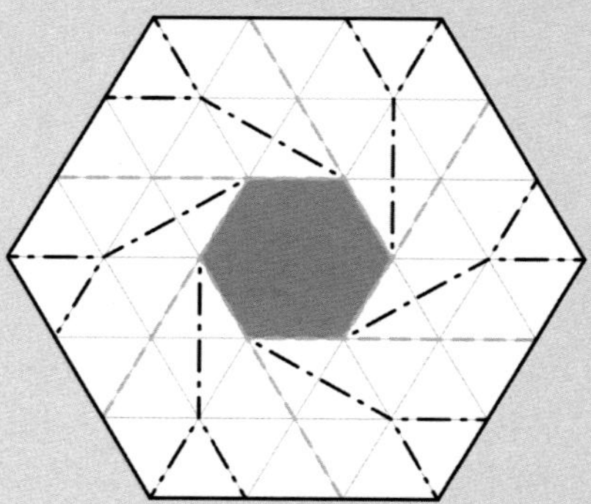

Add the needed mountains. Note that the inner ones are NOT on the grid.

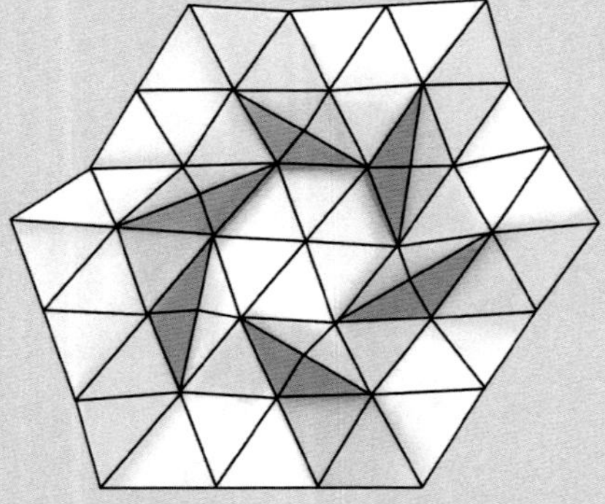

Start the collapse by twisting the inner hexagon, and pinching the off-grid mountains.

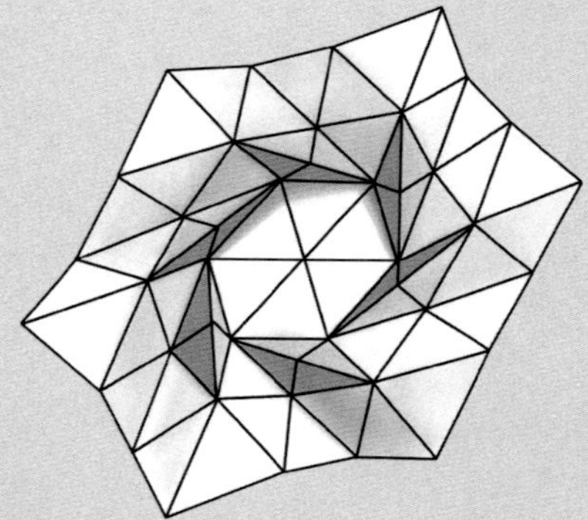

Collapsed. You can tighten the creases even more.

12 Grid Project

Start with a grid of 12 by 12 by 12.

Mark all the molecule-center hexagons.
Add all the precreases around each center.

Note the pattern of the precreases.
Fold a diagonal of a rhombus, and then skip a rhombus to fold another diagonal.

Start the collapse in the center, and add the next molecules, one by one, around it. To complete the collapse on the edges, note that each corner of a hexagon contains a third of the center of a molecule (lighter grey).

Collapse the model by focusing on the triangular waterbombs on the backside of the model. Start in the center and spread out from there. Note that every two parallel mountain-lines have a valley in between.

You can also start from any side as it may be easier to handle the first molecule from the edge of the paper.

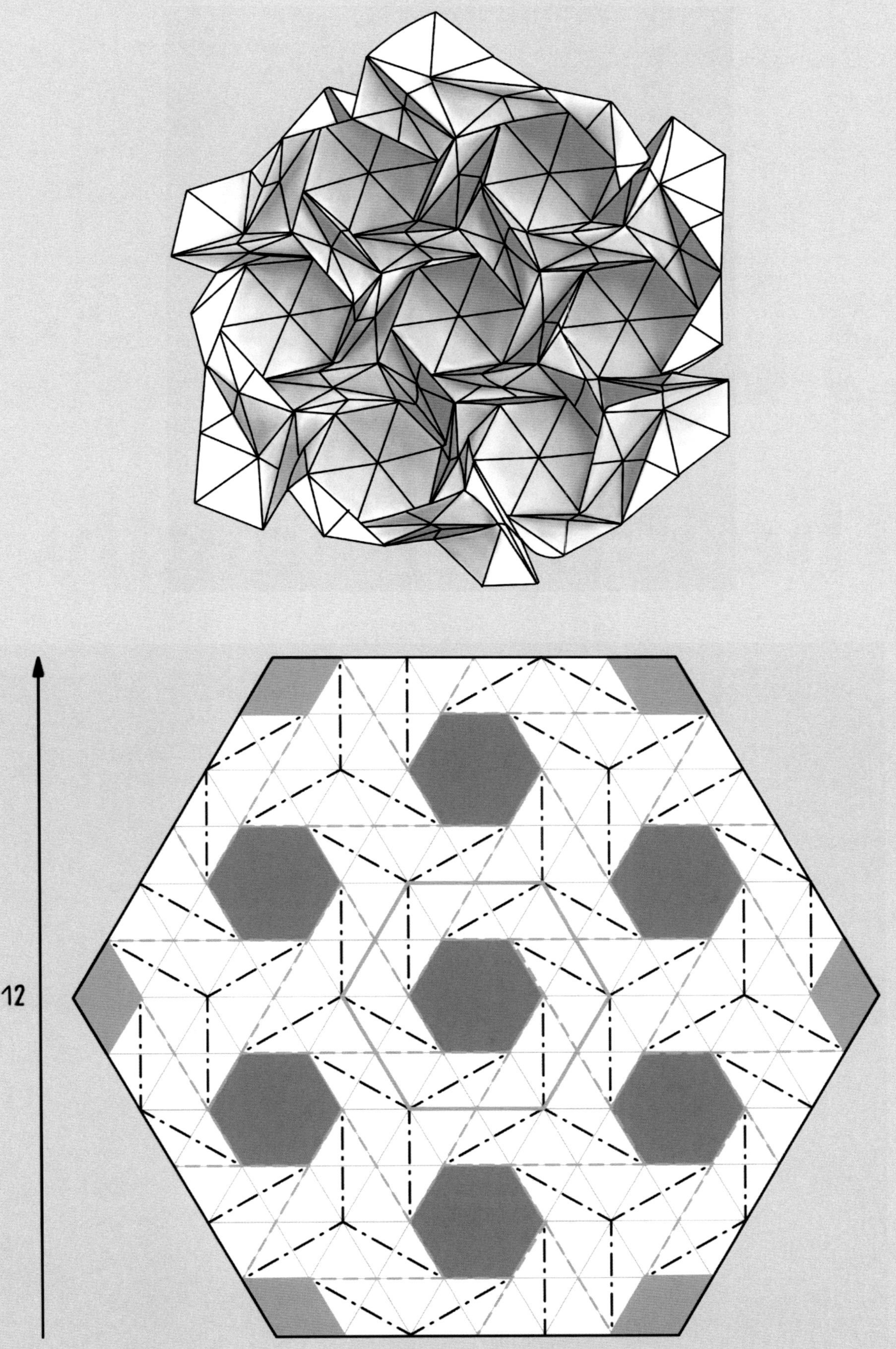
12

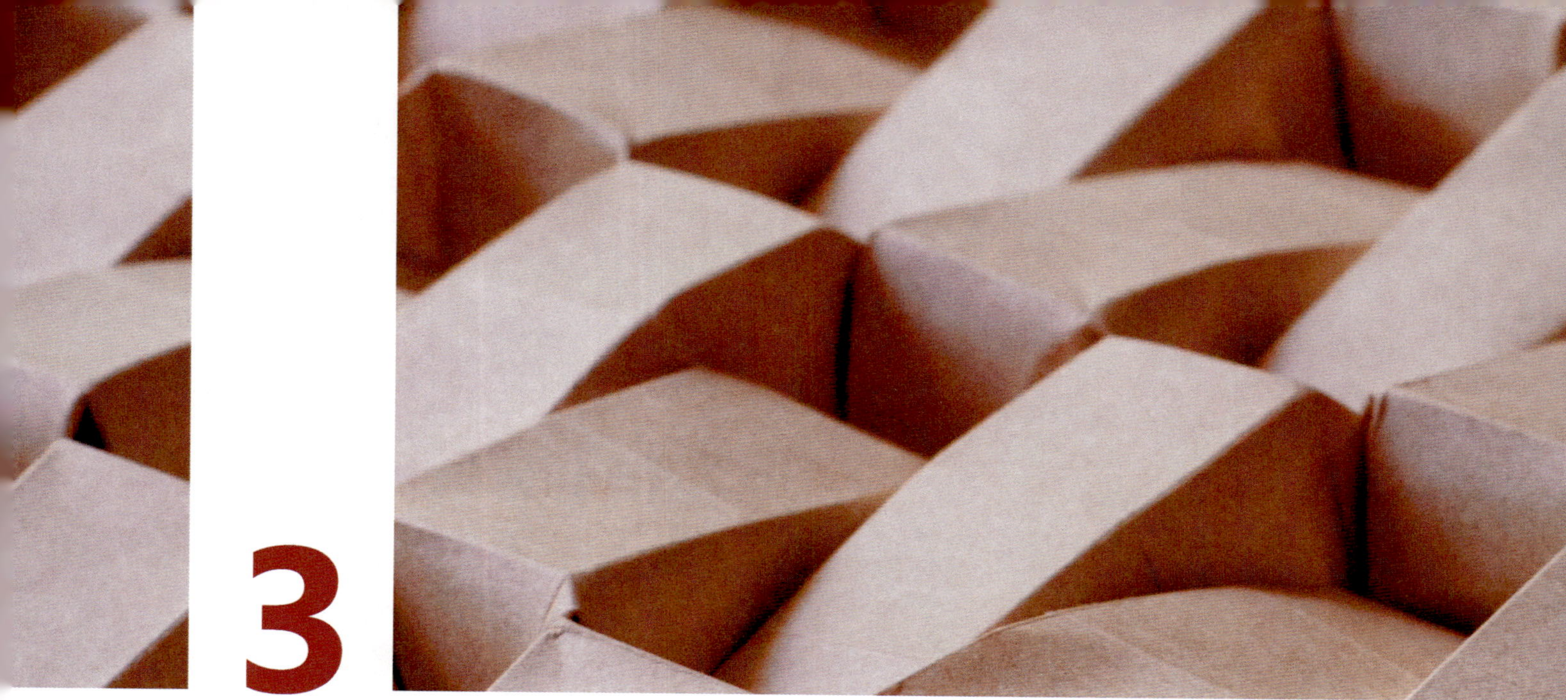

3 The Zipper Family

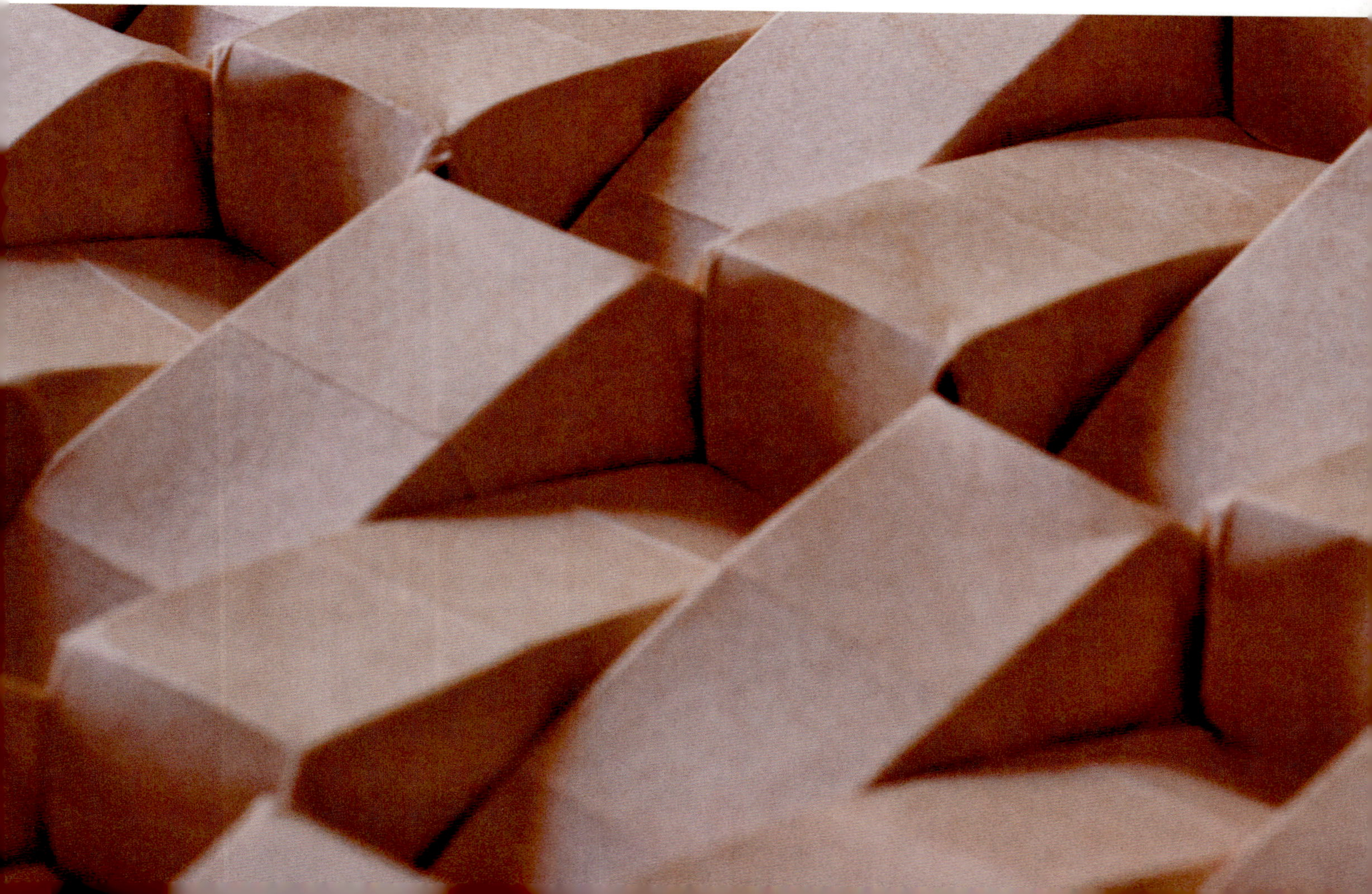

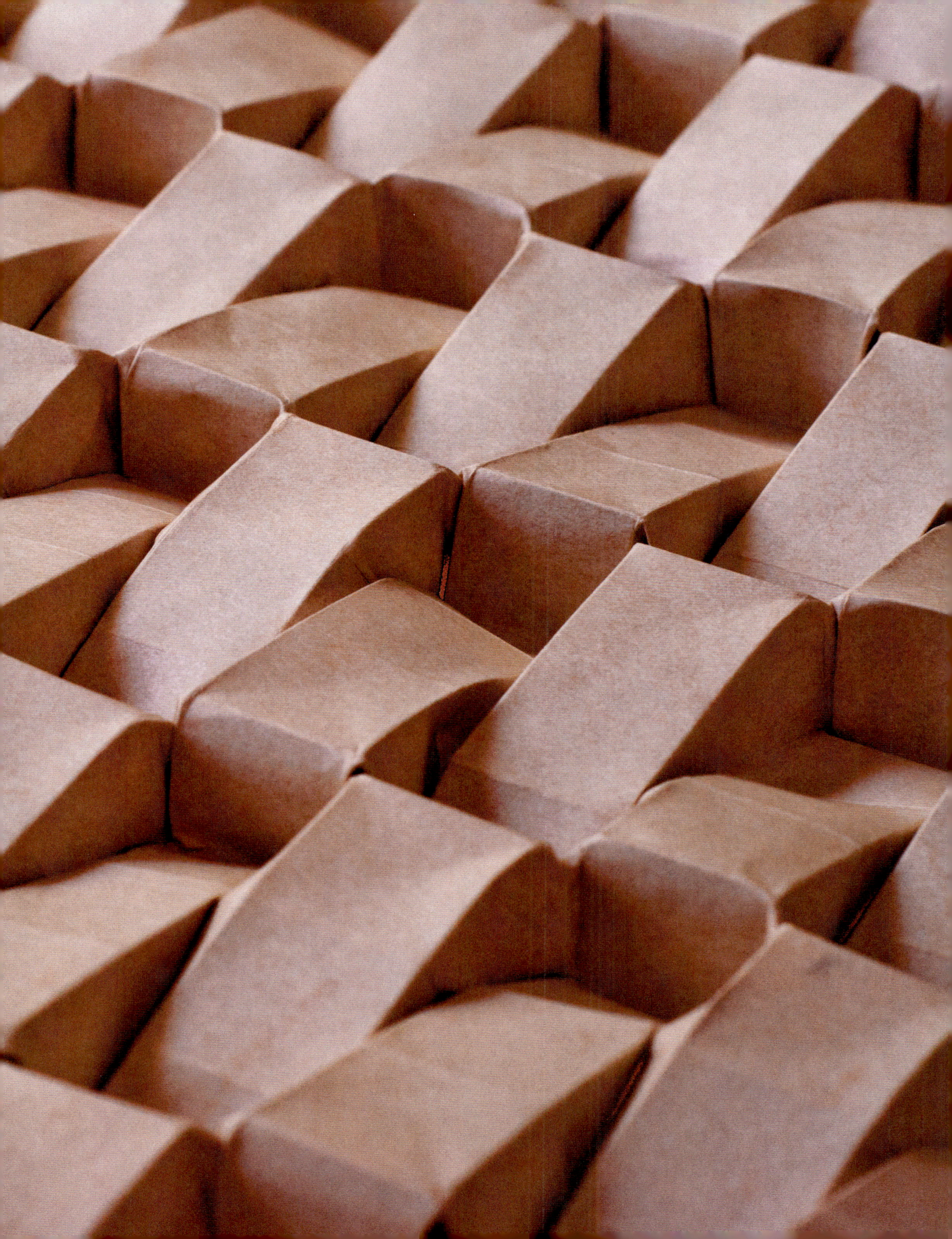

Introduction

The Zipper family is based on two parallel lines of interlocking "teeth", just like a zipper is built.

This molecule does not have four identical edges, but two pairs of them. The top and bottom edges are the same, and so are the left and right ones, but the left is not like the top! For this reason, most of the single-molecule projects here will present one and a half molecules that are easier to collapse.

The molecules in this chapter are narrow, so the last project in each model is a 3 by 5 and not 4 by 4, as the latter result in a narrow model, while the 3 by 5 provides a more balanced look.

3 1 Diamond 1 by 2

The Single Molecule

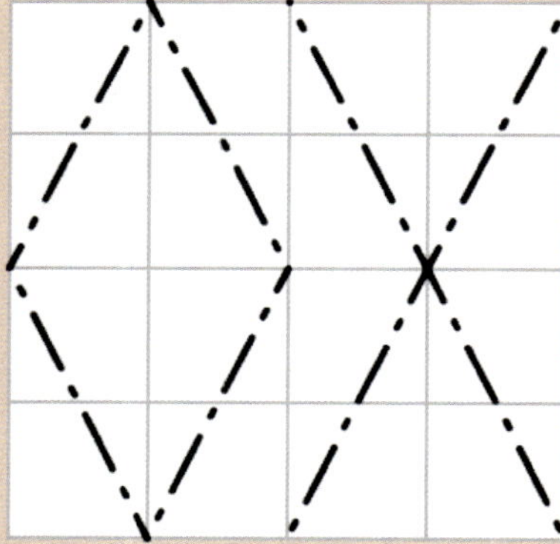

The molecule size is 4 by 4.

It is made from the diagonals of 1 by 2 rectangles, hence the name.

The molecule follows an up-down movement. While some of the areas will stay at the table level, some will raise one square.

The shrinkage differs between the axes. The left-right ratio is 2:1 while the top-bottom is negligible.

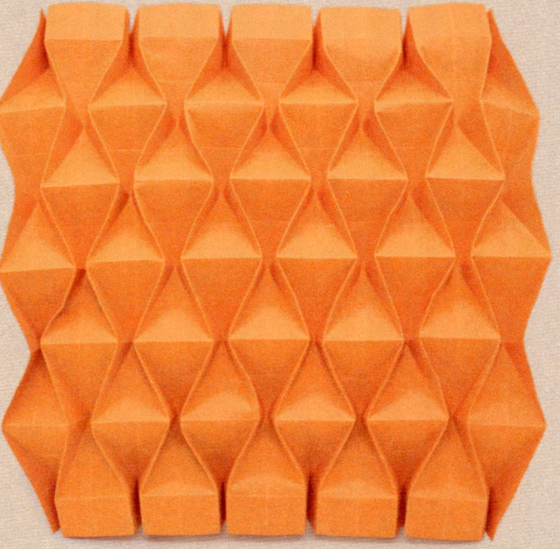

Top: recto view of a 3 by 5–molecule Diamond 1 by 2 tessellation.

Bottom: verso view of a 3 by 5–molecule Diamond 1 by 2 tessellation.

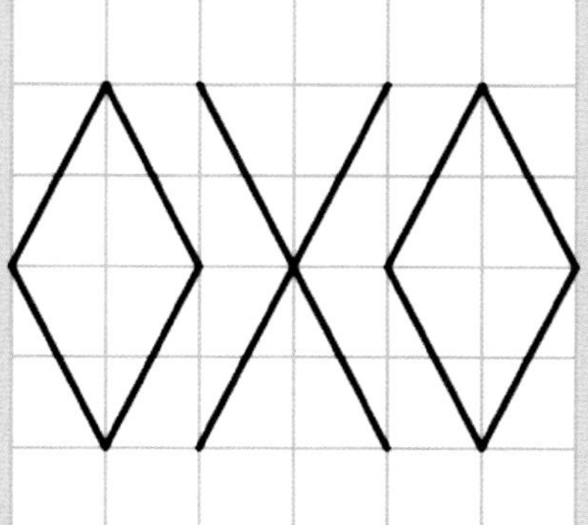

For an easier process, we are going to make one and a half molecules. It is easier to handle the middle part when it is surrounded by molecules.

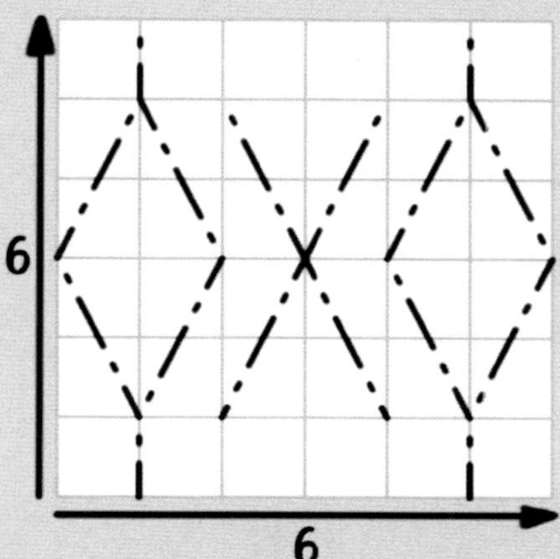

Start with a 6 by 6 grid. Mark the X and the two diamonds.

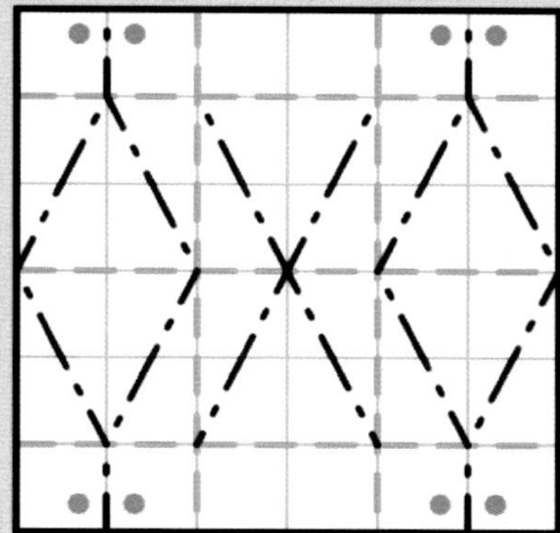

Add all the needed creases. Note the mountain fold lines on the top and bottom rows. Pinch the squares on both sides of the mountains mentioned to start the collapse.

At the same time, make sure the center of the X goes up!

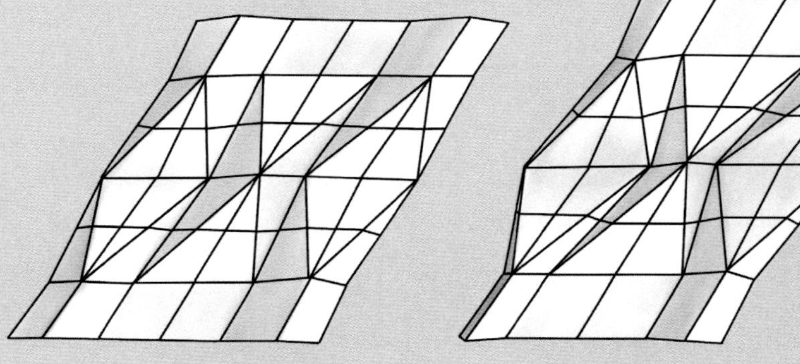

In process

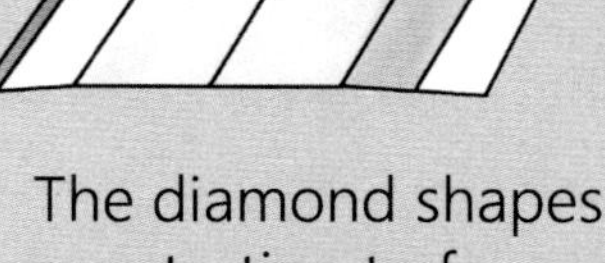

The diamond shapes are starting to form.

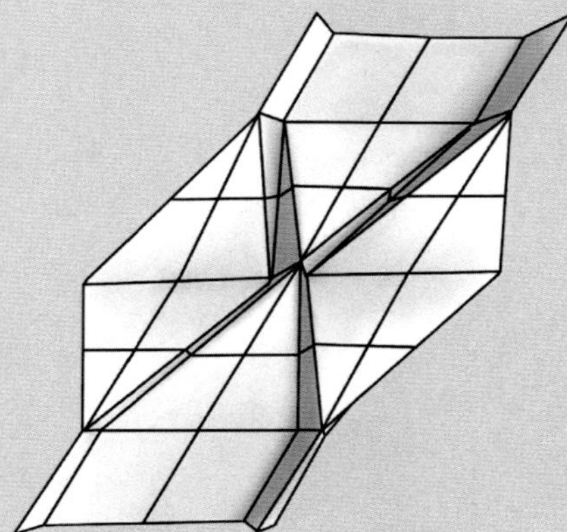

Fully collapsed. Note the rhythm of the edges — two flat squares, bordered by two vertical squares.

Above and Beyond

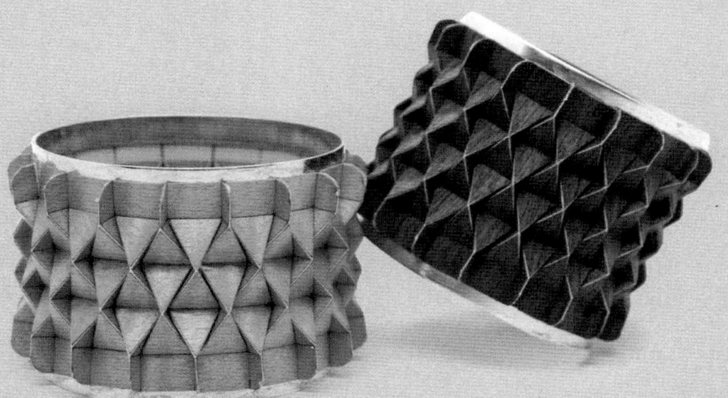

Two wooden bracelets using the Diamond tessellation

2 by 2 Molecules

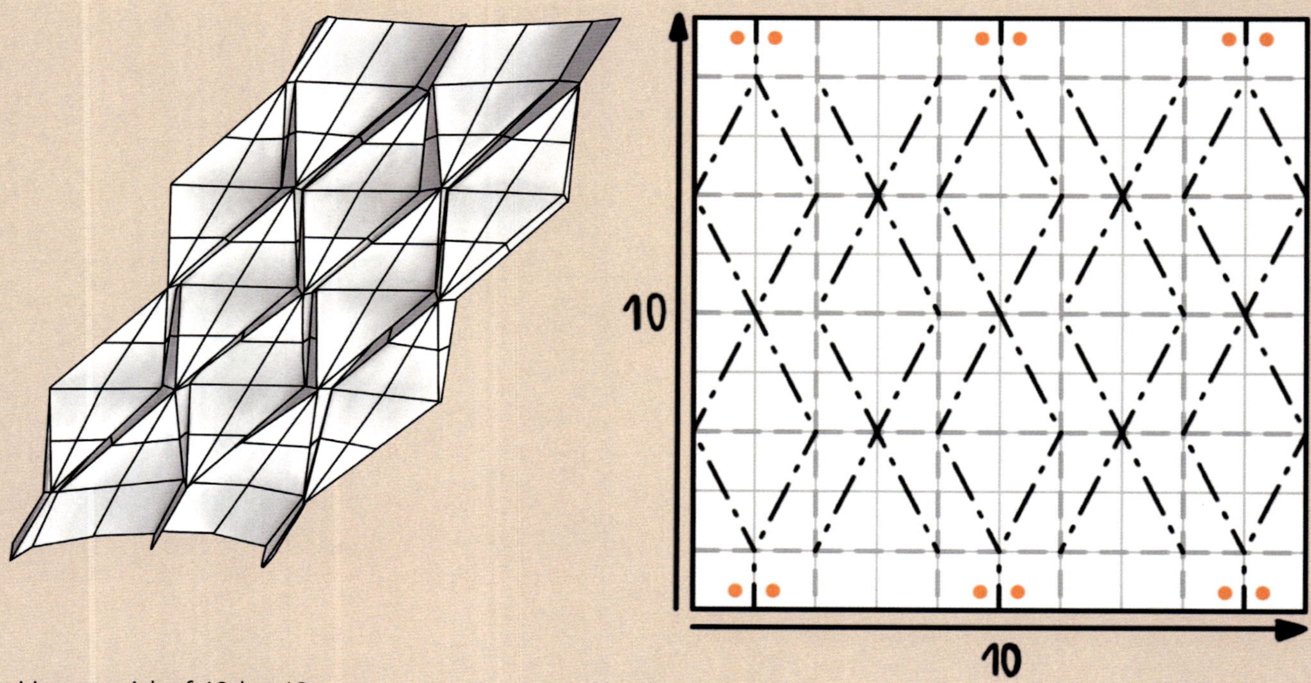

Use a grid of 10 by 10.

For the same reason as with the single molecule, we are going to make a 2 by 2.5–molecule project.

Add all the needed creases, and mark the mountains at the top and bottom rows.

Collapse the model by pinching the mentioned mountains, and making sure every X center is high, while every median of a rhombus stays on the table level.

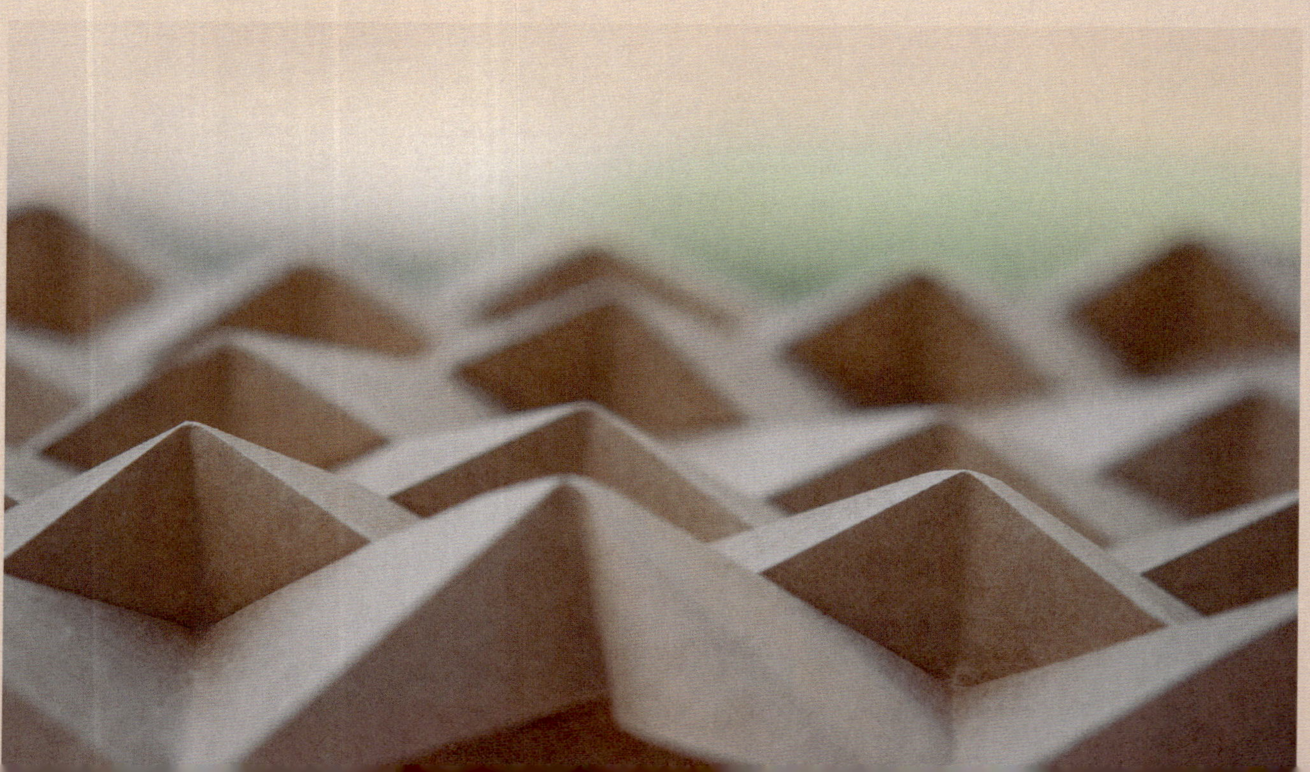

3 by 5 Molecules

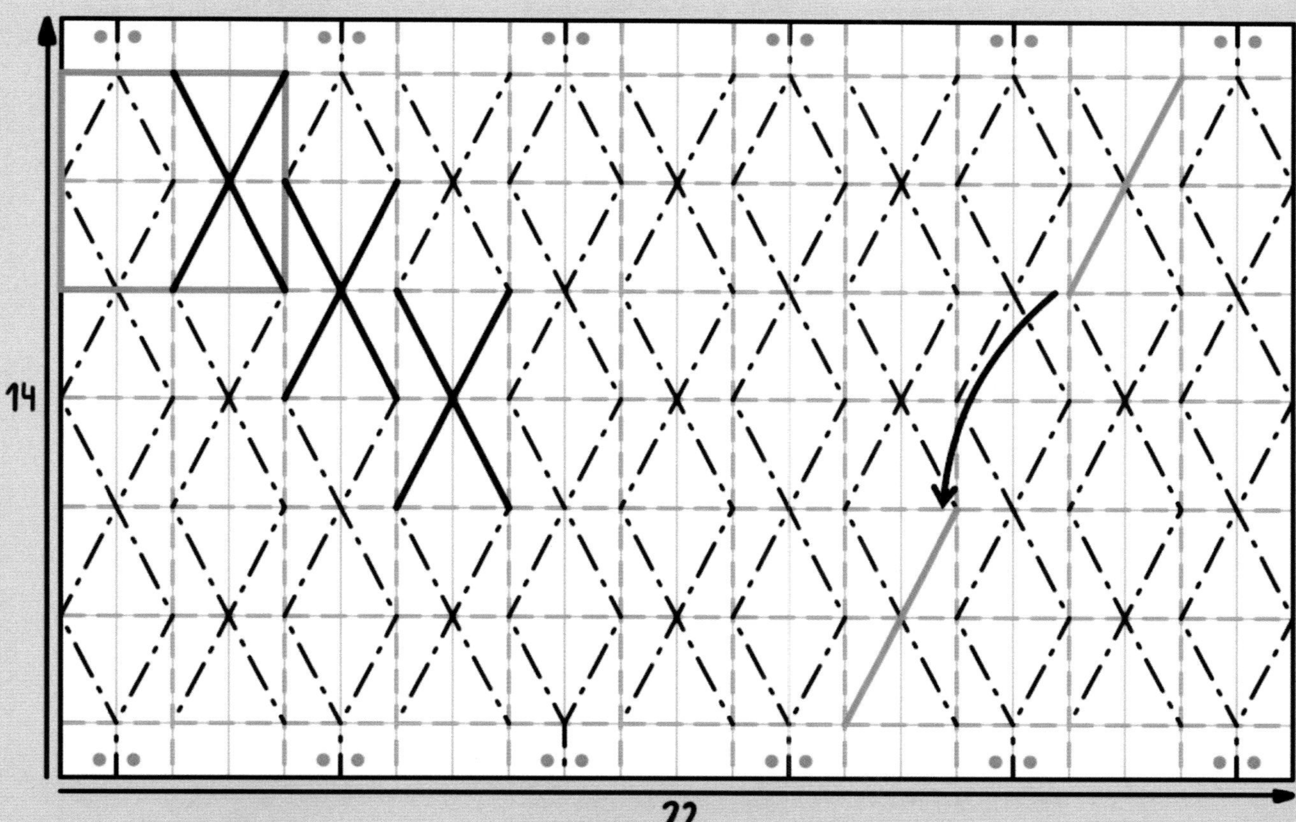

Make a grid of 14 by 22.

The formula for the height is 1 + 3 × 4 + 1 = 14.

For the width, it is 5.5 × 4 = 22.

The final result will be almost 14 squares in height and 12 squares wide.

It is easier to follow the big Xs (in bold black, so you rotate the paper with every X you make), but it is faster if you crease all the lines that go in the same direction (orange lines) one after the other, and only when finished switch to the other direction. In the latter case, the rule is fold four diagonals and jump four.

To collapse, pinch the left mountain on the top and bottom rows and make sure all the Xs centers are poking out. Jump to the next pair of mountains, and repeat the process. Do not hesitate to put pressure on the **complete** sheet of paper from right to left, as it will help you keep the collapsed molecules in place.

Vase Project

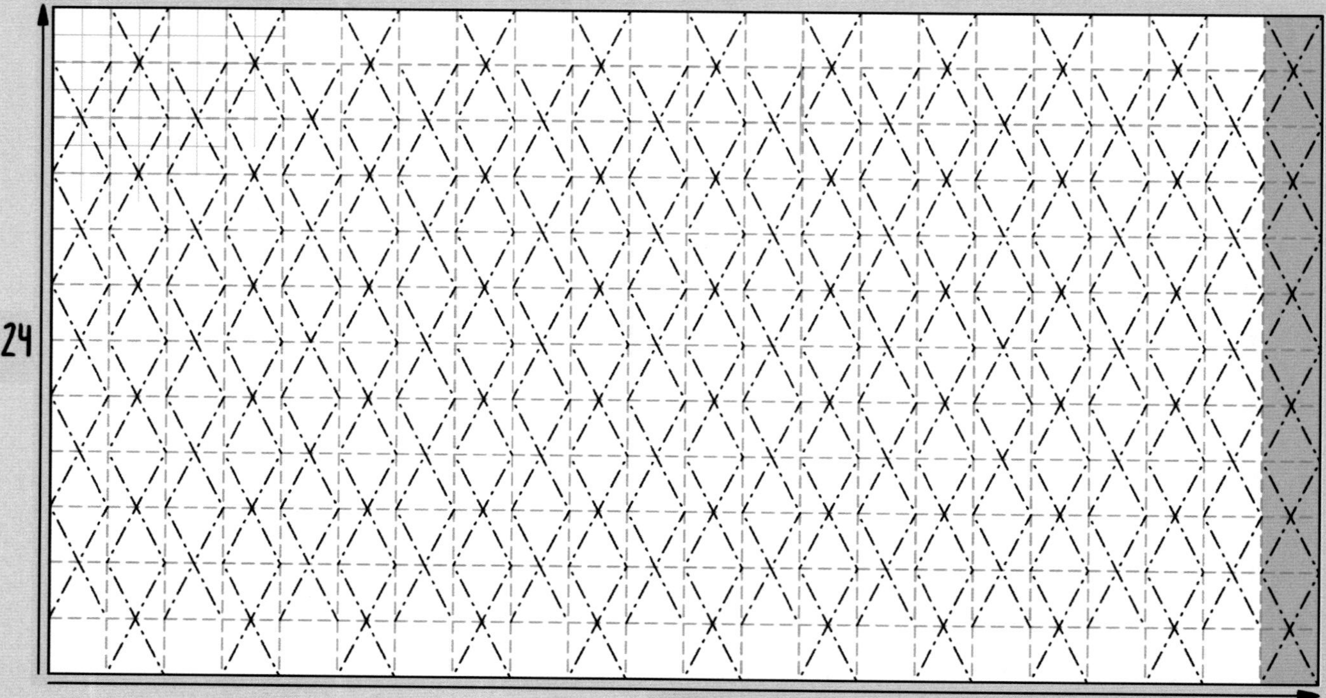

You can make this vase (that could have been in the sixth chapter), if you start with a grid of 24 by 42. Use the last two columns for glueing (in grey). For a cleaner look on the top and bottom rows, skip the half-diamond on the even columns.

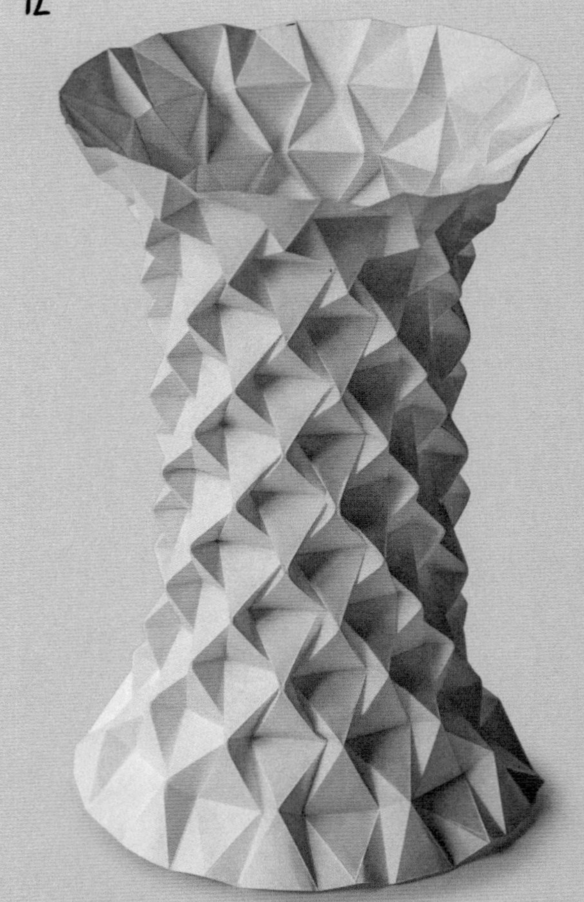

Variations

As always, small modifications in the folding sequence or the crease pattern expands the possibilities of the pattern.

One of them is based on a squash fold that gives it the look of a traffic jam. The other reminded me of stitches, hence the name.

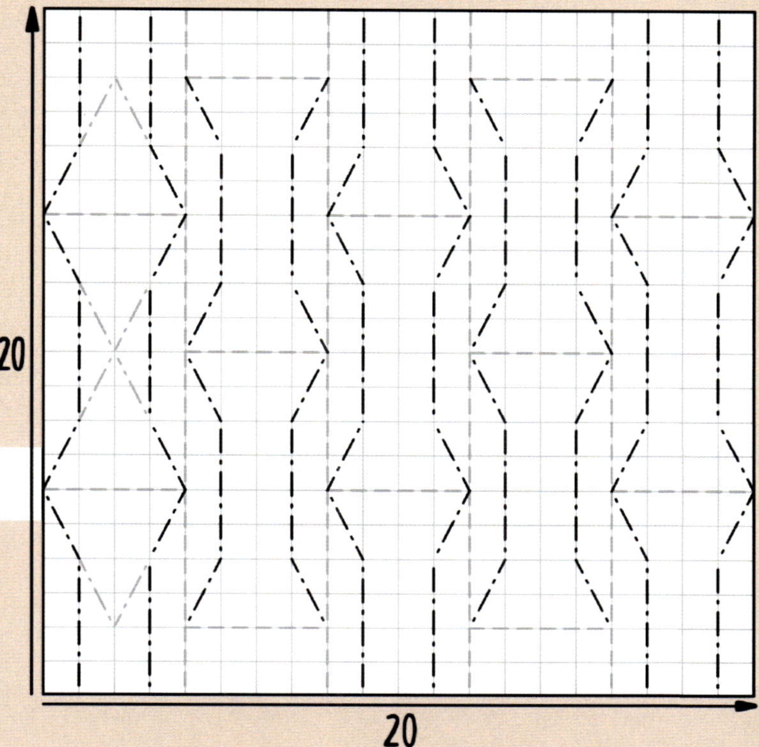

Variation A — Traffic Jam

This is the result of "squashing/flattening" every high point of the X shapes. You can do it during the pre-creases phase, as indicated in the CP.
See the grey mountain lines on the left-most molecules, indicating the original creases.

The model is a bit harder to collapse, since you cannot pinch the mountains as before.

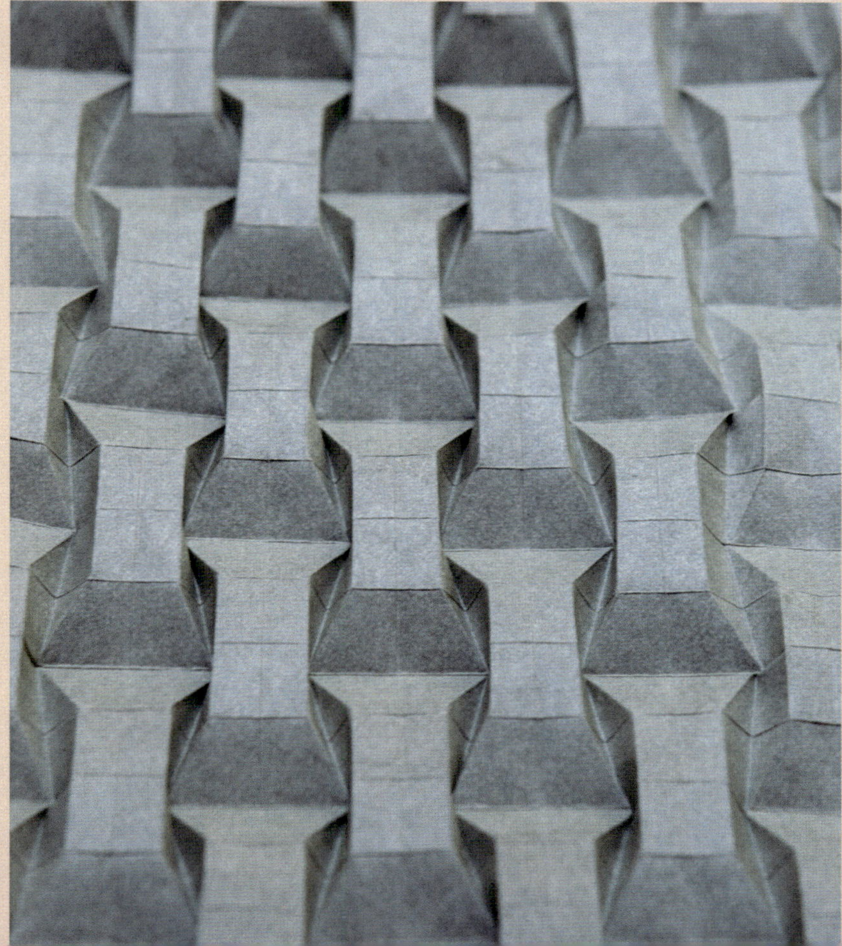

Variation B — Stitched

This variation is using grafting, to add a row of space between the vertical molecules.

The model is a bit harder to collapse, since you cannot pinch the mountains as before.

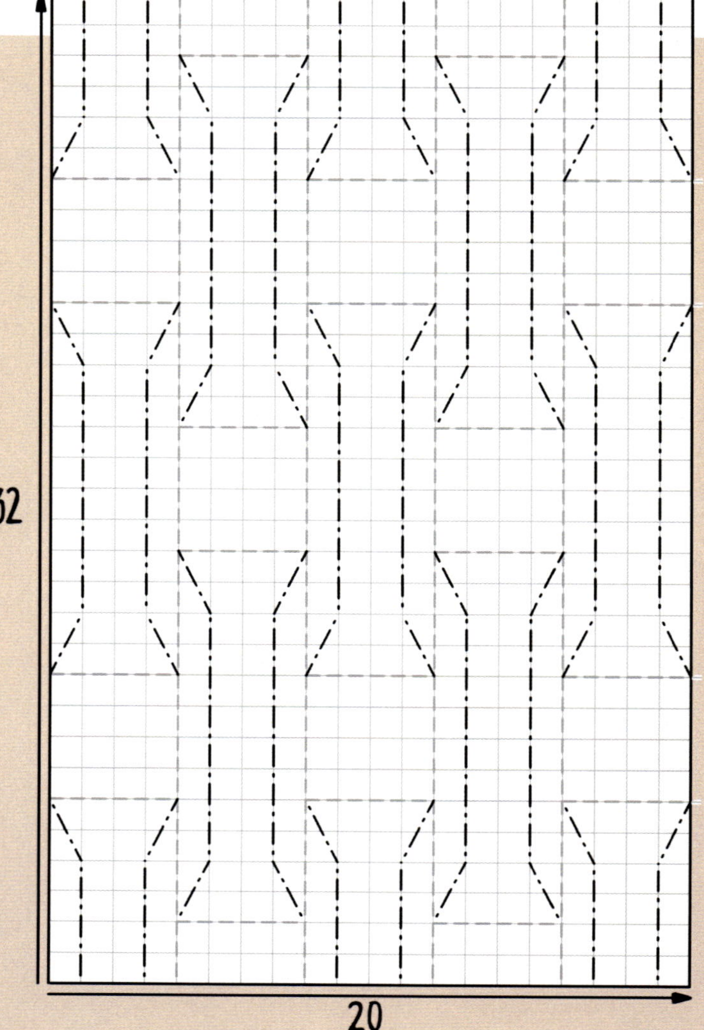

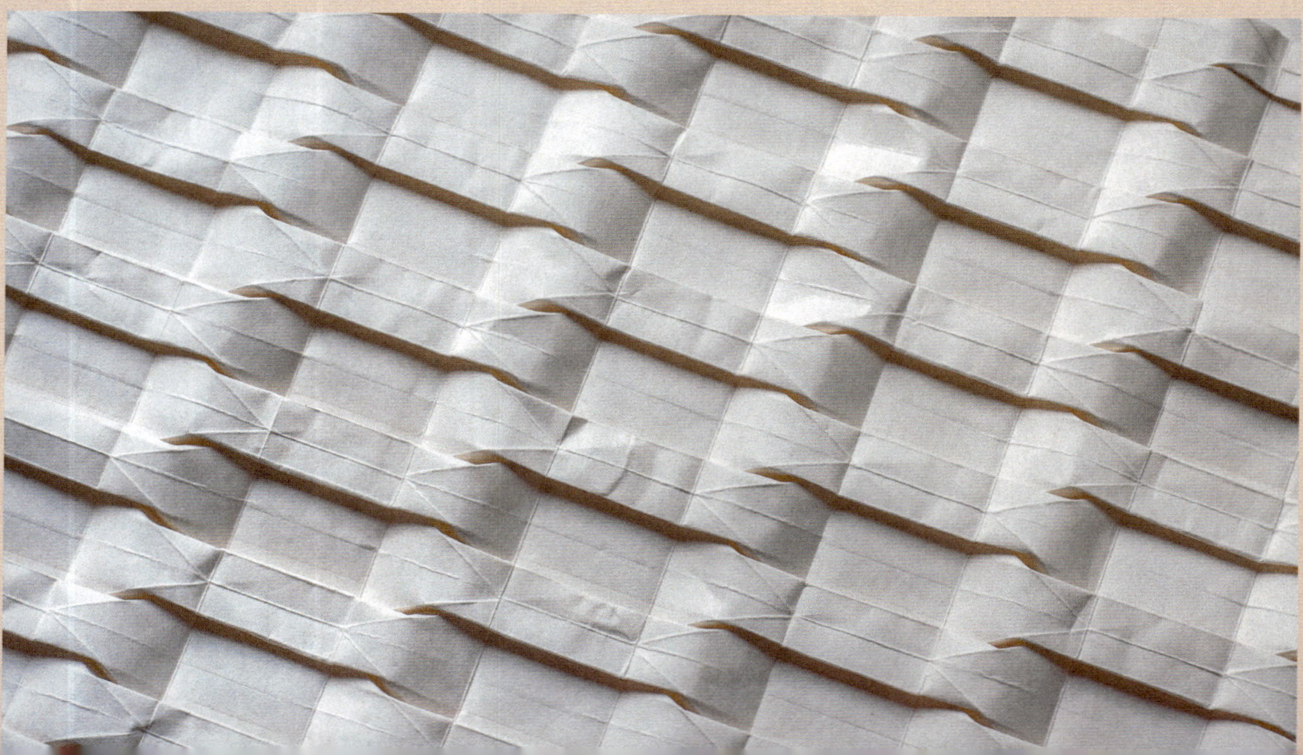

Above and Beyond

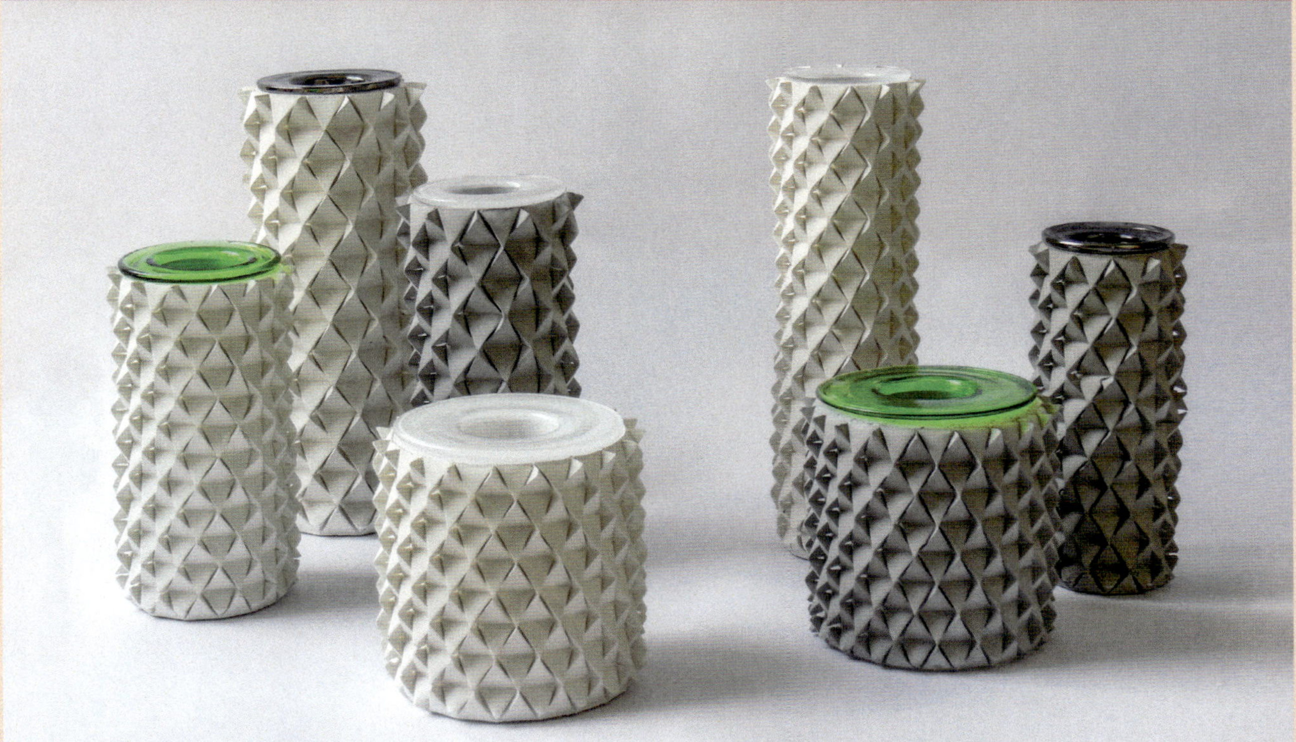

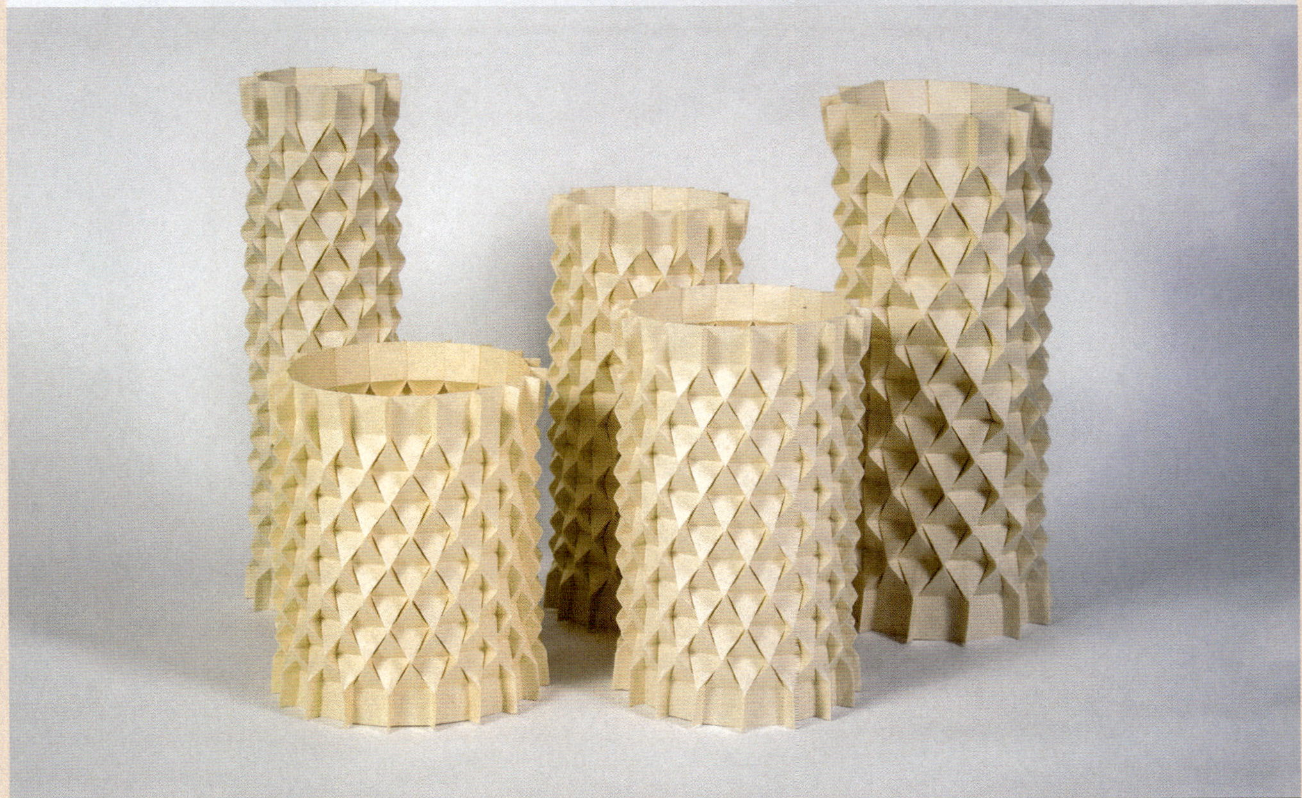

Palmas, concrete vases made by using the paper tessellations as a mold. Designed by Ofir Zucker and me. Image by Ofir Zucker.

3 2 Diamond 1 by 3

The Single Molecule

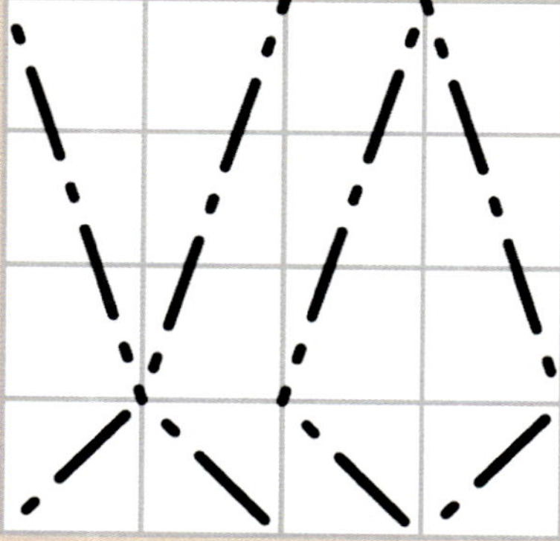

The molecule size is 4 by 4.

In this variation, the center of the X has moved down one square. This made the upper diagonals to be stretched inside a 1 by 3 rectangle, hence the name.

The molecule follows an up-down movement. While some of the areas will stay at the table level, some will raise one square.

The shrinkage differs between the axes. The left-right ratio is 2:1 while the top-bottom is 4:3.

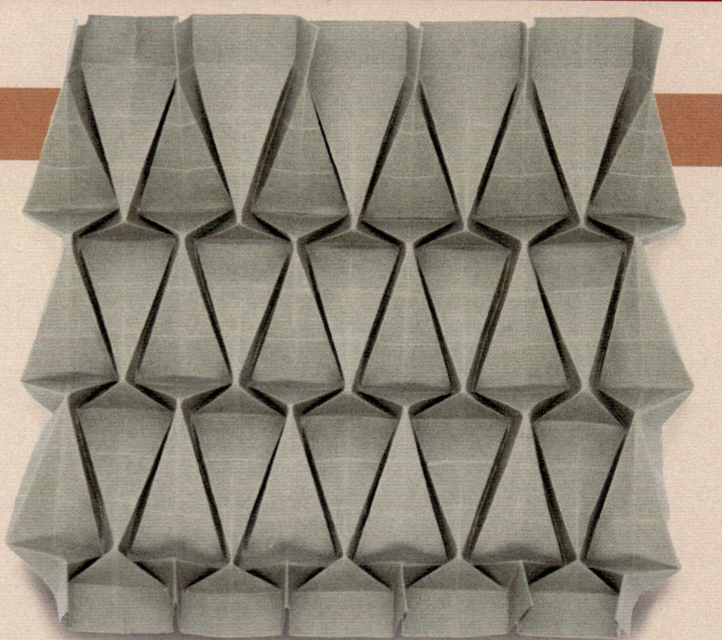

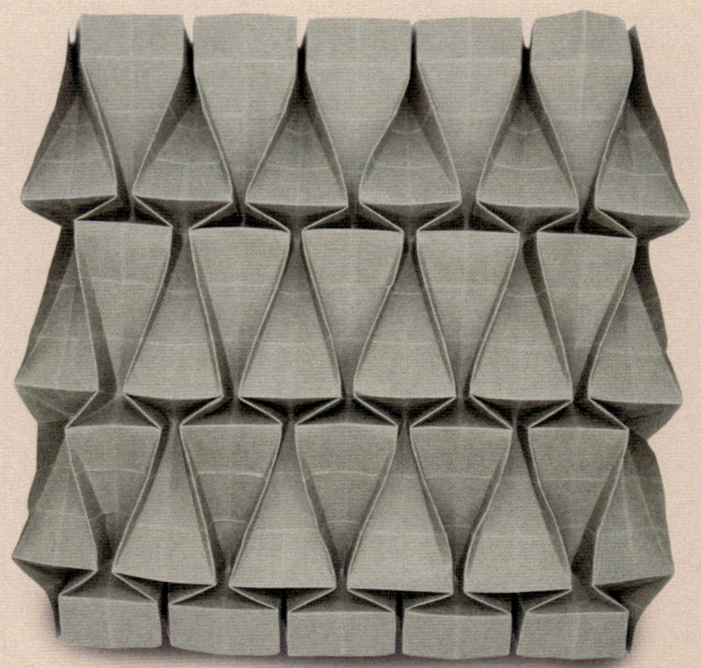

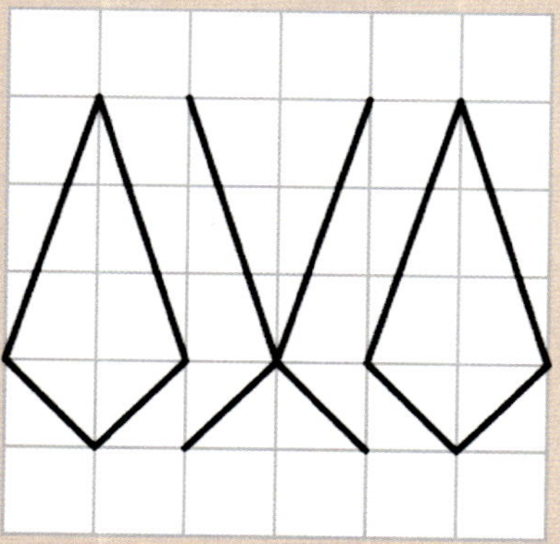

For an easier process, we are going to make one and a half molecules. It is easier to handle the middle part when it is surrounded by molecules.

Top: recto view of a 3 by 5–molecule Diamond 1 by 3 tessellation.

Bottom: verso view of a 3 by 5–molecule Diamond 1 by 3 tessellation.

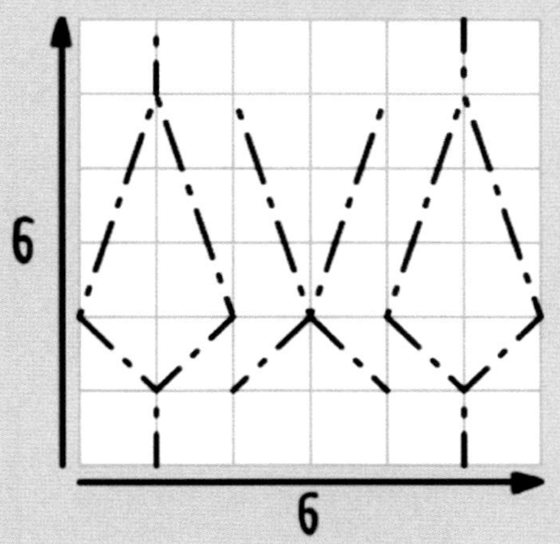

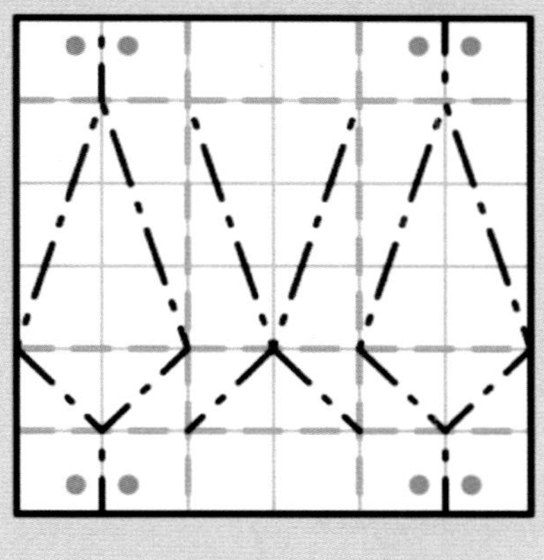

Add all the needed creases. Note the mountain fold lines on the top and bottom rows. Pinch the squares on both sides of the mountains mentioned to start the collapse. Make sure the center of the distorted X goes up!

Start with a 6 by 6 grid. Mark the creases.

In process.

Fully collapsed. Note the rhythm of the edges is exactly like the **1 by 2 Diamond** model (page 54) — two flat squares, bordered by two vertical squares.

2 by 2 Molecules

Use a grid of 10 by 10.

For the same reason as with the single molecule, we are going to make a 2 by 2.5–molecule project.

Add all the needed creases, and mark the mountains at the top and bottom rows.

Collapse the model by pinching the mentioned mountains, and making sure every (distorted) X center is high, while every short diagonal of a kite stays on the table level.

3 by 5 Molecules

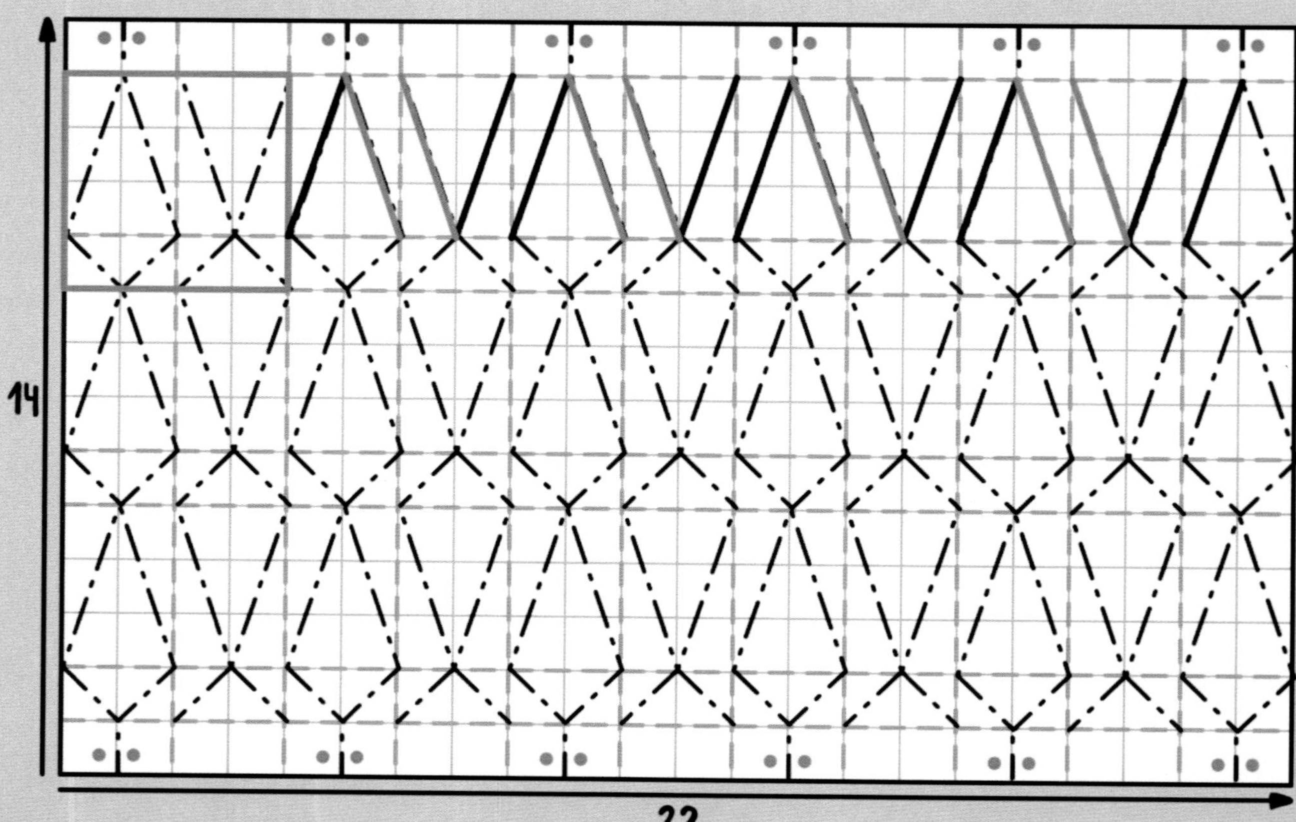

Make a grid of 14 by 22.

The formula for the height is 1 + 3 × 4 + 1 = 14.

For the width, it is 5.5 × 4 = 22.

The final result will be 11 squares high and 12 squares wide.

There are no evident shortcuts here. For better clarity, try to follow all the creases at the same angle in each row (bold black), and return with the other angle (orange).

To collapse, pinch the left-most mountain on the top and bottom rows and make sure all the distorted X's centers are poking out. Jump to the next pair of mountains, and repeat the process. Do not hesitate to put pressure on the complete sheet of paper from right to left, as it will help you keep the collapsed molecules in place.

Variation A — Spacing

It is easy to add columns of spaces and make every molecule wider. The model is a bit harder to collapse, since you cannot pinch the mountains as before.

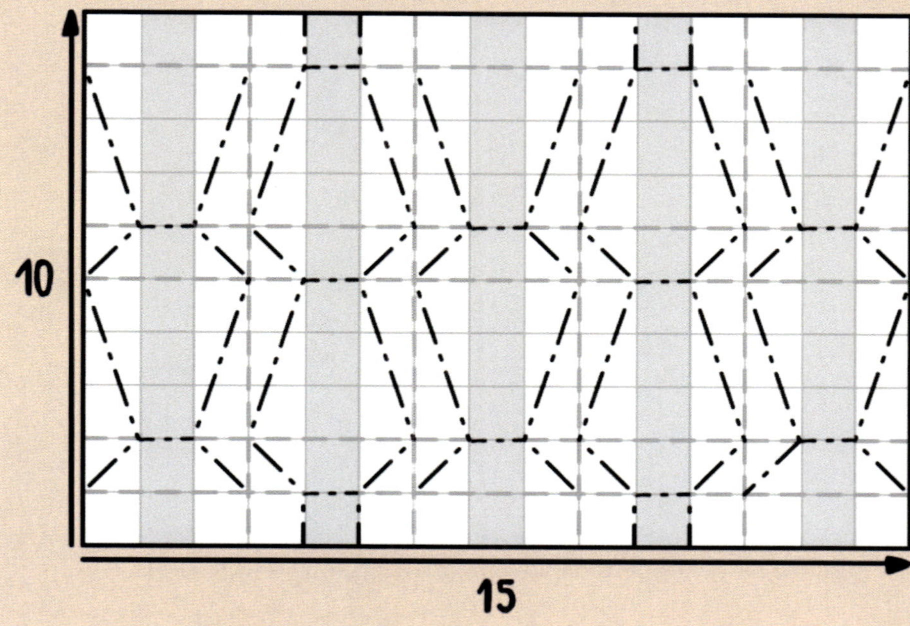

Above and Beyond—A 6 by 8 Project

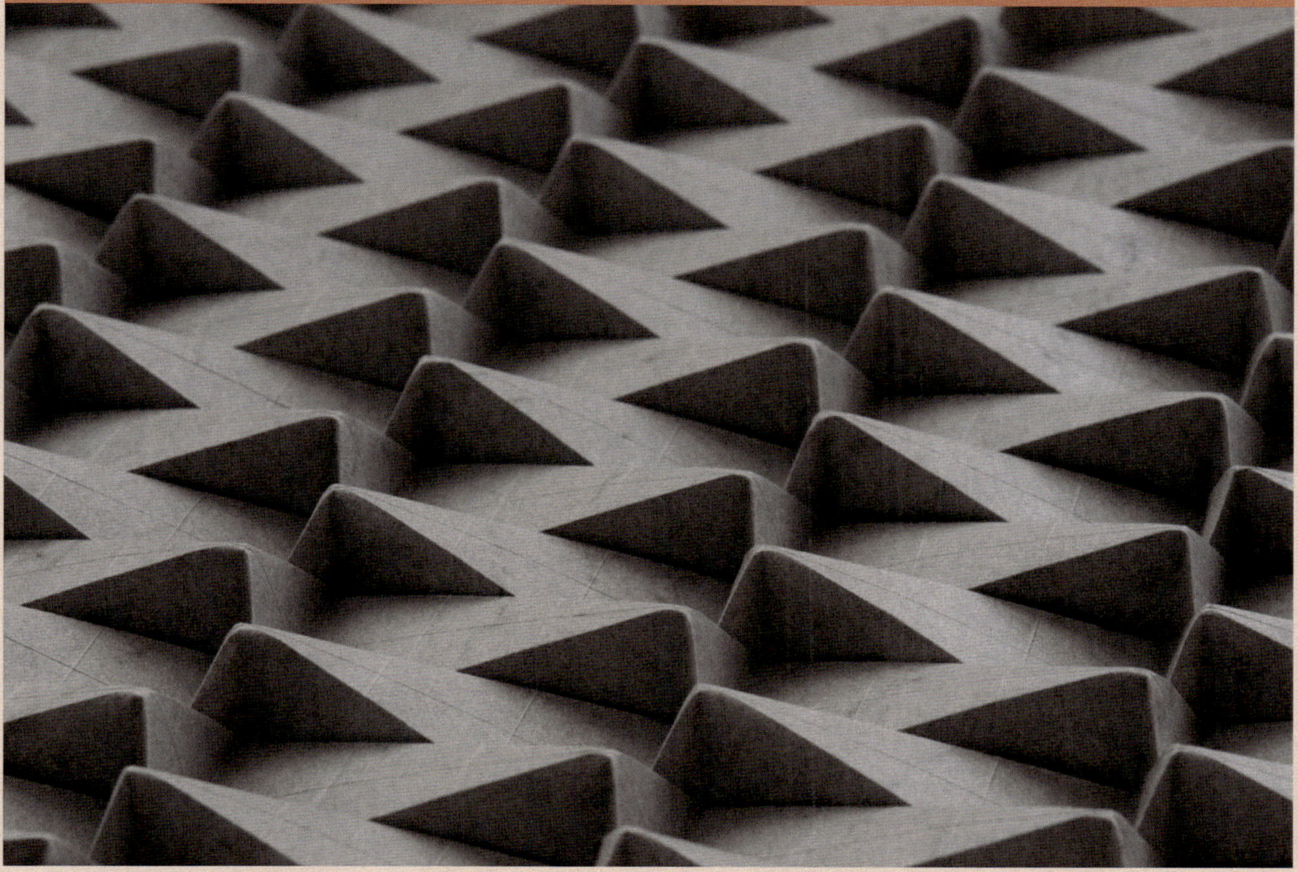

3 3 "Go This Way!"

Please take a good look at the CP. Without the orientation marks (mountains and valleys) it looks exactly like the Diamond corrugations!

Still, this is a different tessellation. The order of the mountains and valleys creates a different effect.

This is the first Iso-Area model I present, which means it looks exactly the same on both sides!

The model gave me a sense of pairs of arrows, pointing in opposite directions and supplying a confusing message — which way should I go? This way!

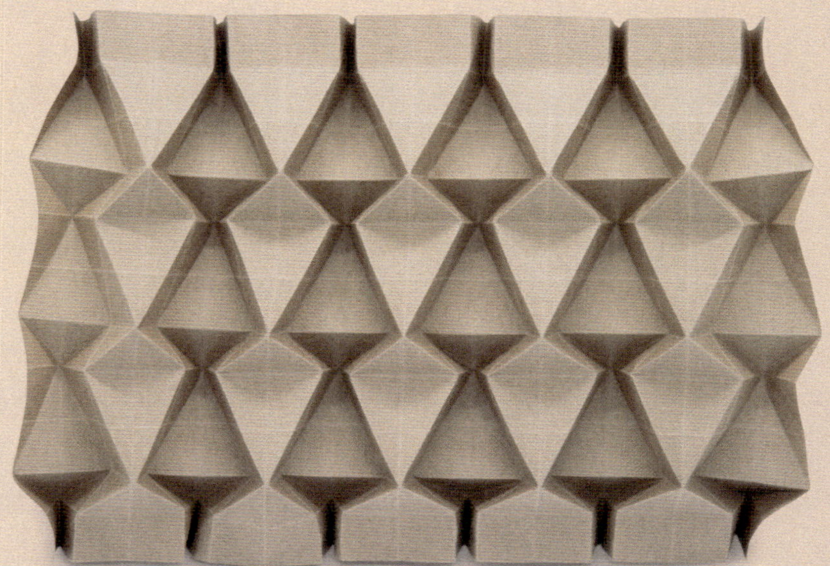

The Single Molecule

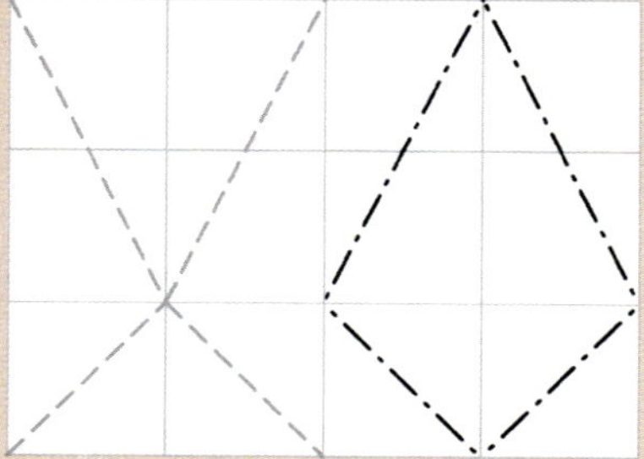

The molecule size is 4 by 3.

This can be changed and one can use many other proportions, like the Diamond 1 by 2 or 1 by 3. It works anyhow.

The shrinkage differs between the axes. The left-right ratio is 2:1 while the top-bottom is negligible.

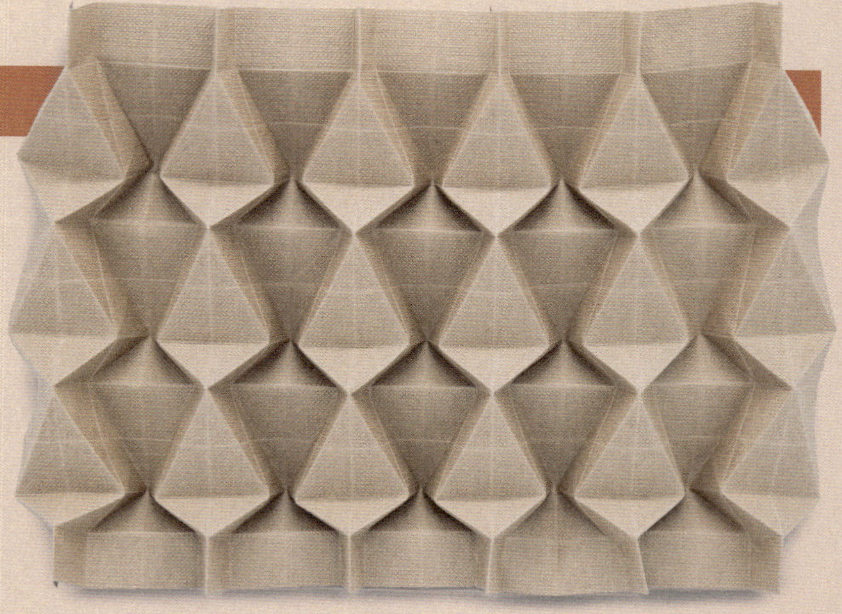

Top: recto view of a 3 by 5–molecule "Go This Way!" tessellation.

Bottom: verso view of a 3 by 5–molecule "Go This Way!" tessellation.

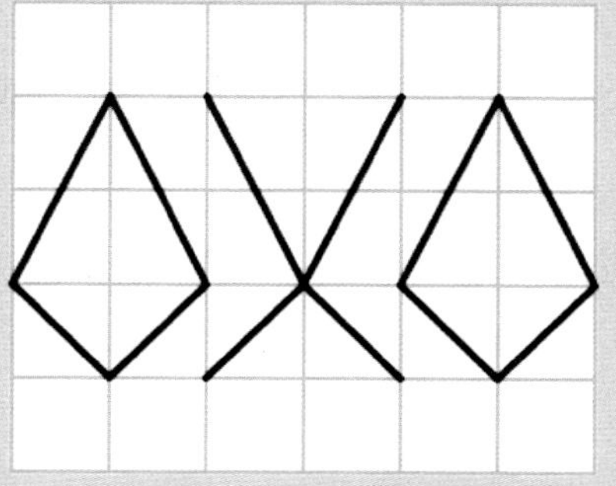

For an easier process, we are going to make one and a half molecules.

It is easier to handle the X part when it is surrounded by molecules.

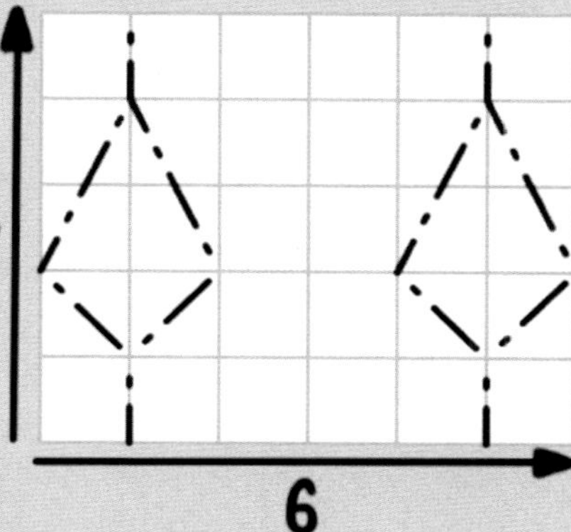

Start with a 5 by 6 grid.
Mark the two kites.

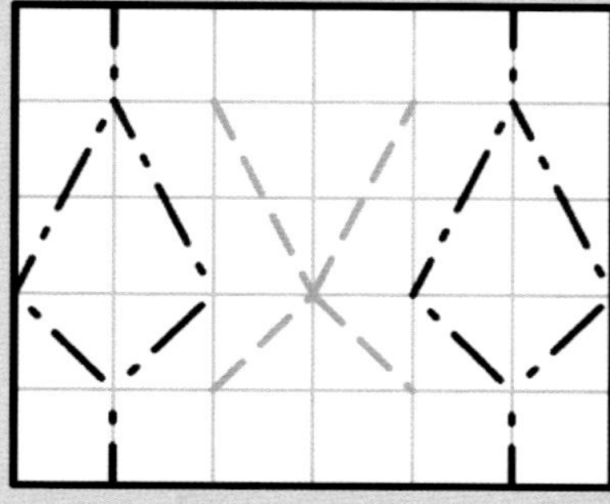

Now mark the distorted X as valleys.

Be aware of the orientation of the creases! The X is valleys, while the kites are mountains!

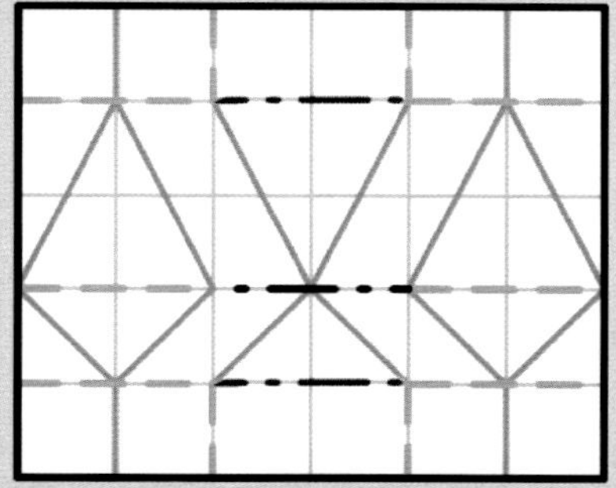

Force the orientation of the creases that align with the grid.

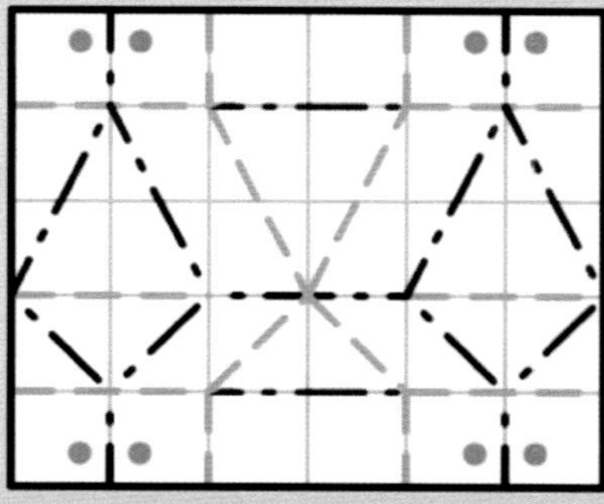

Here are all the needed creases.

Note the mountain fold lines on the top and bottom rows.

Pinch the squares on both sides of the mountains mentioned to start the collapse.

Make sure the center of the distorted X goes **down** while the two kites go **up**!

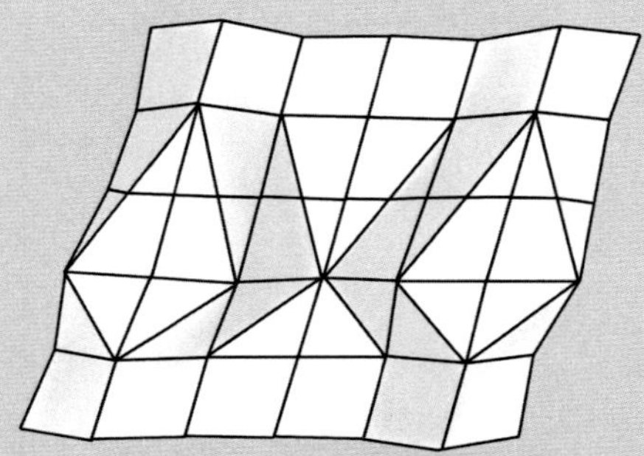

In process

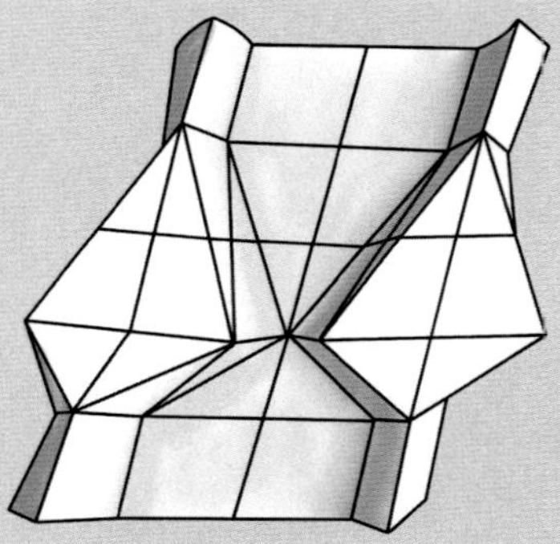

Fully collapsed. Note the rhythm of the edges is exactly like the **1 by 2 Diamond** model (page 54) — two flat squares, bordered by two vertical squares.

2 by 2 Molecules

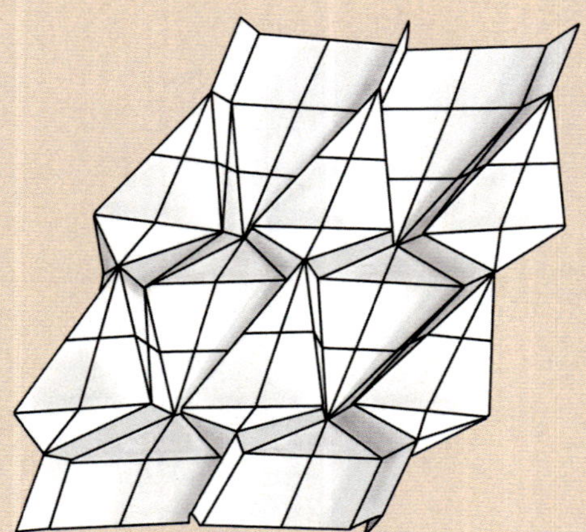

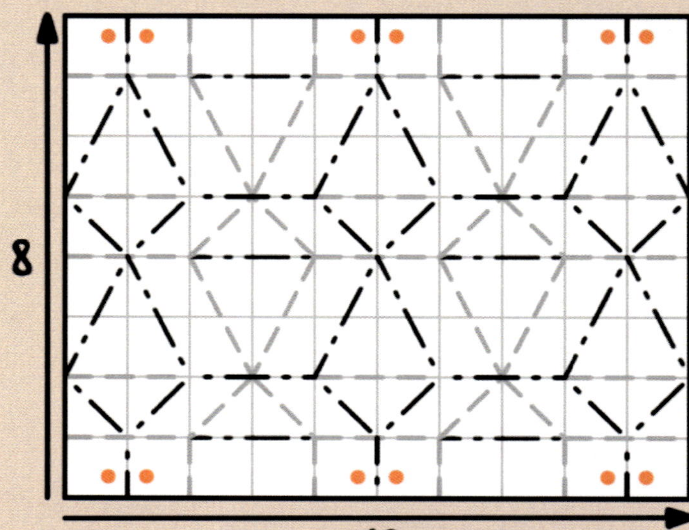

Use a grid of 8 by 10.

For the same reason as with the single molecule, we are going to make a 2 by 2.5–molecule project.

Add all the needed creases, and mark the mountains at the top and bottom rows.

Collapse the model by pinching the mentioned mountains, and force every X to its place. The mountain pops up, while the valley pops down. It is helpful to provide stress from both left and right sides during the collapse, as it helps hold the molecules in place.

Above and Beyond

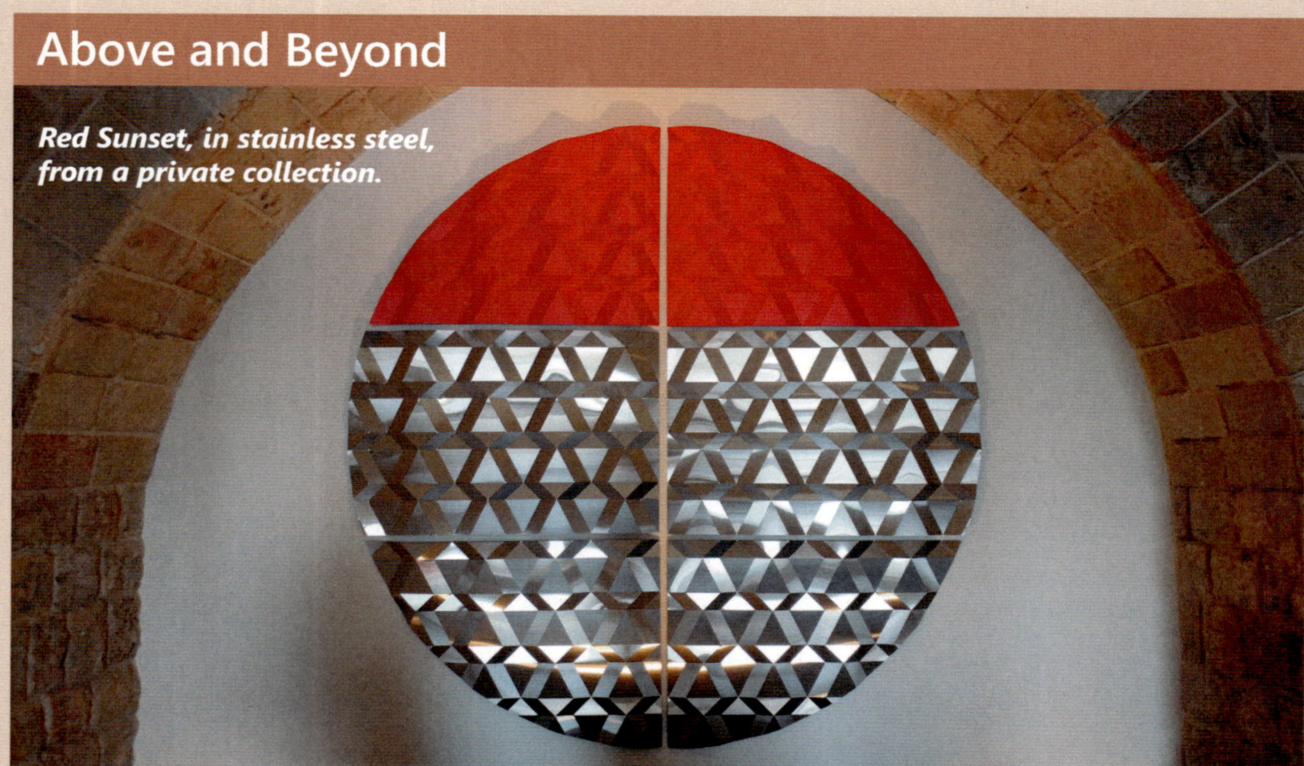

***Red Sunset*, in stainless steel, from a private collection.**

3 by 5 Molecules

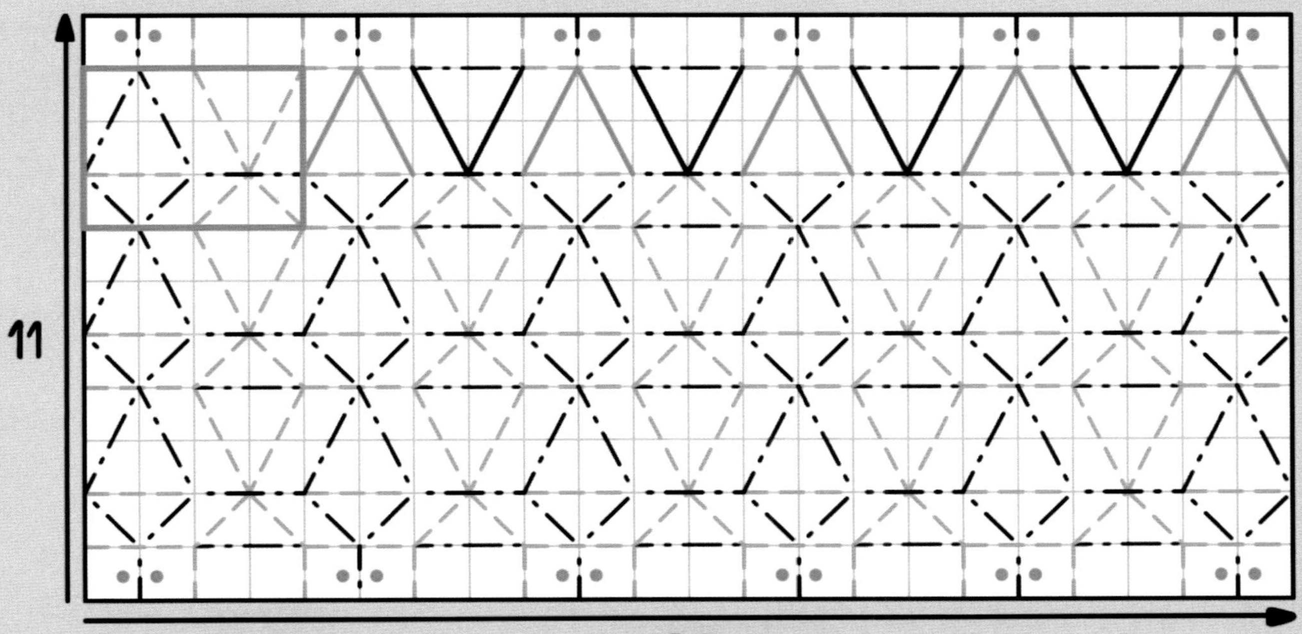

Make a grid of 11 by 22.

The formula for the height is 1 + 3 × 3 + 1 = 11.

For the width, it is 5.5 × 4 = 22.

The final result will be just shy of 11 squares in height and 12 squares wide.

There are no evident shortcuts here. For better clarity, try to follow all the creases at the same angle in each row (bold black), and return with the other angle (orange).

To collapse, pinch the left mountain on the top and bottom rows and make sure all the distorted Xs centers are poking up or down (mountains or valleys). Jump to the next pair of mountains, and repeat the process. Do not hesitate to put pressure on the **complete** sheet of paper from right to left, as it will help you keep the collapsed molecules in place.

3 4 Zipper

The Single Molecule

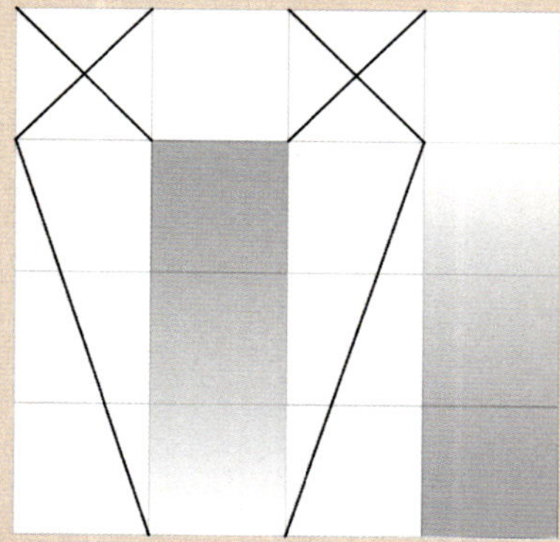

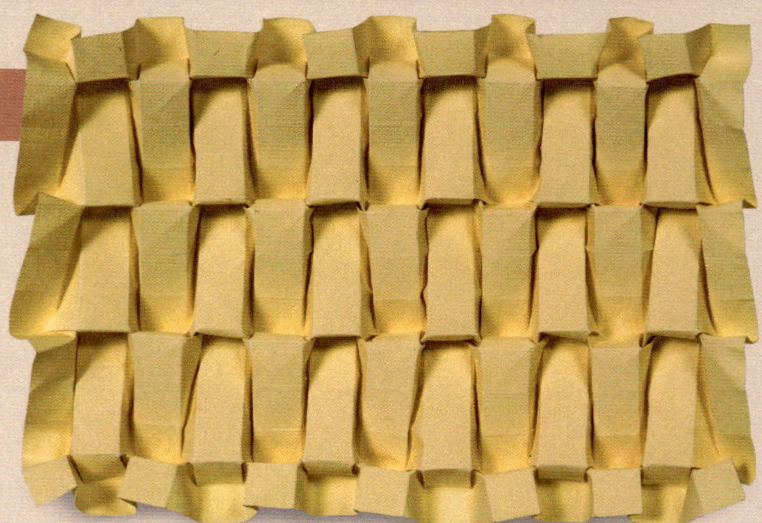

The molecule size is 4 by 4.

The two grey rectangles are slanted in opposite directions, hence the name.

The molecule follows an up-down movement. While some of the areas will stay at the table level, some will raise one square.

The shrinkage differs between the axes. The left-right ratio is 2:1 while the top-bottom is 4:3.

Note that this representation of the molecule creates an asymmetric situation. While the left rectangle has diagonal creases on both sides, the right rectangle has a diagonal crease only to its left. When planning bigger projects, we will have to take this into consideration and add an extra column on the right edge.

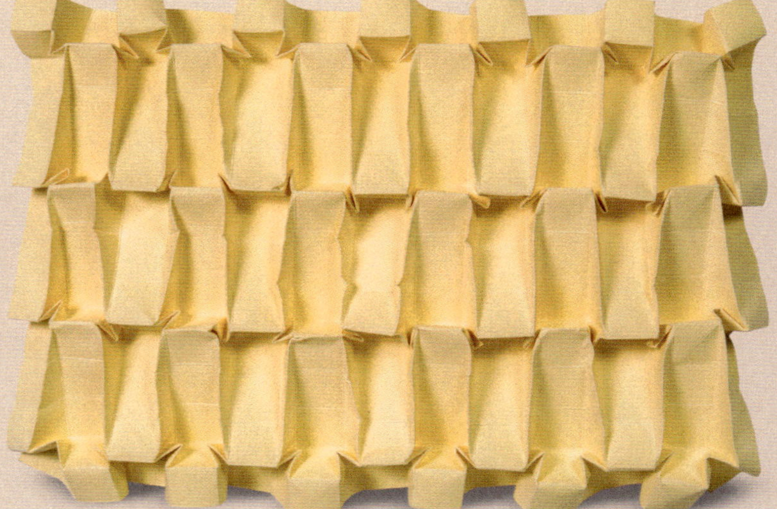

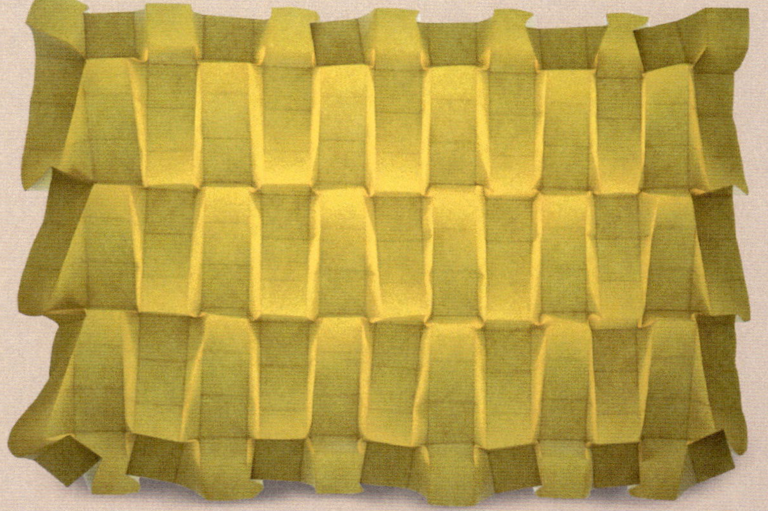

Top: recto view of a 3 by 5–molecule Zipper tessellation.

Center: verso view of a 3 by 5ww Zipper tessellation.

Bottom: recto view with back-light.

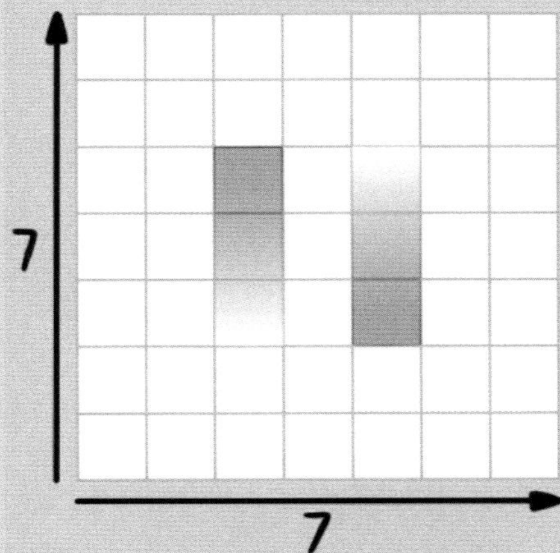

Start with a 7 by 7 grid. Mark the two rectangles.

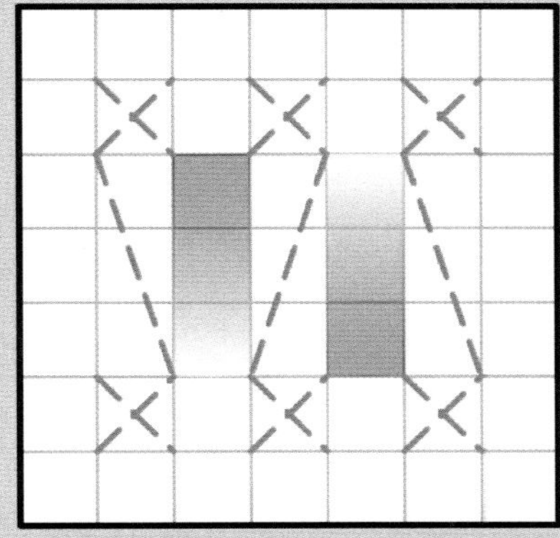

Add all the needed creases. Note the Xs on the top and bottom rows. Although the molecule has only one row of X's, on top, to understand the collapse it is easier if we have another row on the bottom.

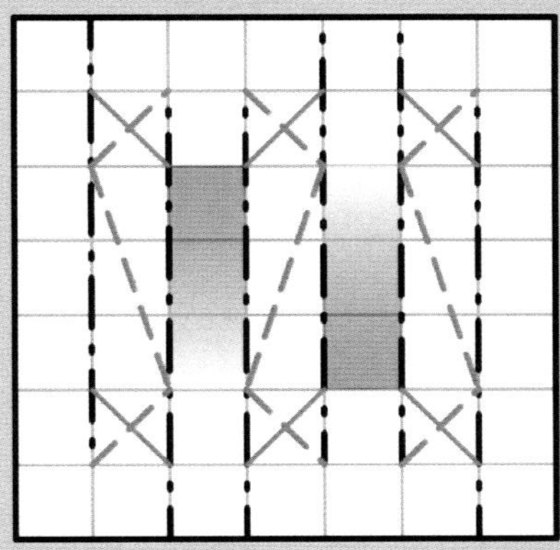

Force the marked mountains on the grid lines. Note the long S shape that is formed from the valleys (ignoring the other part of each X).

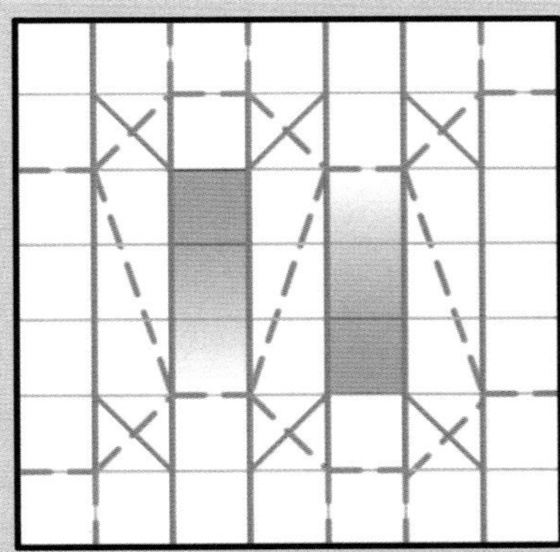

Start the collapse by following the lines shown here (in orange), and only them!

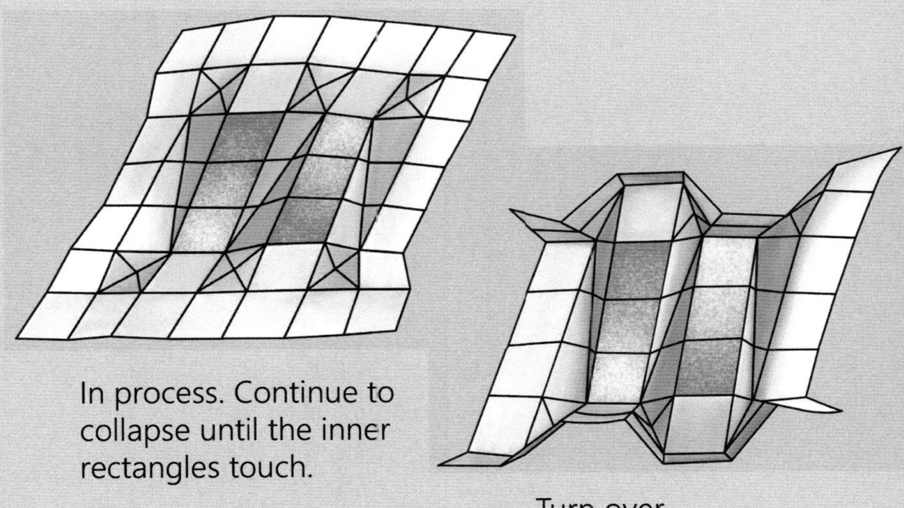

In process. Continue to collapse until the inner rectangles touch.

Turn over.

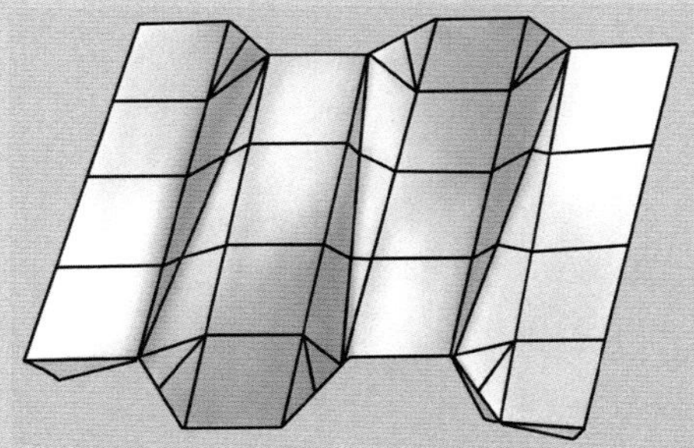

Phase one is fully collapsed.

Now we want to flatten the molecule by adding the second crease of the X's. It is done easily by raising the top and bottom rows, which forces the triangle (see next step) to be folded in half.

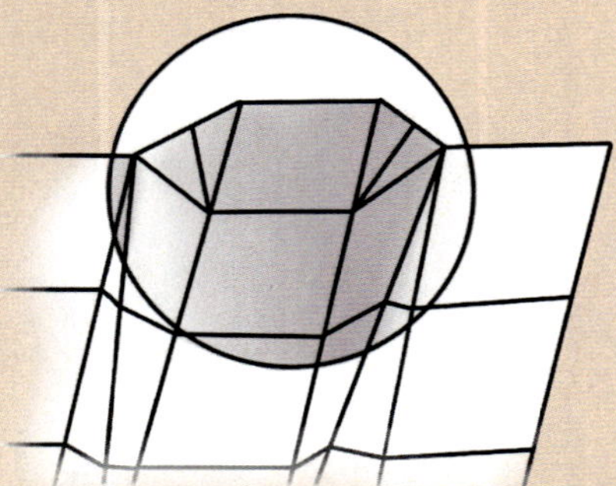

Note the top edge of the molecule. It has two squares folded in half along the diagonal, creating two triangles.

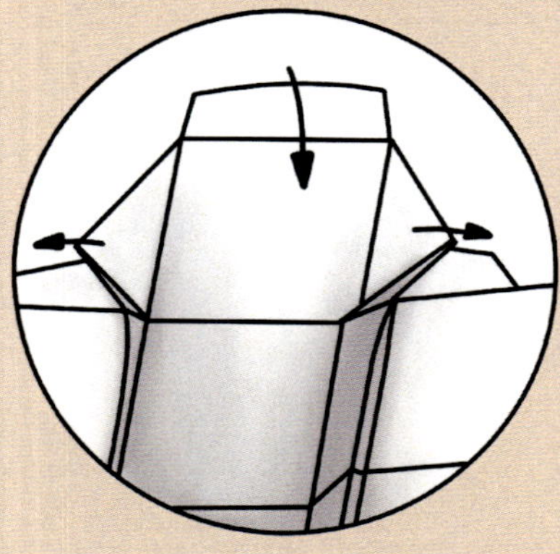

Raise the middle square, and fold each triangle on the side in half as well.

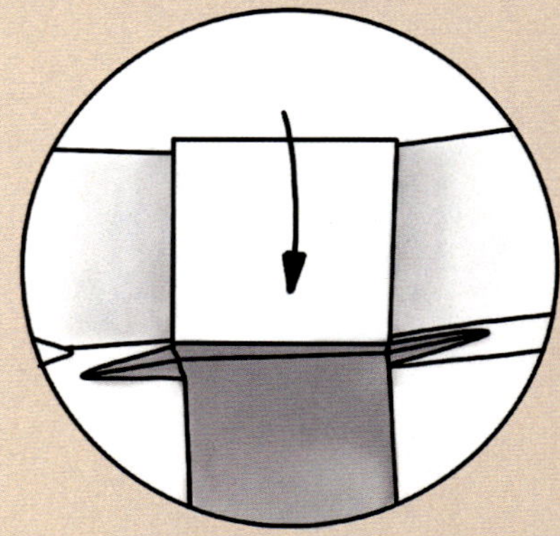

Like so.

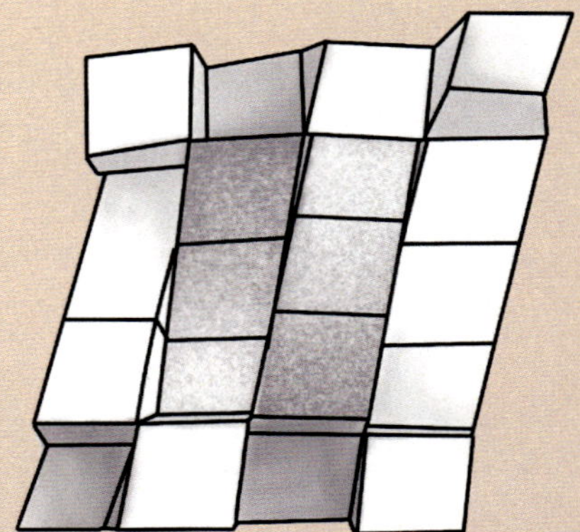

Fully collapsed.

2 by 2.5 Molecules

Use a grid of 11 by 13.

For the same reason as with the single molecule, we are going to make a 2 by 2.5–molecule project.

Add all the needed creases, and mark the mountains at the top and bottom rows.

Collapse the model by following the orange lines first. Do not try to flatten the model until you have all the structure in place. The model will form an incomplete cylinder. We will use this property later, in the next model!

Once you have this cylinder, start and flatten the model, by "breaking" the X's, row by row.

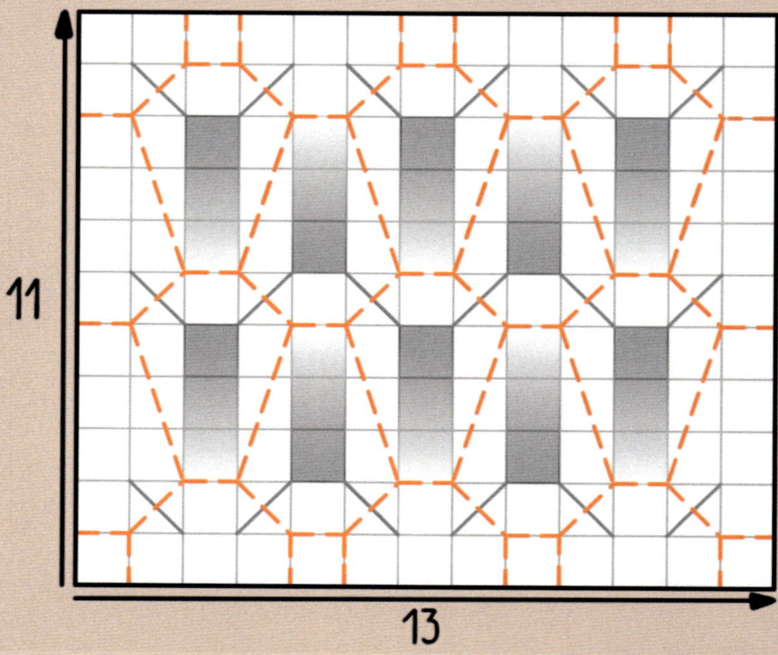

3 by 5.5 Molecules

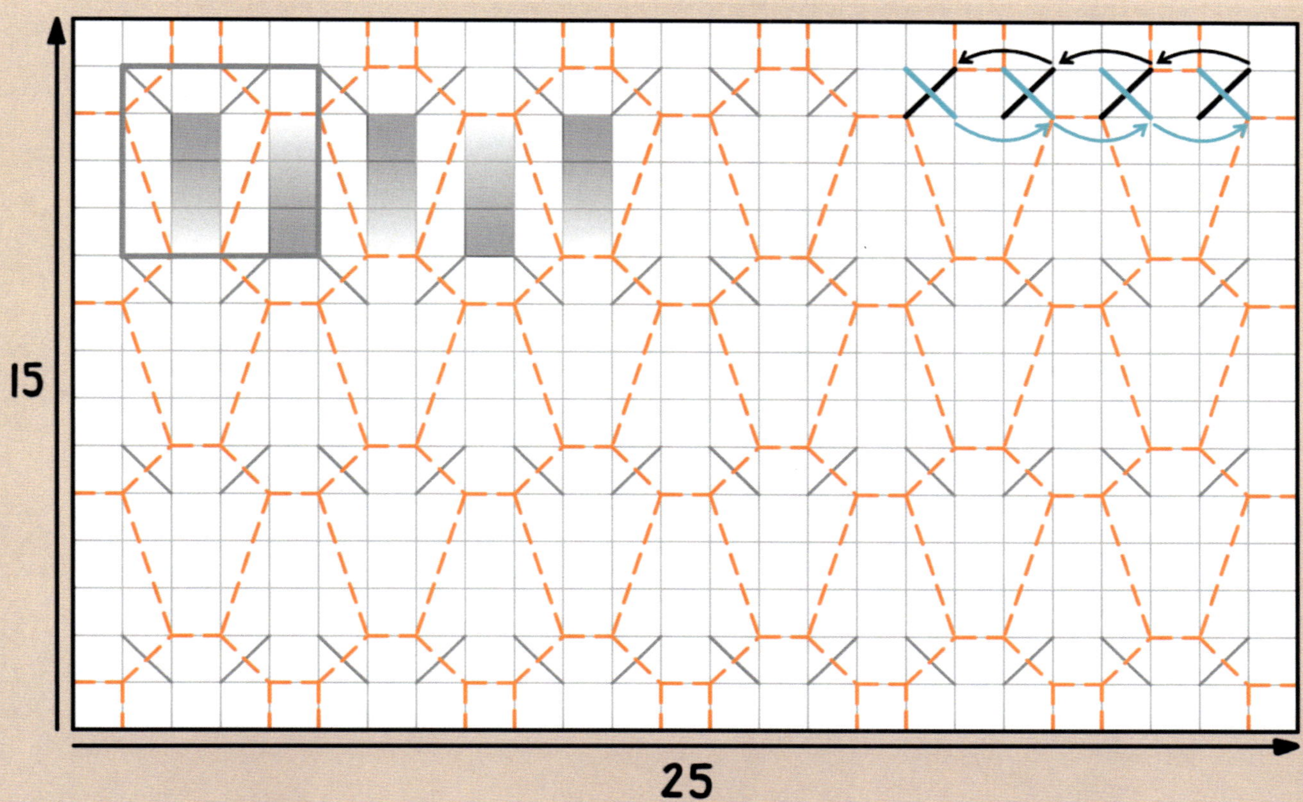

Make a grid of 15 by 22.

The formula for the height is 1 + 3 × 4 + 1 + 1 = 15.

The extra 1 is for the extra row of X's, to allow completion of the bottom of the last row of molecules.

For the width, it is 1+ 5.5 × 4 + 1 + 1 = 25.

Here, the extra 1 is for an extra column to allow a symmetric look on the right.

The final result will be 11 squares high and 13 squares wide.

There are no obvious shortcuts. I prefer to make the rows of X's, and then complete the long diagonals.

To collapse, follow the orange valleys creating an open cylinder. Note that if you plan to make more rows of molecules, the cylinder will close and one side will even overlap the other.

Once you finish that phase, start to force the second crease of the X's. Work on them in pairs, so every two face each other. Keep every collapsed part flat.
This will lock the last creases in place.

Above and Beyond—A 6 by 9 Project

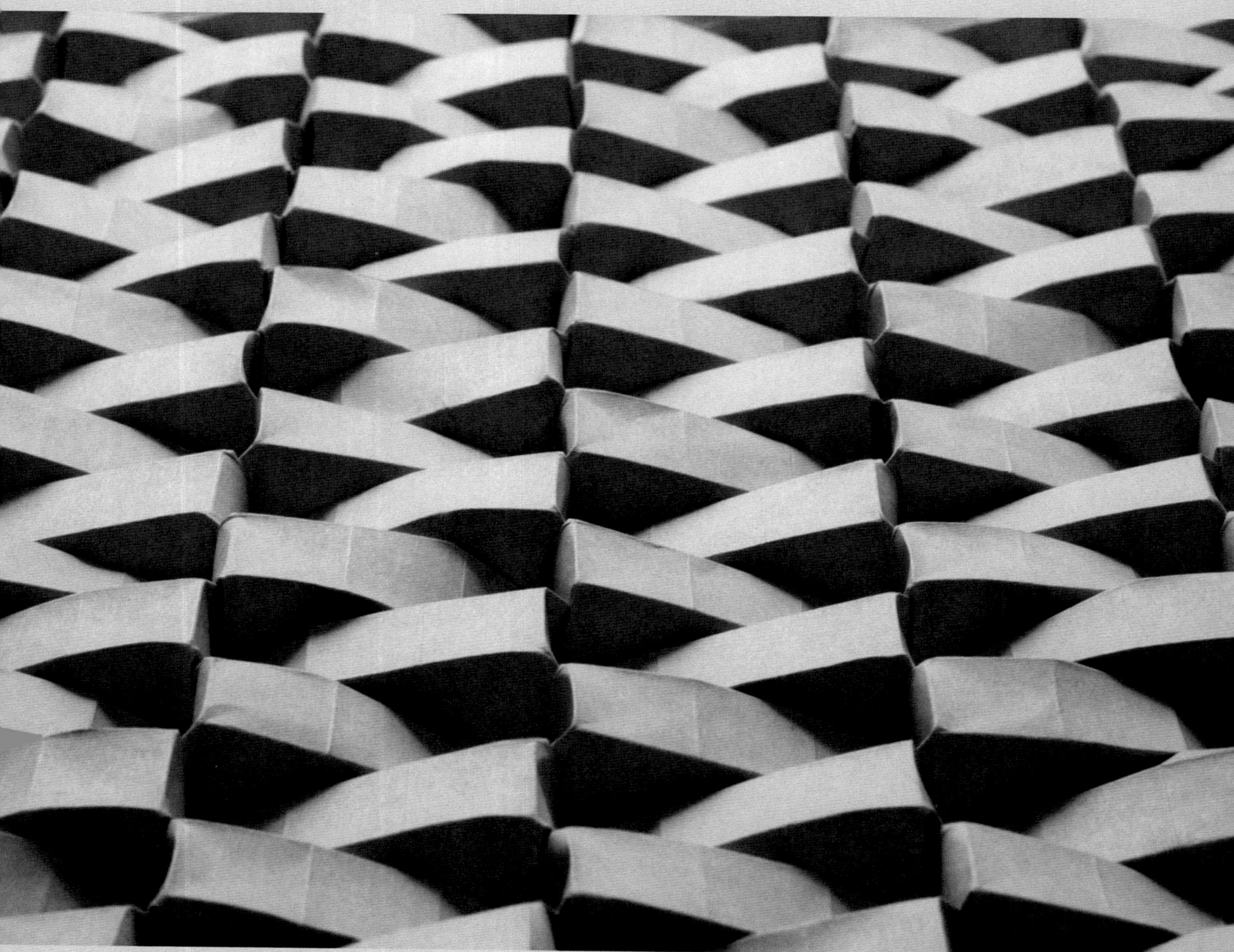

35 Zipper Box

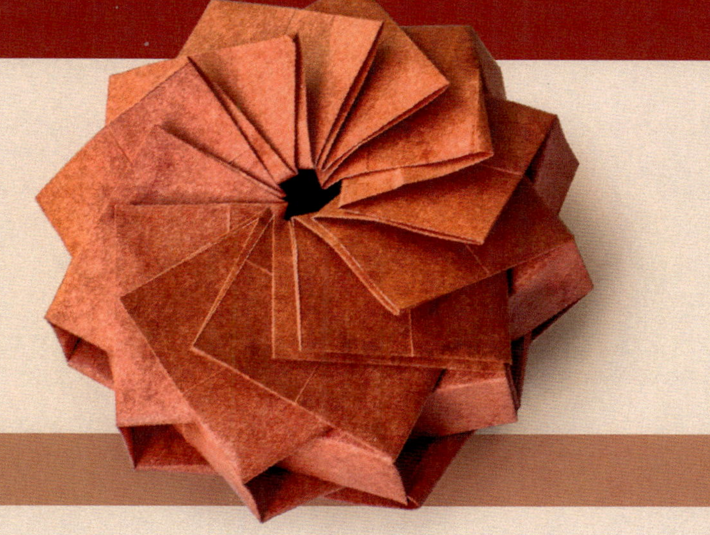

If you do not fold the X's on the previous model, it will not stay flat, but will take a cylinder form. In this model we exploit this property, and we will make a closed shape that can be considered a box.

The Crease Pattern

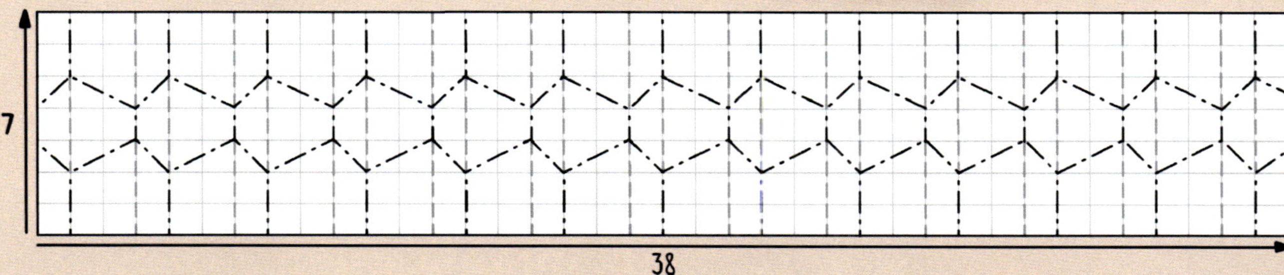

Make a grid of 7 by 38.

The best way to do it is to start with a 5:1 rectangle, and make a grid of 8 by 40. Then cut away two columns and one row.

This model asks for a big paper to start with. Recommended size is 14 by 70 cm (5.5 by 27.5 inch), and no less than 10 by 50 cm (4 by 20 inch).

The grid is all bi-directional folds.

All pre-creases (the zig zag part) are mountain folds.

Start with folding the grid, and finish all grid creases as mountains. Add all the pre-creases.

Folding Sequence

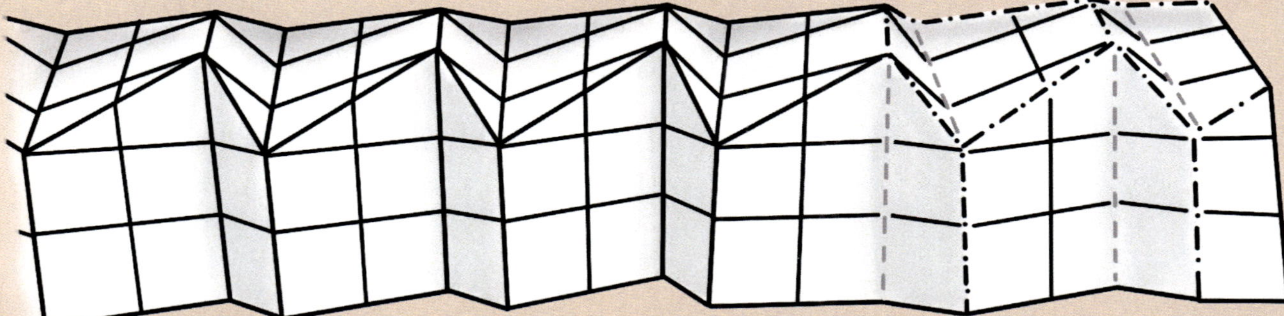

Fold the sheet into this position, creating a "caterpillar" with a zig zagged back.

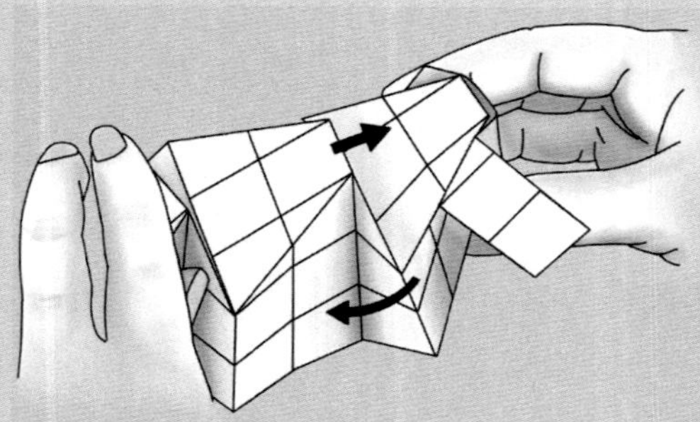

Collapse is done in a repetitive way: hold on the far right link with the right hand and with the left hand push forward the link before that. See how the sides of the far right molecule encompass the sides of the next molecule to the left.

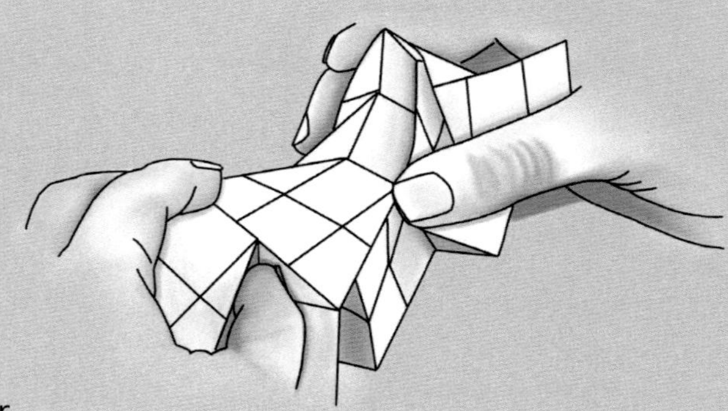

The result.

Collapse more molecules in the same way.

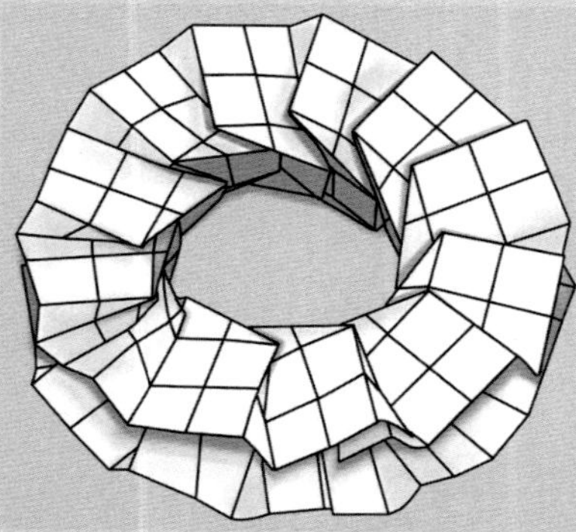

The result is an open ring. The last (the 13th) molecule is made from two squares instead of three. Use it to close a ring by overlapping the last molecule with the first one.

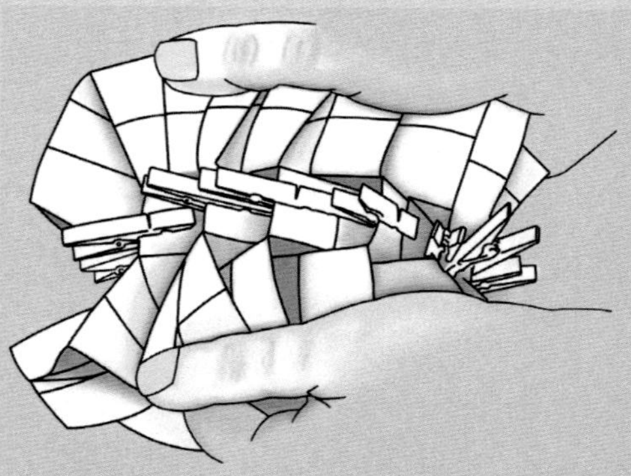

It is helpful to use clips on the middle row of the ring to hold it in place.

Mountain-fold the two outer rows of squares, as shown.

Hold the model as shown and expose the clipped area by folding every flap inward. Fold all flaps as shown and keep folding them to the centre, one by one. Since every flap is attached to the next one, this is done simultaneously.

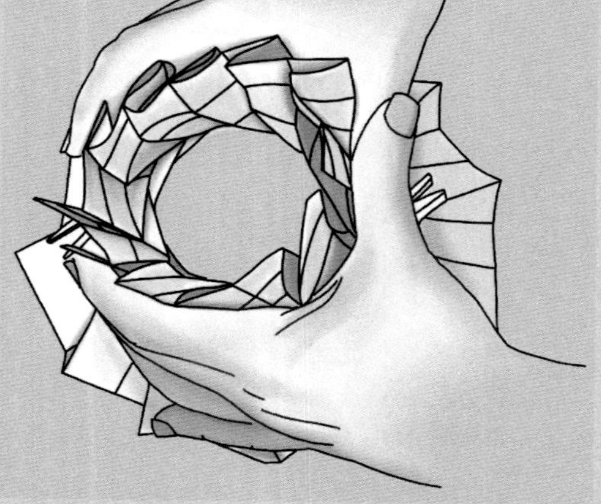

A new valley fold is formed in this stage.

Repeat on the other side.

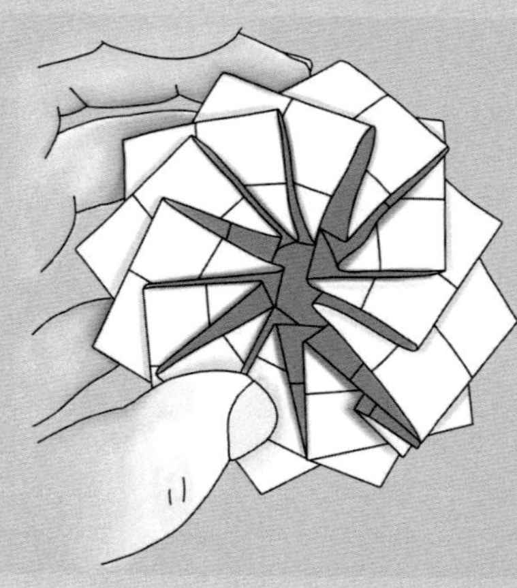

Force all the creases and remove the clips. There is no lock to the sides. You can open the box from each side.

Variations

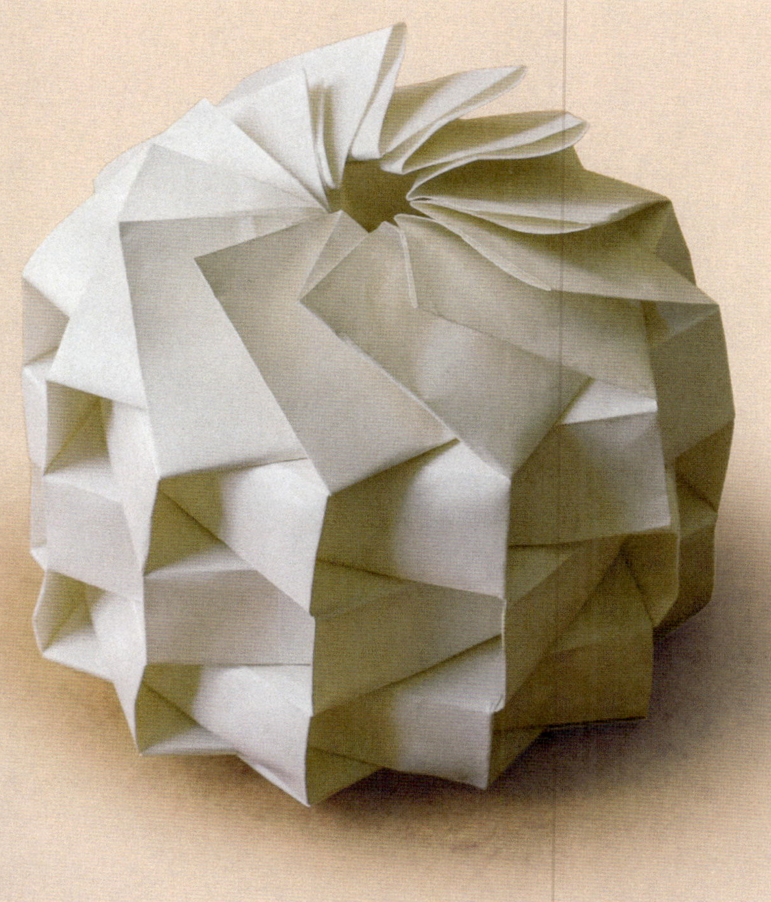

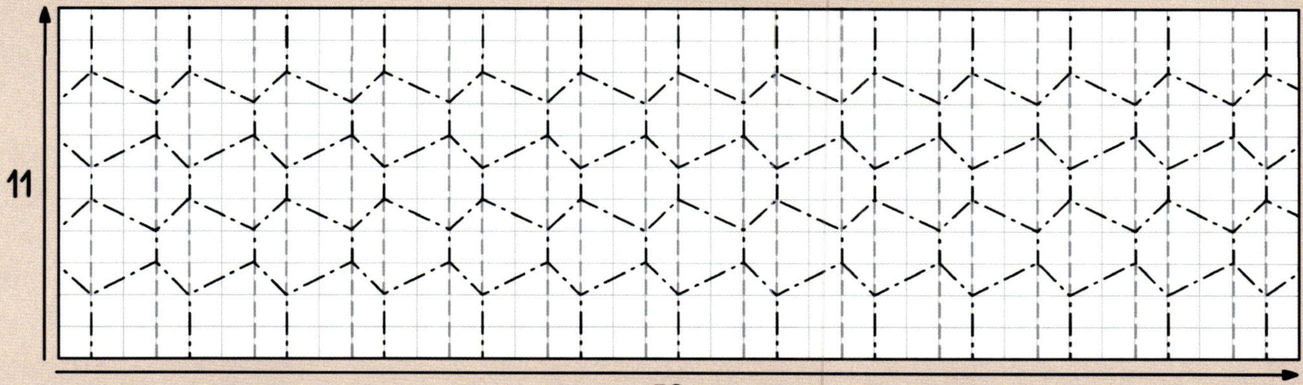

Since this is a tessellation, you can have more than one row of molecules, just by adding more zig zagged rows.

This is the CP for a three-layer ring. A two-layer project is easier, and one can challenge himself with five and even eight layers.

Changes can be done with the size of the molecule. Here you zig on one square and zag on two squares. You can try to zag on three squares instead of two and see what happens.

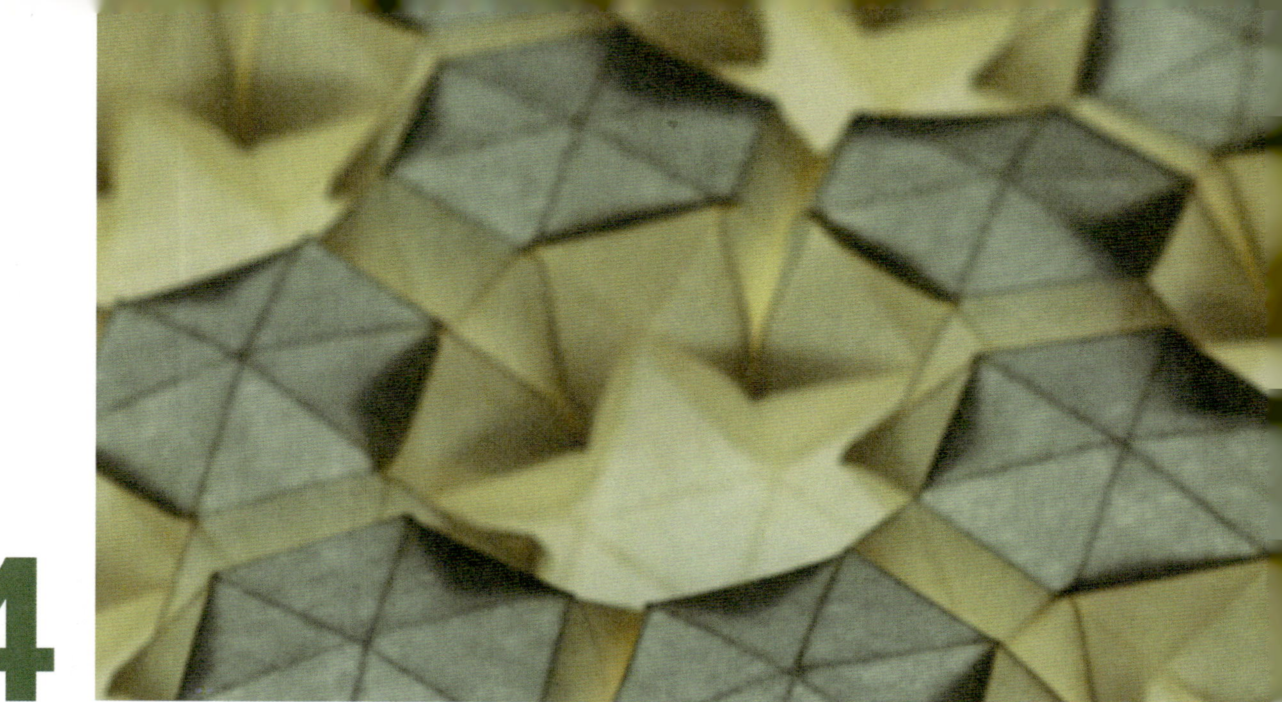

4 The Concinnous and Heptamerous Family

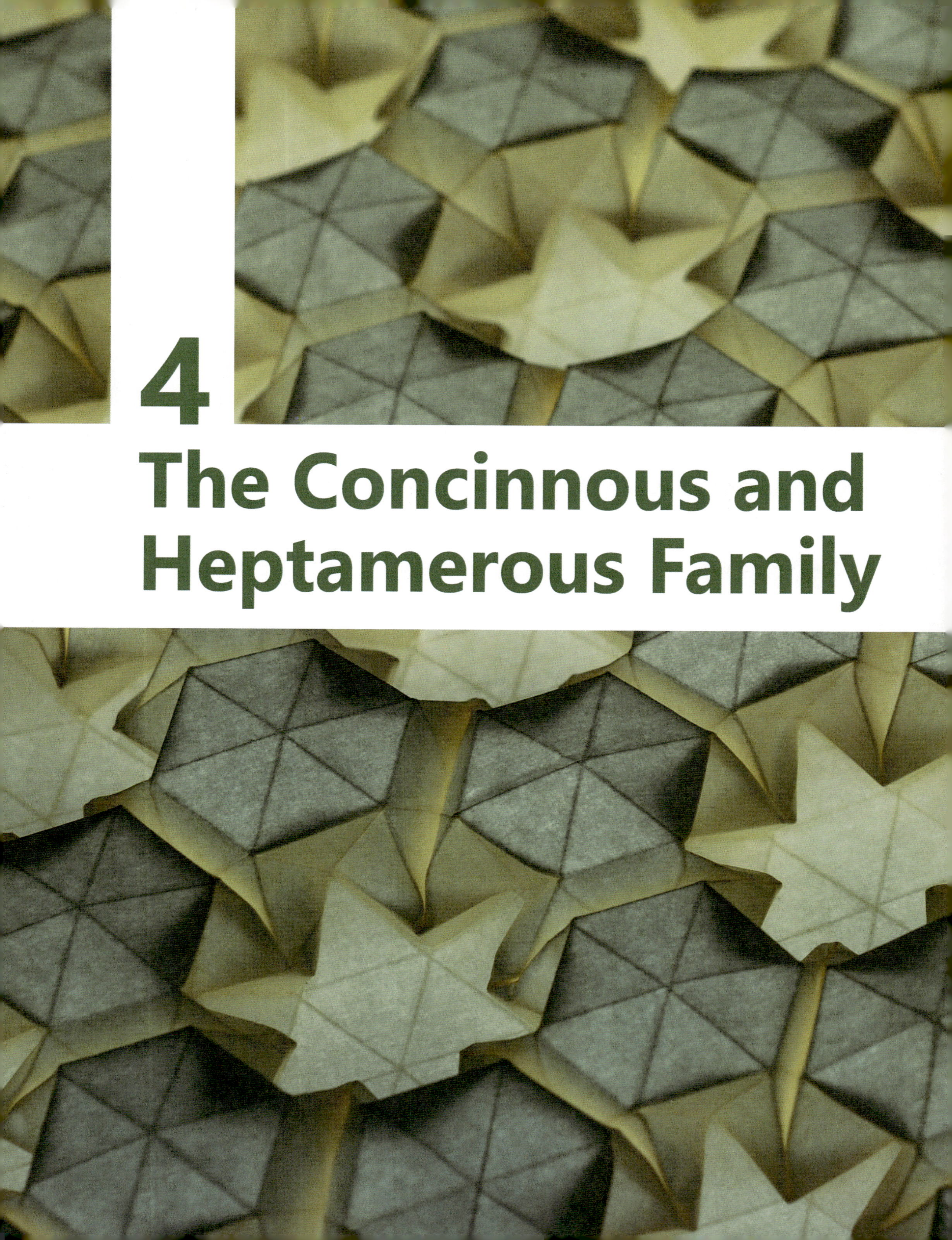

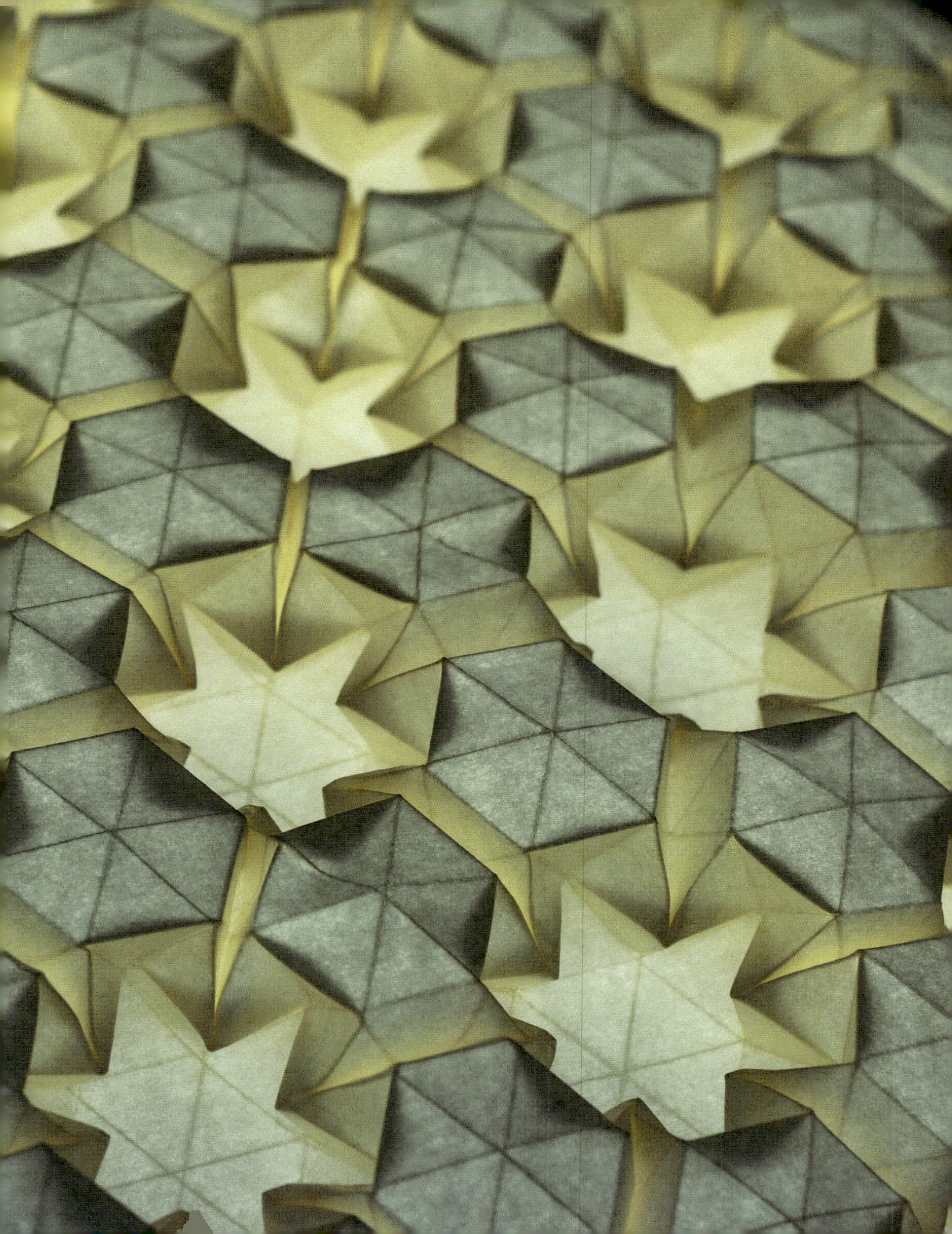

Introduction

Concinnous means "harmony or elegance of design especially of literary style in an adaptation of parts to a whole or to each other". I found it on a list of the most beautiful words in English (which I use quite often to find names for my models). Since it perfectly portrays what tessellations are, it was an easy decision.

This family includes two cousins and each has many brothers.

I found **Heptamerous** on the same list. This word means "consisting of or divided into seven parts". The second hexagonal model here is made out of seven hexagons, and once again the name fits perfectly.

The main idea behind this design is to create small cocoons that are connected with bridges. As before, the variations are made by grafting a line or two, or by increasing the central part.

For all the 4 by 4-projects in this chapter, it is better to have a frame of two squares, not one. However, the instructions for the single-molecule, as well as the 2 by 2 project, are still with a single-square frame.

4 1 Concinnous

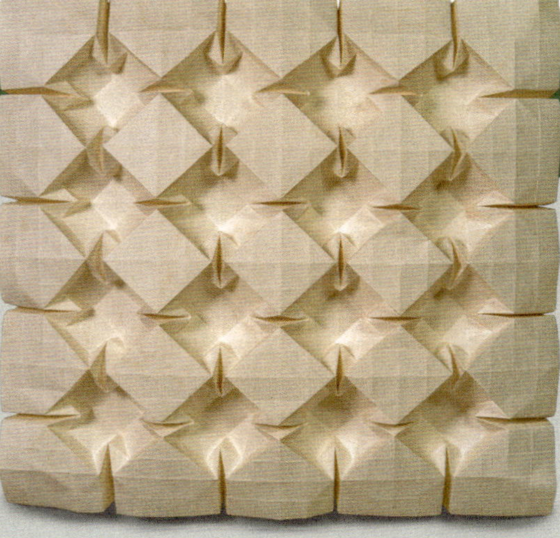

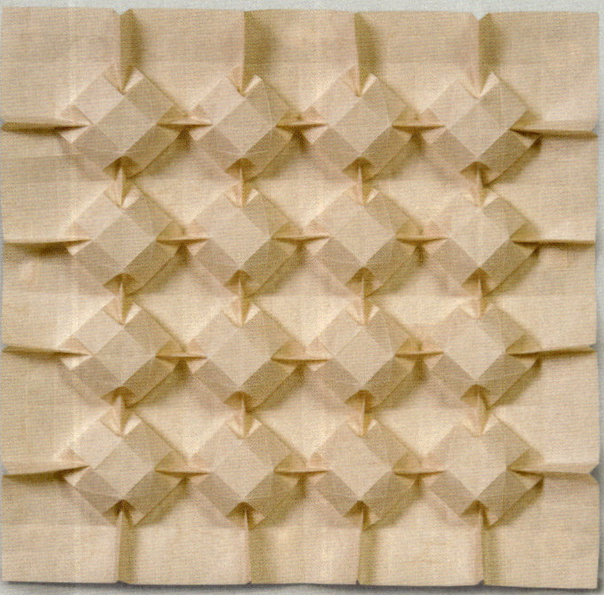

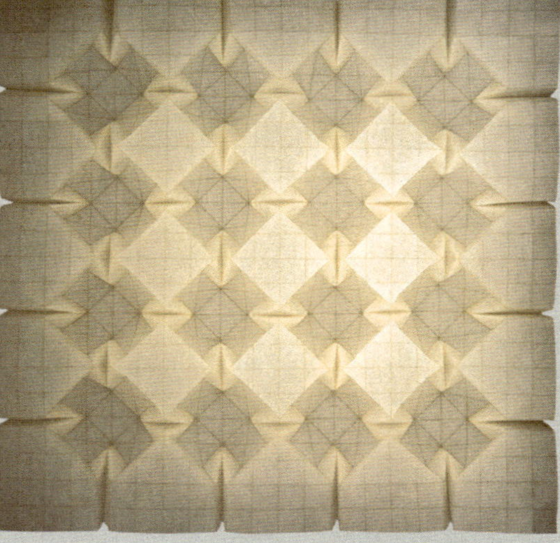

Top right: verso view of a 4 by 4–molecule Concinnous tessellation.

Left: recto view of a 4 by 4–molecule Concinnous tessellation.

Bottom right: recto view with back-light.

The Single Molecule

This molecule is tilted by 45° on the grid and is two-square high. It is connected to the other molecules via a bridge. You can change the width of this bridge, to create variations.

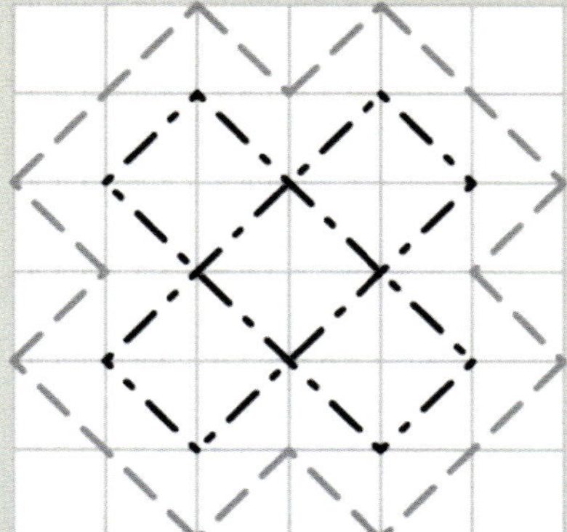

The molecule size is 6 by 6.

It is based on a cross shape, rotated 45° on the grid. Around it, there is a wider cross, as valleys.

There is no rotation during the collapse, and the height is two squares.

The shrinkage ratio is 3:2.

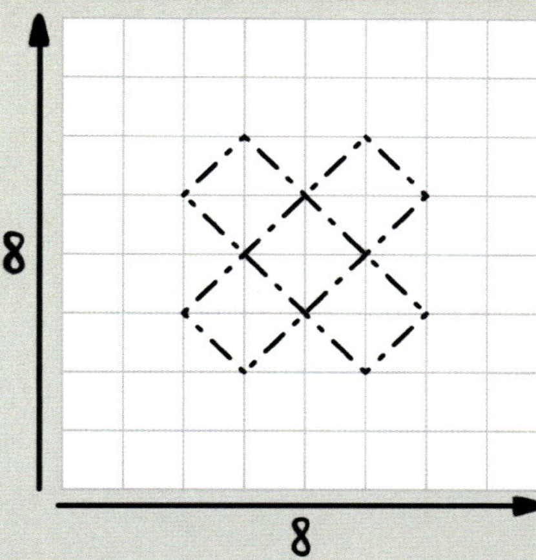

Start with a grid of 8 by 8, to allow extra rows and columns on all four sides.

Mark the inner cross with mountains.

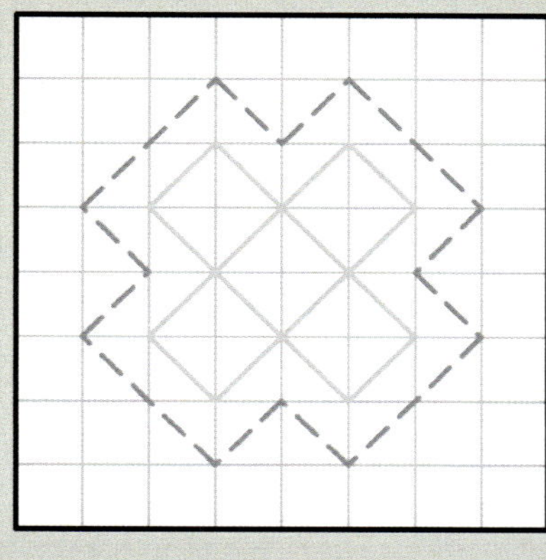

Add the bigger cross with valleys.

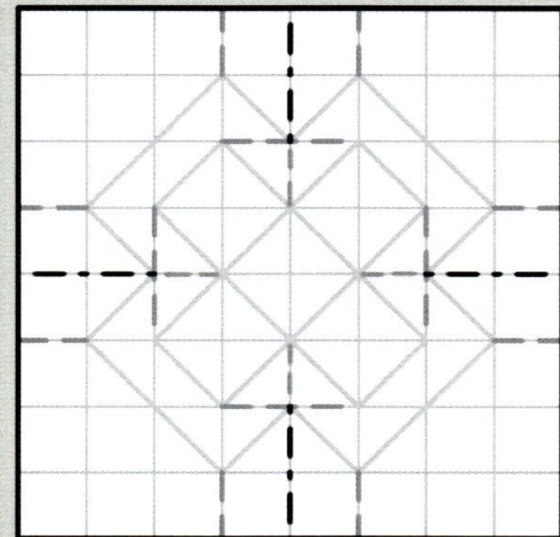

Force the needed creases on the grid in the right direction, as indicated.

Note the mountain fold lines that reach the four edges. They will form the bridges.

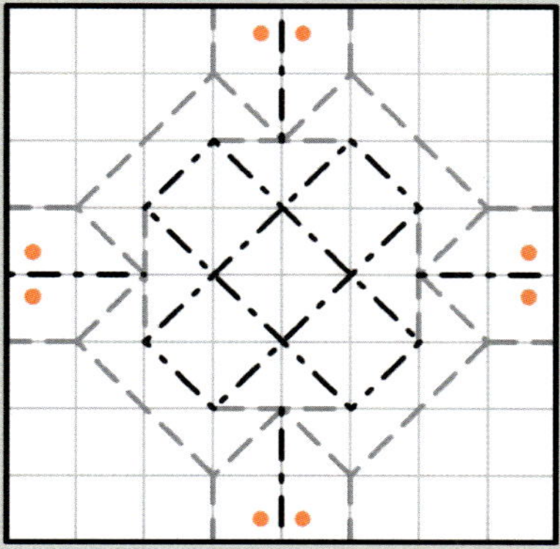

These are all the needed creases.

Pinch the squares on both sides of the mountains mentioned, starting the collapse.

Make sure the center tilted square (the center of the inner cross) goes up, while all the four surrounding it are sloping down!

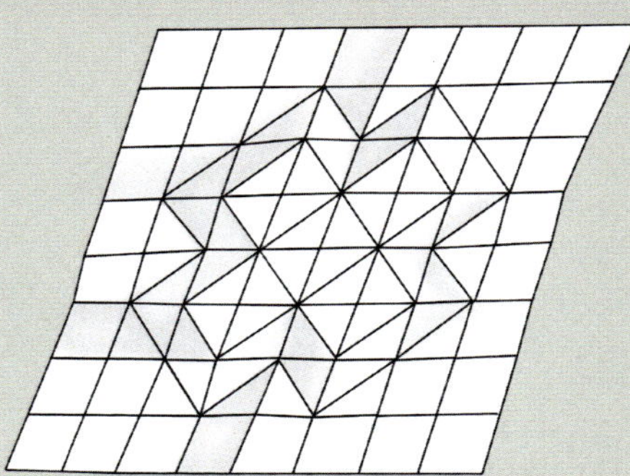

In process. The inner cross should rise up.

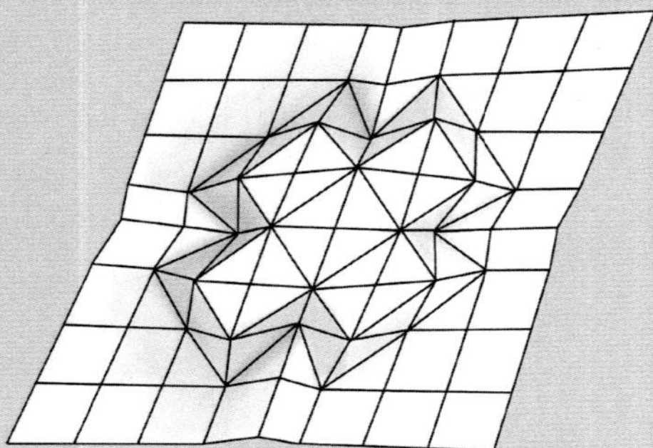

In progress. Make sure the outer creases of the wide cross are set as valleys. This will form the wanted shape. Continue to pinch the bridges.

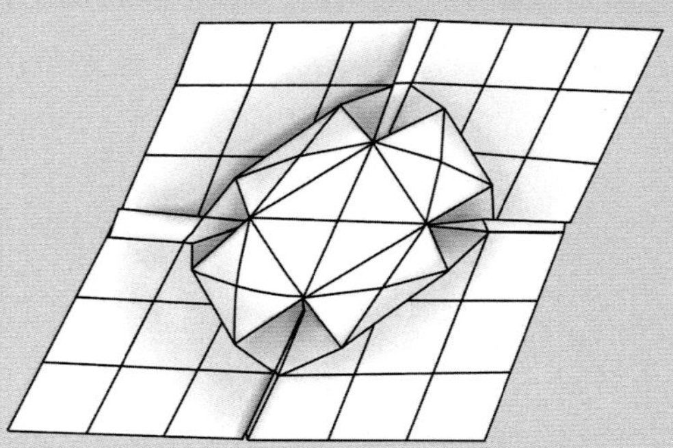

Fully collapsed. The bridges here have no width.

2 by 2 Molecules

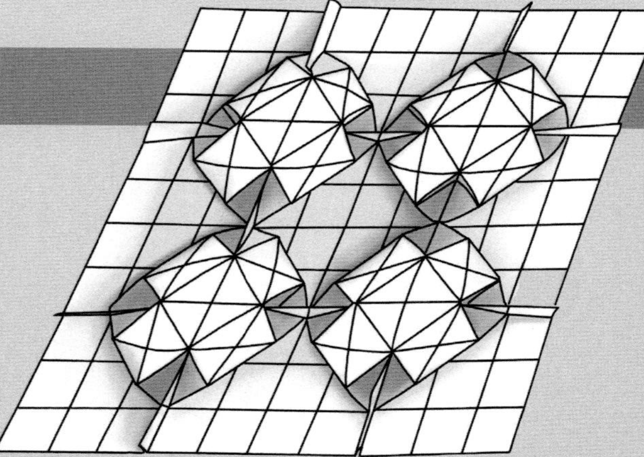

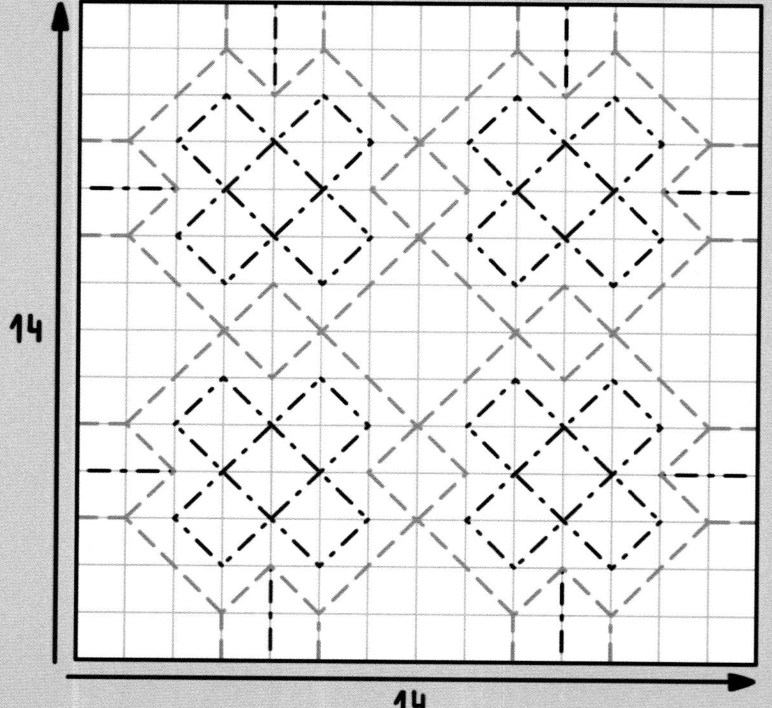

Use a grid of 14 by 14.

Collapse the model one molecule at a time, but make sure the adjacent molecule is slightly folded (mainly the inner mountains cross) before you collapse the molecule. The best way to do it is by pinching the bridges on the outer edges and then completing the inner bridges.

4 by 4 Molecules

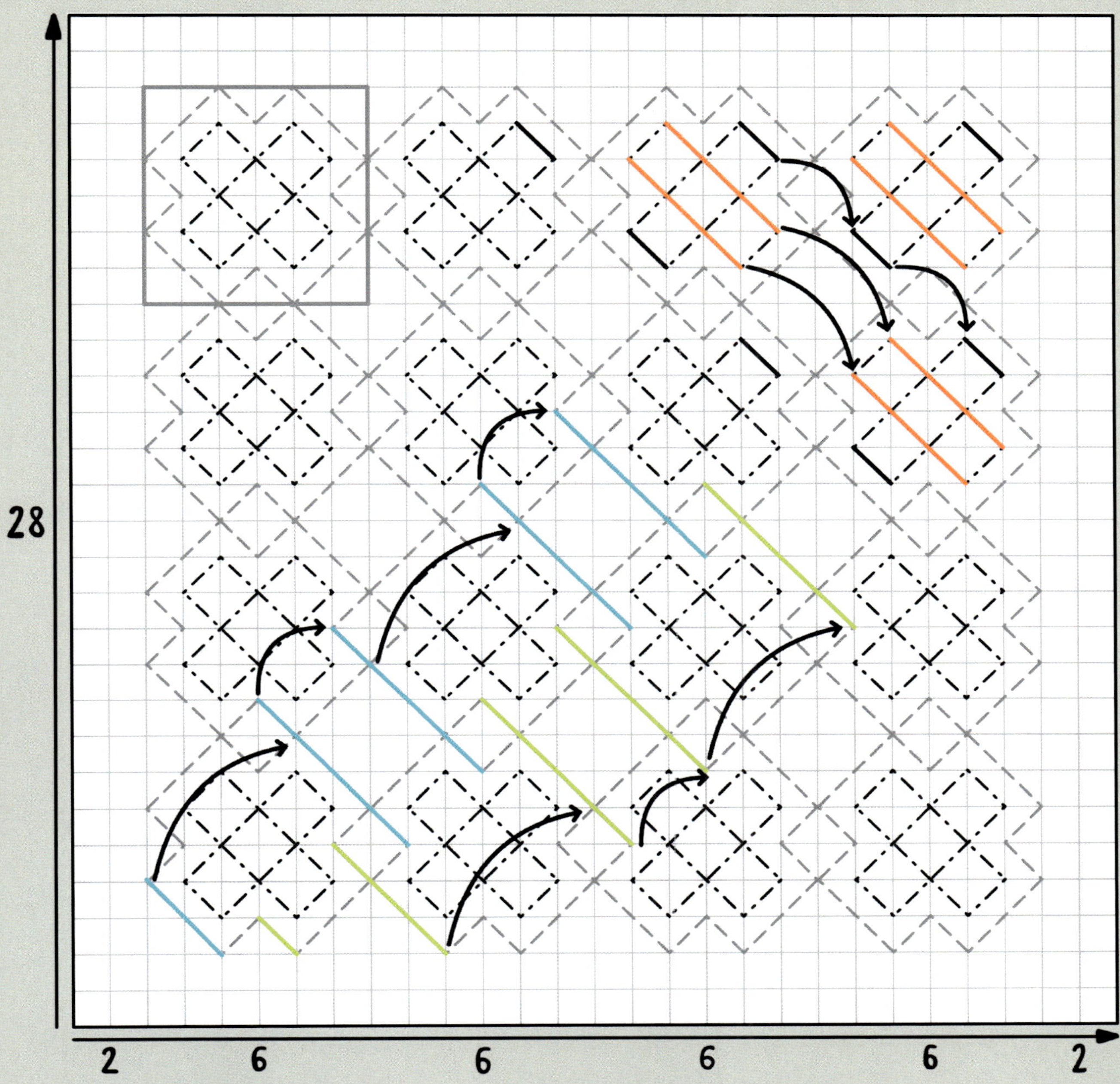

Make a grid of 28 by 28. This family benefits from a wider frame, made of two-square rows and columns.

The formula for the grid is 2 + 4 × 6 + 2 = 28.

The final result will be 18 squares wide.

This is a multi-fold pattern and there are many possible shortcuts to complete the CP. The inner crosses can be made by marking the orange lines first (crease three diagonals and skip three). Complete the longer lines of the cross in the other direction (top-right to bottom left, not marked here) so it will be easy to complete the crosses with the short lines.

Once the inner crosses are ready, it will be easier to add the outer ones, following the pattern suggested here with the light blue and bright green lines.

To collapse, start with a corner molecule, and use the bridge to the next molecule as a guideline to collapse the second molecule. It is wise to fold the bridges of the first row all the way to the far edge of the paper, so when the first row is complete the model lies flat.

Complete the rest of the rows in the same manner.

Variations — Concinnous; Single Space

The Single Molecule

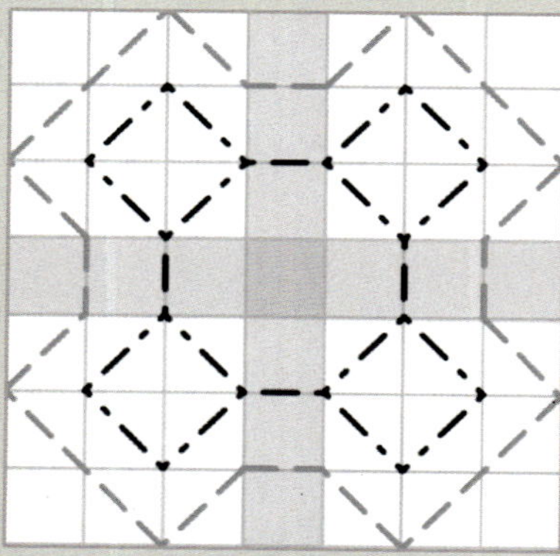

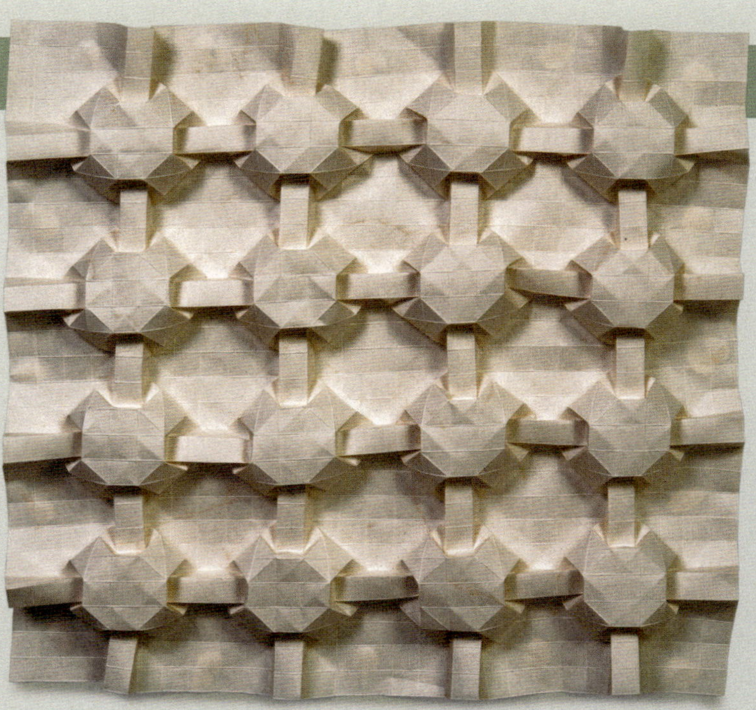

Verso view of a 4 by 4–molecule Concinnous tessellation with a single space.

This version is made by adding an extra column and row in the middle of the molecule.

What was a square in the center of it is now an octagon and the gray parts on the edges give a better explanation of why I chose to call it a bridge, as now the molecule is connected with a square-wide connection. This increases the molecule grid to 7 by 7.

To practice your folding, start with a grid of 9 by 9.

The height of this molecule is around two squares.

The shrinkage ratio is 7:5.

4 by 4 Molecules

Make a grid of 35 by 35. This family benefits from a wider frame, made of two-square rows and columns.

You need seven squares for four molecules and three spaces in between the four.

The formula for the grid is $2 + 3 \times 1 + 4 \times 7 + 2 = 35$.

The final result will be 27 squares wide.

This is a multi-fold pattern but unlike the original version, the extra rows shifted the folds to a position that only a few align.

Follow the orange lines: fold 1, skip 2, fold 1, skip 4, and repeat. Once you have a pair of fold lines, it is easy to complete the small squares.

Once the inner crosses are ready, it will be easier to add the outer ones, following the light blue pattern: fold 2, skip 6.

To collapse, start with a corner molecule, and use the bridge to the next molecule as a guideline to collapse the second molecule. It is wise to fold the bridges of the first row all the way to the far edge of the paper, so when the first row is complete the model lies flat.

Complete the rest of the rows in the same manner.

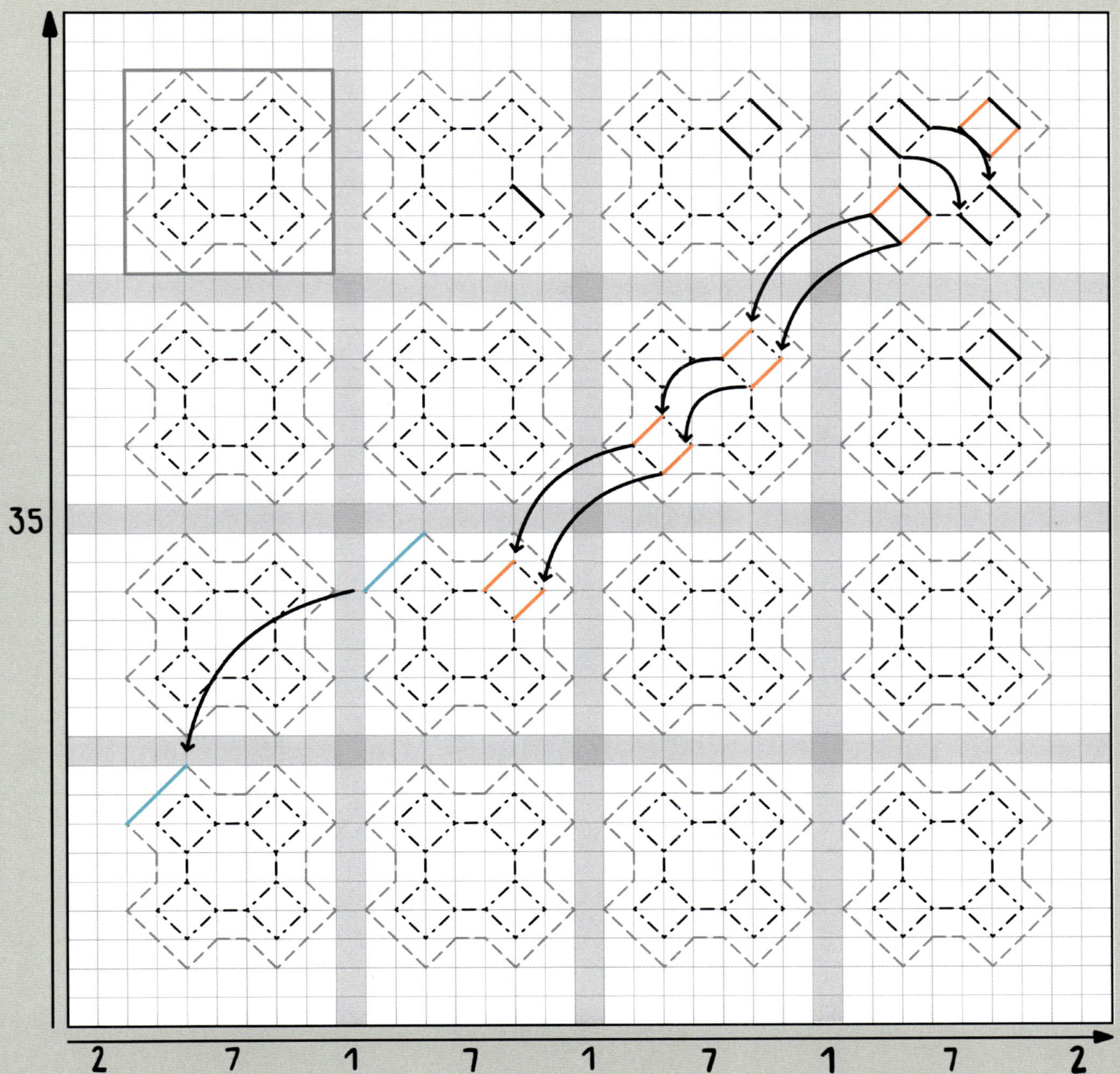

Concinnous; Double Space

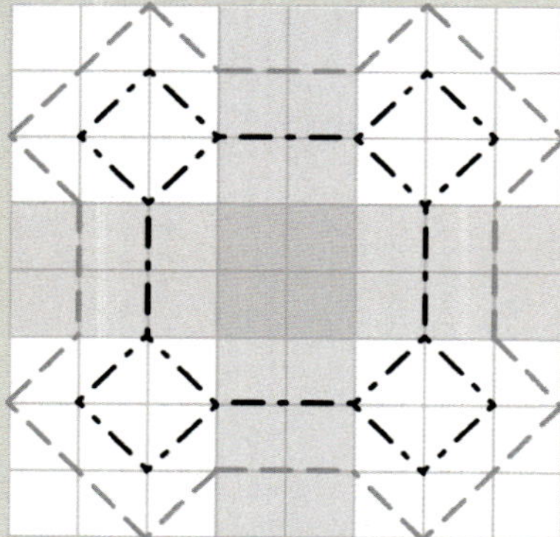

This version is made by adding **two** extra columns and rows in the middle of the molecule. The inner octagon is wider now, and the fact that the bridge is two-square wide allows us to flatten it on top of the two adjacent squares, on left and right. This creates an effect that transforms the molecule structure into a closed box. The height of the box is the length of a square diagonal.

The molecule grid is 8 by 8.

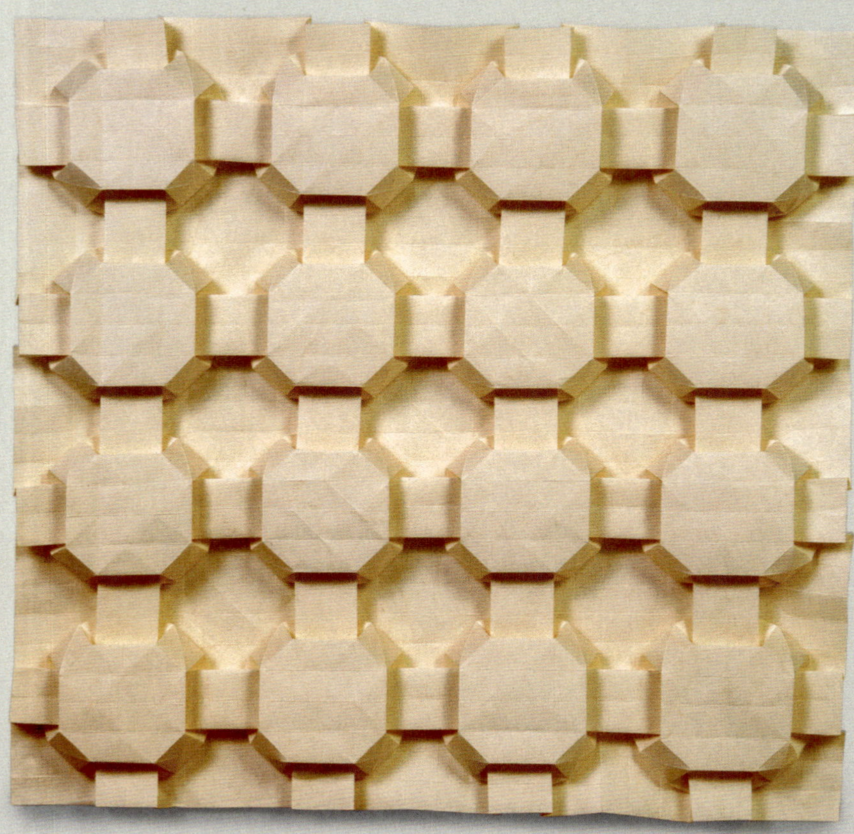

Verso view of a 4 by 4–molecule Concinnous tessellation with a double space.

To practice your folding, start with a grid of 10 by 10.

The shrinkage ratio is 2:1.

3 by 3 Molecules

Make a grid of 30 by 30. This family benefits from a wider frame, made of two-square rows and columns. You need seven squares for three molecules and two spaces in between the three.

The formula for the grid is 2 + 2 × 1 + 3 × 8 + 2 = 30.

The final result will be 18 squares wide.

This is a multi-fold pattern but unlike the original version, the extra rows shifted the folds into a position where they are no longer aligned.

To collapse, start with a corner molecule, and use the bridge to the next molecule as a guideline to collapse the second molecule. It is wise to fold the bridges of the first row all the way to the far edge of the paper, so when the first row is complete the model lies flat.

Complete the rest of the rows in the same manner.

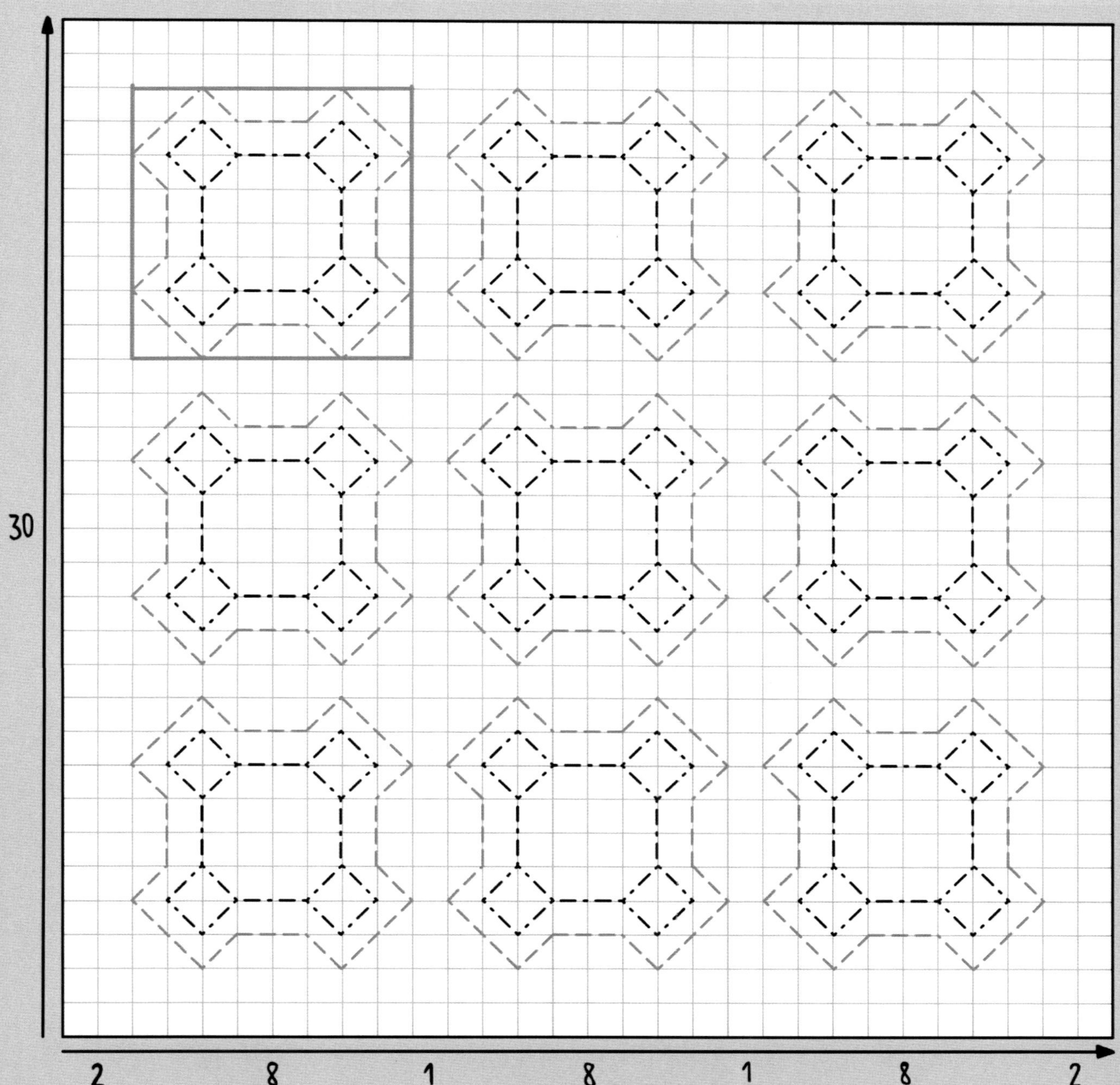
30
2
8
1
8
1
8
2

Concinnous; Alternate Collapse

This molecule has all the off-grid creases exactly like the original version. The difference is the way we collapse the molecule. Note the new mountain folds on the corners. They create a three-level molecule.

The Single Molecule

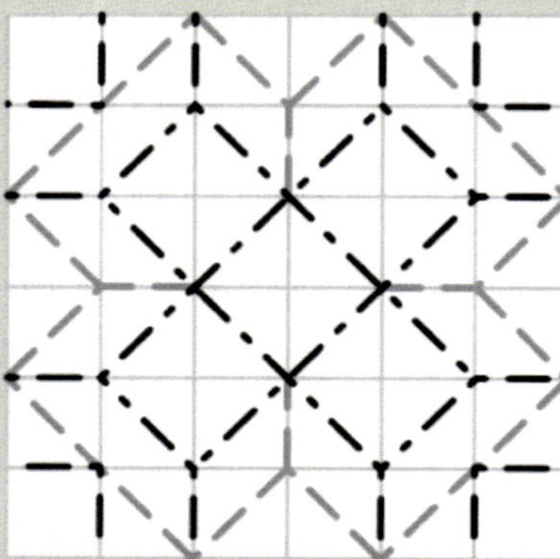

The molecule size is 6 by 6.

To practice your folding, start with a grid of 8 by 8.

The shrinkage ratio is 3:2.

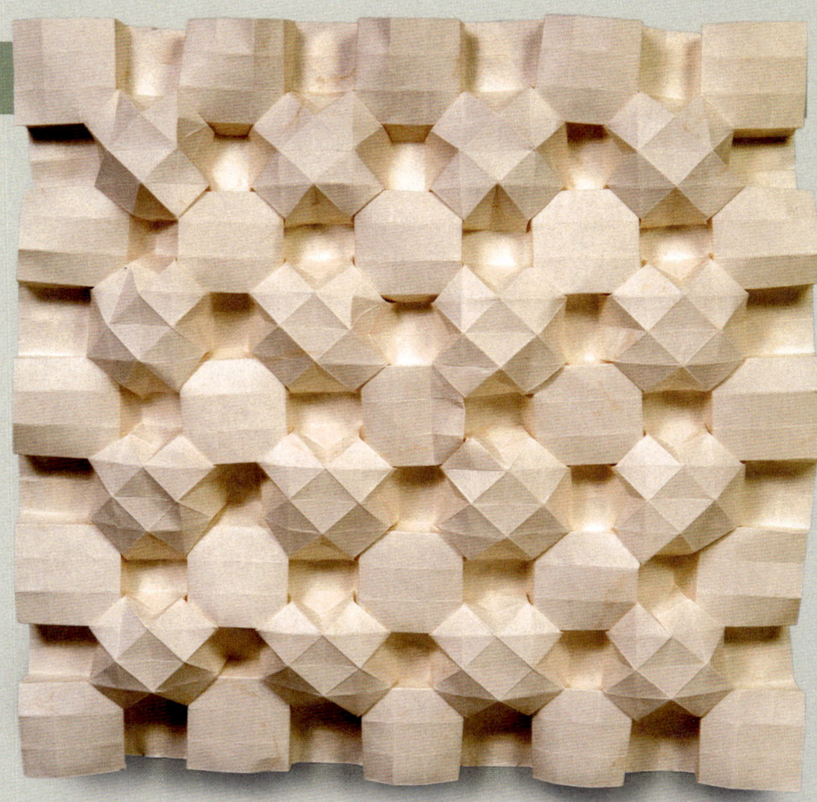

Verso view of a 4 by 4–molecule Concinnous tessellation with an alternate collapse.

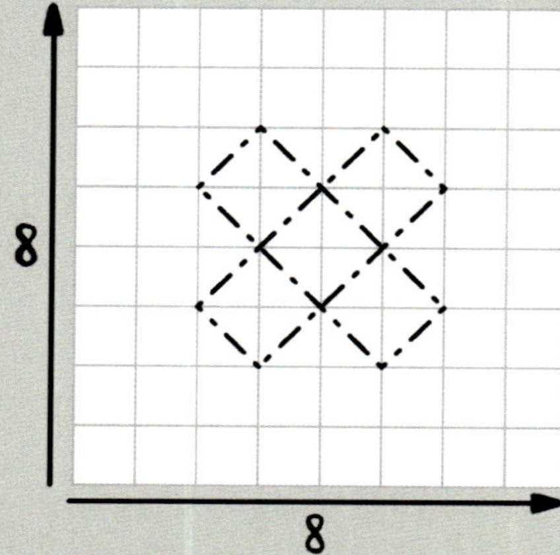

Start with a grid of 8 by 8, to allow extra rows and columns on all four sides.

Mark the inner cross with mountains.

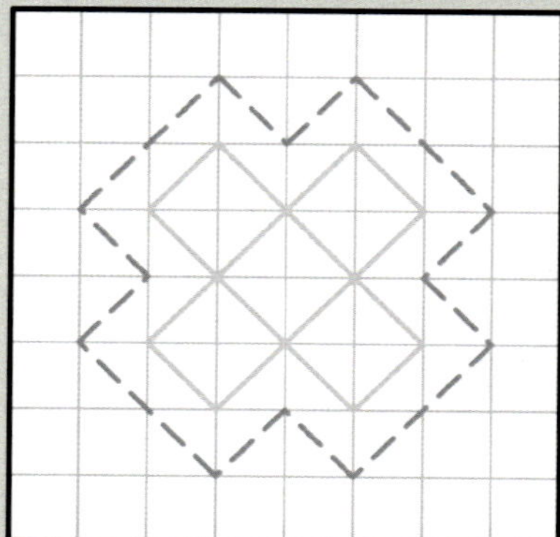

Add the bigger cross with valleys.

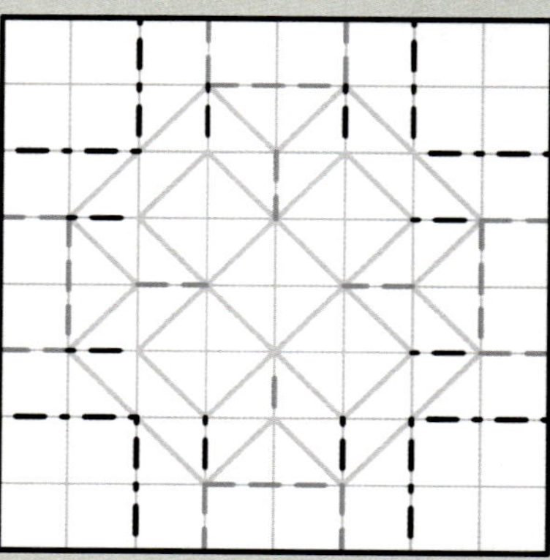

Force the needed creases on the grid in the right direction, as indicated.

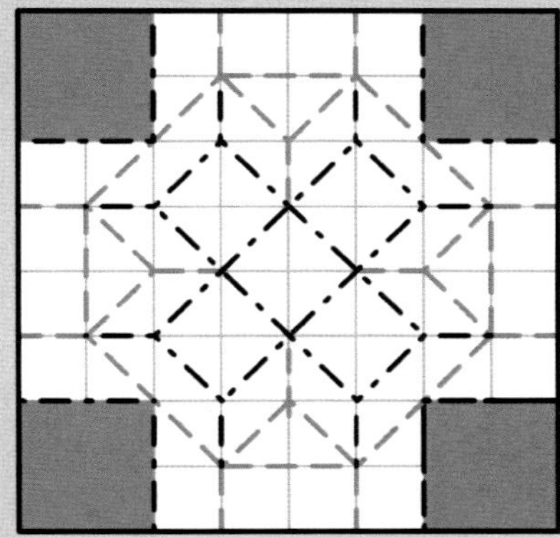

These are all the needed creases. Note the 2 by 2 squares in the four corners (in dark gray), as you will start the collapse with them.

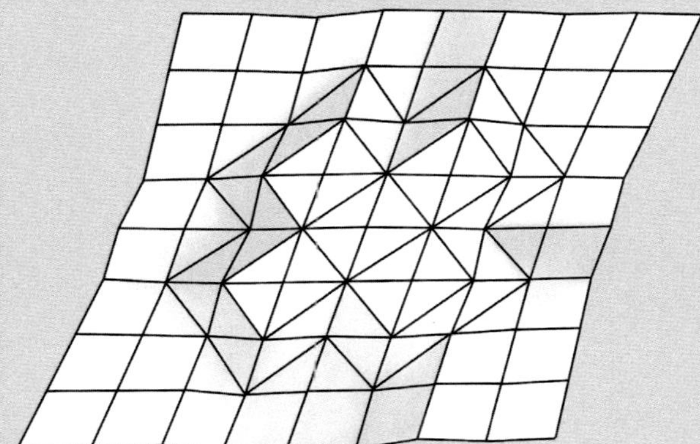

Push up the 2 by 2 squares in the four corners, and at the same time keep the bridge flat on the table.

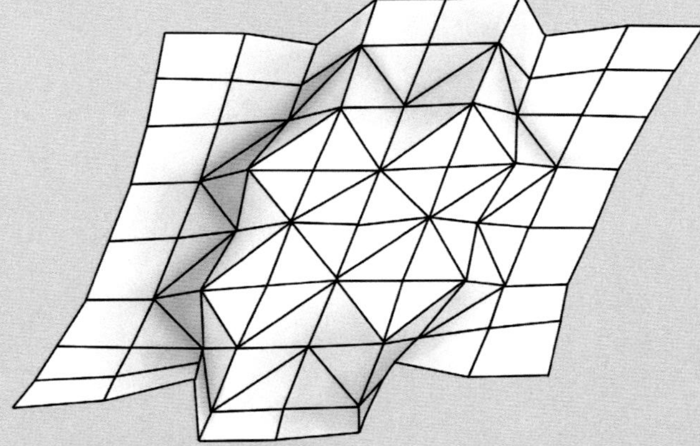

In process.

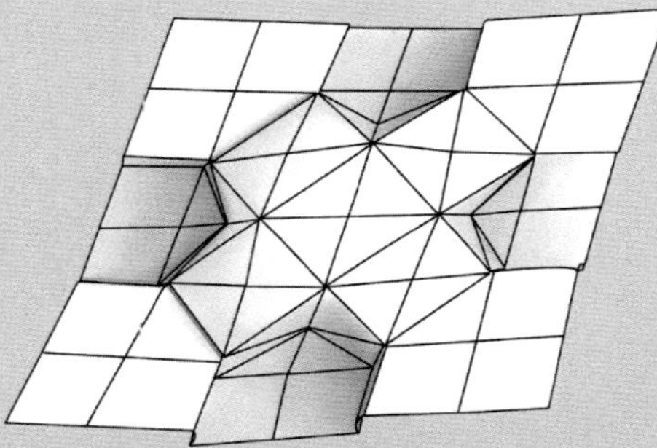

Fully collapsed. The 2 by 2 squares are one-square height, and the bridges are on the table level. The final result has three levels.

4 by 4 Project

Make a grid of 31 by 31. This family benefits from a wider frame, made of two-square rows and columns. Molecules should have spaces between them, to emphasize the three levels, and for easier collapse.

The formula for the grid is $2 + 4 \times 6 + 3 \times 1 + 2 = 31$.

The final result will be 23 squares wide.

For the precreases, you can find the pattern on the **Concinnous; Single Space** model (page 84).

To collapse, start with a corner molecule, and use the bridge to the next molecule as a guideline to collapse the second molecule. It is wise to fold the bridges of the first row all the way to the far edge of the paper, so when the first row is complete the model lies flat.

Complete the rest of the rows in the same manner.

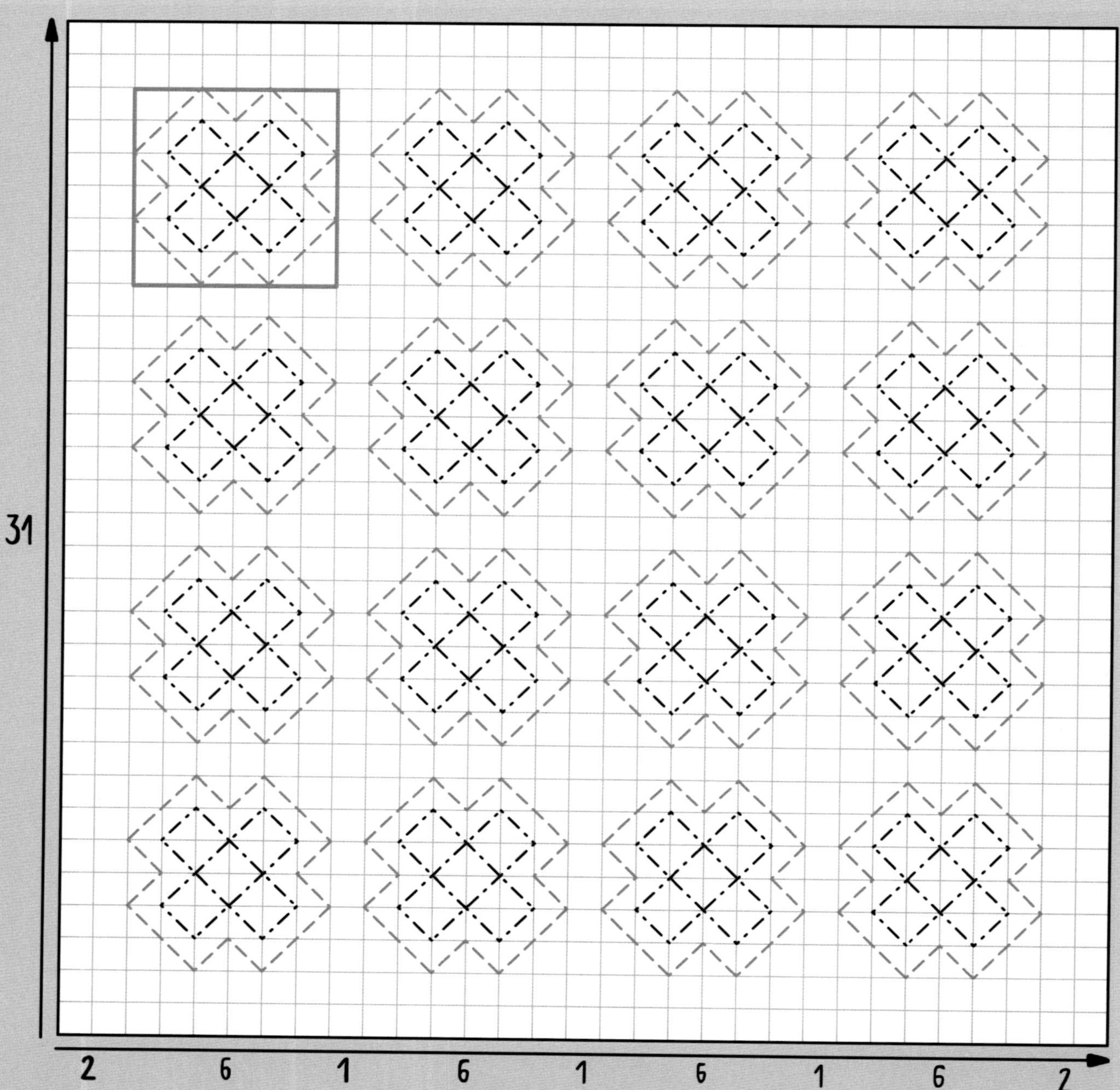
31
2
6
1
6
1
6
1
6
2

4 2 Concinnous B

This molecule is the natural evolution of the previous one. It follows the same logic, but it goes one level higher. To have this extra height the grid is increased by two rows and columns.

There are two ways to collapse the molecule, differing only on the last step.

The Single Molecule

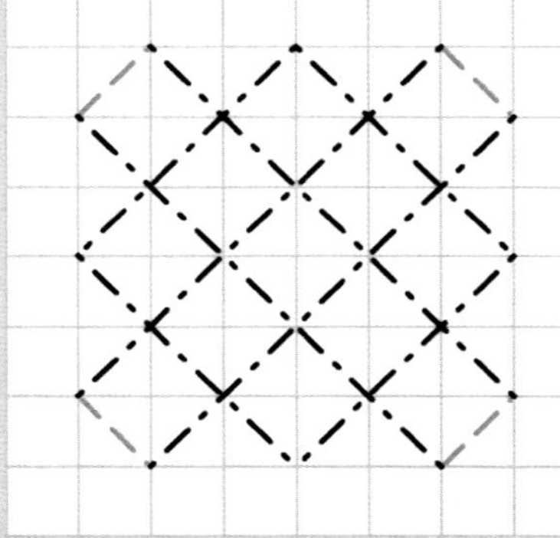

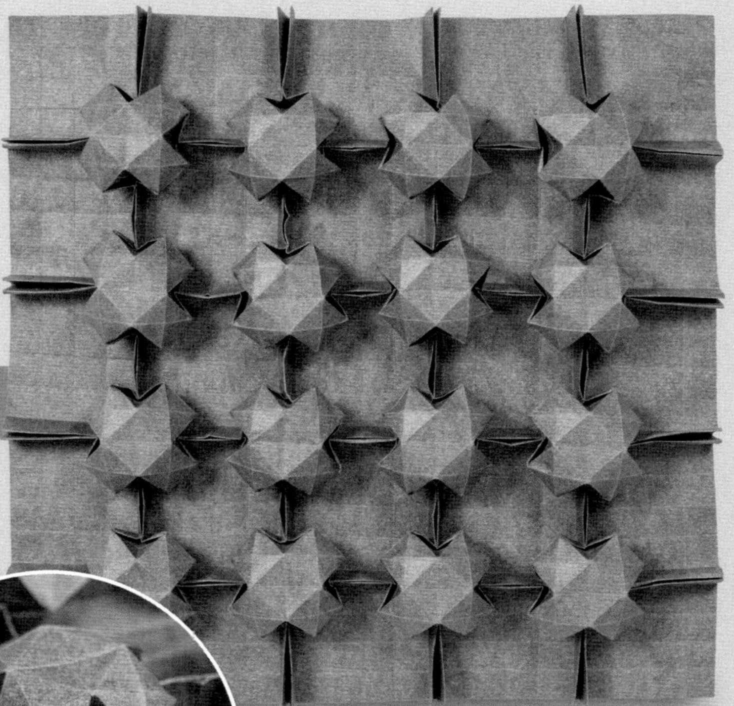

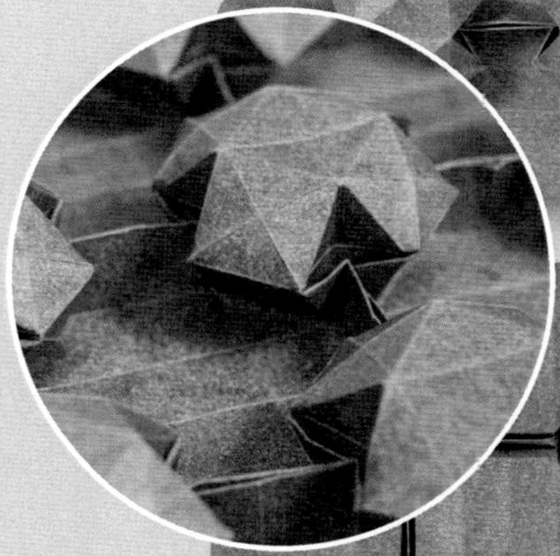

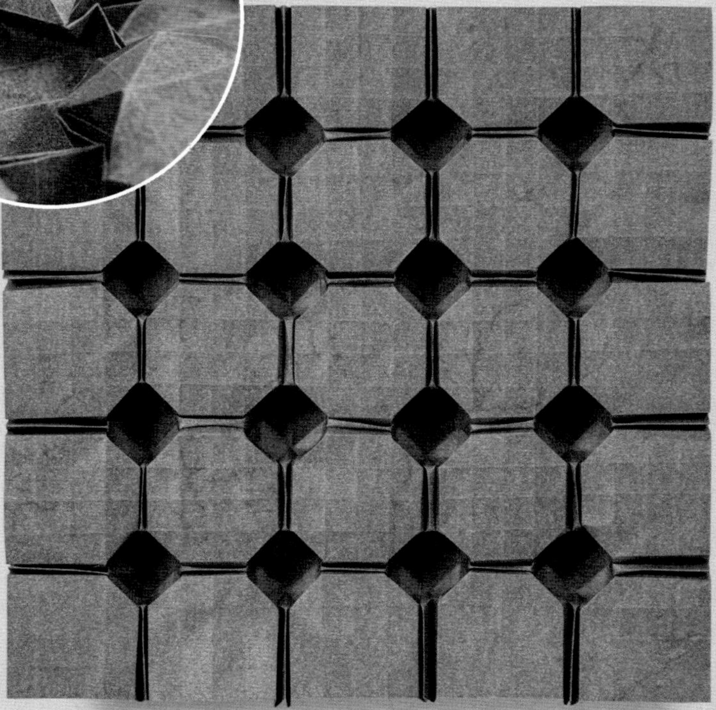

The molecule size is 8 by 8.

It is based on a wide cross shape, rotated 45° on the grid. Every leg of the cross is made out of two squares. On top of it, there is a tilted square, three-diagonal in length.

There is no rotation during the collapse, and the height is two square diagonals.

The shrinkage ratio is 3:2.

Top: recto view of a 4 by 4–molecule Concinnous B tessellation.
Bottom right: verso view of a 4 by 4–molecule Concinnous B tessellation.
In circle: detailed view.

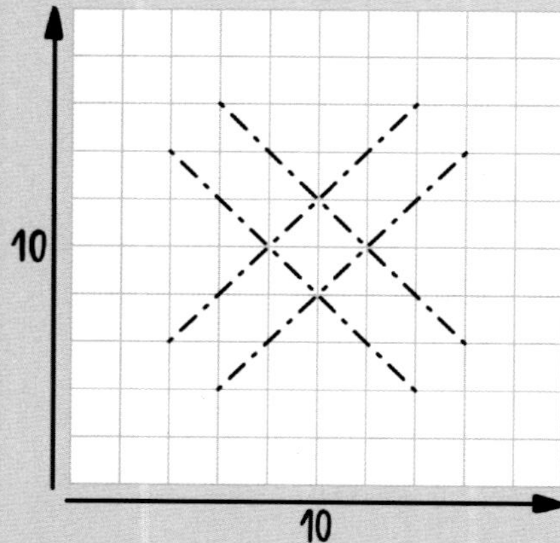

Start with a grid of 10 by 10, to allow extra rows and columns on all four sides.

Mark with mountains the long lines of the inner cross.

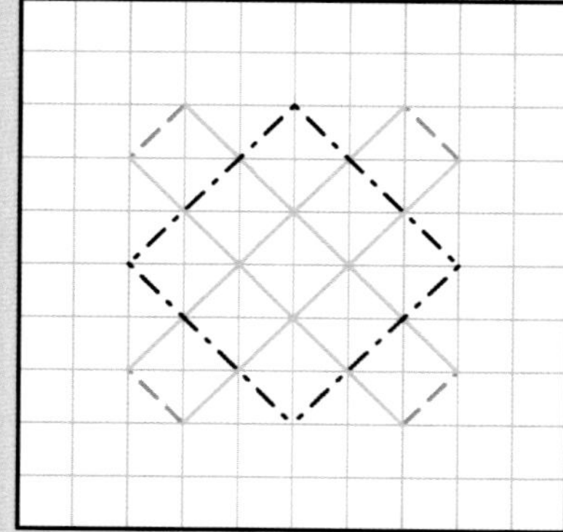

Add the valleys at the ends of the long mountains. This finishes the cross.

Now fold the tilted square with mountains.

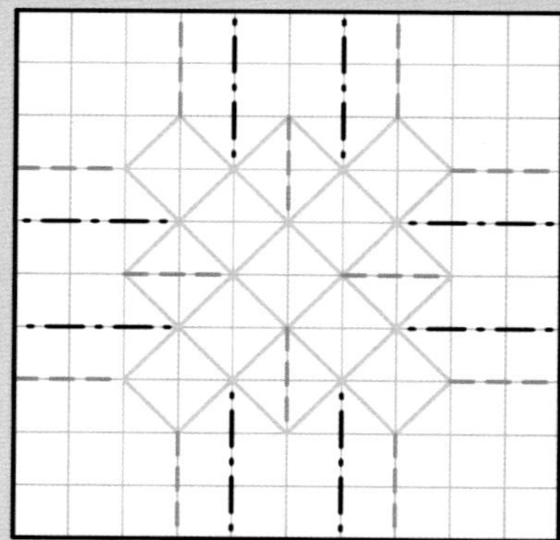

Force the folds on the grid lines in the right direction.

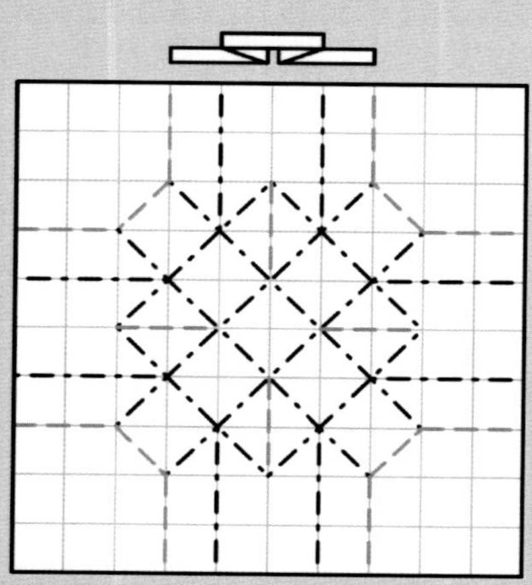

These are all the needed creases. Note the edges of the square — the layers will lie flat at the end of the collapse. The center square will rise up, taking with it the four legs of the cross.

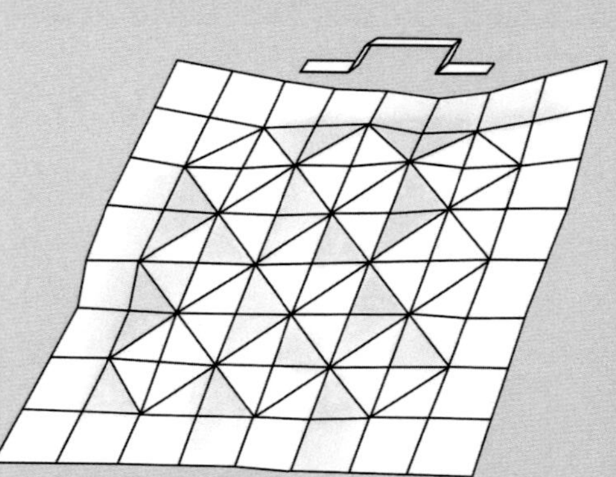

Start the collapse by building the bridges, while pushing up the center (from below!).

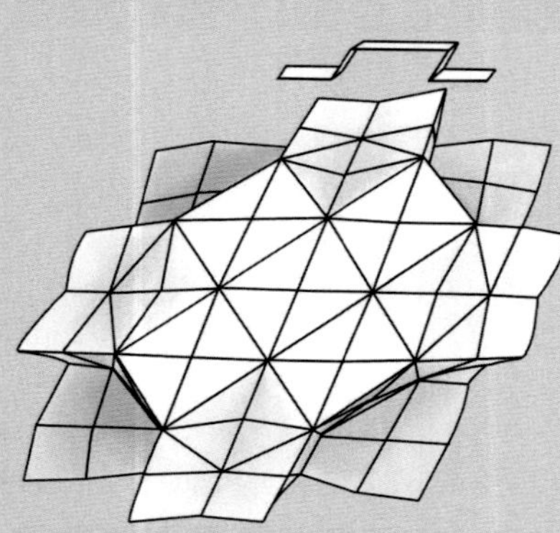

In process. Once the bridge is high, start to flatten it back, following the Zig Zag pattern (see the next step).

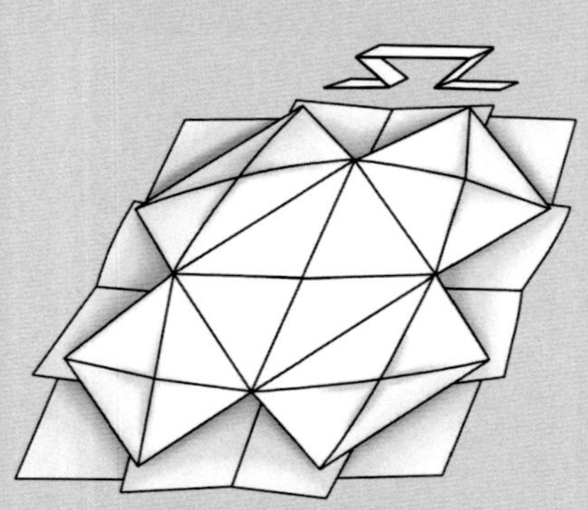

Fully collapsed.

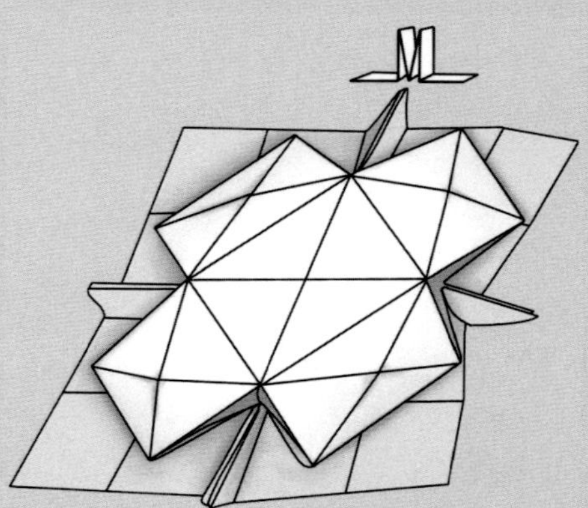

By pinching the sides, you can have this result:

2 by 2 Molecules

Use a grid of 18 by 18.

Collapse the model one molecule at a time, but make sure the adjacent molecule is slightly folded (mainly the inner mountain cross) before you collapse the molecule.

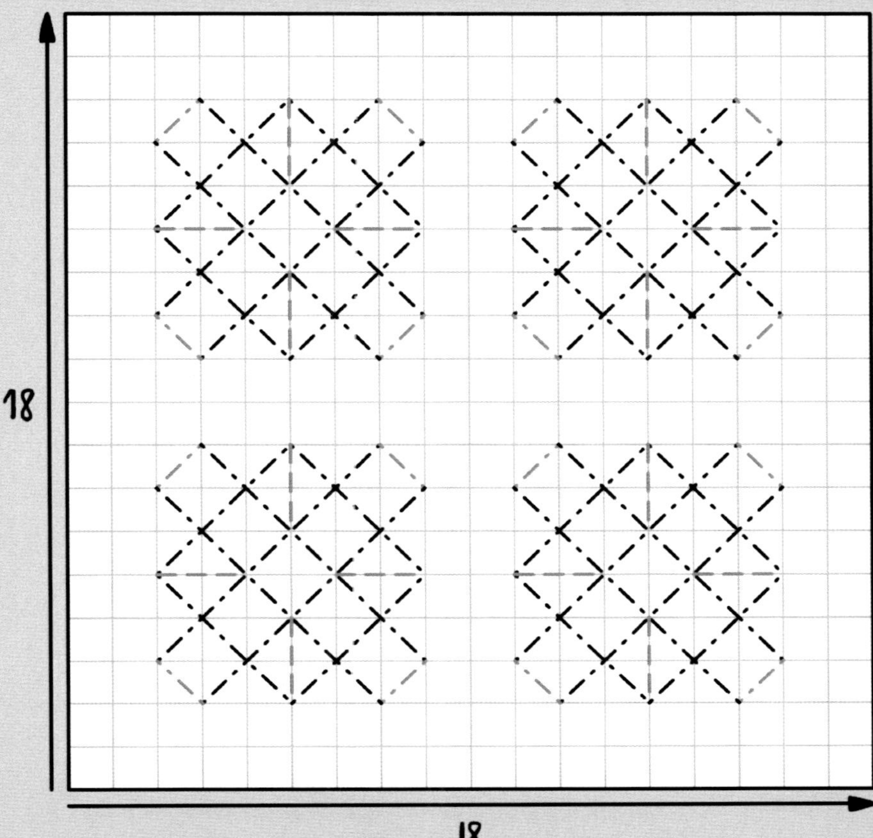

4 by 4 Project

Make a grid of 36 by 36. This family benefits from a wider frame, made of a two-square row and column all around.

The formula for the grid is 2 + 4 × 8 + 2 = 36.

The final result will be 18 squares wide.

Start with the longest, inner lines, in black. The sequence is: fold 4, skip3, repeat. If you rotate the paper 90° and repeat the process, you will have all the inner crosses as a clear reference to the next folds.

The orange lines are following this rhythm: fold 3 and skip 5. Now you may rotate the paper and complete the orange square.

The blue lines are valleys! Fold 1 and skip 7 is a helpful beat, but it is just easier to make sure every valley completes the black crosses.

To collapse, start with a corner molecule, and use the bridge to the next molecule as a guideline to collapse the second molecule. It is wise to fold the bridges of the first row all the way to the far edge of the paper, so when the first row is complete the model lies flat.

The best way to complete the model is by building the bridges on the outer edges and then completing the inner ones.

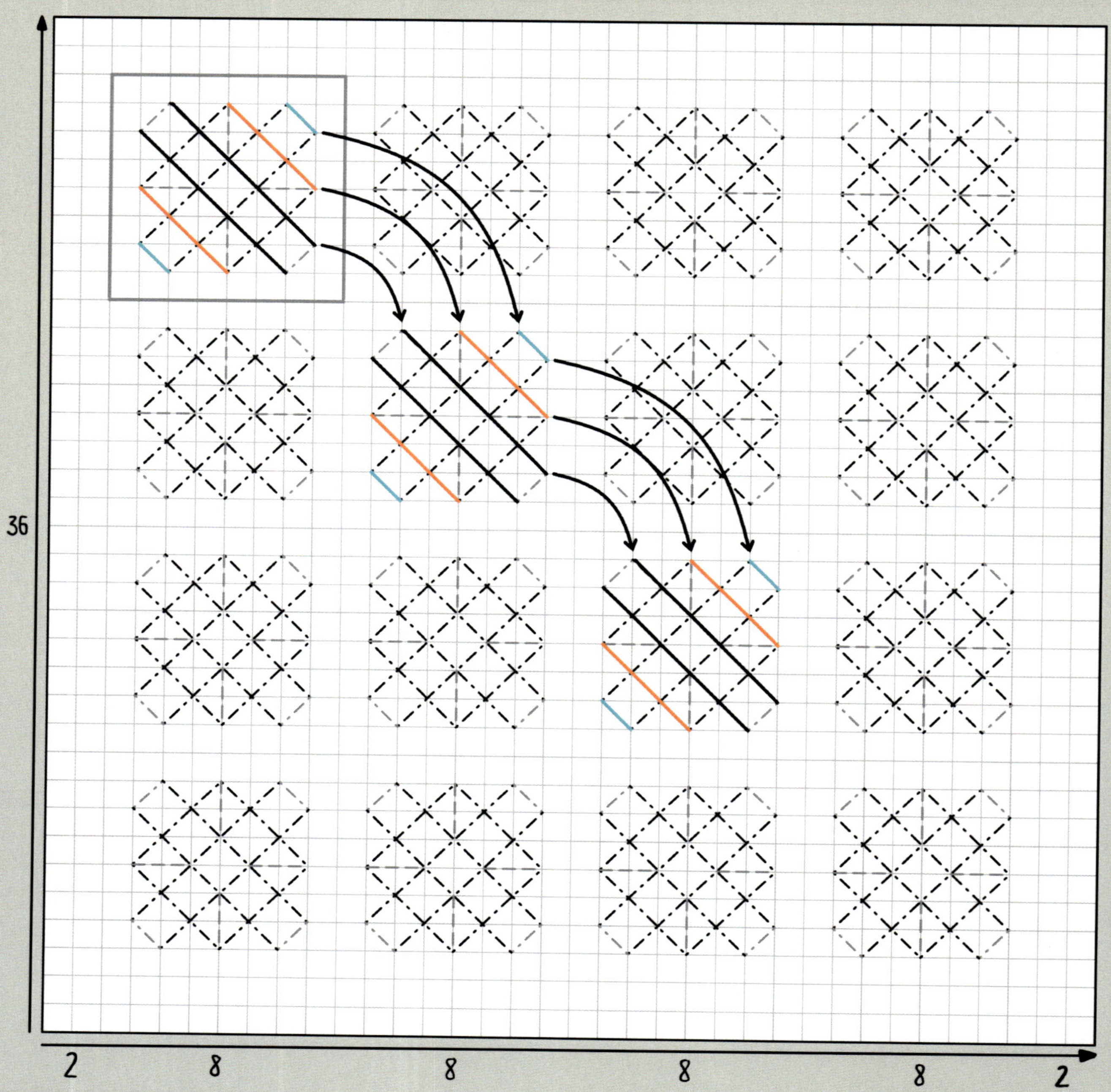
36
2
8
8
8
8
2

Variations - Concinnous B - Single Space

The Single Molecule

This version is made by adding an extra column and row in the middle of the molecule. What was a square in the center of it is now an octagon. This increases the molecule grid to 9 by 9.

To practice your folding, start with a **grid of 11 by 11**.

The height of this molecule is around two squares.

The shrinkage ratio is 9:5.

There is no CP for a complete project with this molecule.

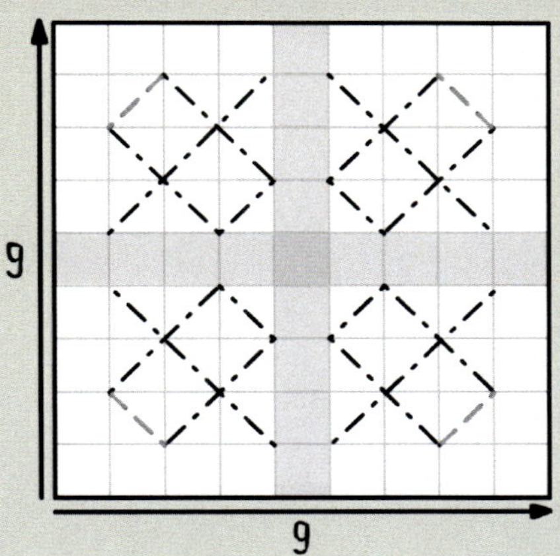

Concinnous C

There is one last step in the evolution of this molecule, and here it is. No, it's not elegant, maybe too much of everything, but I did design it, and it makes the chapter a whole.

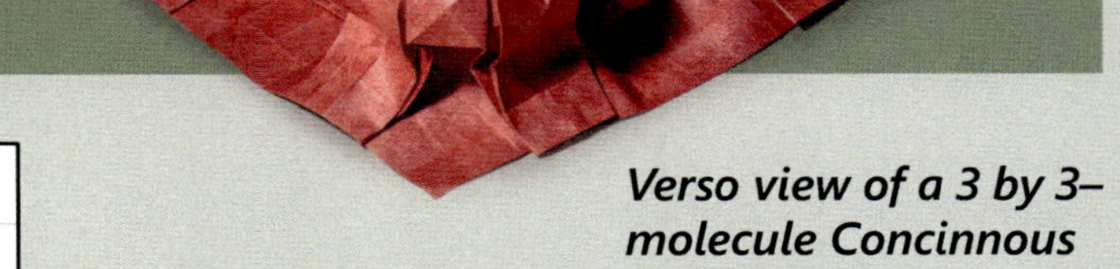

Verso view of a 3 by 3–molecule Concinnous C tessellation.

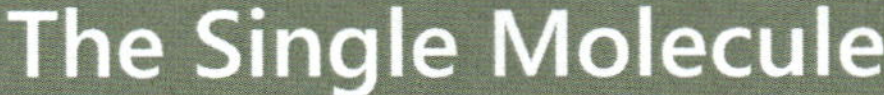

The Single Molecule

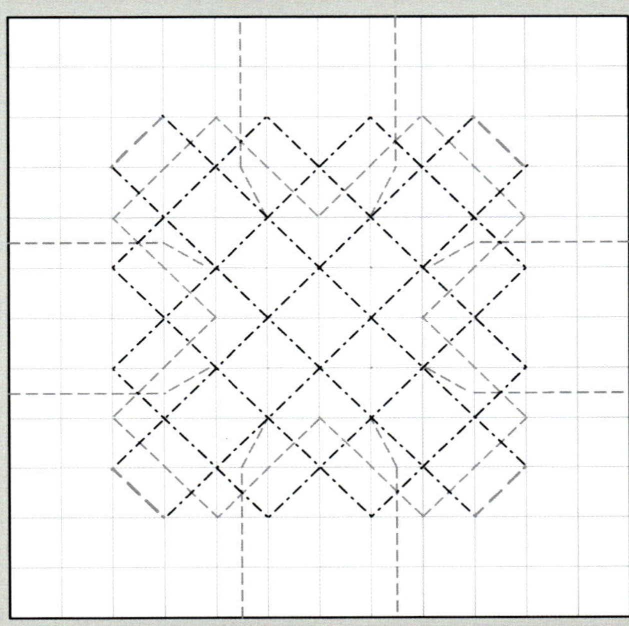

This version has a seven-square cross. Its height is a little above two squares (although it can be flattened to a square height if you flatten all the creases.

The molecule grid is 10 by 10.

For easier folding practice, use a grid of 12 by 12.

The shrinkage ratio is 5:2.

There is no CP for a complete project with this molecule.

4 3 Heptamerous

This hexagonal molecule is the natural evolution of the square one. It follows the same logic, on a hexagon grid.

There are two ways to collapse the molecule, differing on the last step only.

Variations are based on "inflating" the inner hexagon.

The Single Molecule

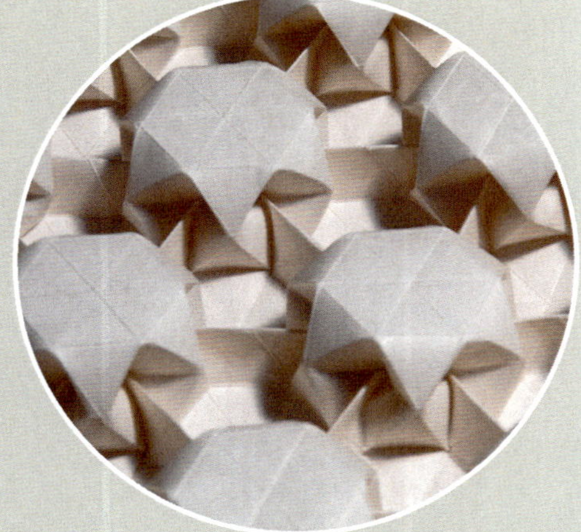

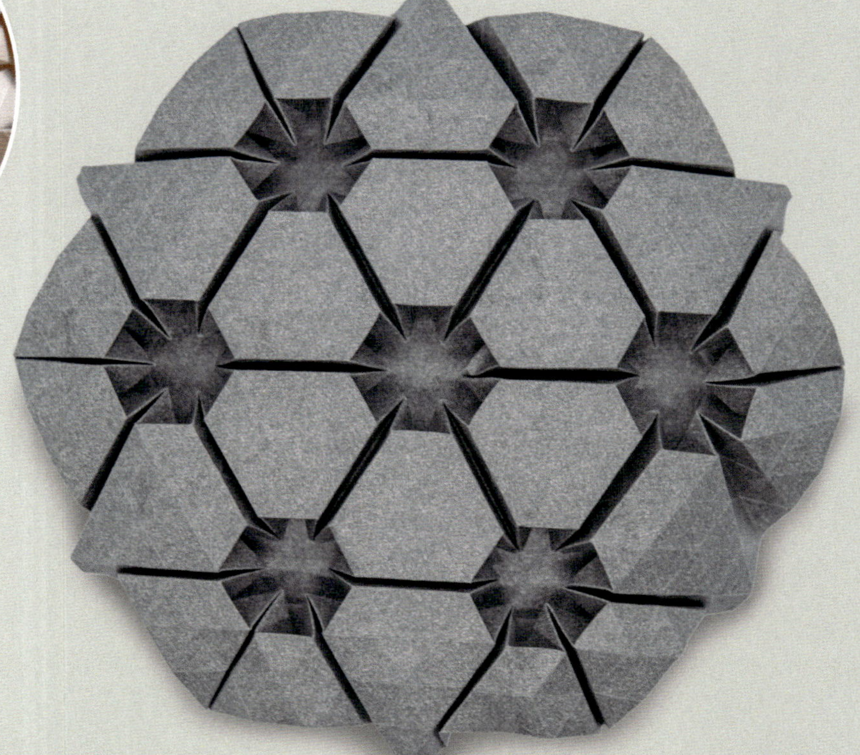

Top: recto view of a 24 grid Heptamerous tessellation.

Bottom: verso view of a 24 grid Heptamerous tessellation.

In circle: Heptamerous with a single space between molecules.

The molecule size is 6 by 6 by 6.

It is based on a six-point star puff, made by six mountain folds, on the grid lines.

The height of the molecule is just shy of two triangles.

The shrinkage ratio is 3:1.

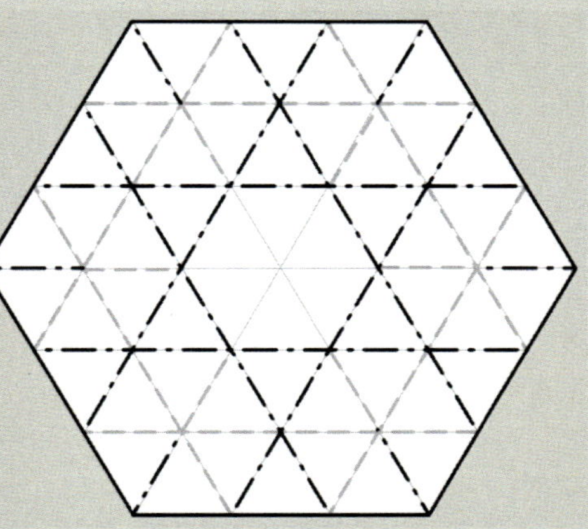

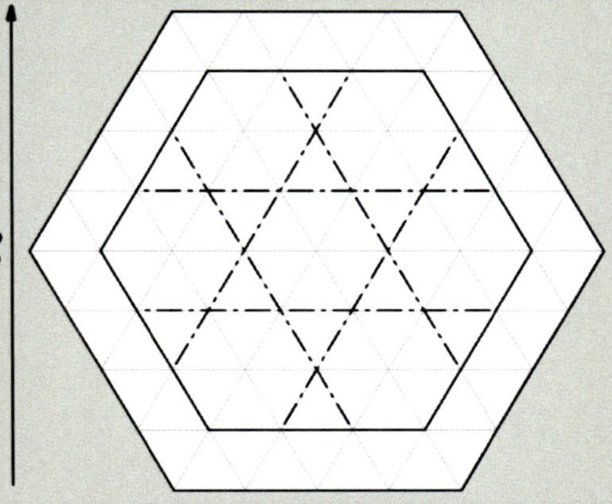

Use a grid of 8 by 8 by 8.

Force on the grid the six mountains, and see the six-point star emerges in the center.

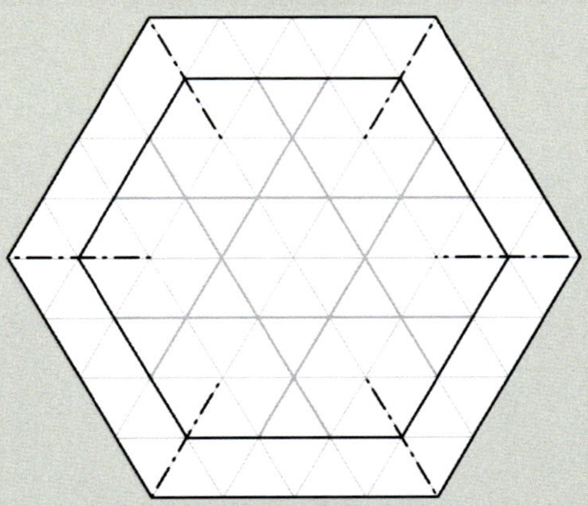

Force mountains at the six corners.

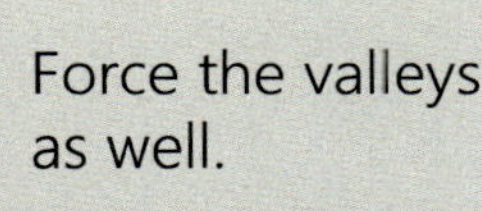

Force the valleys as well.

To start the collapse, pinch the orange dots while forcing the inner hexagon to rise.

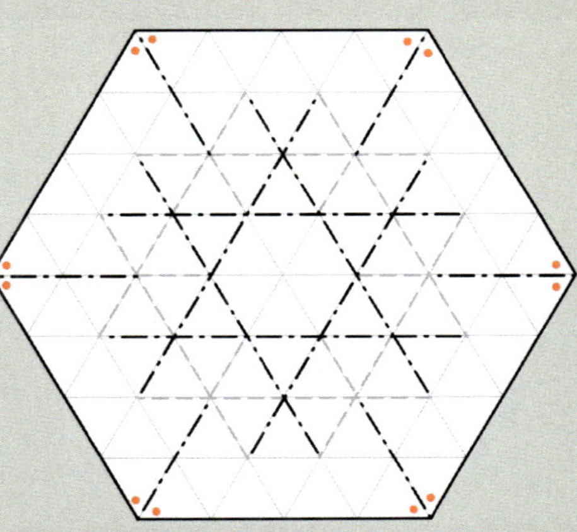

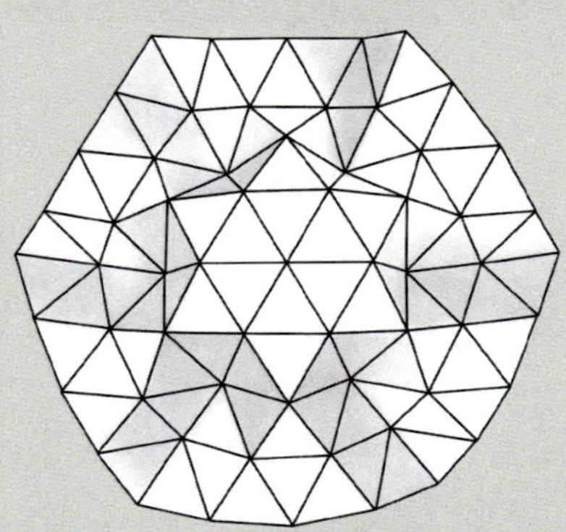

Every mountain is surrounded by 5 valleys, which form a four-side concave shape.

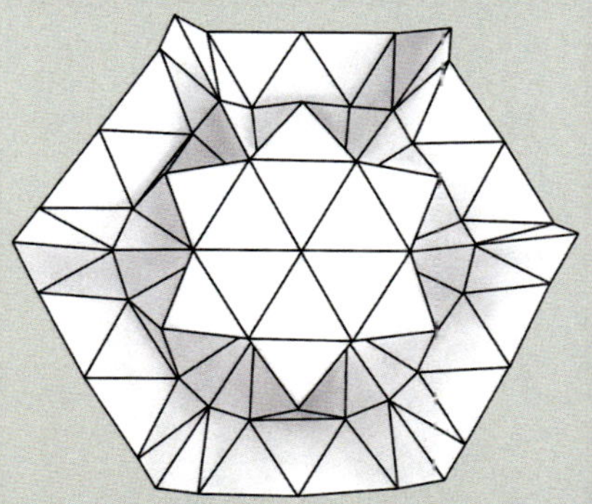

In progress.

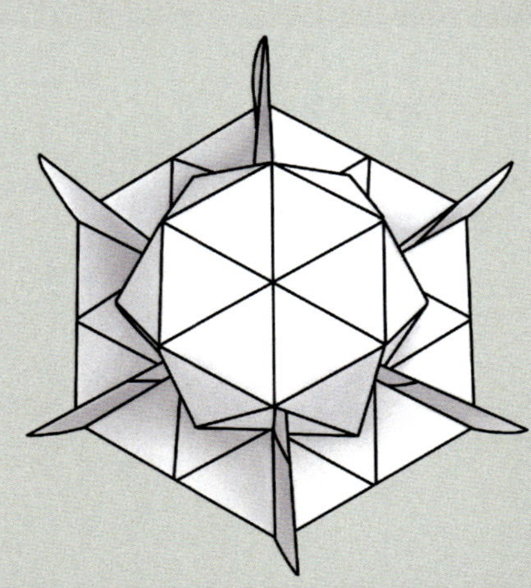

Fully collapsed.

24-Grid Project

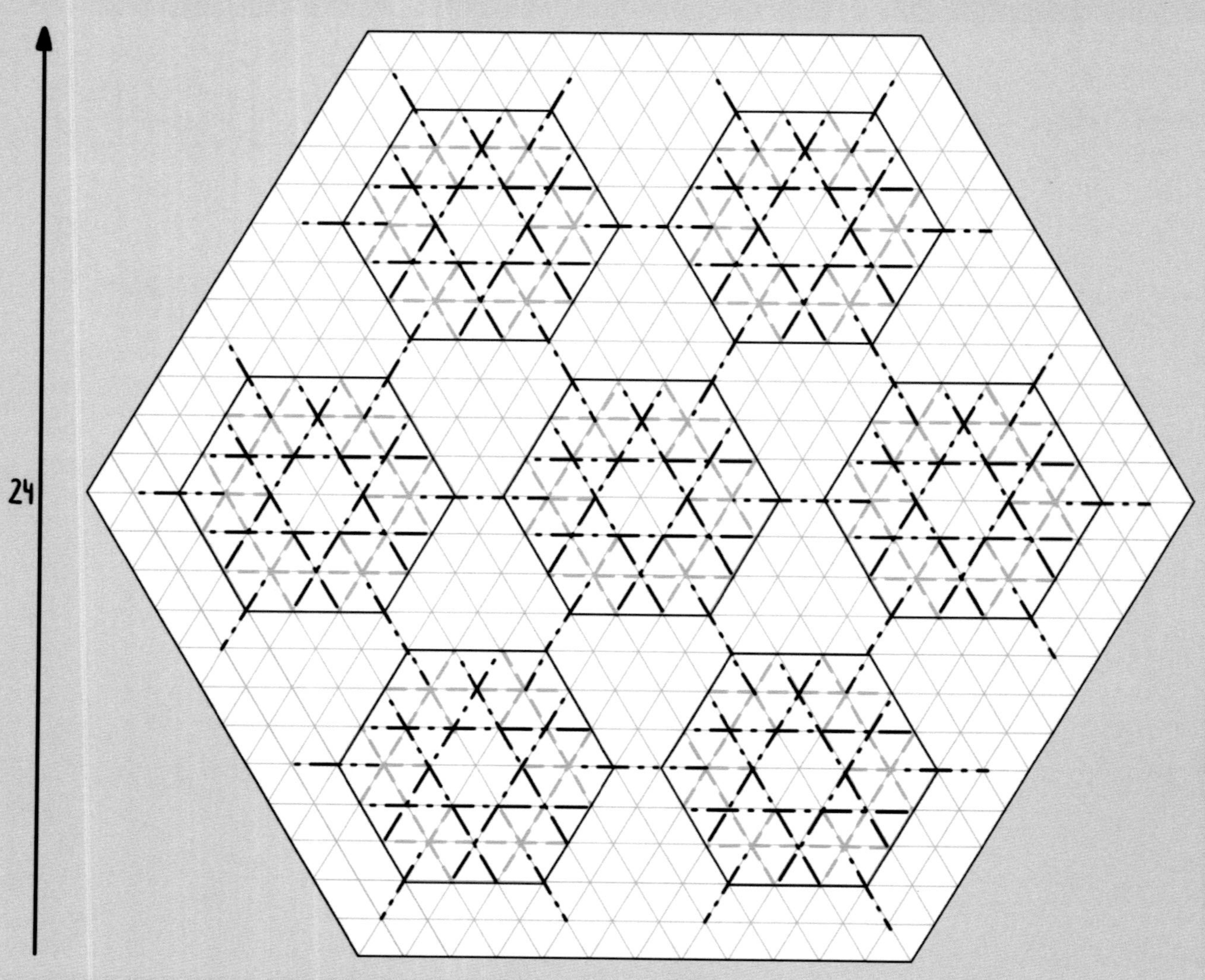

Start the collapse from the center molecule. You can mountain-fold the six bridges all the way to the corners of the paper.

Having the first molecule fully collapsed, add a new molecule. Some of the bridges (those that point to other unfolded molecules) will intersect with the existing bridges of the first molecule. Don't force this junction. Allow the bridges to flatten there, and once you finish the second molecule, you can collapse the molecule that sits on this junction.

Repeat all around.

Variation

This was actually my first design from this family. The previous model was a simplification of this one.

You can see the seven hexagons forming the molecule, hence the name of this model.

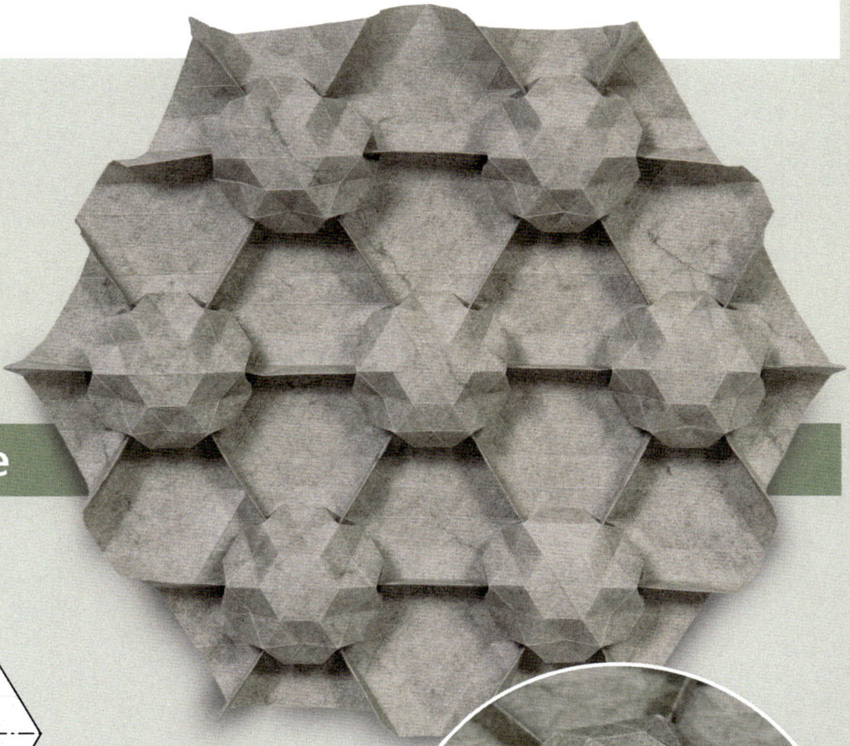

The Single Molecule

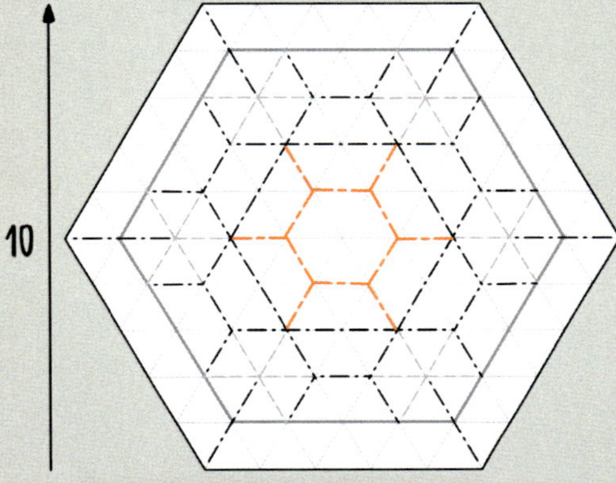

The molecule size is 8 by 8 by 8. Use a grid of 10 by 10 by 10, to allow extra space on all sides.

It is based on an enlarged center — seven hexagons instead of one.

To get the six hexagons around the center you have to add the mountain lines marked in orange.

The height of the molecule is just shy of two triangles.

The shrinkage ratio is 3:2.

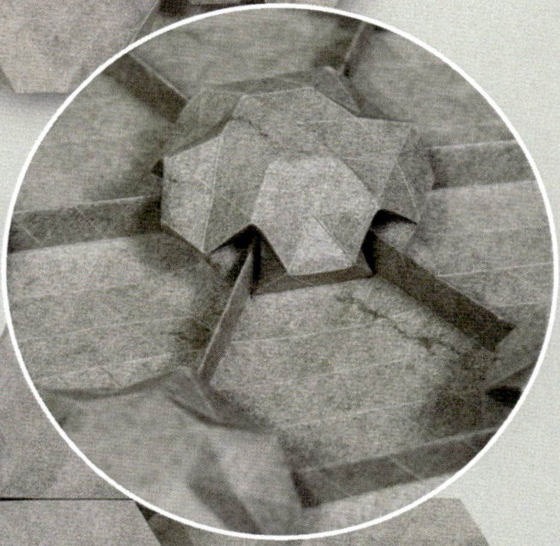

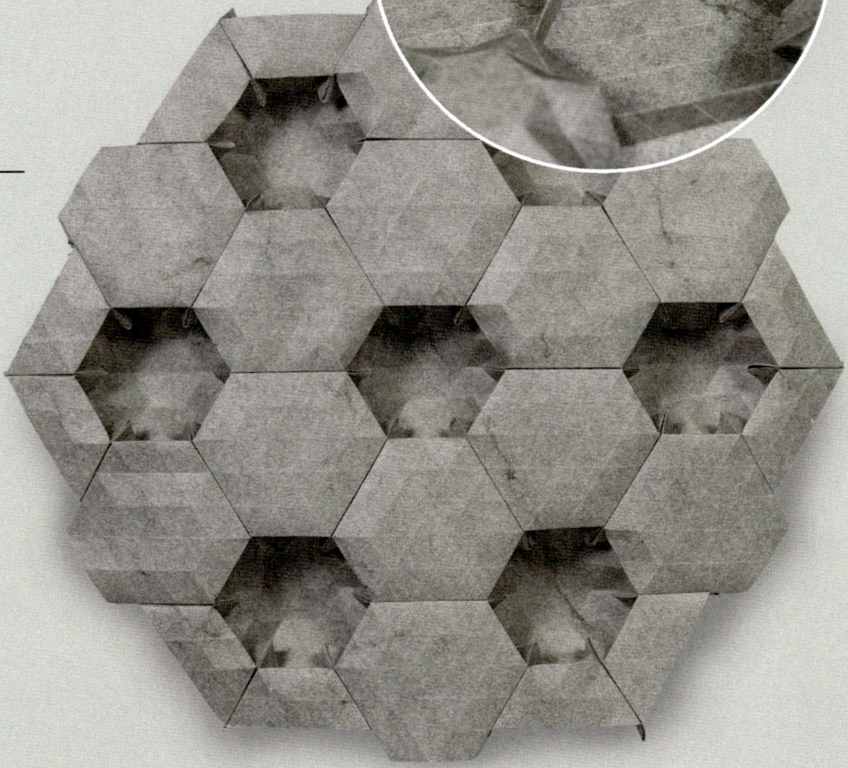

Top: recto view of a 32 grid Heptamerous variation.

Bottom: verso view of a 32 grid Heptamerous variation.

In circle: detailed view.

32-Grid Project

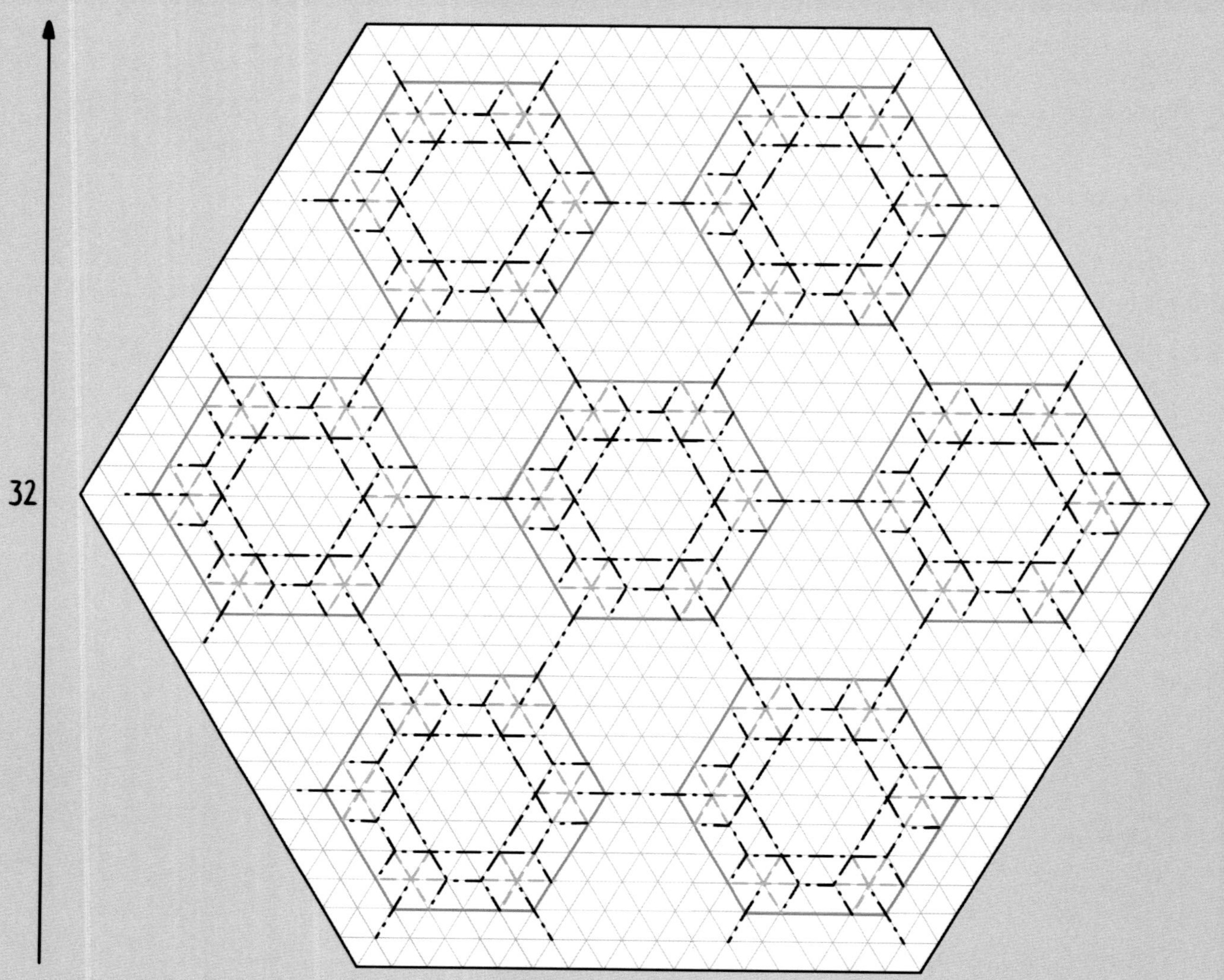

Start the collapse from the center molecule. You can mountain-fold the six bridges all the way to the corners of the paper.

Having the first molecule fully collapsed, add a new molecule. Some of the bridges (those that point to other unfolded molecules) will intersect with the existing bridges of the first molecule. Don't force this junction. Allow the bridges to flatten there, and once you finish the second molecule, you can collapse the molecule that sits on this junction.

Repeat all around.

Above and Beyond

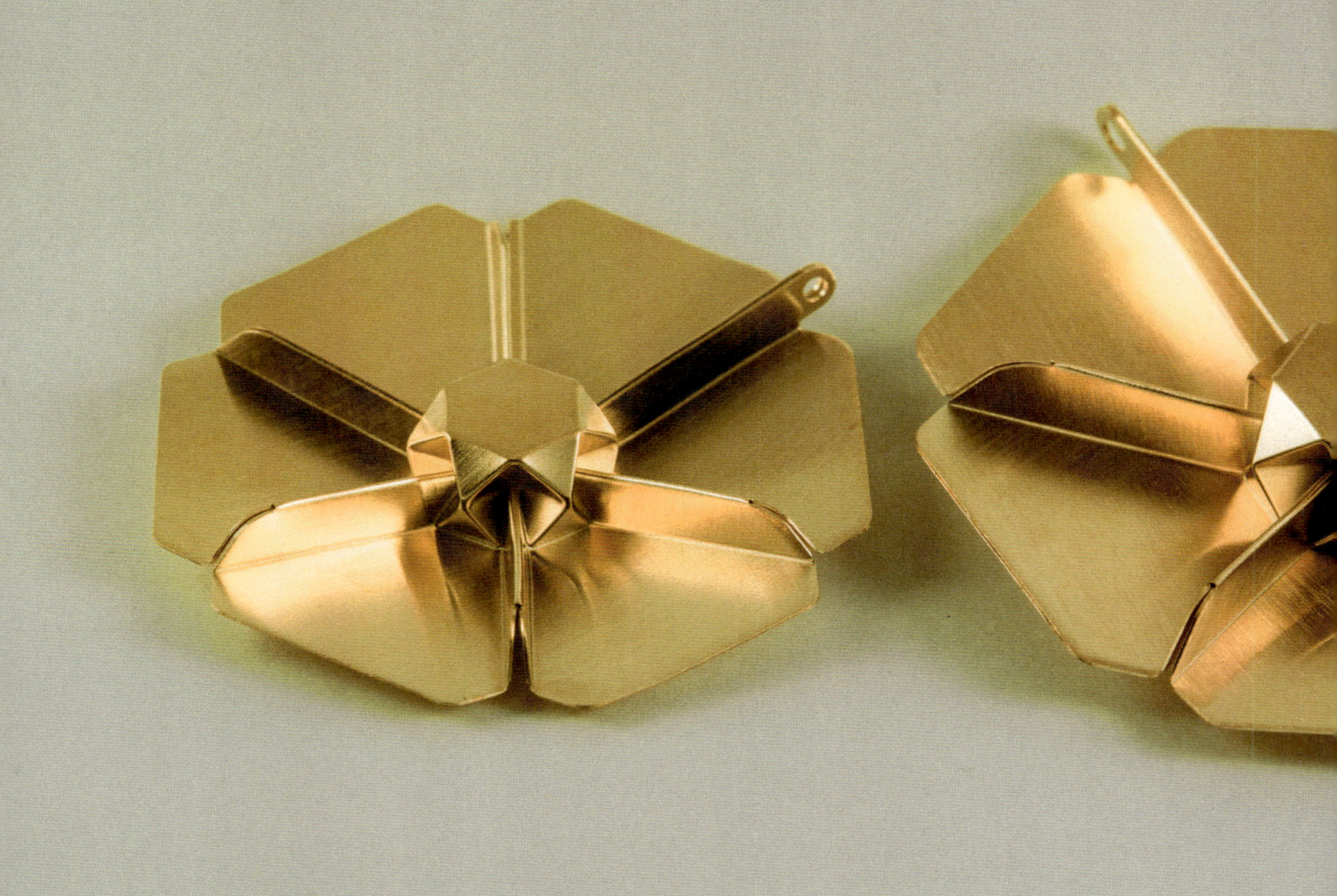

This pattern is a perfect fit for pendants, hand-folded from a single sheet of gold-plated brass.

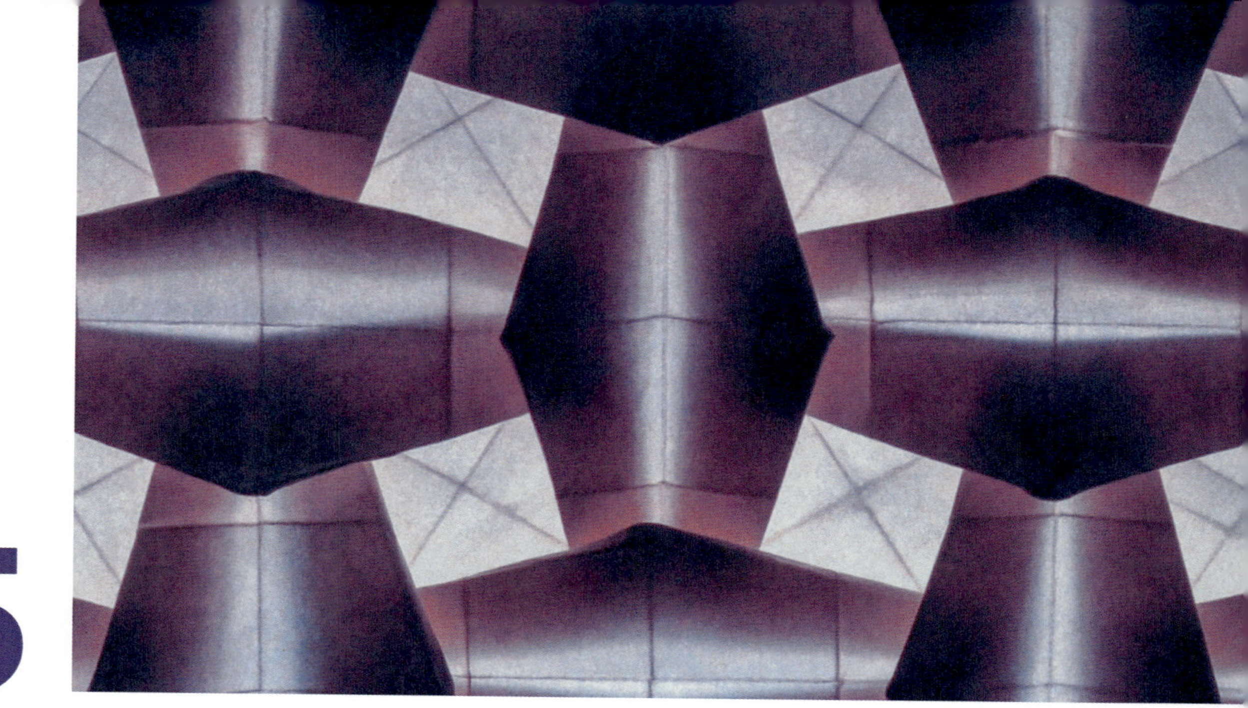

5 The Flat Models Family

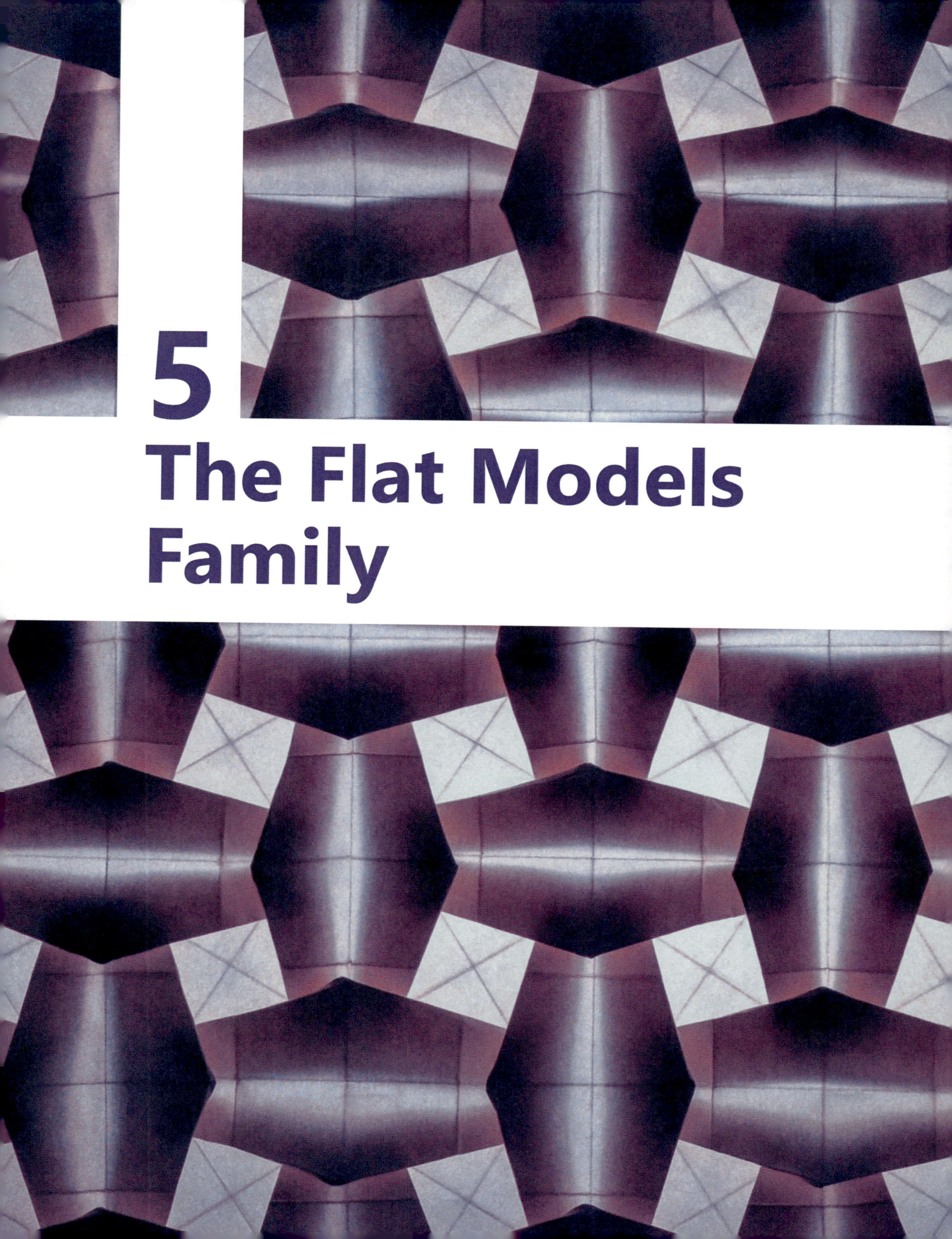

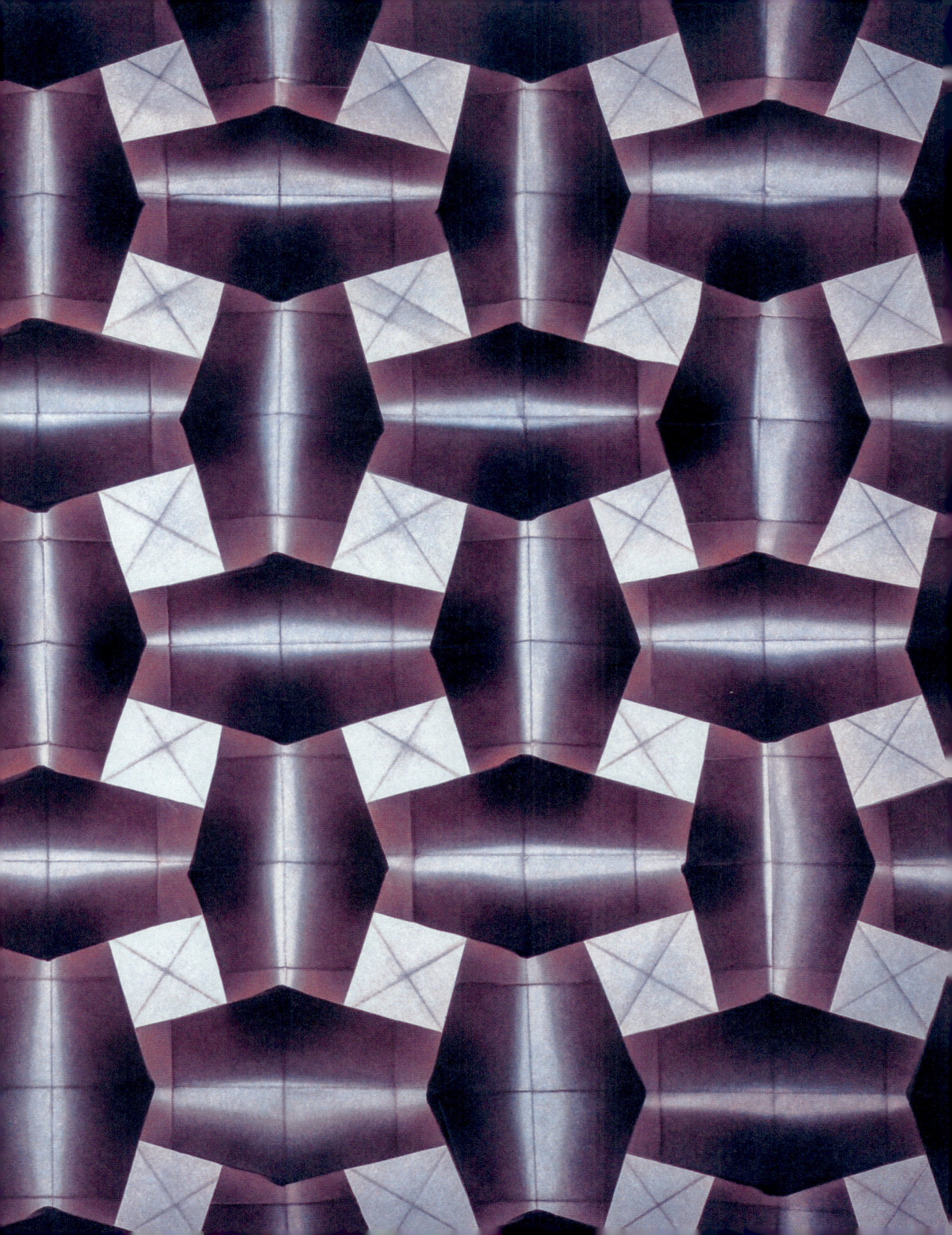

Introduction

To be honest, this is not a family but a group.

I usually do not design flat models. The vast majority of my work has volume, but not here. Three out of the four are from my earlier period, and they explore known areas, and I am sure I was unknowingly following others who already found them before me.

The latter two present a new idea in my books, Self Similarity. It means you repeat the process on a smaller scale.

The last model is a new entry I designed after I realized three are not enough for a chapter.

5 1 Flambuginous

I named it after I saw the backside. Seeing the simple tiled square could not explain the beauty of the front side!

This molecule performs a twist and stays flat.

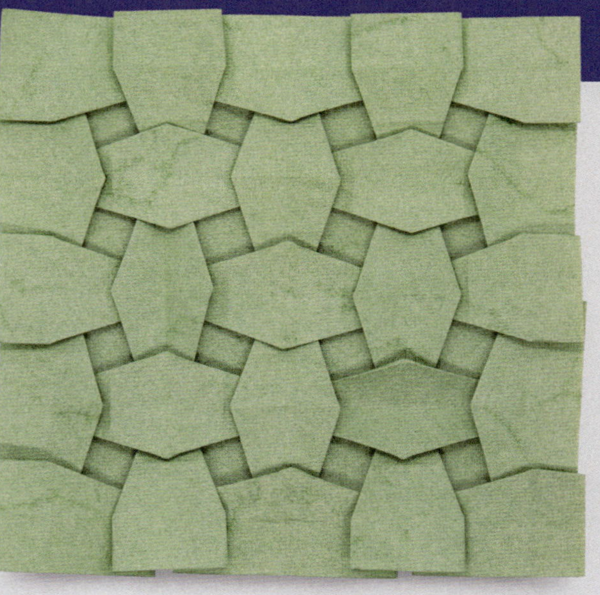

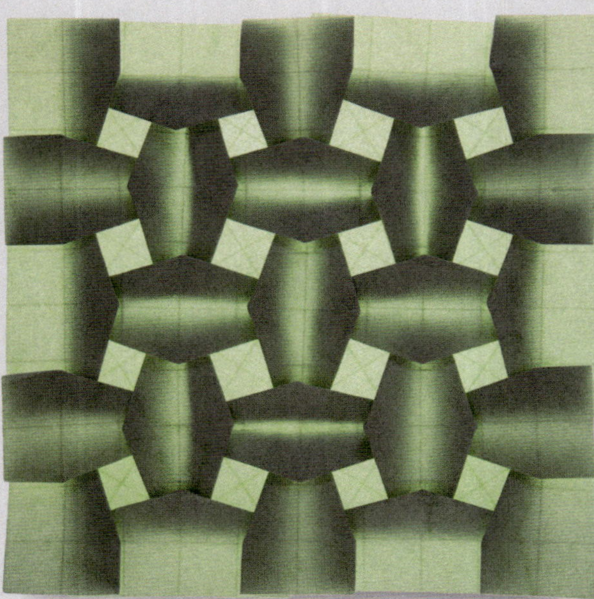

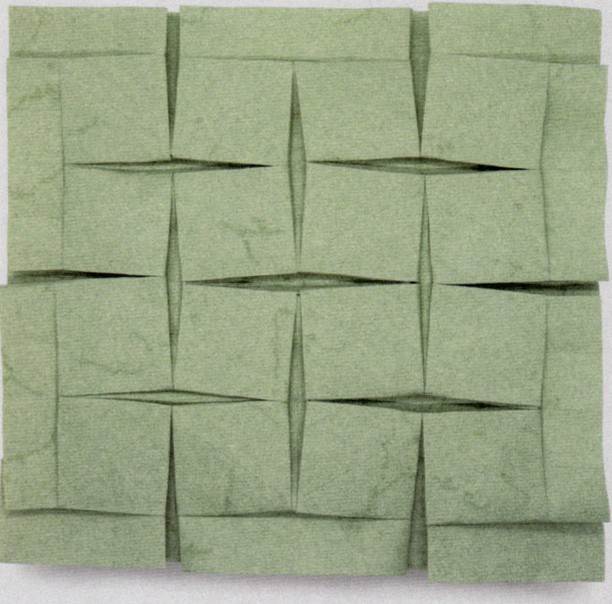

Top right: recto view of a 4 by 4–molecule Flambuginous tessellation.

Bottom right: verso view of a 4 by 4–molecule Flambuginous tessellation.

Left: recto view with back-light.

The Single Molecule

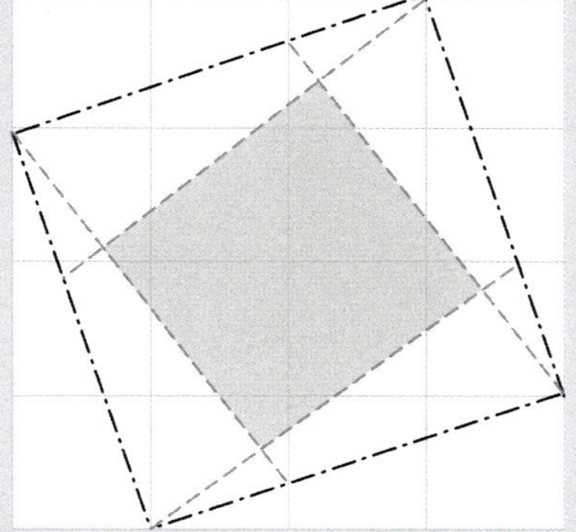

The molecule size is 4 by 4.

It is based on a slanted inner square, made from diagonals of 1 by 3 rectangles.

The inner grey square performs a slight twist, but the molecule stays flat.

The shrinkage ratio is 2:1. The final molecule size is shown as the grey square.

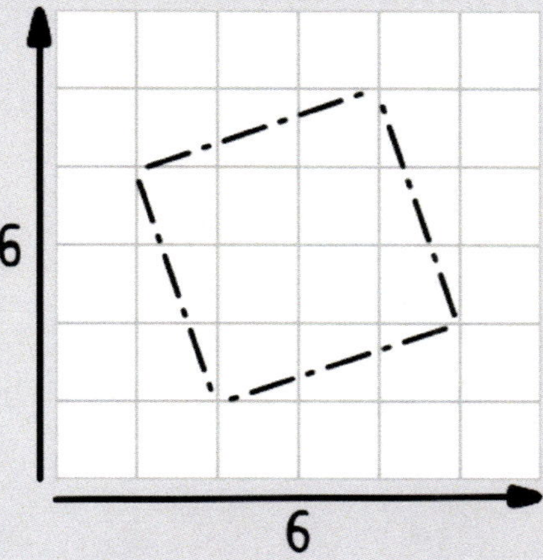

Start with a grid of 6 by 6, to allow extra rows and columns on all four sides.

Mark with mountains the inner tilted square.

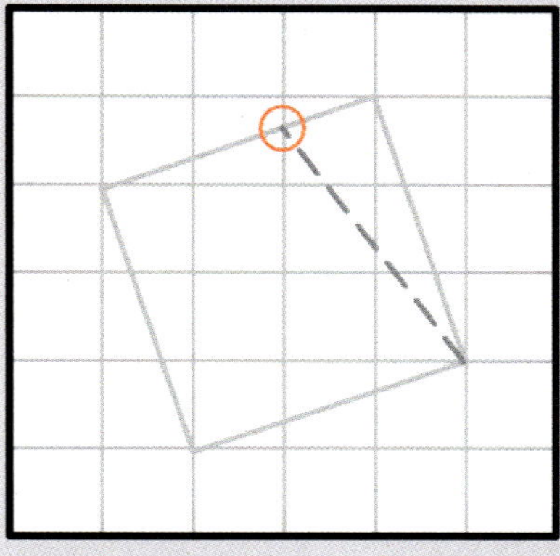

Add the first valley from a corner to the intersection of the square with the grid, as shown.

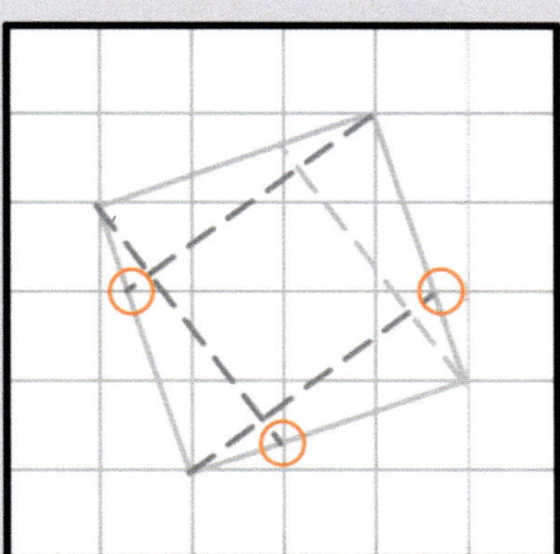

Continue to add those valleys in counterclockwise order, to make sure you have no conflict which intersection to choose for the second and third lines.

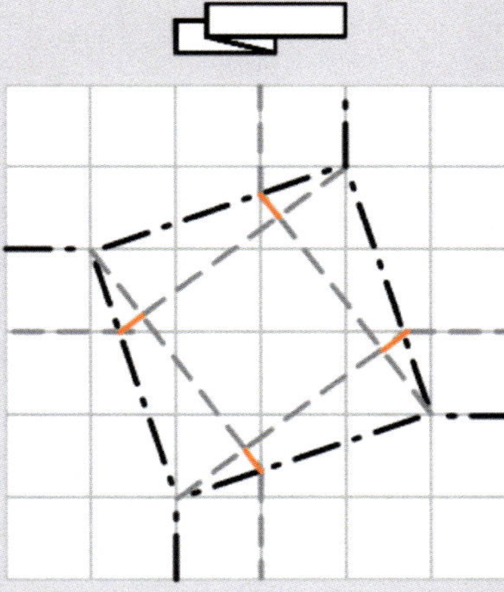

The complete set of creases. Note the edges will perform a zig-zag pattern all around.

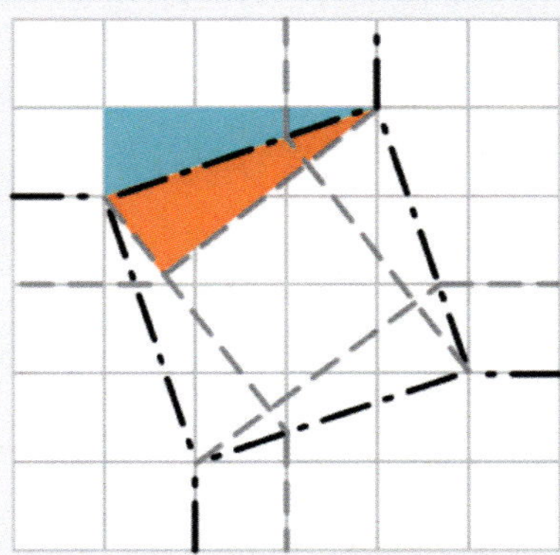

Note the marked areas, they are the same in size and shape! They will overlap after the collapse.

While folding the fourth line notice you cross a valley to reach the mountain! Remember this whenever you decide which way to go when you fold the inner valleys!

If you went clockwise, every valley would meet its predecessor and this would get you confused!

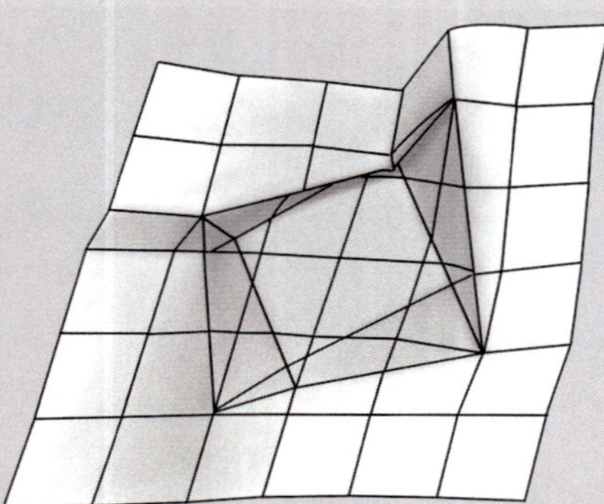

Start the collapse by forcing the outer square of mountains, **and** the mountains that connect its corners to the edge of the molecule.

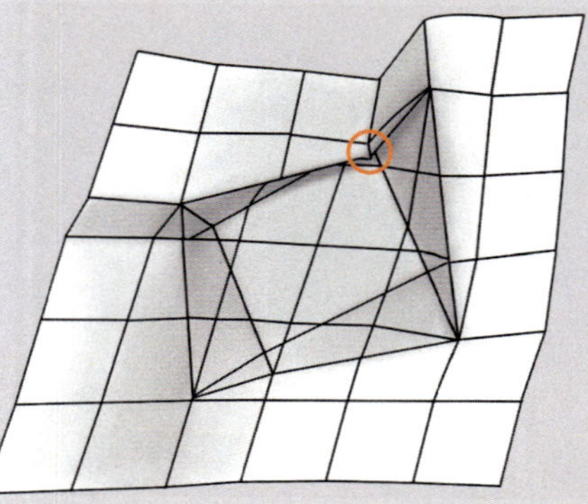

In process. This is a simultaneous step! When you start to force the valley to form the pleat pattern, note the marked area and make sure it happens on all four interactions!

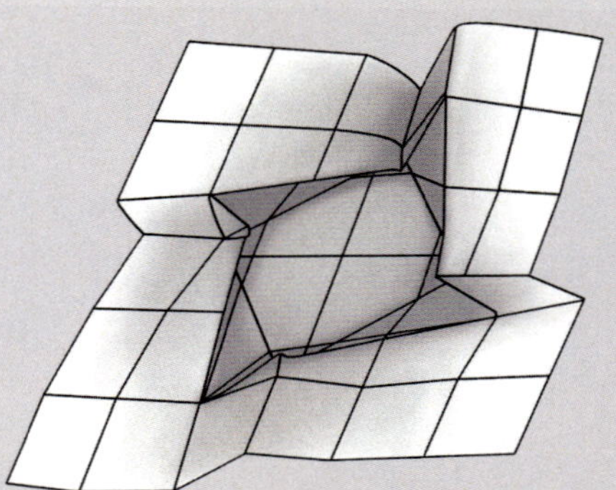

In process.

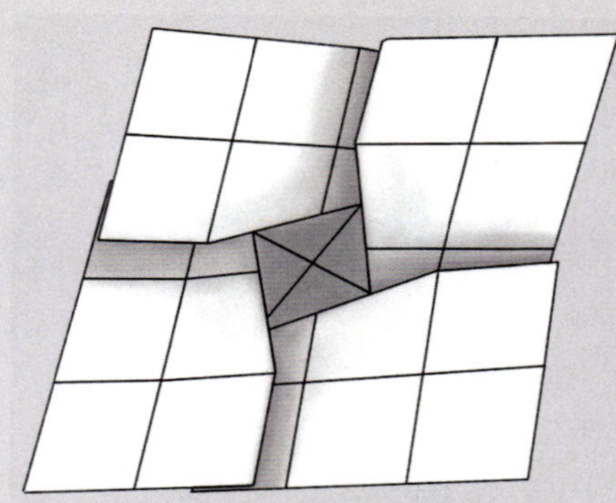

Fully collapsed.

2 by 2 Molecules

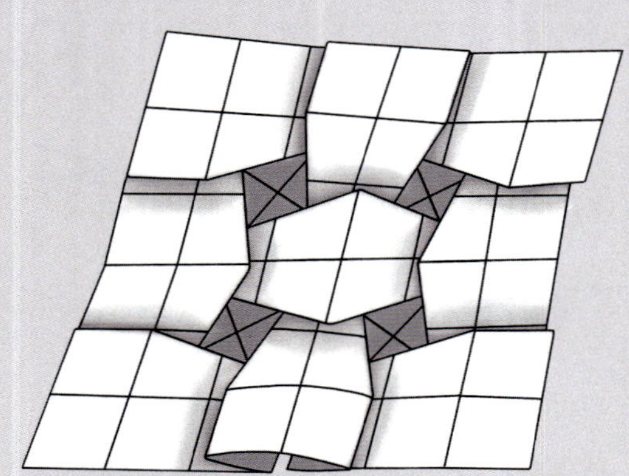

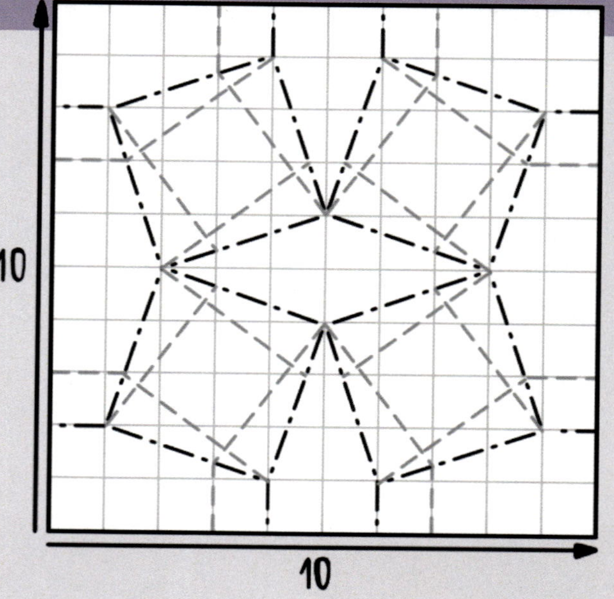

Use a grid of 10 by 10.

This is one of the hardest collapses to explain. You can not use the row-by-row method, as every molecule twists the complete paper. It has to be done as an all-at-once process.

Note the sharp diamonds, as they will help you through the process. Follow the zig-zag pattern of the edges, form the two half-diamonds on the top and the bottom, and then work on the inner diamond.

4 by 4 Molecules

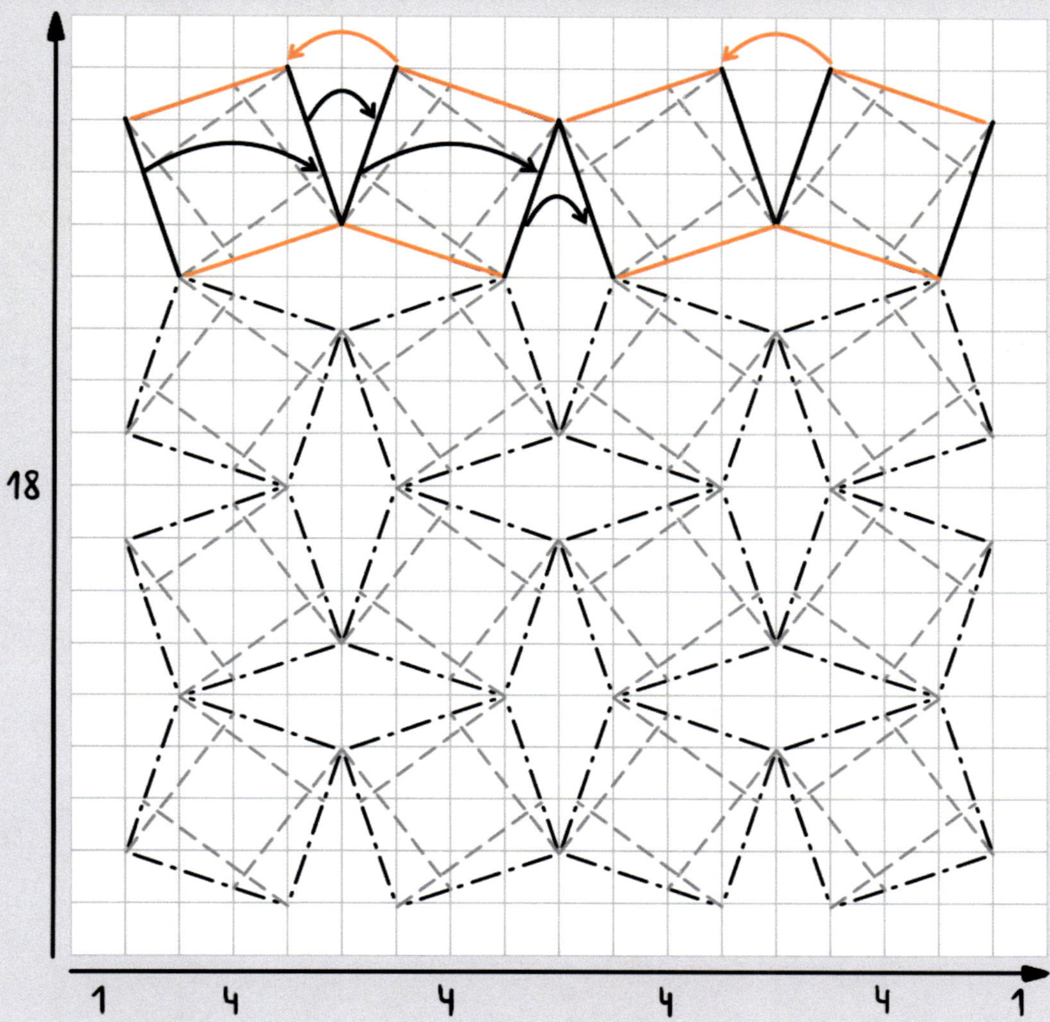

Make a grid of 18 by 18. A single-square width of a frame is enough and helpful.

The formula for the grid is 1 + 4 × 4 + 1 = 18.

The final result will be 10 squares wide.

This is the hardest collapse yet, so make sure you fold and collapse the 2 by 2 project first!

Mark the outer tilted squares first. There is no easy pattern that allows you to mark many molecule parts easily.

I prefer to make the squares by making the black Vs and return with the orange lines to complete them. This asks for just little rotations as you advance.

Note the order of the inner valleys! Make sure you don't get confused about which intersection to choose. The rule is simple: your first valley creates a triangle, the corner to start the next valley must be the right angle of this new triangle!

The collapse, I have no easy way to say it, has to be done simultaneously. The sharp tips of the diamond are going to be covered at the end, so do not worry if you cannot get them folded cleanly! It is wise to curve the paper as deep as needed to perform the zig-zag-zag-zig of those tips.

5 2 Blue Tessellation

This is the first model that is based on Self-Similarity, and as such, it has the beauty to stand alone as a project, with a single molecule. The most I reached was eleven iterations. You may try to get more, but you need a huge piece of paper for that!

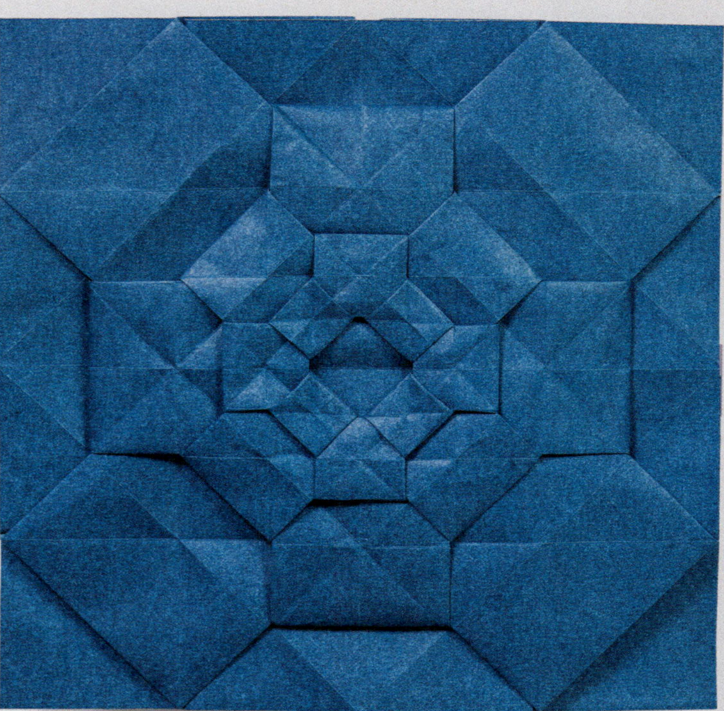

The Single Molecule

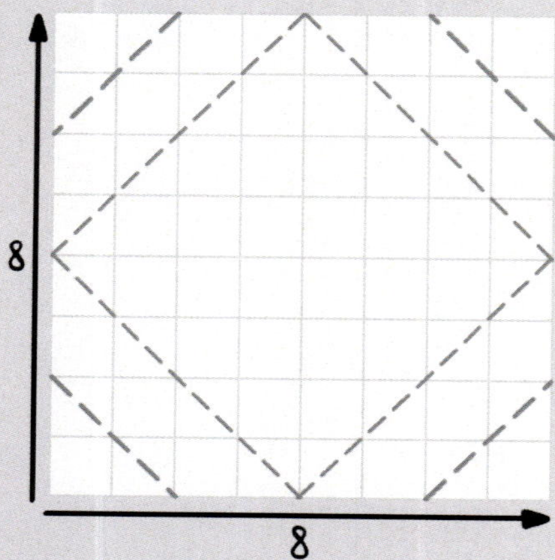

The molecule starting point is a grid of 8 by 8, to make a windmill base. For practice, use 25 cm square. For a full project, go as big as you can.

The base itself does not have all the original edges of the paper on the edges of the molecule, so we need to add a few folds, to make it so. This will make it tessellatable.

Since we work on both sides, this is a gray/white duo paper. Start with color-side up.

The shrinkage ratio is 2:1.

Mark the valleys, creating an edge-to-edge tilted square in the center, and a parallel line two units out of each edge. Turn the paper over.

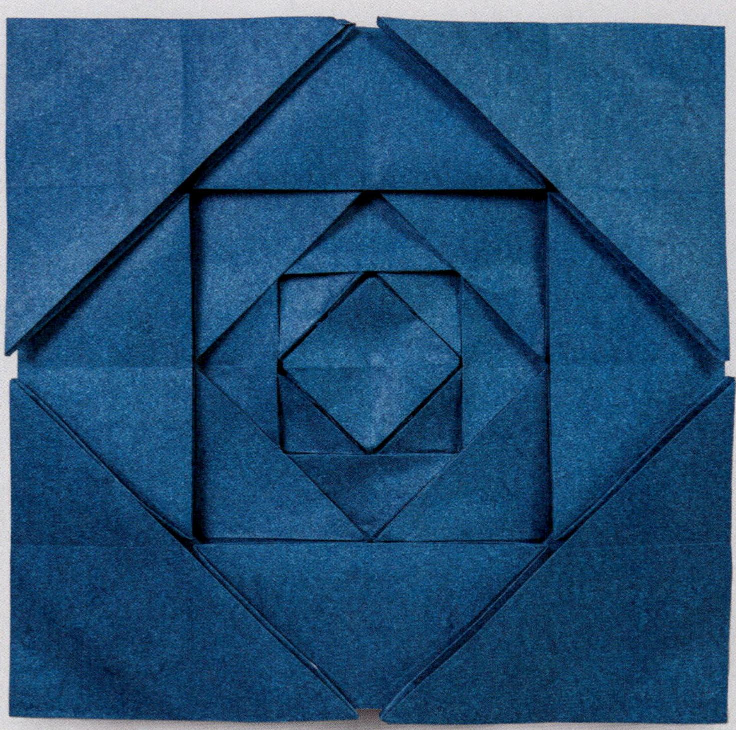

Top: recto view of a 5–level Blue tessellation.
Bottom: verso view of a 5–level Blue tessellation.

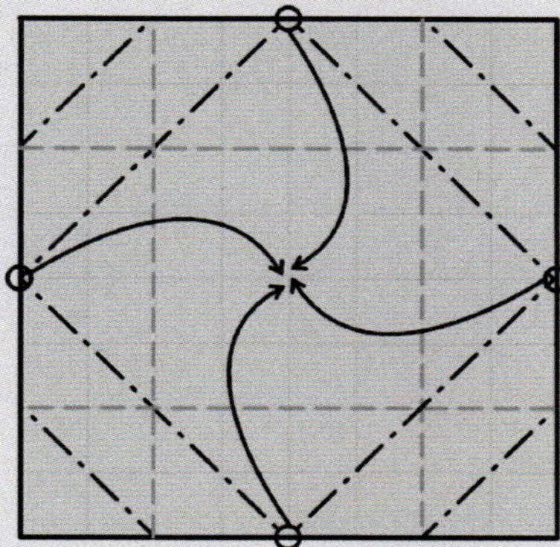

Force all the needed creases as indicated. Collapse by bringing the four marked points to meet in the center, creating the Windmill base.

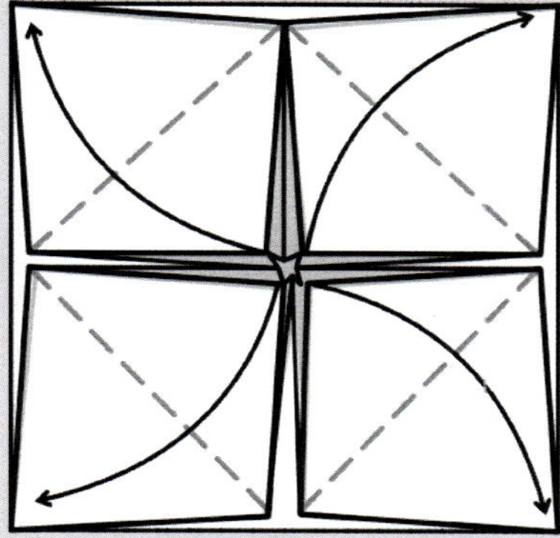

From here we will bring the edges of the paper to be on the edges of the molecule.

Fold the original corners out.

For better clarity, the grid lines are not shown until the eighth step.

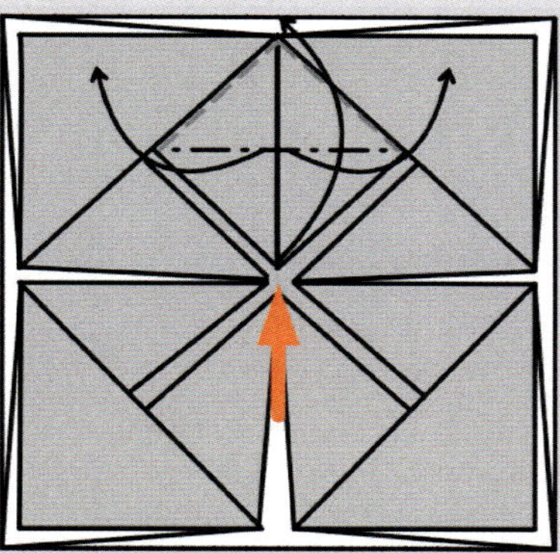

Squash-fold the marked corner. This will align the edges of the paper with the edge of the molecule.

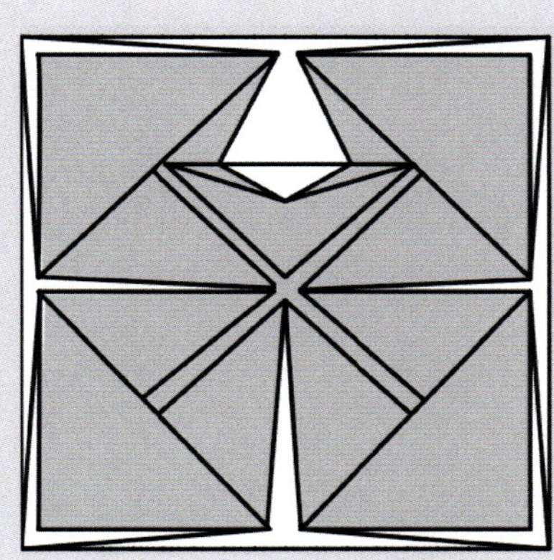

In process.

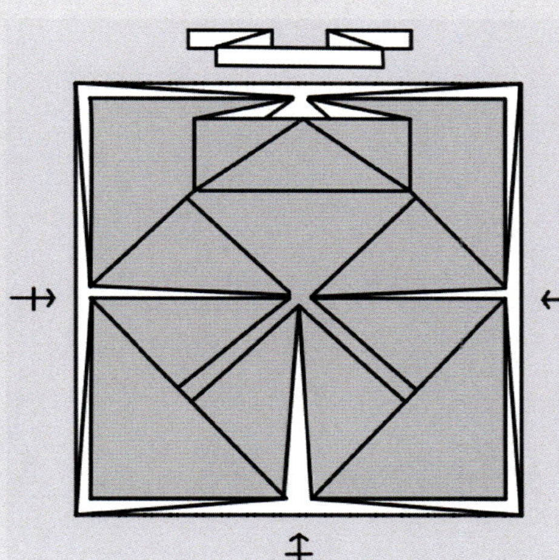

Squash completed.

Repeat on the other three sides.

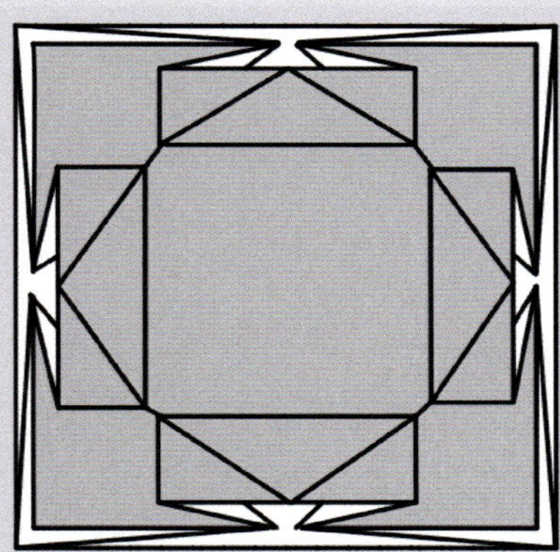

The finished collapse. Turn over.

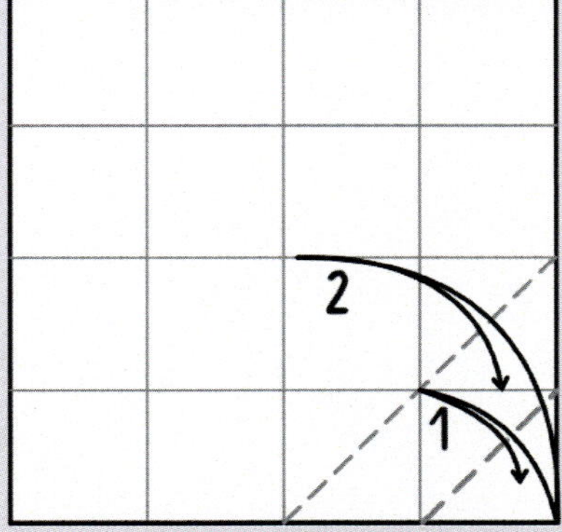

Fold and unfold the corner to the opposite corner of the unit.

Fold and unfold the corner to the center of the molecule.

Spread-open the corner completely.

Next step is shown from an isometric point of view.

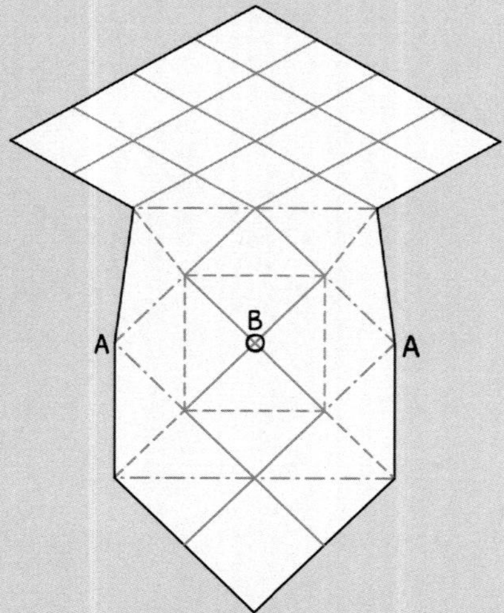

Collapse back while sinking the inner square, marked with valleys. Points **A** are going to meet at point **B**, while the two mountain lines (top and bottom) are meeting as well.

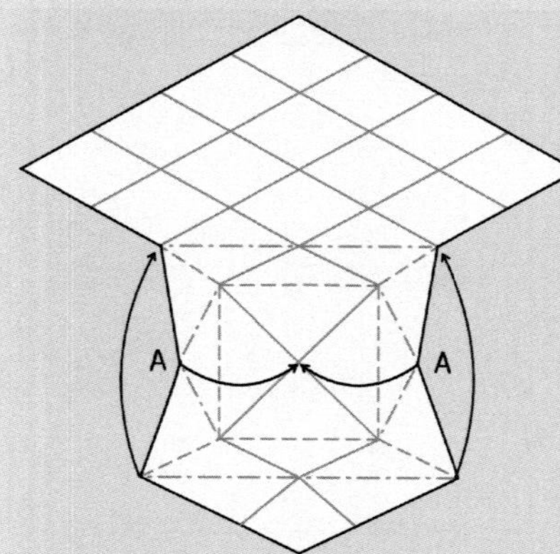

In process.

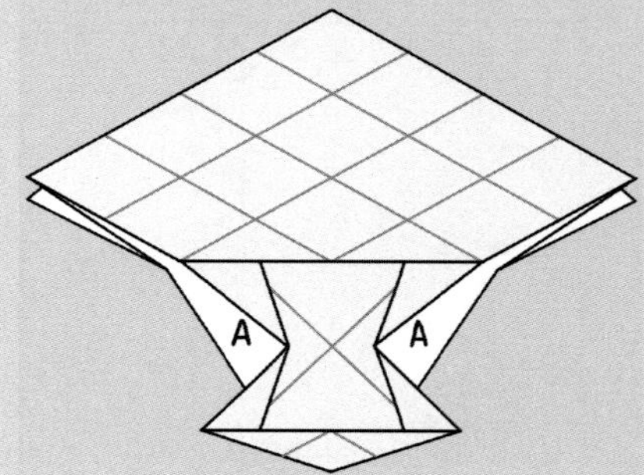

Almost there...

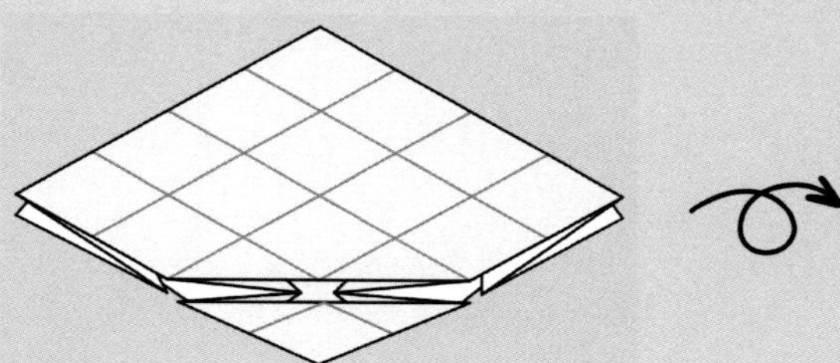

Finished. Turn over.

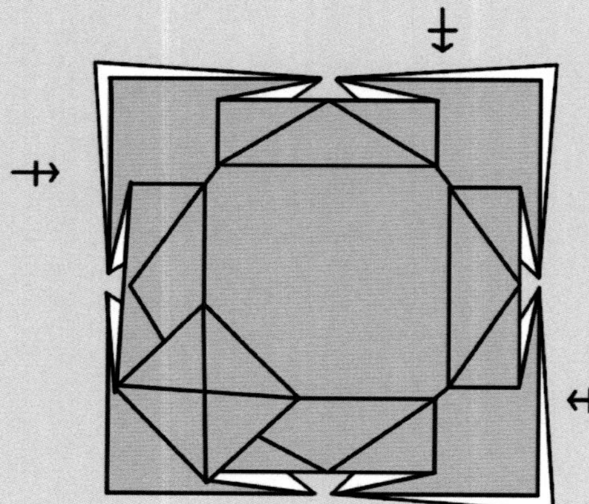

You can see the first squashed square, and its center is point **B** (on the other side).

Repeat all around.

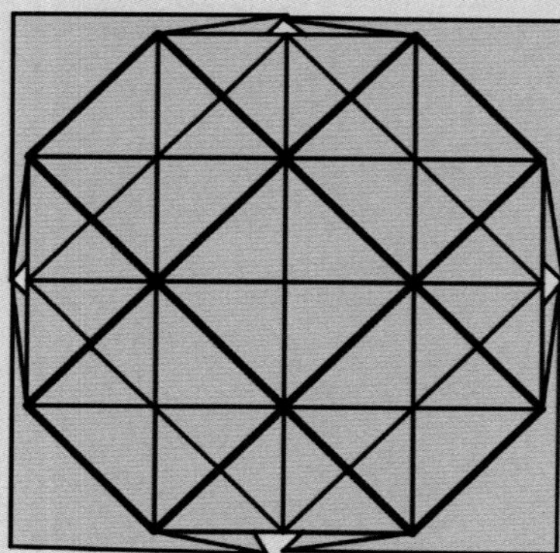

The four corners are done. Turn over.

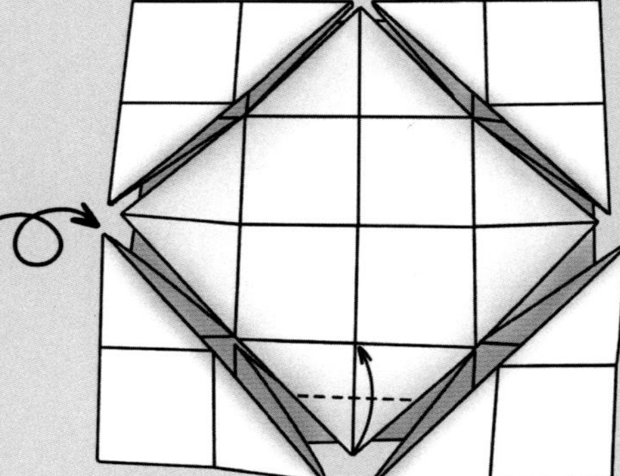

It is time for the second iteration, creating a new level of squashed squares. Valley-fold the corner of the new, smaller, square. Spread open this corner. Try not to unfold everything around it.

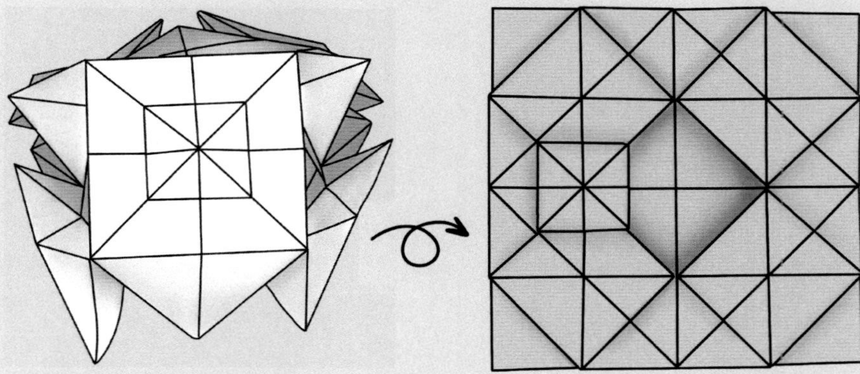

Collapse the corner, as we did with steps 9 to 12.

Turn over.

And now we have a new square emerging between the two first squashed squares we made.

Repeat all around.

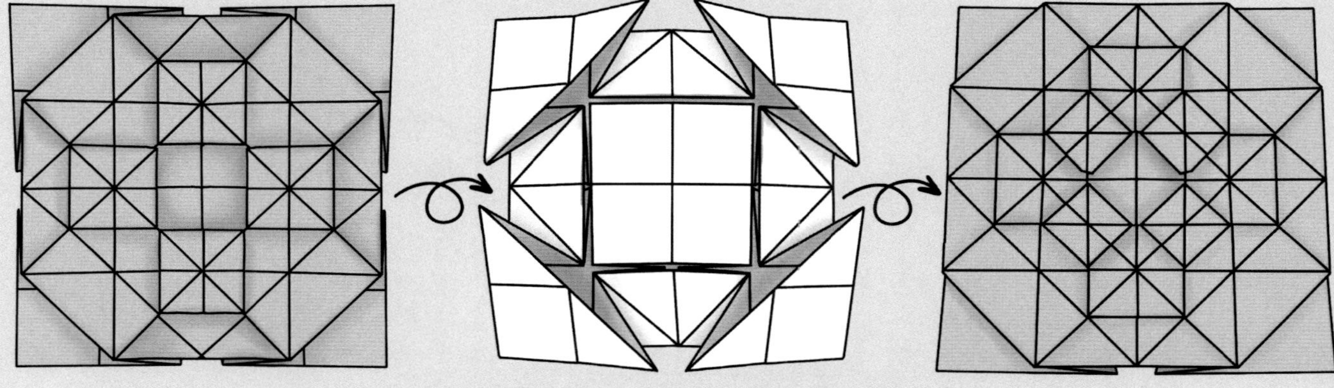

This is the result.

Turn over.

Do you want to continue?

If you do, turn over again.

Here is another iteration.

Let's stop here, ok?

Well done!

Variation - Tessellated

If you are brave enough, you can tessellate this molecule, since this molecule answers the two criteria needed: all the original edges of the paper are on the edge of the molecule, and all four sides are the same.

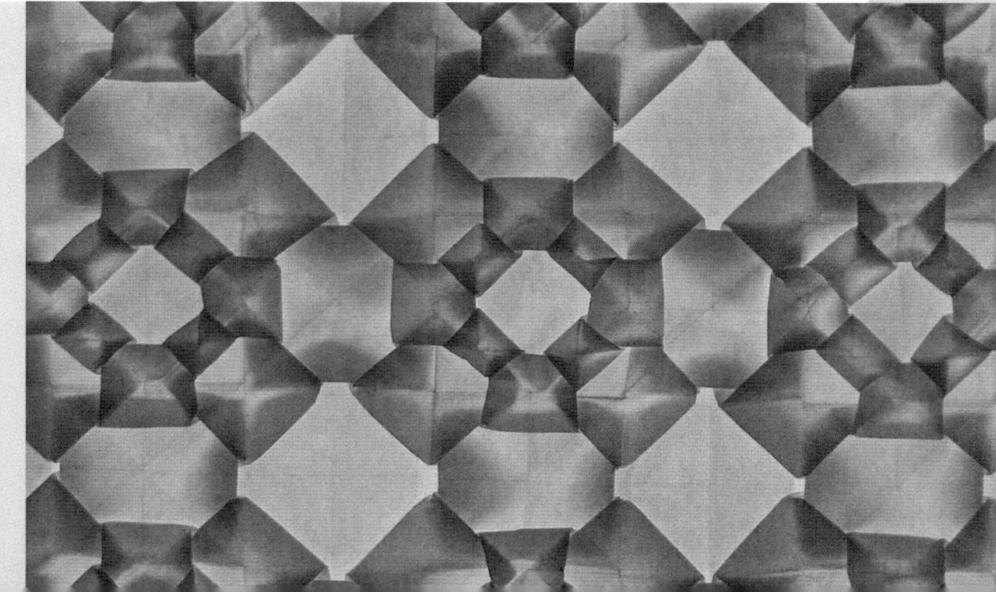

5 3 Hydrangea for the Simple Man (HFTSM)

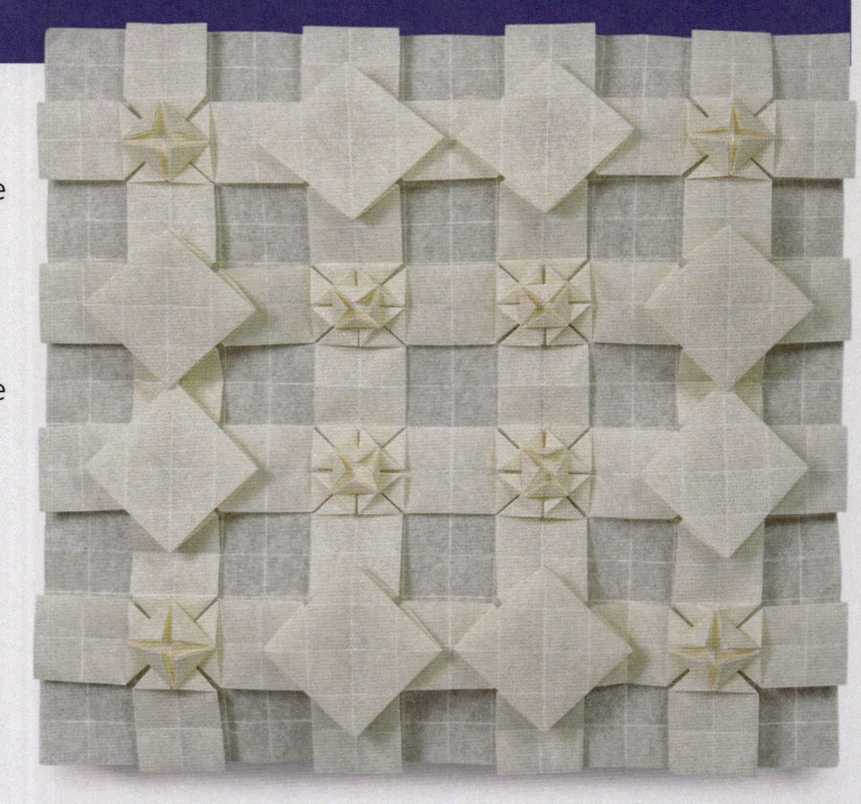

This molecule was discovered before me by quite a few, probably because it has a simple logic to it. One example is J.C. Nolan, who named it Andrea's Rose.

I love this molecule since it has self-similarity in the central piece - you can repeat the process in the central part since every iteration results in a smaller square that allows another iteration. The shape reminded me of the famous Hydrangea by Shuzo Fujimoto, but it is way simpler, hence the name I chose for it. After playing with it, I was overjoyed to find it can be tessellated, as well!

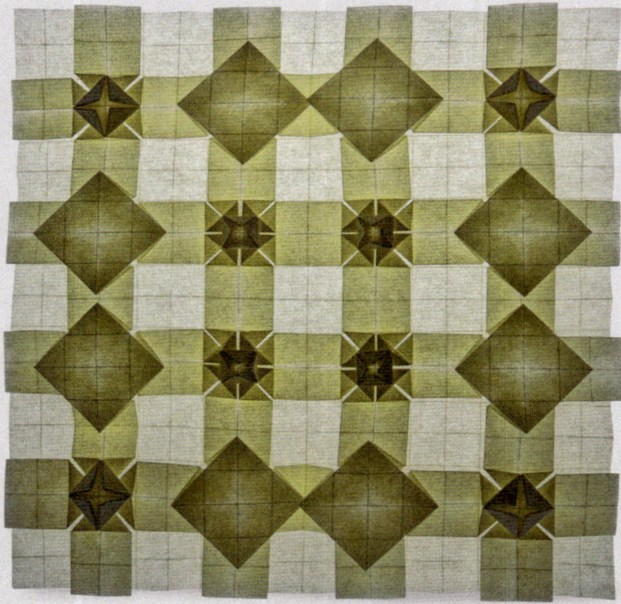

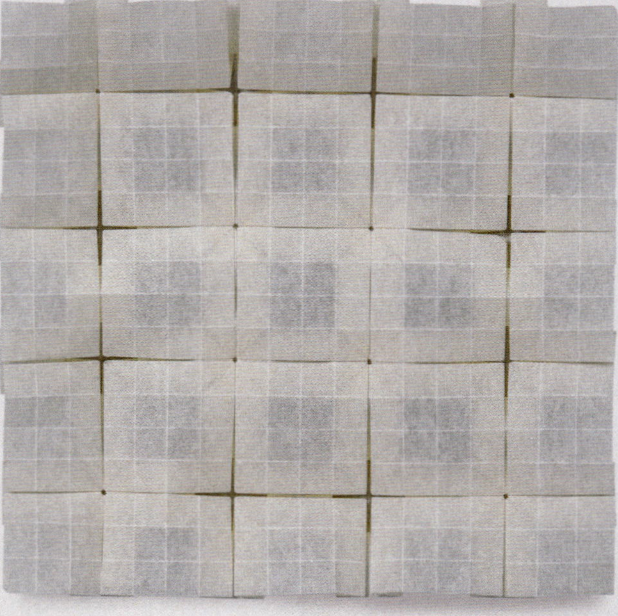

Top right: recto view of a 4 by 4–molecule HFTSM tessellation, with spacing.

Bottom right: verso view of a 4 by 4–molecule HFTSM tessellation, with spacing.

Left: recto view with back-light.

The Single Molecule

The molecule size is 8 by 8.

It is based on a wide cross shape, rotated 45° on the grid. The center square (marked in gray) is unfolded at the first stage of the collapse, and on every corner, there will be a preliminary base (with the help of the four valleys (as part of the grid lines)).

The possible iterations, to reduce the central square, are not shown here!

There is no rotation during the collapse, and the model stays flat.

The shrinkage ratio is 2:1.

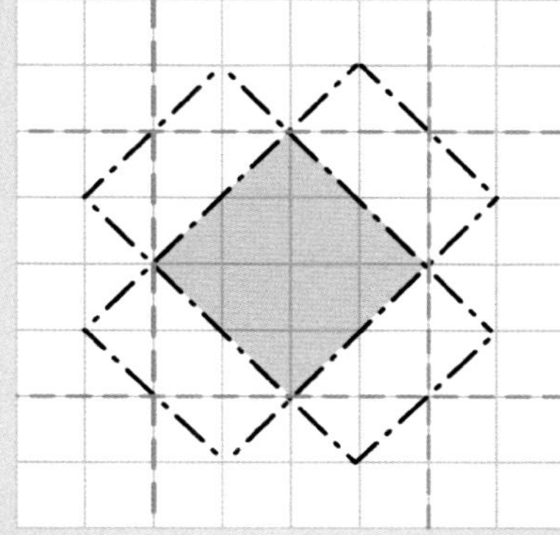

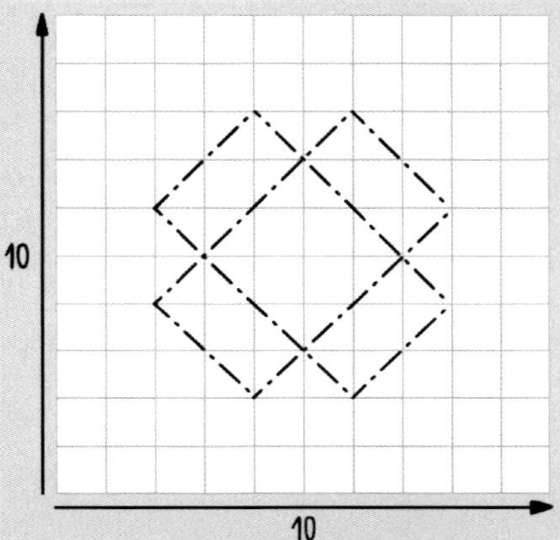

Start with a grid of 10 by 10, to allow extra rows and columns on all four sides.

Mark with mountains the wide cross.

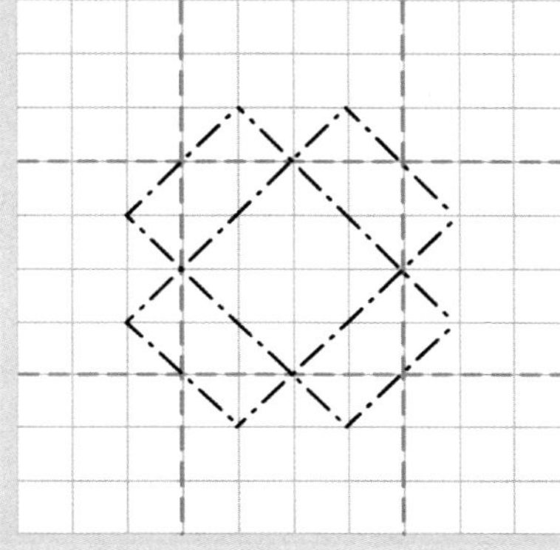

Force the folds on the grid lines.

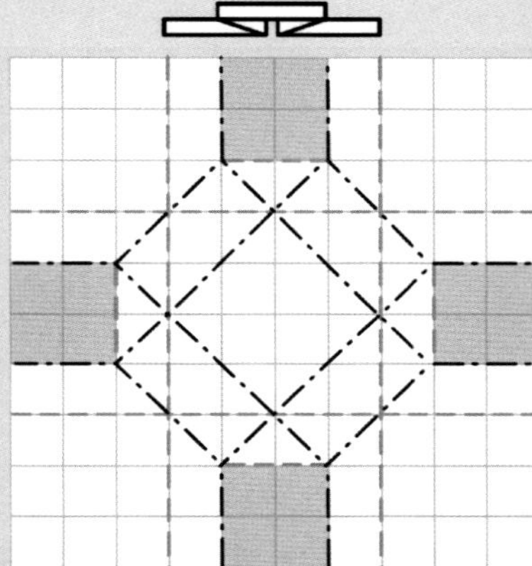

Those are all the needed pre-creases. The marked lines of the grid are valleys. Please note the gray areas, they are the "bridges" to the adjacent molecules

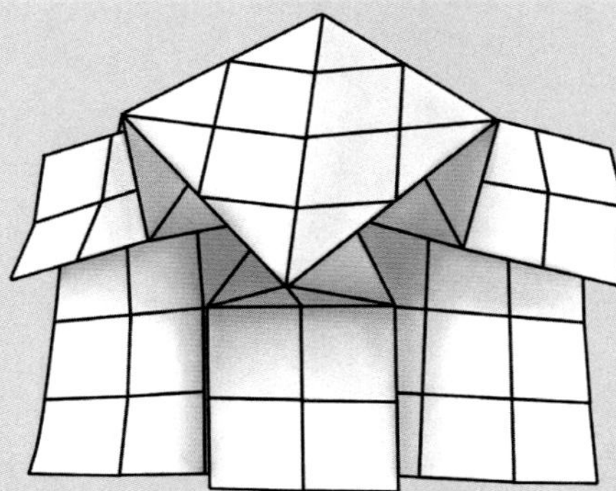

Start by creating the bridges on the sides, while at the same time raise the central tilted square.

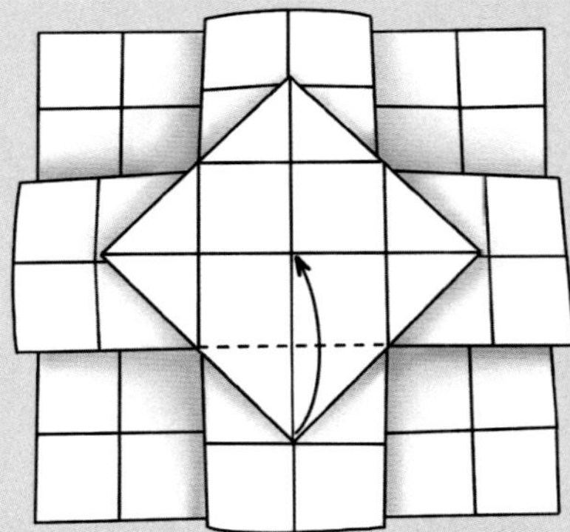

Fully collapsed.

Fold the four corners of the inner square to the center and unfold. Mark strongly.

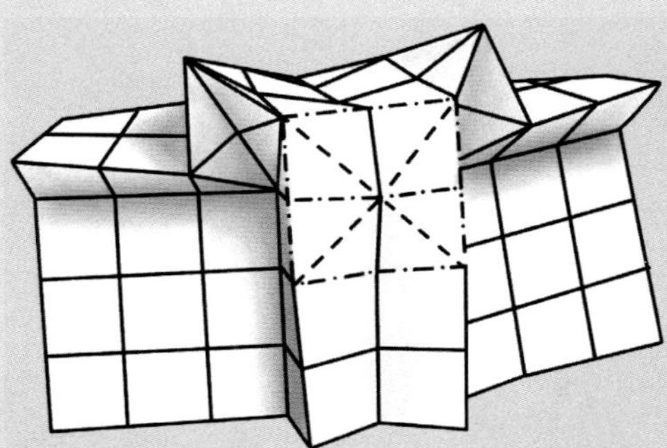

Open-sink the top corner. You may need to open the folds to allow that step!

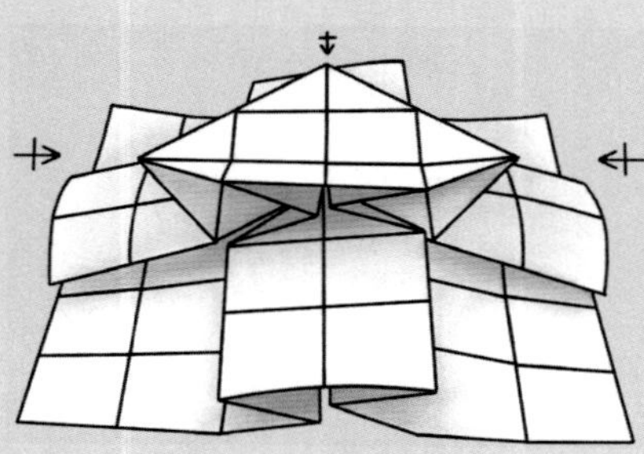

Repeat on the other three corners.

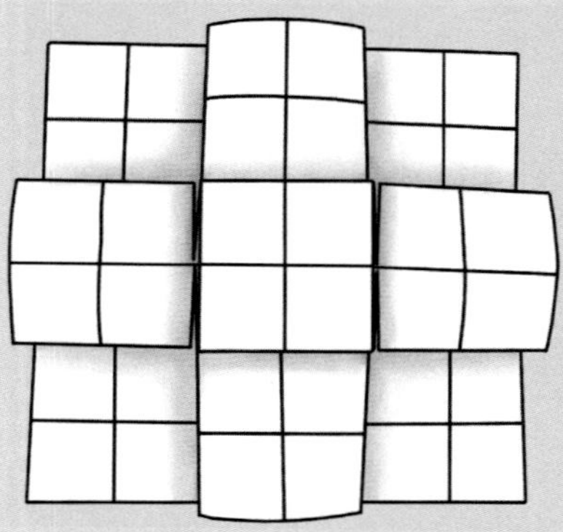

Now there is a new, smaller, square in the center. You can stop here, or sink its four corners as well!

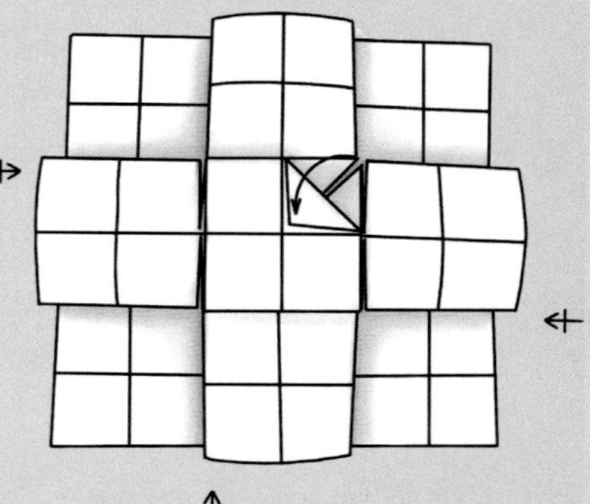

Fold the corner to the center.

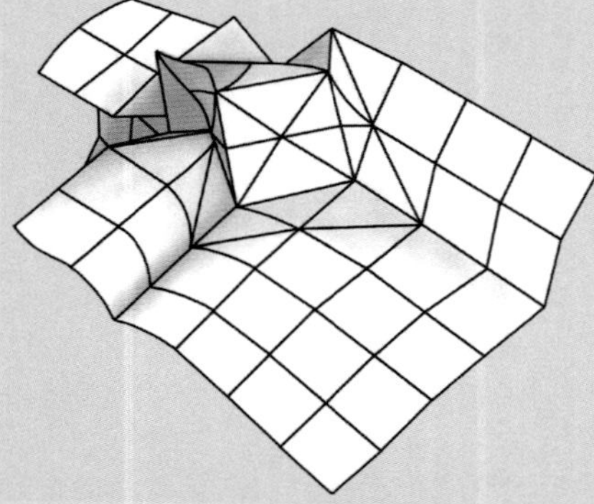

Unfold and spread the square, like we did on steps 6 and 7.

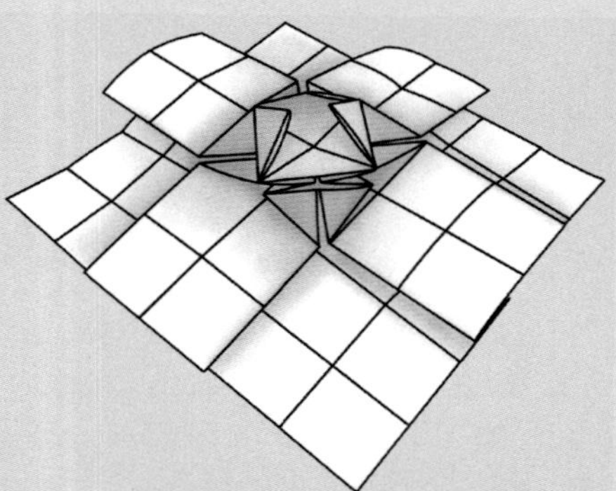

Repeat all around.

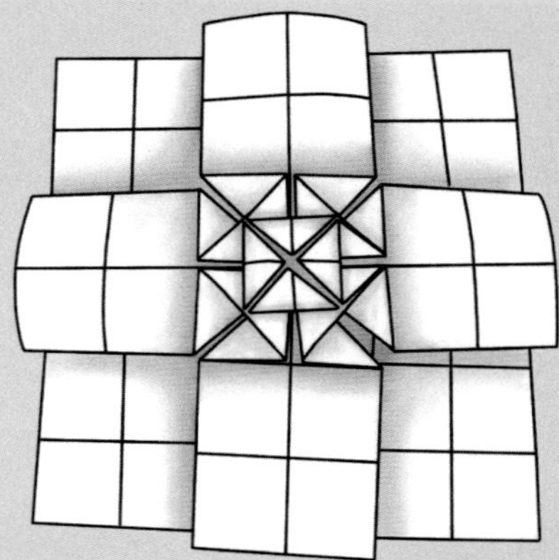

You can continue with that until your fingers are too big to go so small!

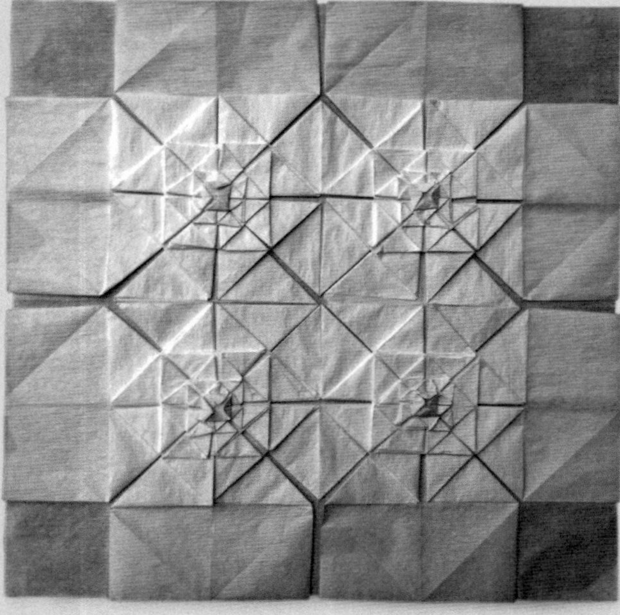

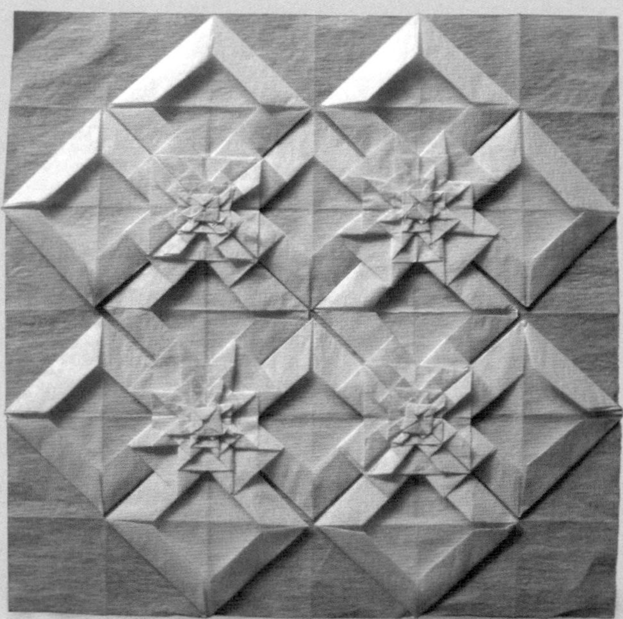

Two ways to tessellate the HFTSM.

2 by 2 Molecules

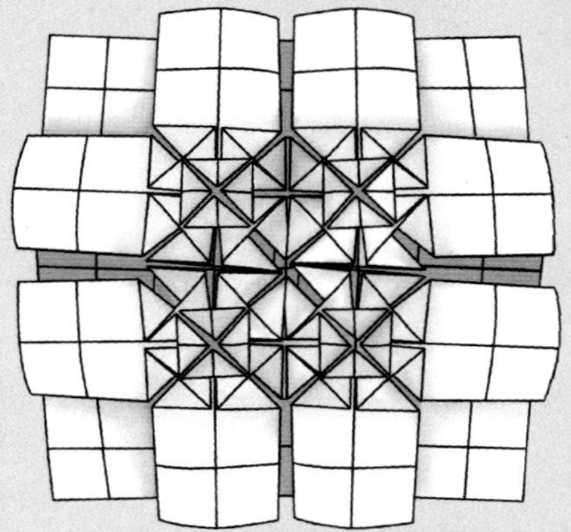

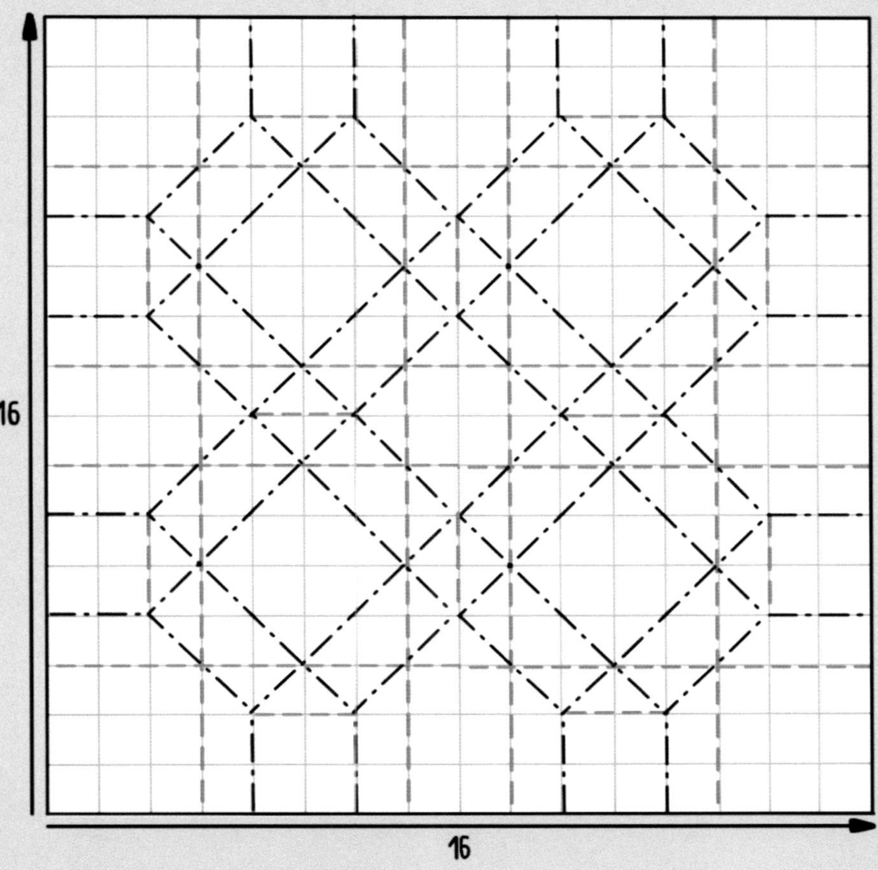

Use a grid of 16 by 16.

In this project we discard the spaces between the molecules, to create a denser look.

Collapse the model one molecule at a time, but make sure the adjacent molecule is slightly folded before you collapse the molecule.

4 by 4 Molecules

This project uses back again the more spacious version, unlike the 2 by 2 project. It will make the collapse more accessible.

Make a grid of 34 by 34.

The formula for the grid is 1 + 4 × 8 + 1 = 34.

The final result will be 18 squares wide.

Start with the longest, inner lines, in orange. The sequence is fold 4, skip 4, repeat. If you rotate the paper 90° and repeat the process, you will have all the inner crosses as a clear reference to the next folds.

The light-blue lines complete the wide crosses, and they are following this rhythm: fold 2 and skip 2.

To collapse, start with a corner molecule, and use the bridge to the next molecule as a guideline to collapse the second molecule. It is wise to fold the bridges of the first row all the way to the far edge of the paper, so when the first row is complete the model lies flat.

Complete the rest of the rows in the same manner.

Once you collapse all you can add iterations to each square, as much as you want.

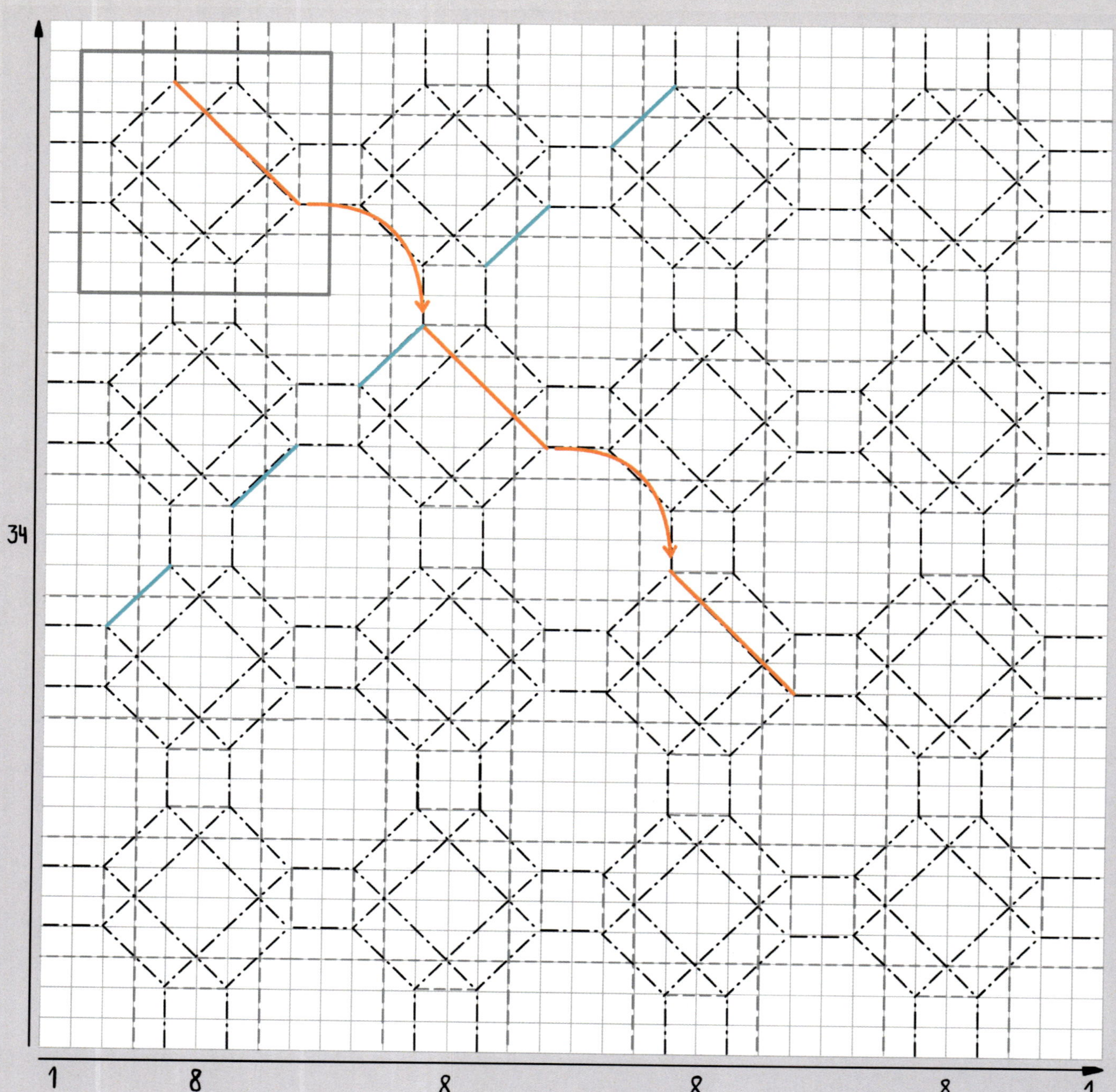
34
1
8
8
8
8
1

Above and Beyond

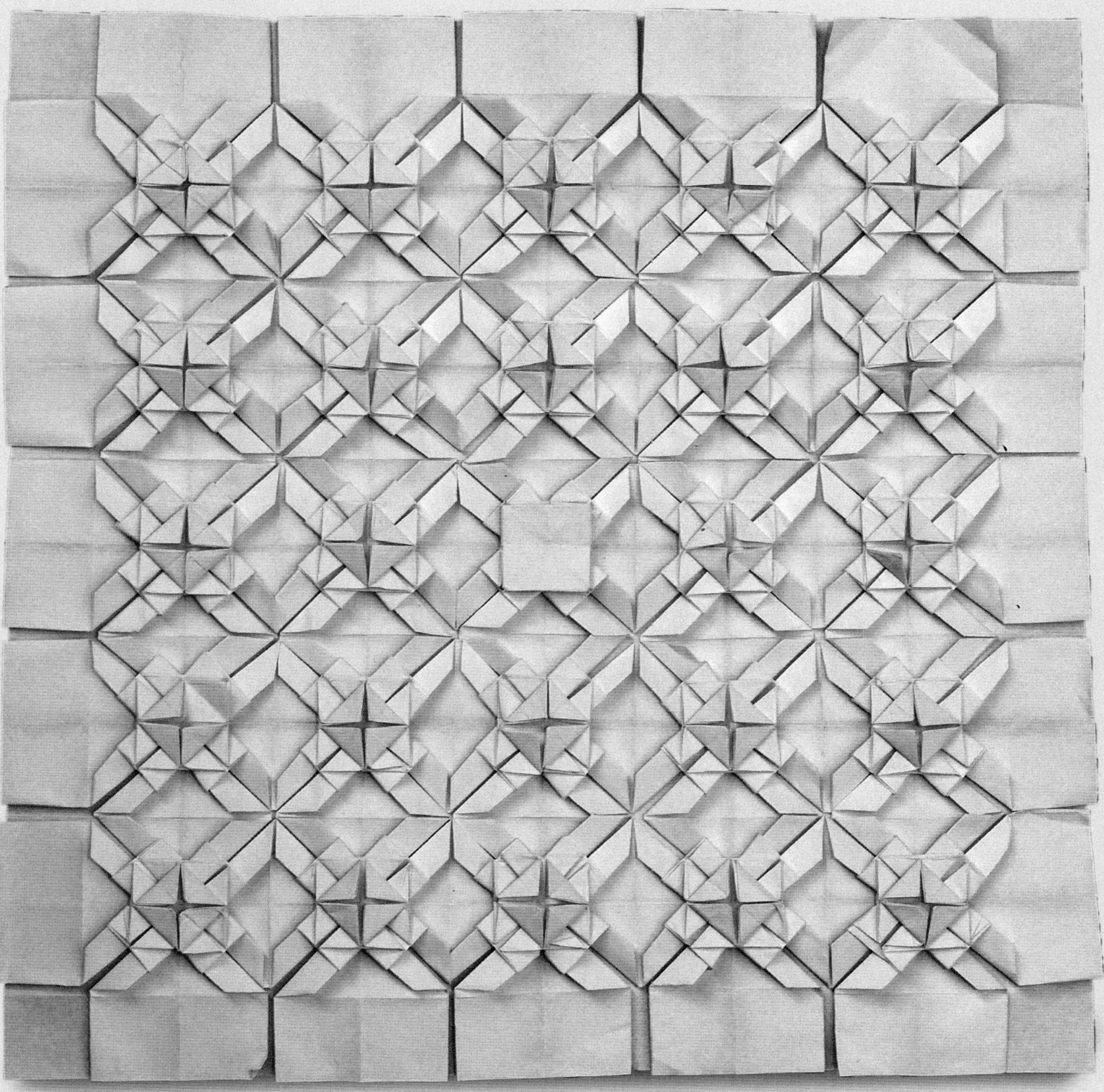

5 by 5-molecule project, with two different ways of finishing the model.

5 4 Windmill

This model is based on a unique "twist" that does not rotate the central square! The result is a five-layer construction that strangely enough is quite easy to collapse.

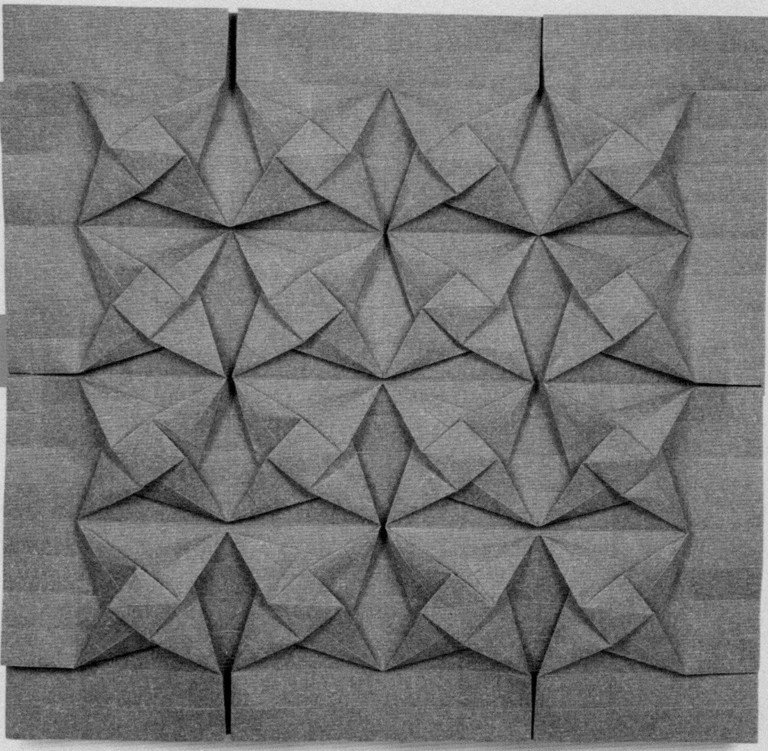

The Single Molecule

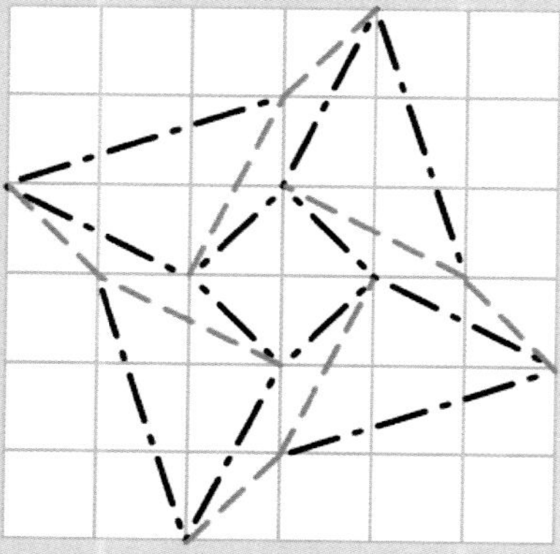

The molecule size is 6 by 6.

It is based on a rotated square in the center, and with a total of 20 creases, it is one of the most demanding designs in this book.

The shrinkage ratio is 3:1.

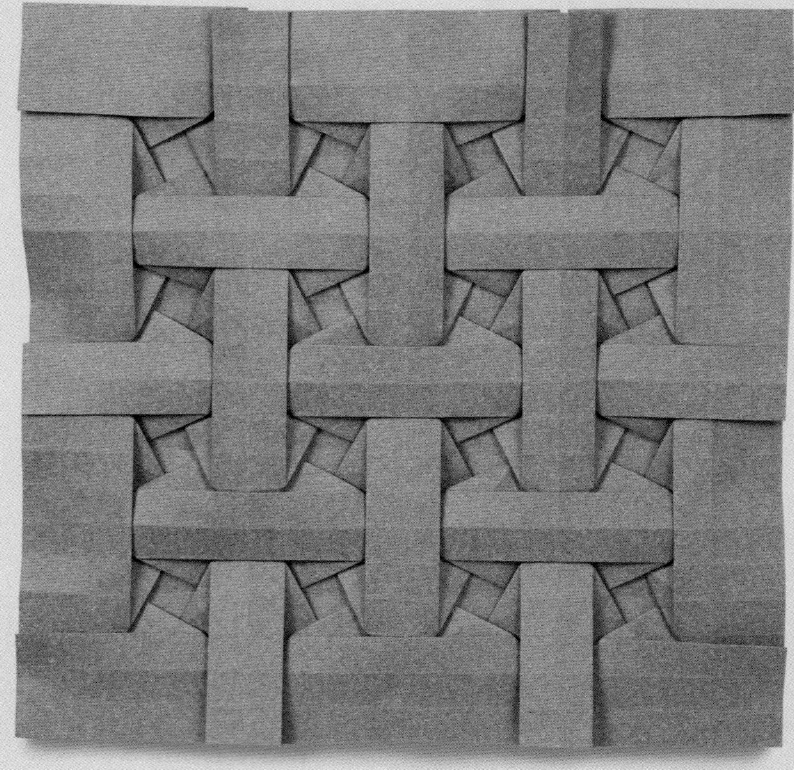

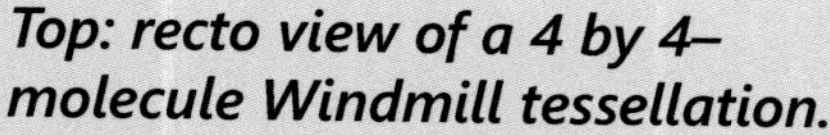

Top: recto view of a 4 by 4–molecule Windmill tessellation.

Bottom: verso view of a 4 by 4–molecule Windmill tessellation.

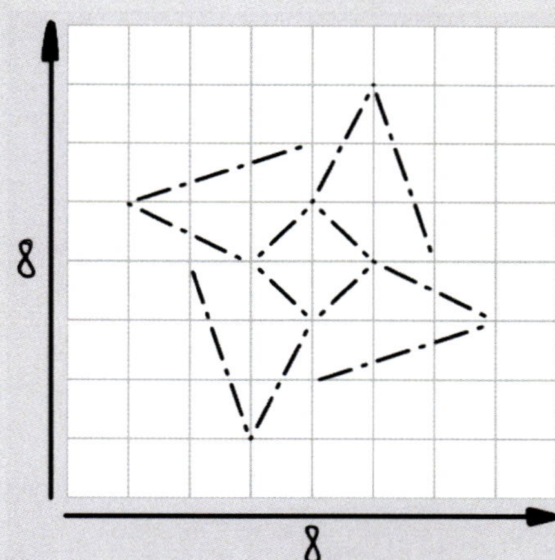

Start with a grid of 8 by 8, to allow extra rows and columns on all four sides.

Mark with mountains the inner tilted square.

Add more mountains. Note that the four that emerge from the center square are at the length of two units, while the outer mountains are 3-unit long.

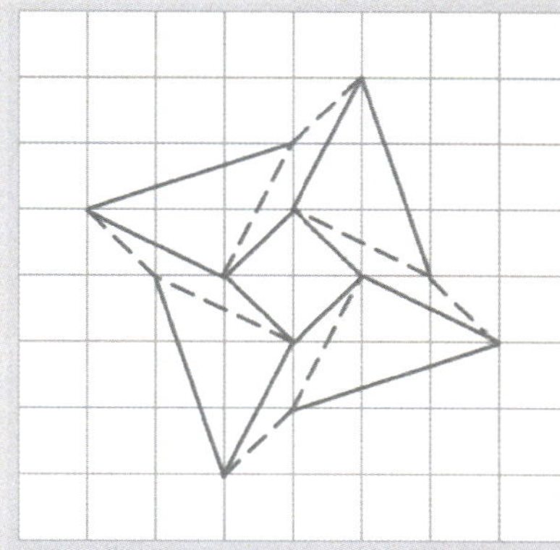

It is time to add valleys. Note there are eight lines altogether, not four, as the valley changes direction after two units!

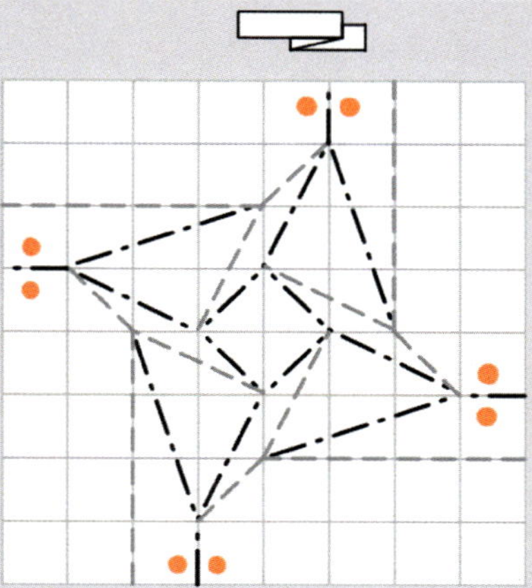

Start the collapse by zig-zagging the edges, while raising the inner square. Pinch the marked points and shift the ridge clockwise.

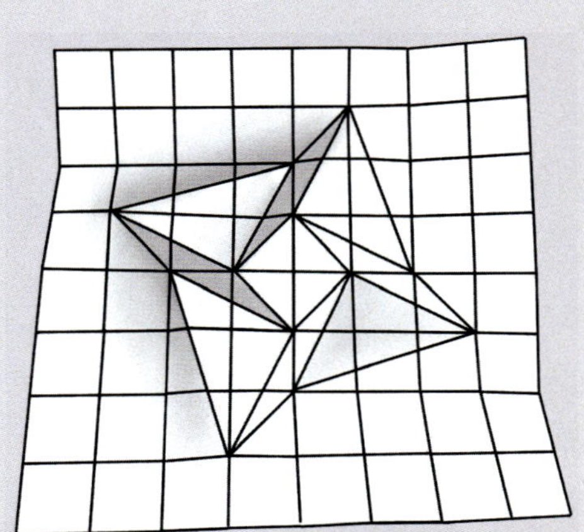

In process. Continue to rotate and flatten again. The center does not rotate at all!

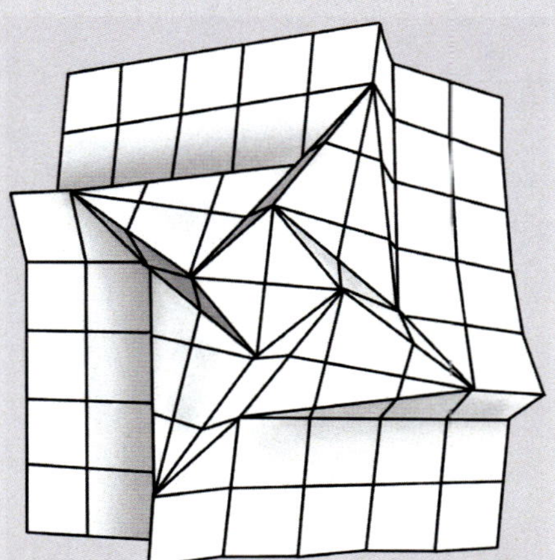

Almost there.

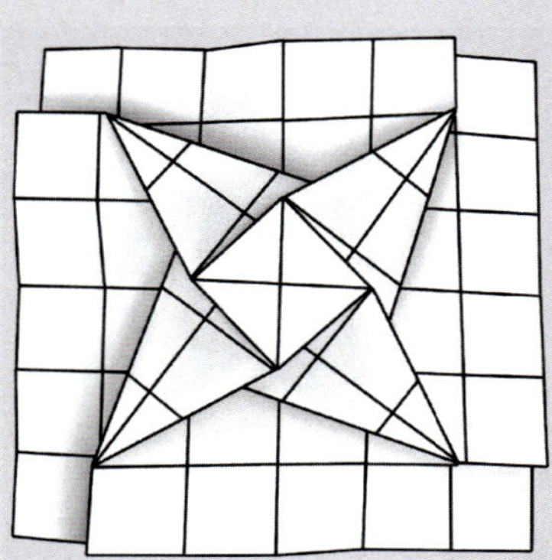

Fully collapsed.

2 by 2 Molecules

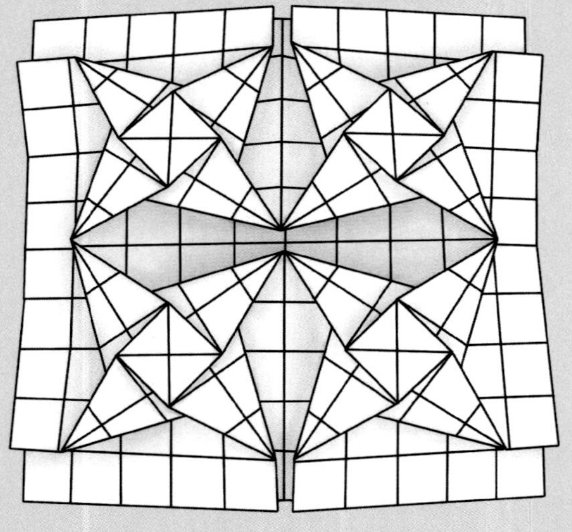

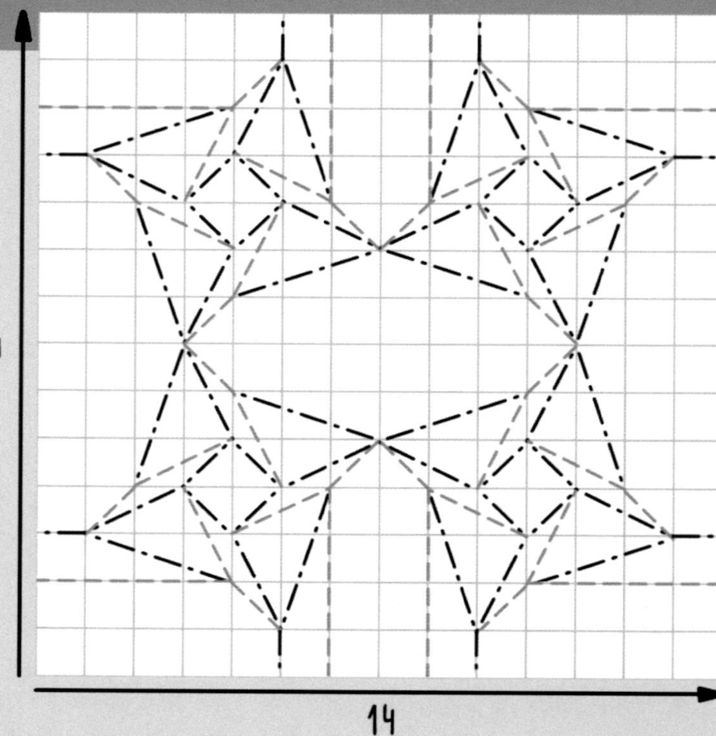

Use a grid of 14 by 14.

This model is collapsed by applying pressure on the sides. Do not press before you raise the four center squares. Once you do that, gently push every crease in the right direction, and start to press. It is helpful to make sure all the inner corners of the four stars are meeting in the center.

4 by 4 Molecules

Make a grid of 28 by 28, which will allow for a two-unit frame.

The formula for the grid is 2 + 4 × 6 + 2 = 28.

The final result will be 14 squares wide.

Start the pre-creases with the inner squares (in light blue). The rhythm is fold 1, skip 5. That will be the only shortcut here. I advise you to make the next pre-crease molecule by molecule.

Add around each square the green lines.

Continue with the orange mountains. Make sure each molecule is the mirror image of the adjacent one.

Turn over the paper and complete the valleys. I find it easier to complete the outlines first, and then the inner valleys (in purple).

For the collapse, since the center does not rotate,it's all about rearranging the layers. Once you pleat the edges of the first molecule, you can hold the edges with a clip and force the complete first row. Each molecule should stay flat after it collapses.

Note the shape of each windmill that you make and make sure they are layered correctly, it is easy to get confused!

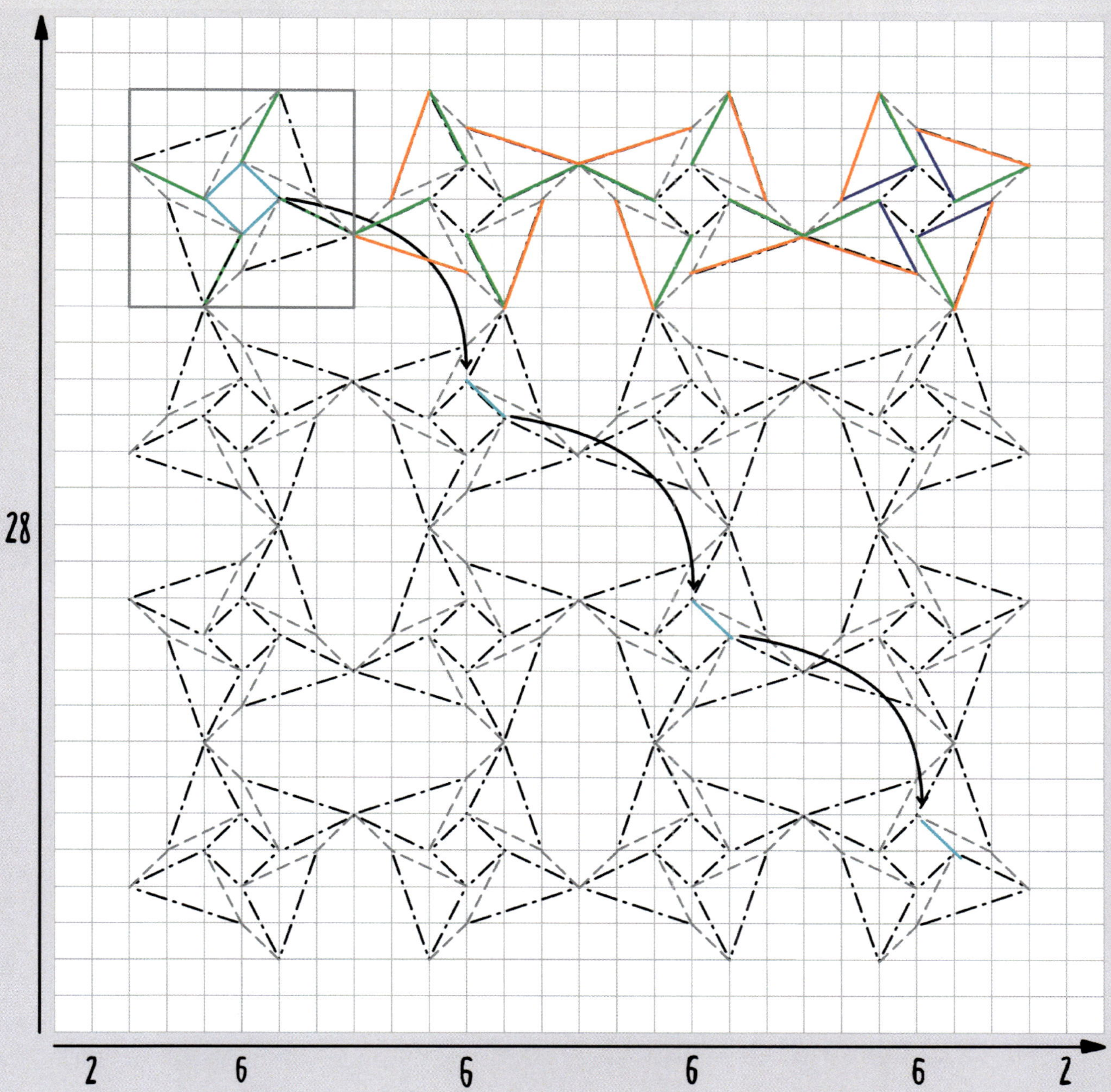
28
2
6
6
6
6
2

6
The Circular Models Family

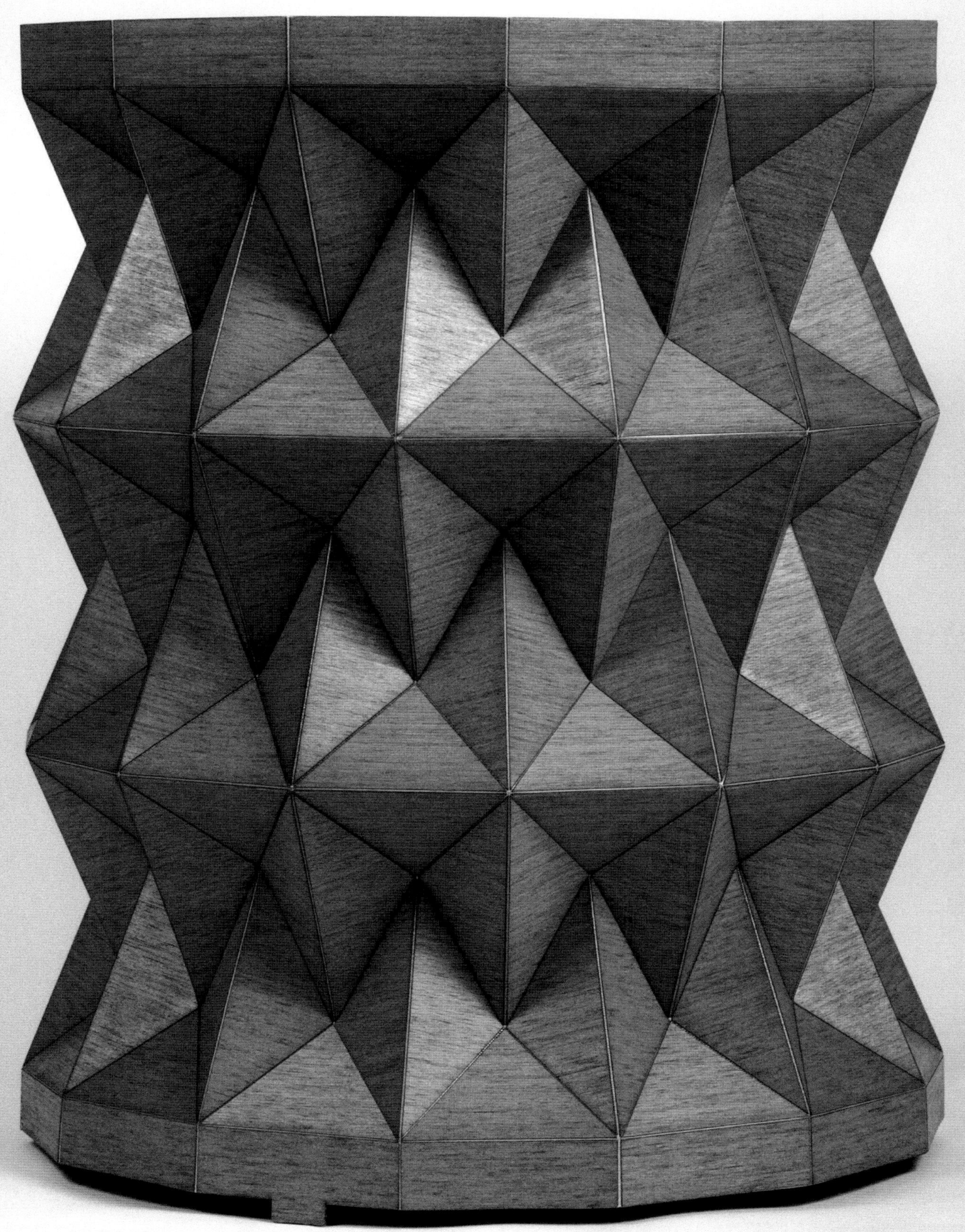

Introduction

There are a few ways to create a circular model. The first is to design it going around its center, and the only model in this book as such is the **Braided Bowl**.

Another way is to create a flat design and roll it onto a tube. From that point of view, almost all the models in the book can be considered as circular, and for some, like the Zipper family, I did find nice uses of this property.

The most interesting type is the one that cannot lie flat. The **Tavolini** family is the only one I found.

And yes, you do need to use glue to connect edge to edge, and hold the tube shape.

6 1 Fabergé Egg

This model is a brother to the famous Magic Ball.

The base is the result of a mistake I made with the calculations, not leaving enough paper to fit in the last molecule, and this extra paper became the natural base for the egg.

In truth, this is an action model, as you can play with the extra paper as a handle, and by changing its shape the whole model twists and modifies.

This tessellation spread differently left-to-right than top-to-bottom.

Fabergé Egg with a flat base.

The Single Molecule

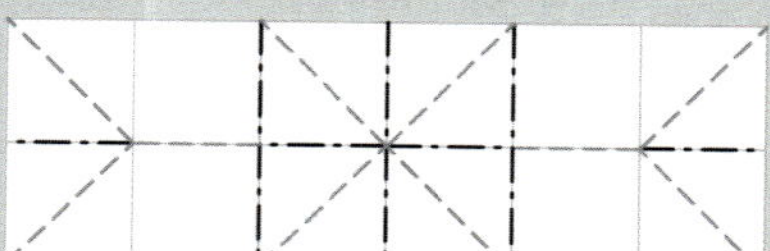

The molecule size is 2 by 6.

It is based on a Waterbomb base in its center, and two inside reverse folds at the ends, to allow connection to the next molecule.

There are two variants to the molecule: the edge molecule, and the middle molecule. Both the first and the last molecules do not need to connect to any other molecule, so this edge will look a bit different.

The shrinkage ratio is 3:1 on the long side. On the width, you can collapse the molecule to be totally flat.

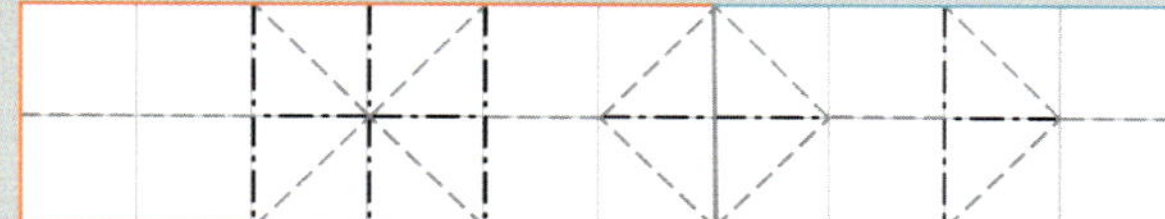

To practice, we are going to fold a hybrid of the first and the last molecule.

The starting molecule is on the left, marked with red, and the last one is on the right, marked in light-blue.

Start with a grid of 2 by 10.

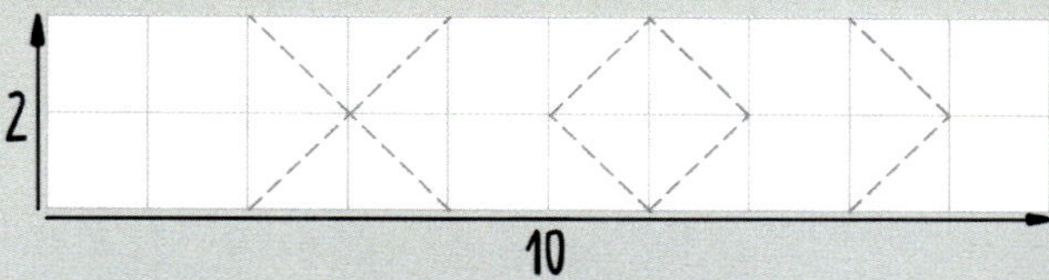

Mark with valleys the X lines to form later the waterbomb base. Next, add a tilted square. This will be the connection between two molecules. Last, on the right, this is a half waterbomb base, and this is also the way to end the last molecule.

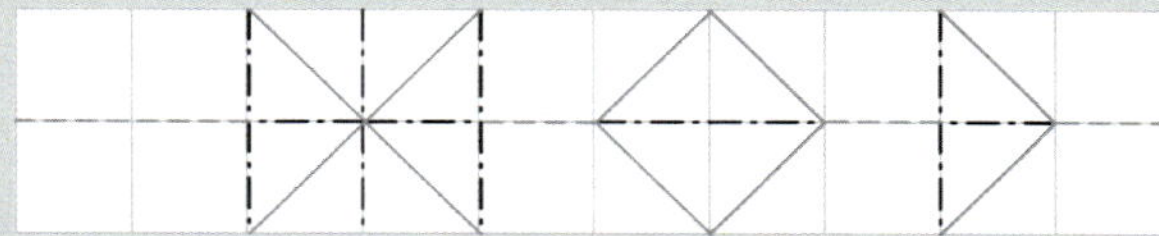

Now force all the needed mountains on the grid.

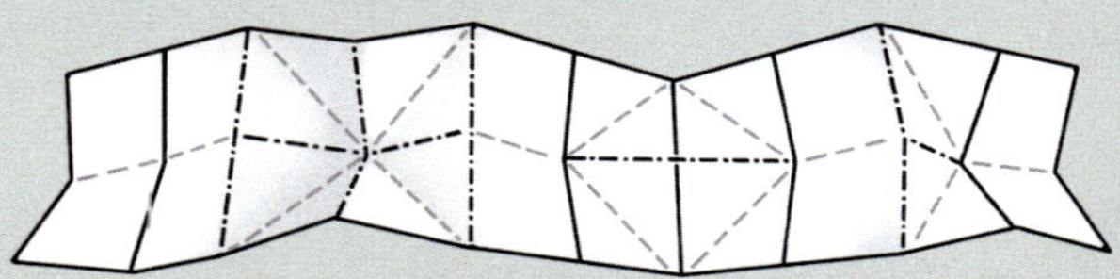

Force all the creases in the right orientation.

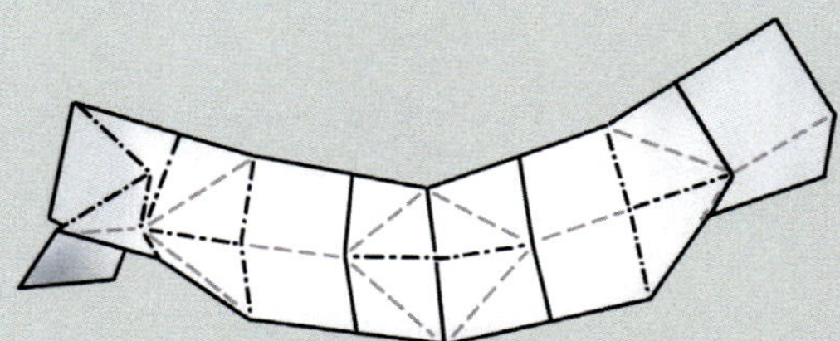

Start the collapse on the left side. Force the left-most valley, and see how the left side of the waterbomb base is formed.

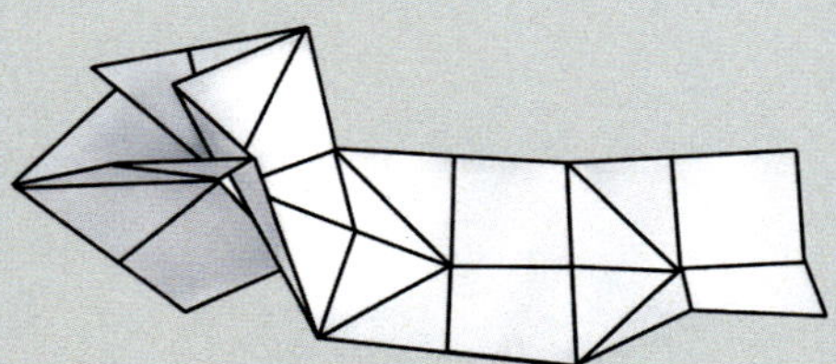

Repeat the same step on the right side of the waterbomb base.

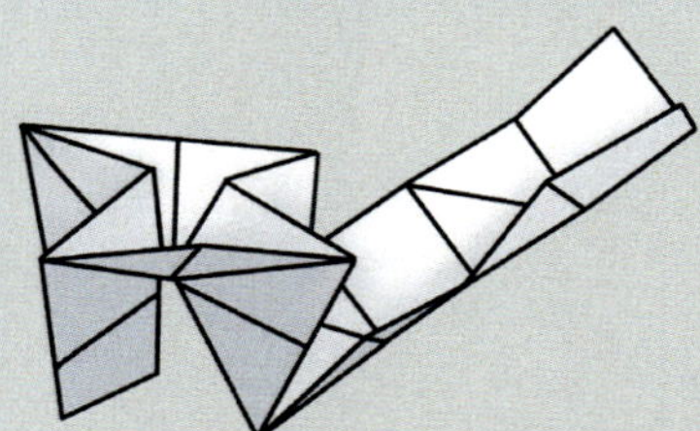

Now make an inside-reverse fold twice, using the valleys of the tilted square.

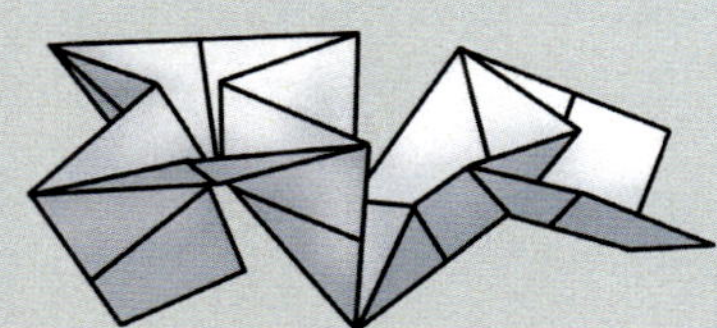

Fold the last mountain fold, and outside-reverse fold the last V-shaped valleys.

The molecule is finished.

2 by 2 Molecules

Use a grid of 4 by 16.

In this stage, we are practicing the first molecule, a middle molecule, and the last molecule.

Collapse this from left to right. First, repeat the step you made on the first molecule with the second one, and then move to the right.

It may look complicated, but once you get used to the process, it will go smoothly.

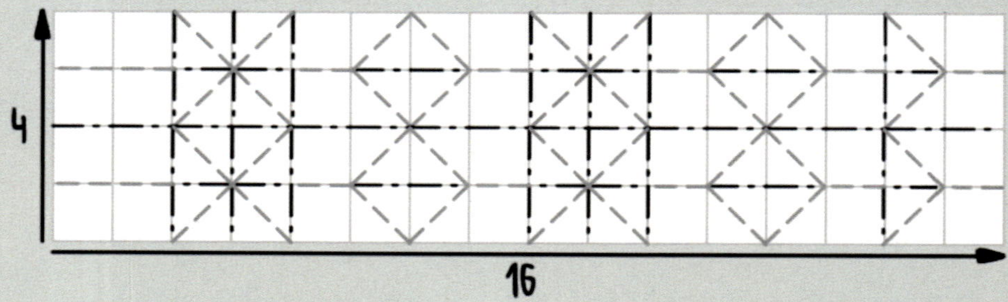

Tip:

If you want to save time, you can simplify the precrease phase. All the diagonal lines align, so you can just fold them all! This will make it work faster, but you will get some extra lines on the paper.

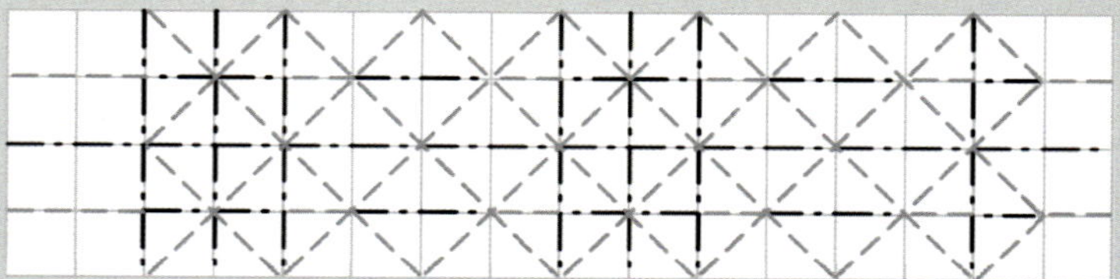

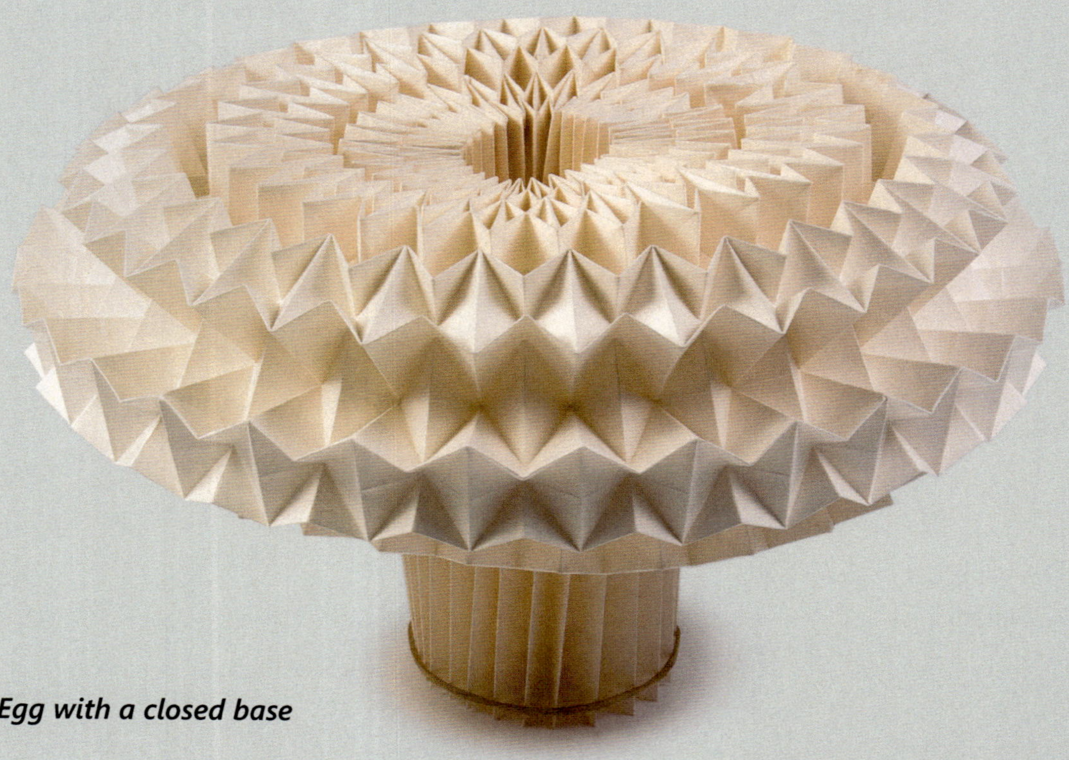

Fabergé Egg with a closed base

31 by 6 Molecules—Full Project

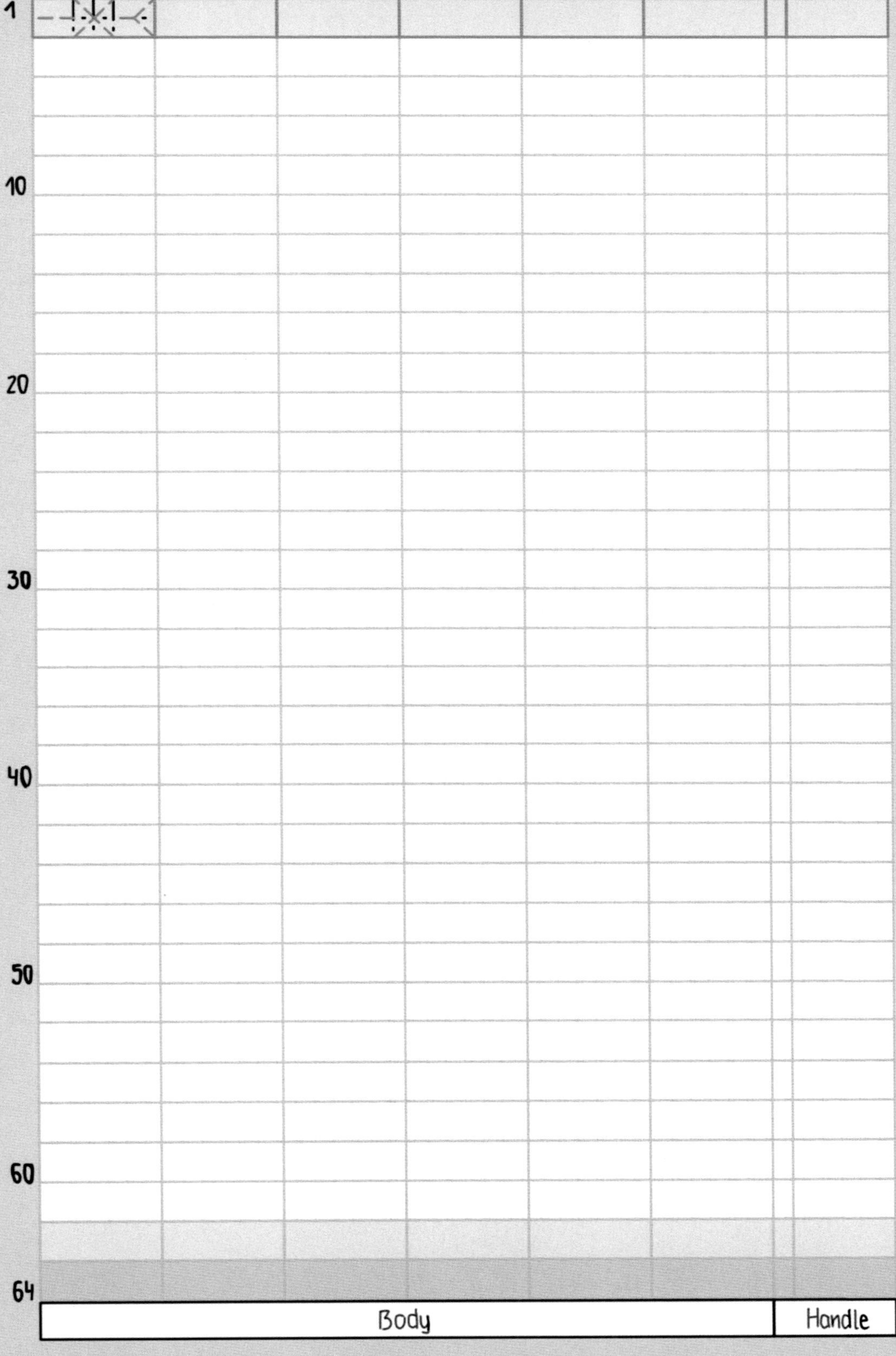

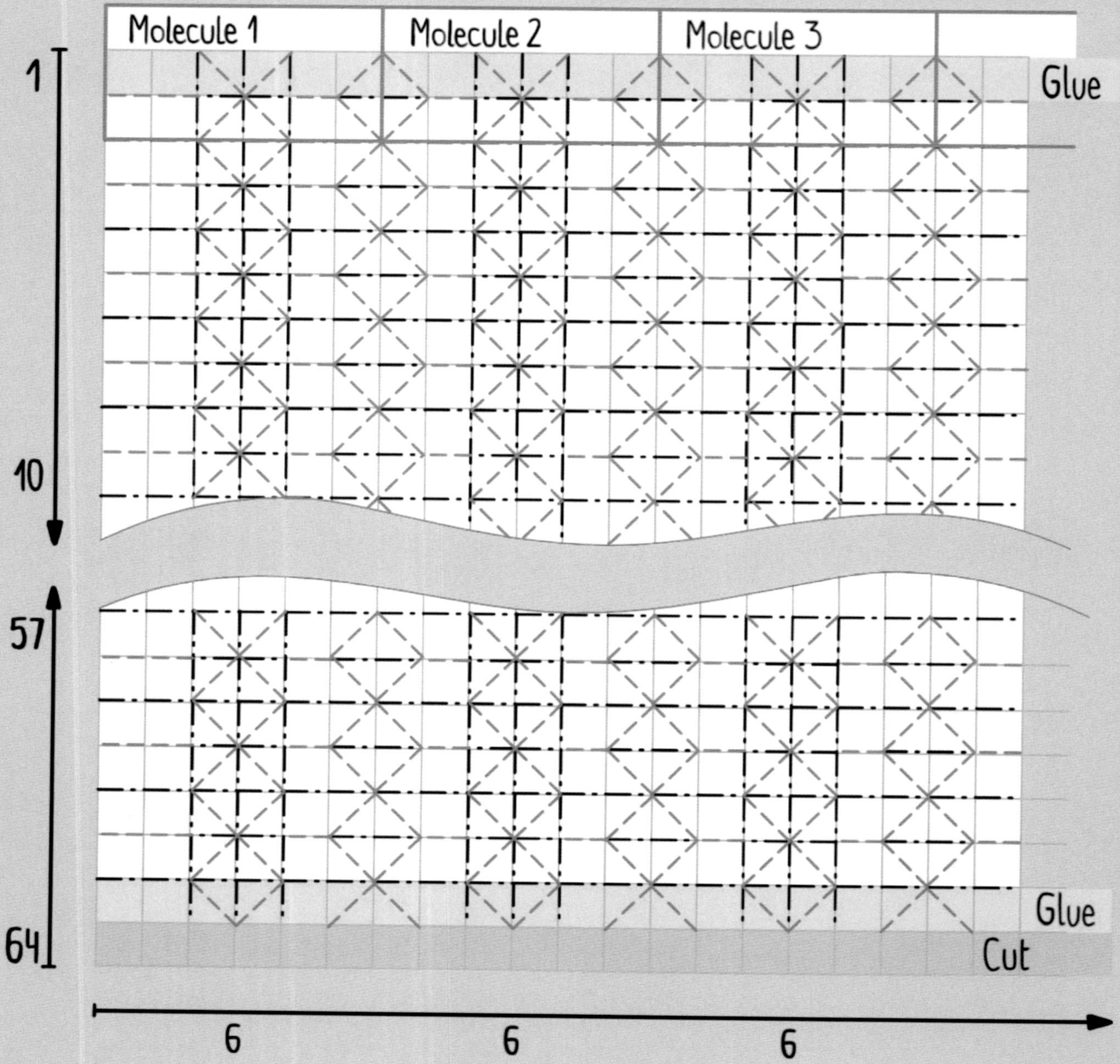

Make a grid of 64 by 37. If you are using a full sheet (70 by 100 cm), this will leave you with a handle of about 12 cm. There is no need to grid the handle.

The final result will be 12 squares high.

Pre-crease the diagonals on every square on the second column (from the left). If you want to save time, make the complete grid of diagonals. If you want a cleaner result at the cost of extra time, notice that each diagonal goes through two units, and skips one. You can also see that columns, 1, 2, 5, 8, 11, etc. are kept unfolded!

To collapse, start on the left. With every element that you fold, complete all 31 molecules. Once finished, move to the next element.

Start with the left-most waterbomb base. If you are comfortable with this, fold both sides of the base at once. This will ask for six iterations, to complete the model.

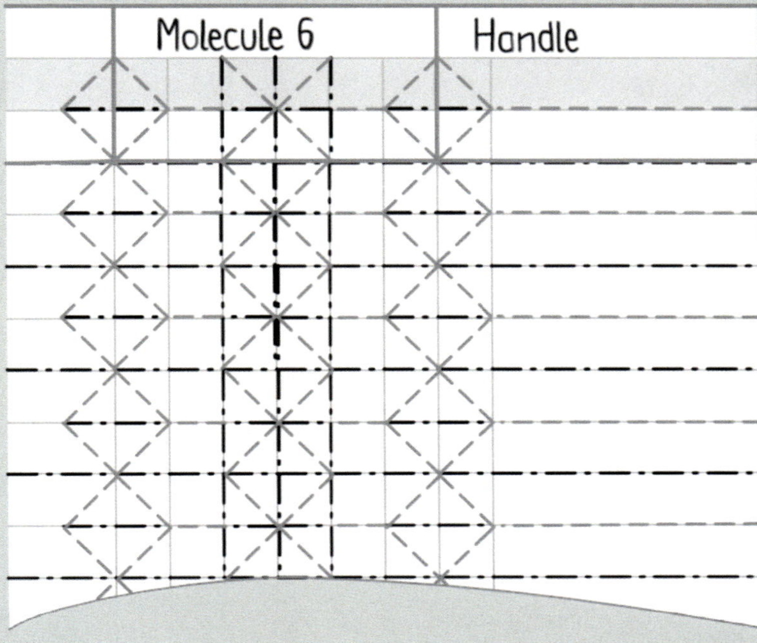

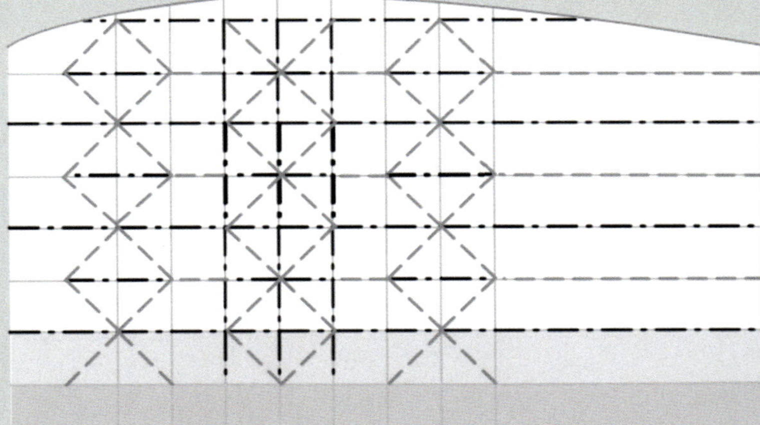

6 1

If not, you can start with the left half of the waterbomb base through the 31 rows, and then complete the base on all of them.

Next will be the inside-reverse fold and the outside-reverse fold.

Now go for the second waterbomb base.

Complete six waterbomb bases and make only the last inside-reverse fold for the handle.

The last step is to glue edge to edge. I use only a single row to overlap. Unfold both the first and the last rows. You may consider unfolding two rows on each edge. Fold one row to lay on the previous row completely and apply the glue. Now attach to it the other edge and hold them together with clips.

Once the glue is dry, refold the molecules. Make sharp creases to eliminate the molecule's wish to expand, because of the excessive layer.

You can play with the handle to create various looks. Spread it open or hold it tight with a rubber band.

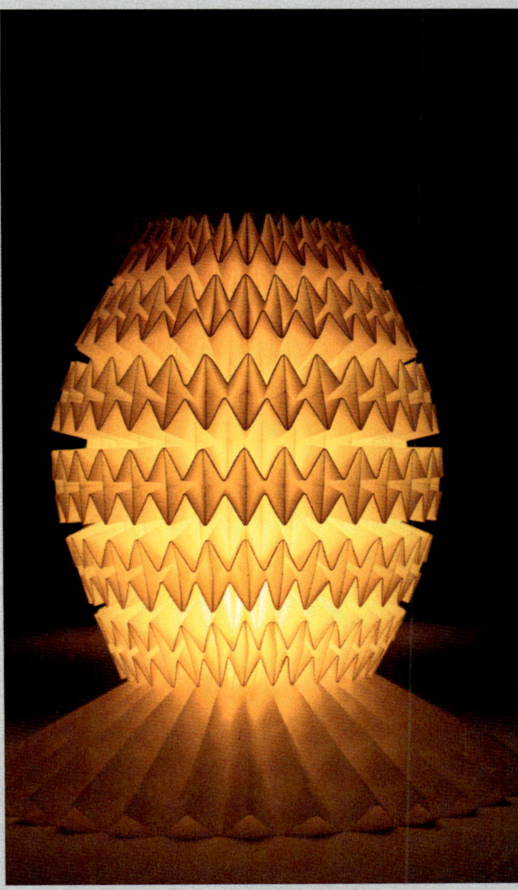

Fabergé Egg with inner light.

6 2 Braided Bowl

This bowl is my only circular design and you may not consider it as a tessellation at all, being so different from all the other models here. Still, it has a repetitive molecule, you must admit that!

There are several possible variations. The trivial ones are the polygon you start with. I prefer the 12-side one, as it balances well between the roundness and the size of the molecule. A 16-sided polygon creates small molecules that are hard to handle, and an octagon results with big molecules.

More variations are hidden in the distances between the three "rings" of folds you start with. Change their locations, and you can get many different bowls, changing the height and the depth.

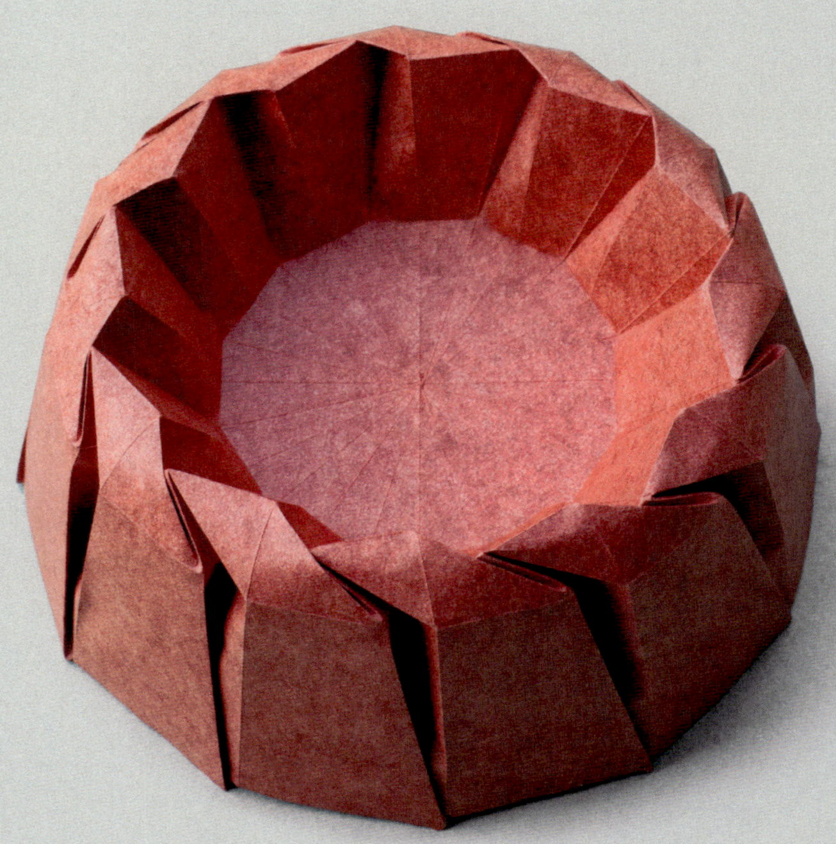

12-side Braided Bowl.

The Single Molecule

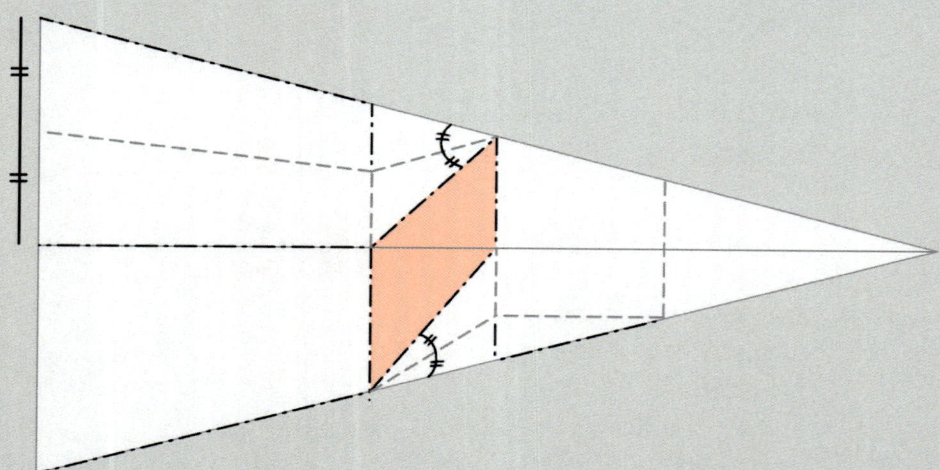

The molecule has a pizza-slice shape. The red part is braided by the opposite bisectors, folded in a mountain-valley pleat.

The shrinkage ratio is 2:1. Start with a 30 cm square to get a bowl with 15 cm in diameter.

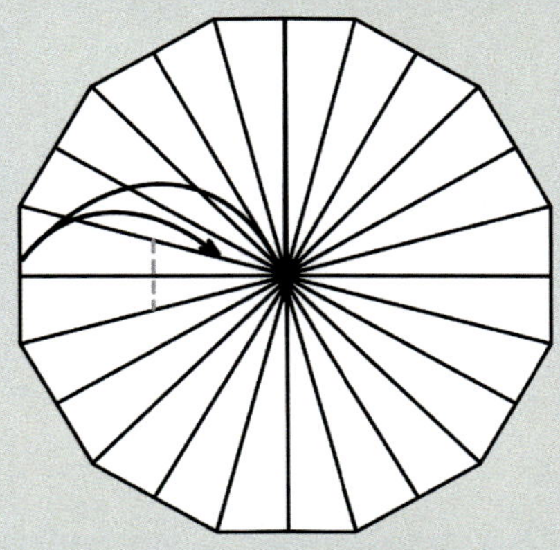

Start with a 12 sided polygon. Fold all medians and diagonals.

Fold and unfold the edge to the center, marking only between two adjacent diagonals.

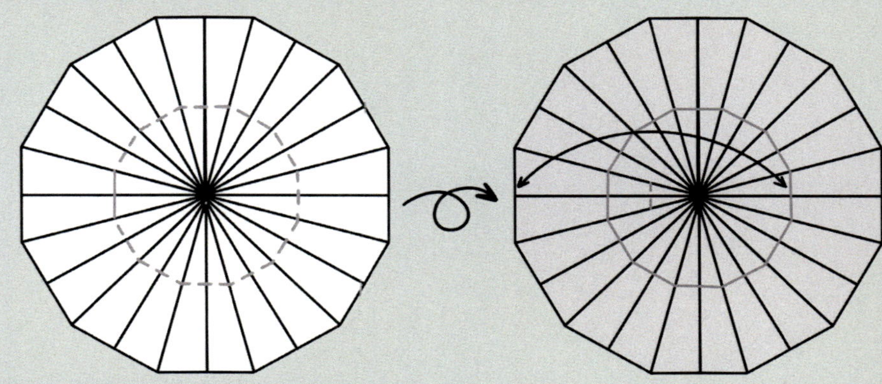

Repeat all over.

Turn over.

Fold and unfold the edge to the far crease line. Mark only between the diagonals.

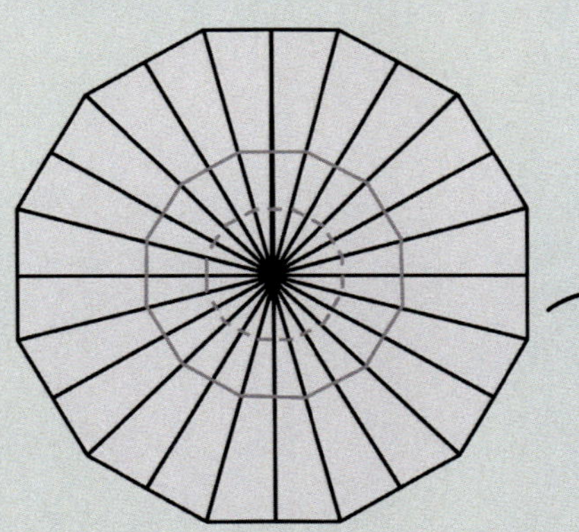

Repeat all over.

Turn over again.

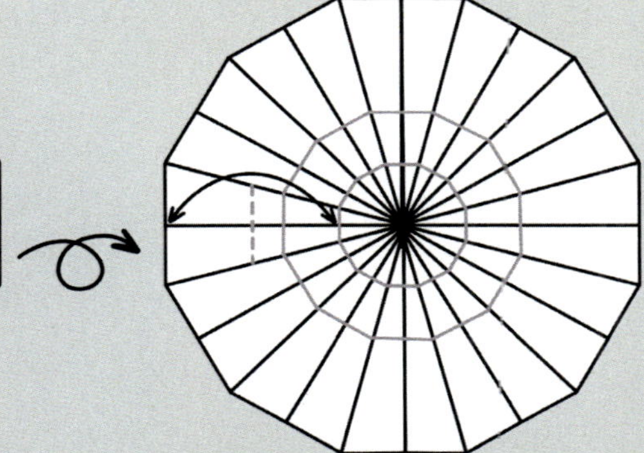

Fold and unfold the edge to the inner crease line.

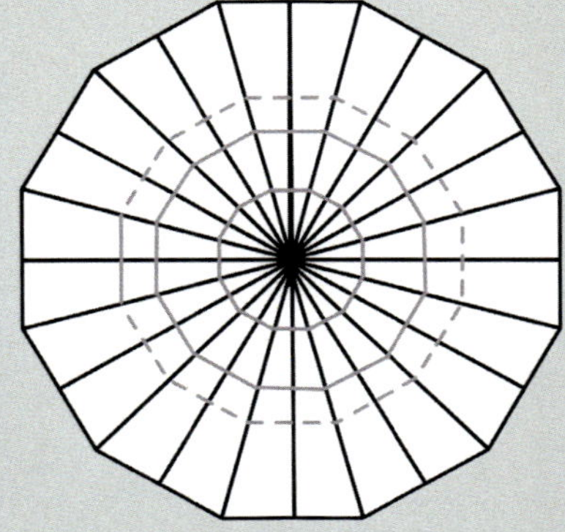

Repeat all over.

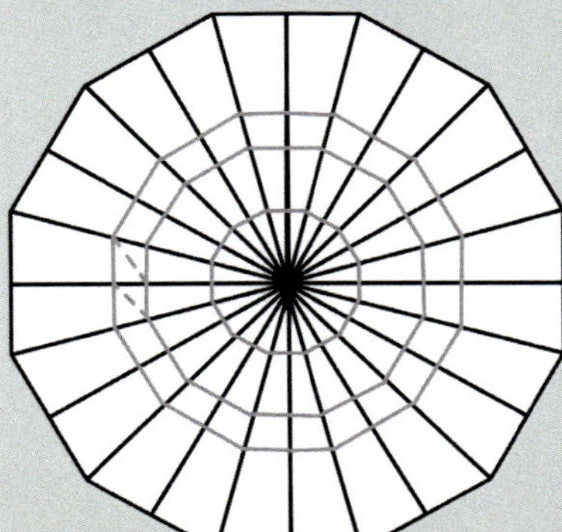

Fold and unfold the diagonals of the marked trapezoids.

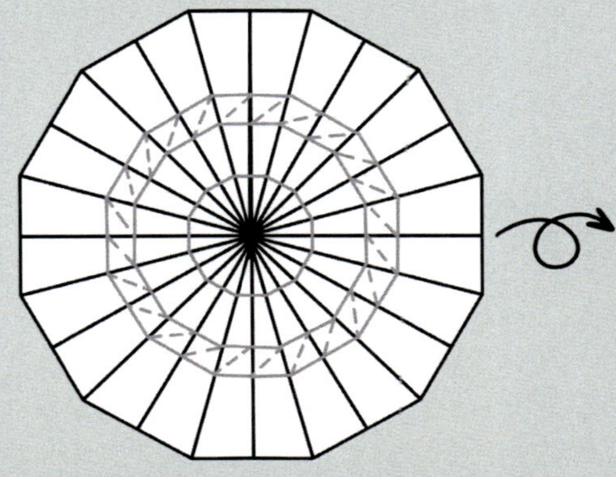

Repeat all over.

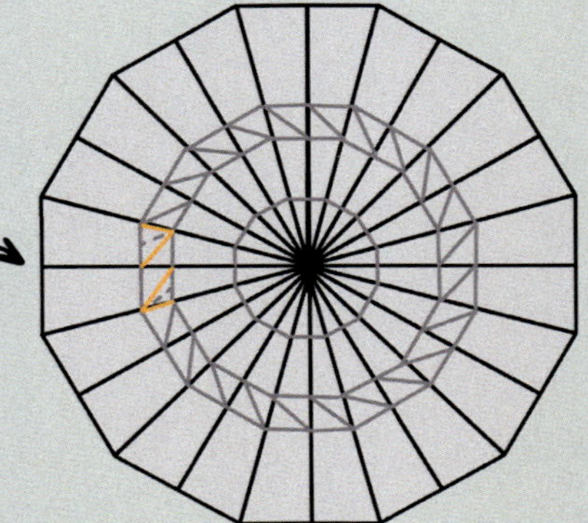

Fold and unfold the bisectors of the orange angles. Look at the single molecule to see the exact location of the folds.

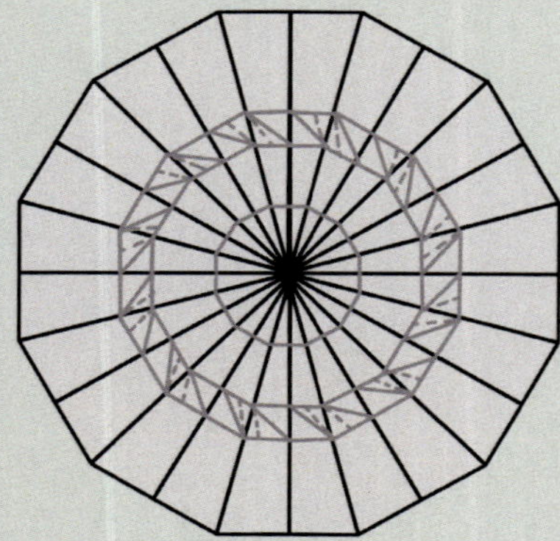

Repeat all over.

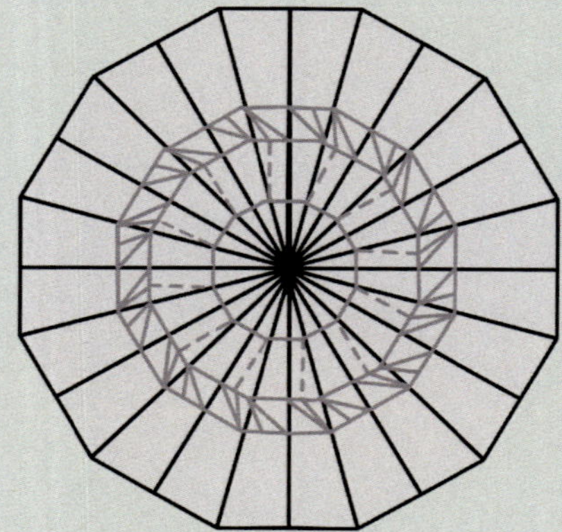

Fold and unfold the marked valleys.

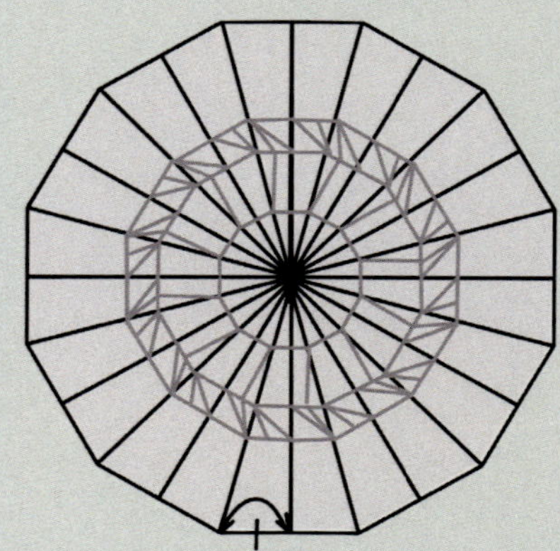

Mark by a pinch the centre point of the left half of the edge. Repeat all over.

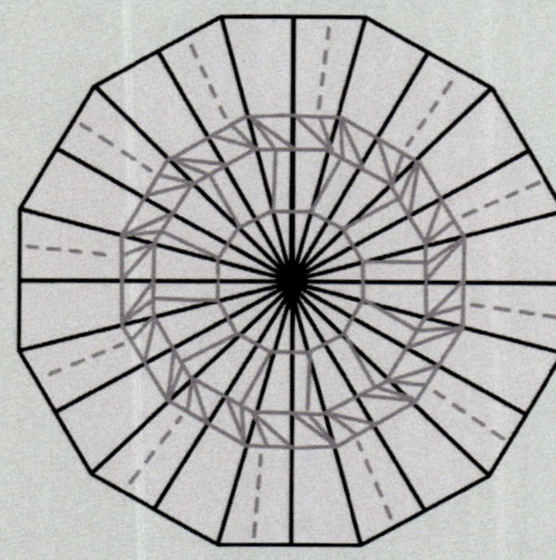

Valley-fold all lines connecting the bisectors to the pinches. Repeat all over.

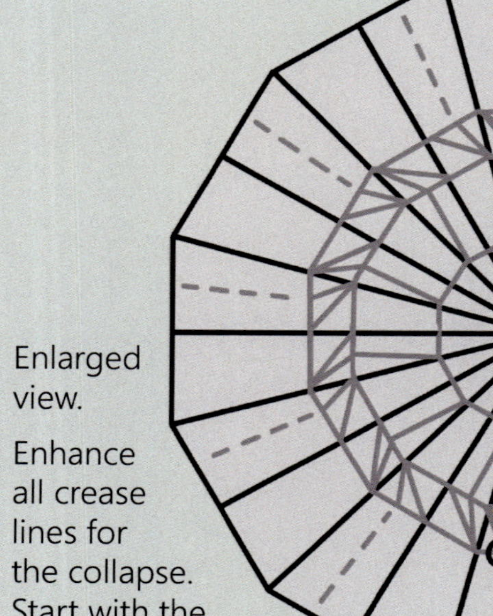

Enlarged view.

Enhance all crease lines for the collapse. Start with the marked area (in orange), and shape the valley folds on the left and the right. Make sure the marked intersections are sunk.

Now bring a corner (marked as *) to the median (as shown with the arrow). Repeat all over.

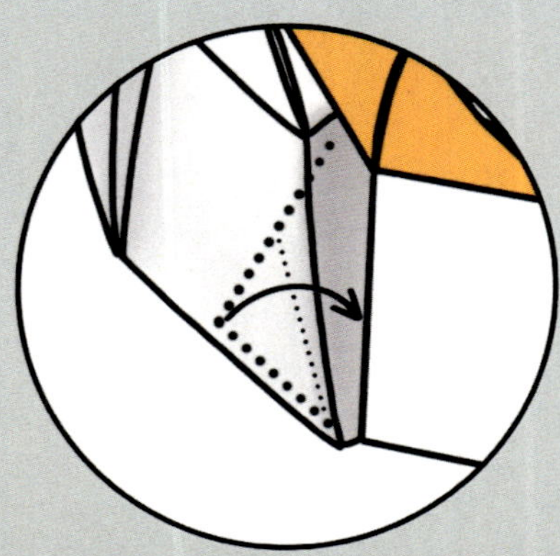

Lock all the inner tabs by folding a bisector.

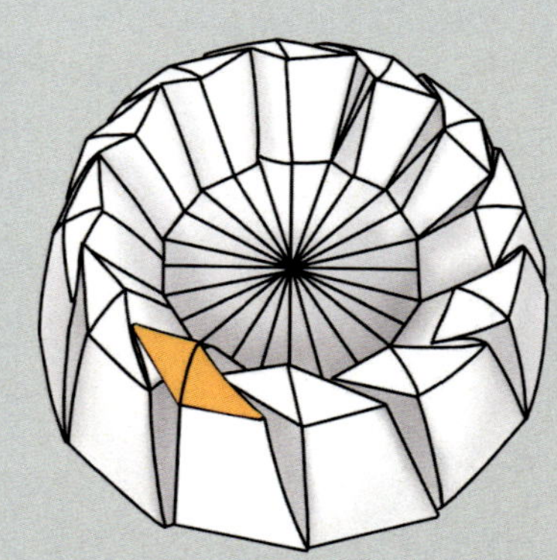

Finished!

6 3 Tavolini

This is the only molecule in this book that cannot lie flat. Its only way to exist is in a circular shape. It is a highly robust construction and this was my reason to make tables out of it, from metal, wood, or both.

As always, the basic molecule has many variations, and one can play with the proportions, density, angles, and even the inner structure of the molecule.

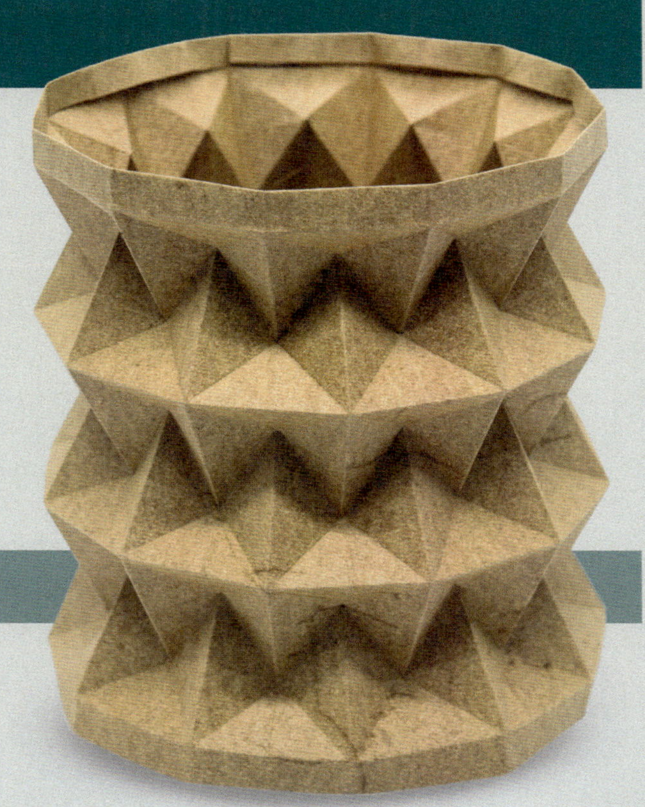

12-side Tavolini.

The Single Molecule

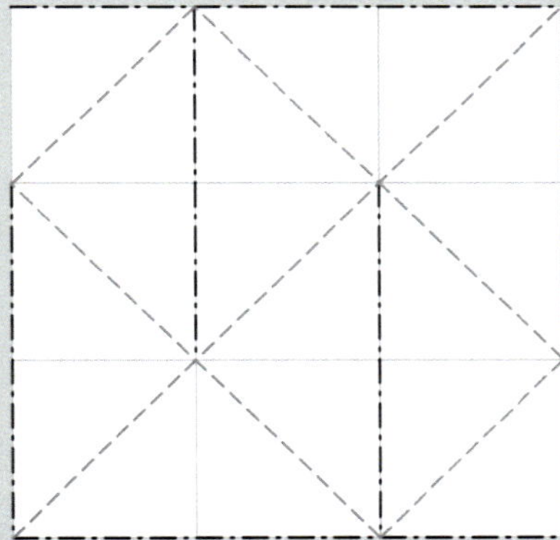

The molecule size is 3 by 3.

It is based on a pair of mountain folds, two-square in length and a grid of diagonals, as valleys.

This combination allows sinking the intersection of the mountain with the diagonals.

The shrinkage ratio differs between the width and the height.

The width does not shrink at all.

The height shrinkage is about 6:5.

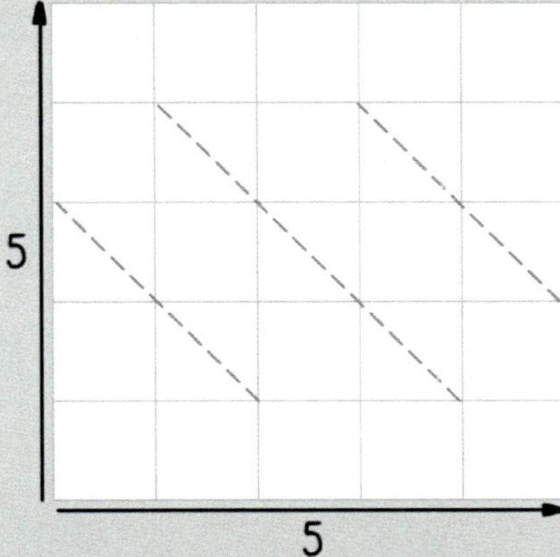

Start with a grid of 5 by 5, to allow extra rows on top and bottom.

Mark with valleys the diagonals.

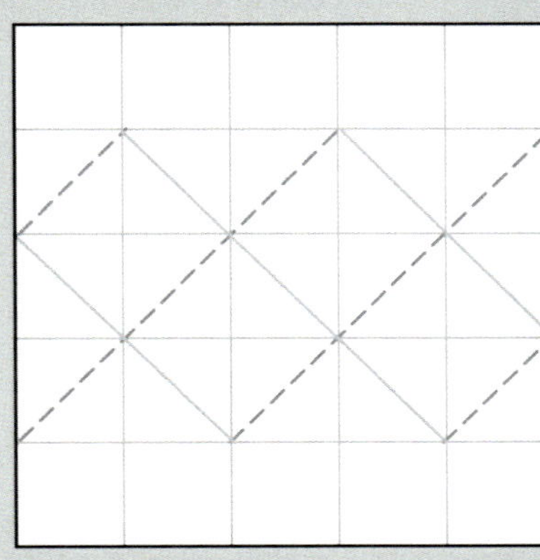

Complete the diagonal grid with more valleys.

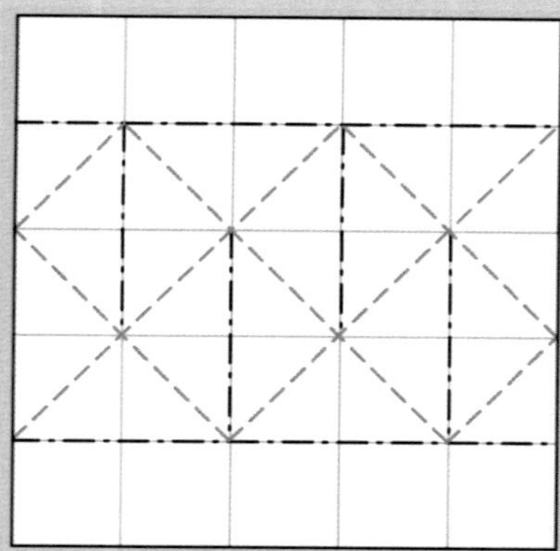

Those are all the needed pre-creases. The marked lines of the grid are mountains. Note the top and lower rows. They are not critical for the design to stand, but they do give a lovely frame and help with the collapse.

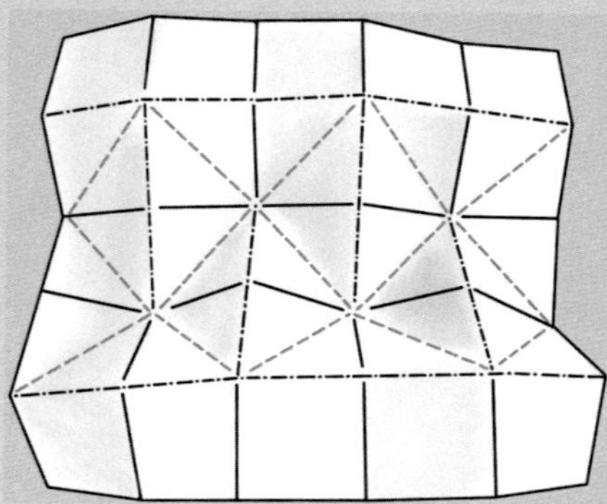

Start the collapse by forcing the valleys that meet the edges, and move inward. Use a little force to bend the center part toward you while pushing away the left and right edges. Make sure the mountains are mountains, and everything will just pop into place. Done!

2 by 2 Molecules—Full Project

Use a grid of 8 by 8.

Collapse the model from both left and right edges inward. It is highly important to maintain the horizontal mountains in the right orientation during the complete process. Do that and everything will jump into place, just by curving the paper.

I prefer to shorten the top and bottom rows. You can cut it or fold it inward.

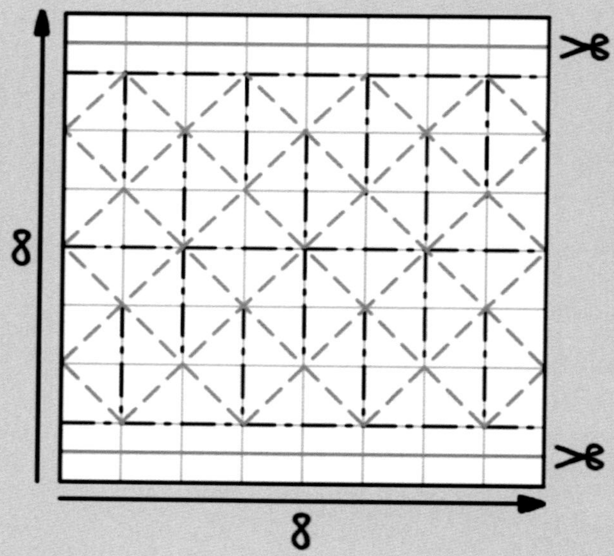

12 by 3 Molecules—Full Project

Make a grid of 11 by 25.

The formula for the grid is dependent on the number of rows you want to have. For every row count 3 squares.

For the width, you can again choose any number between 8 to 14. That will change the density of the folds when you form a tube.

Crease the diagonal grid as valleys.

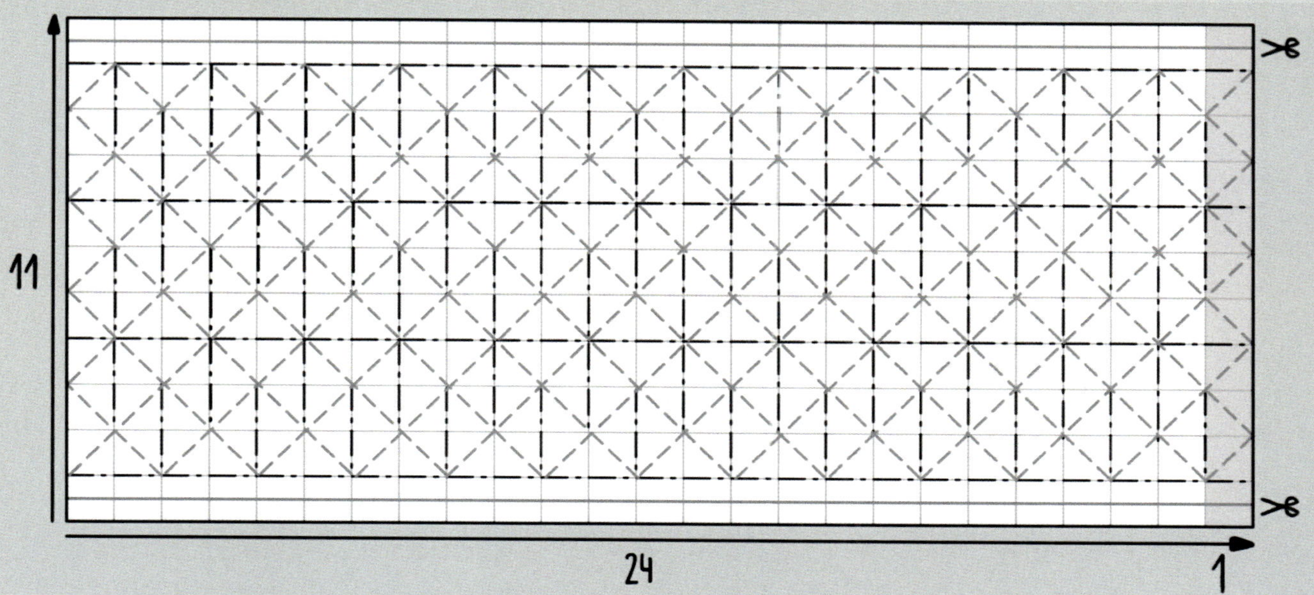

To collapse, start with the edges, and apply force to bend the paper into a curve. It is easier to work row by row, but you can just as well work on the columns.

Once you collapse you can glue the first column to the last.

Above and Beyond

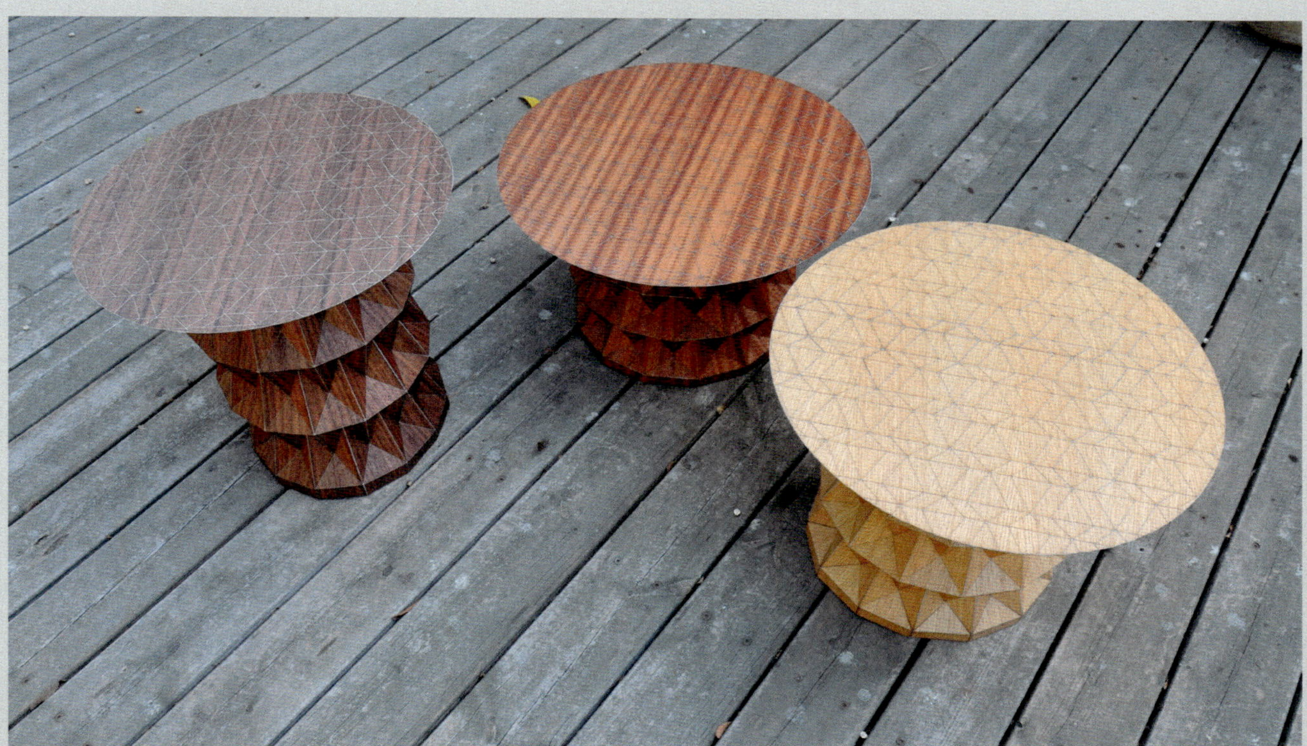

Three Tavolini, folded from metal and wood sheets.

Variations

Every parameter can be changed here.

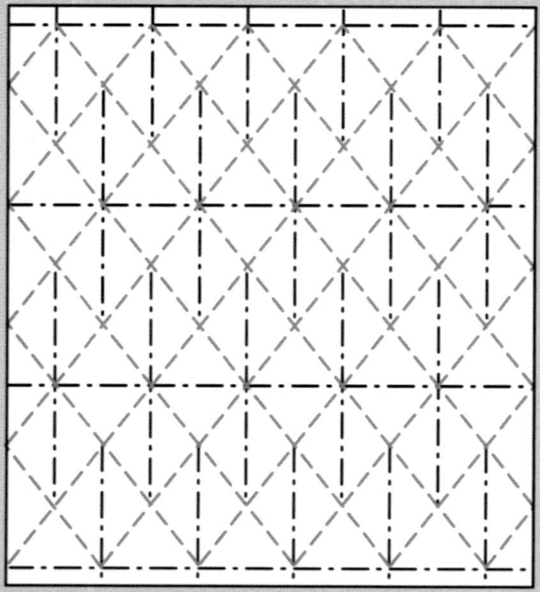

You can make the angles sharper by making the grid narrower.

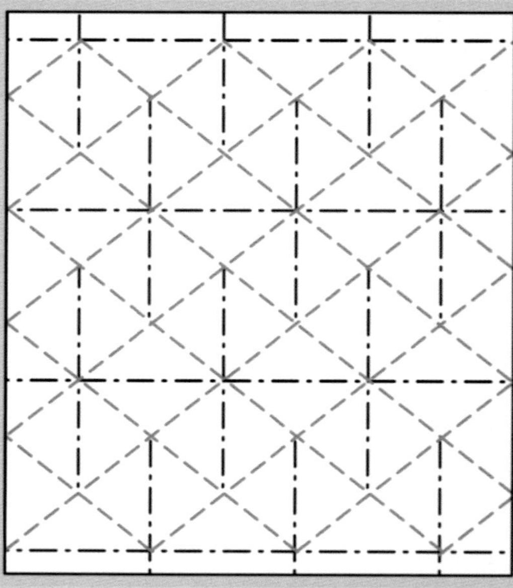

You can make it wider.

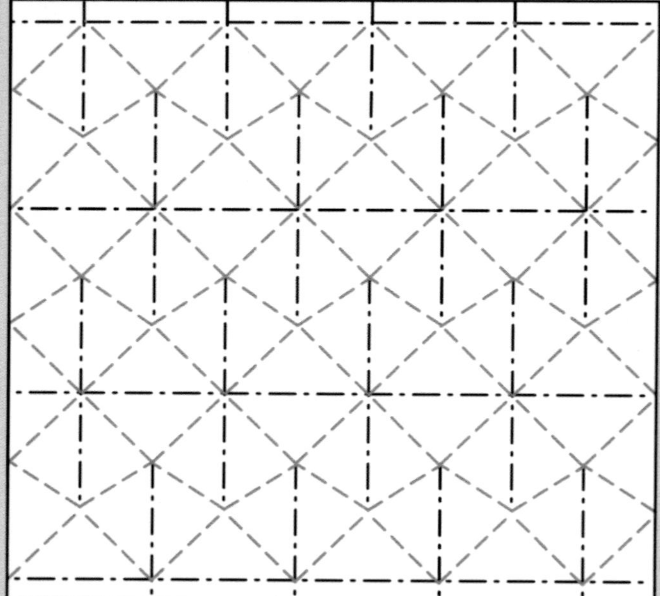

You can play with the location of the inner intersection between the mountain and the valleys. This creates an asymmetric pattern.

This variation was revealed by **Riccardo Foschi.**

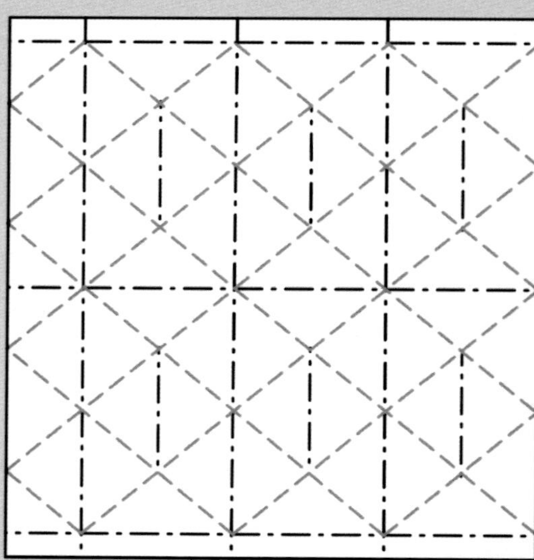

You can have more iterations **within** the rows! Instead of having the rows made from three units, you can use four units, like here, or even more!

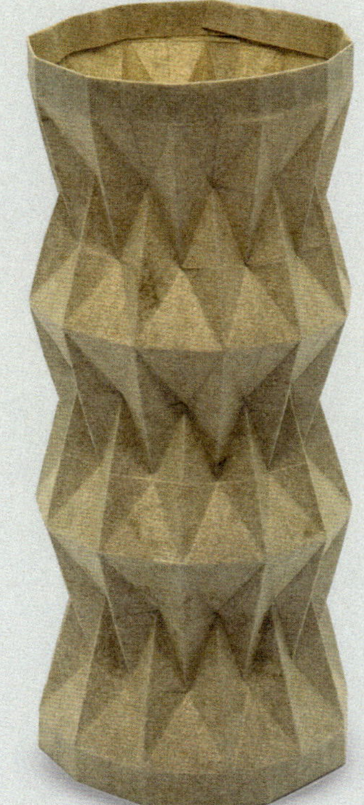

12-side narrow Tavolini.

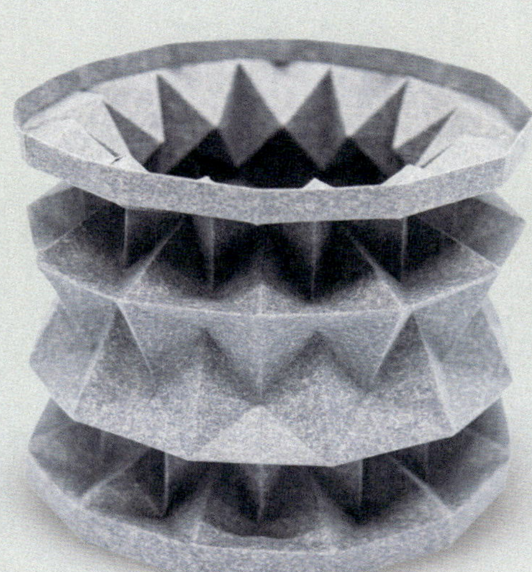

12-side Tavolini, with rows 1 and 3 made from 2 iterations each.

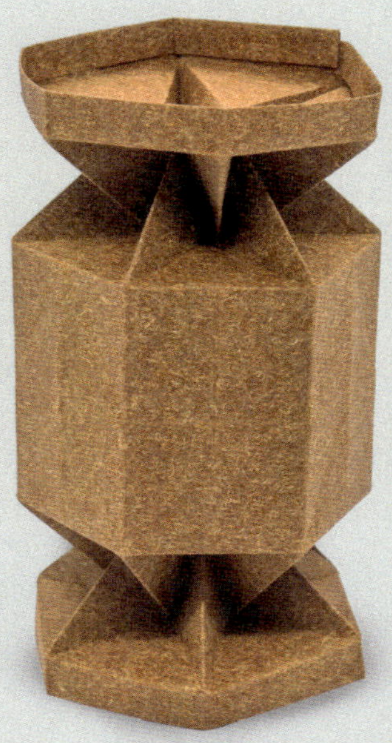

6-side Tavolini, with an unfolded center row.

Above and Beyond

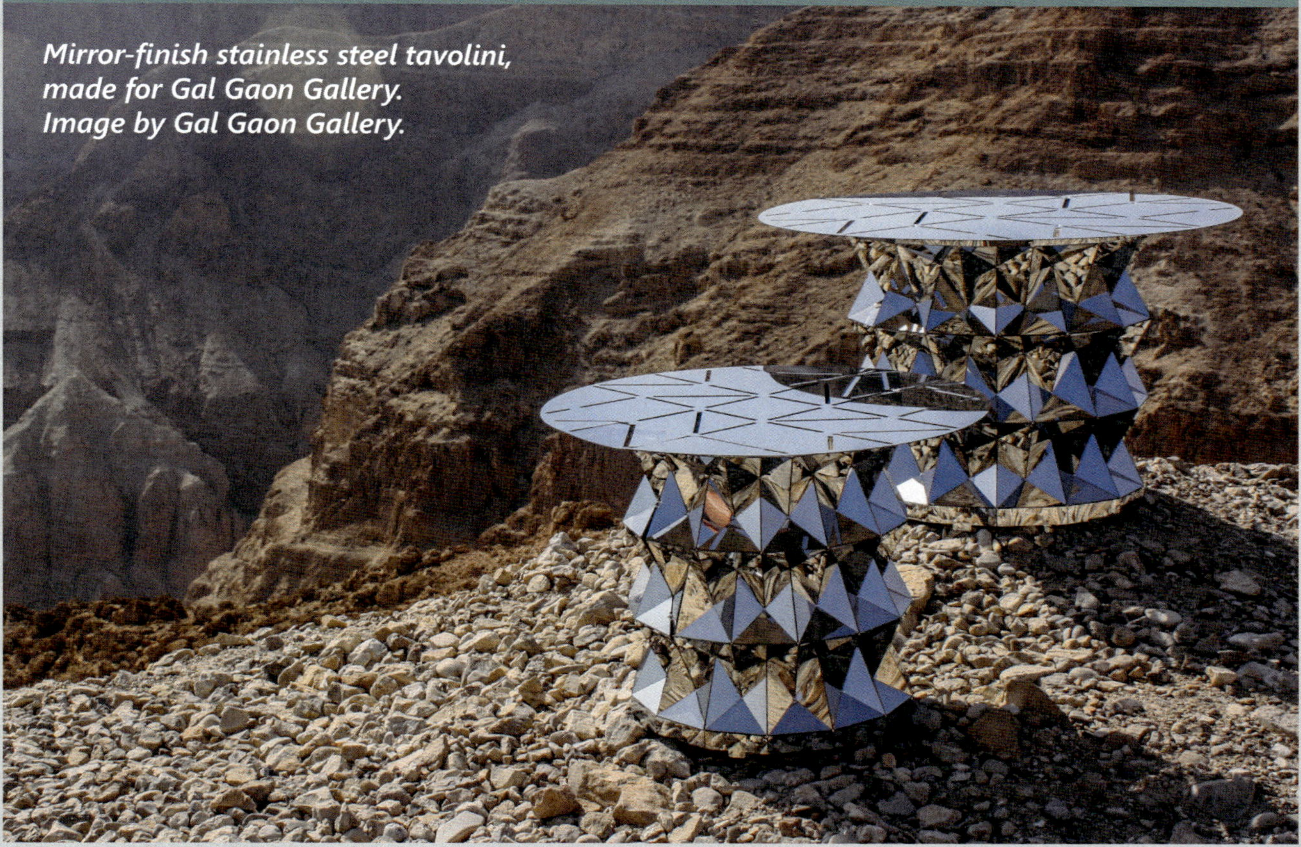

Mirror-finish stainless steel tavolini, made for Gal Gaon Gallery. Image by Gal Gaon Gallery.

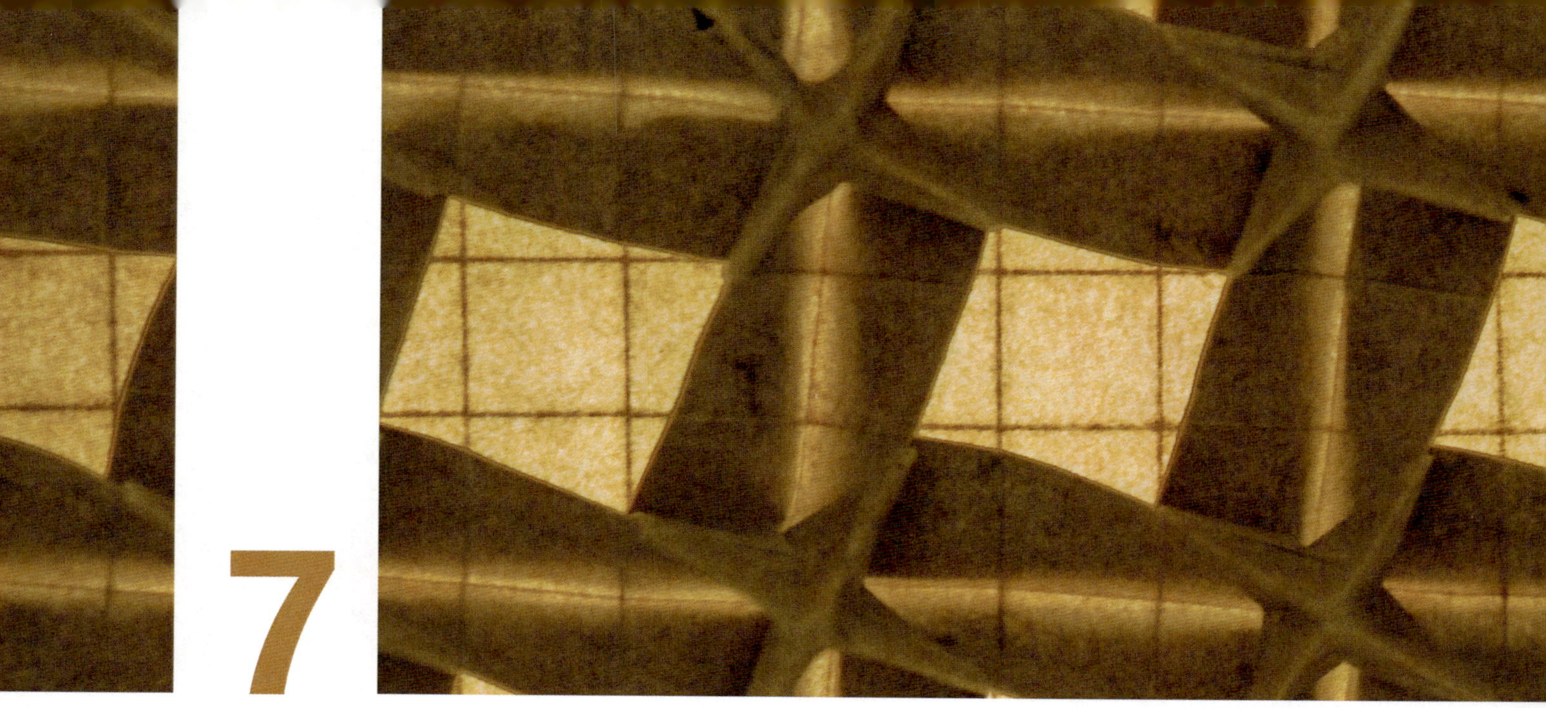

7 Advanced Models

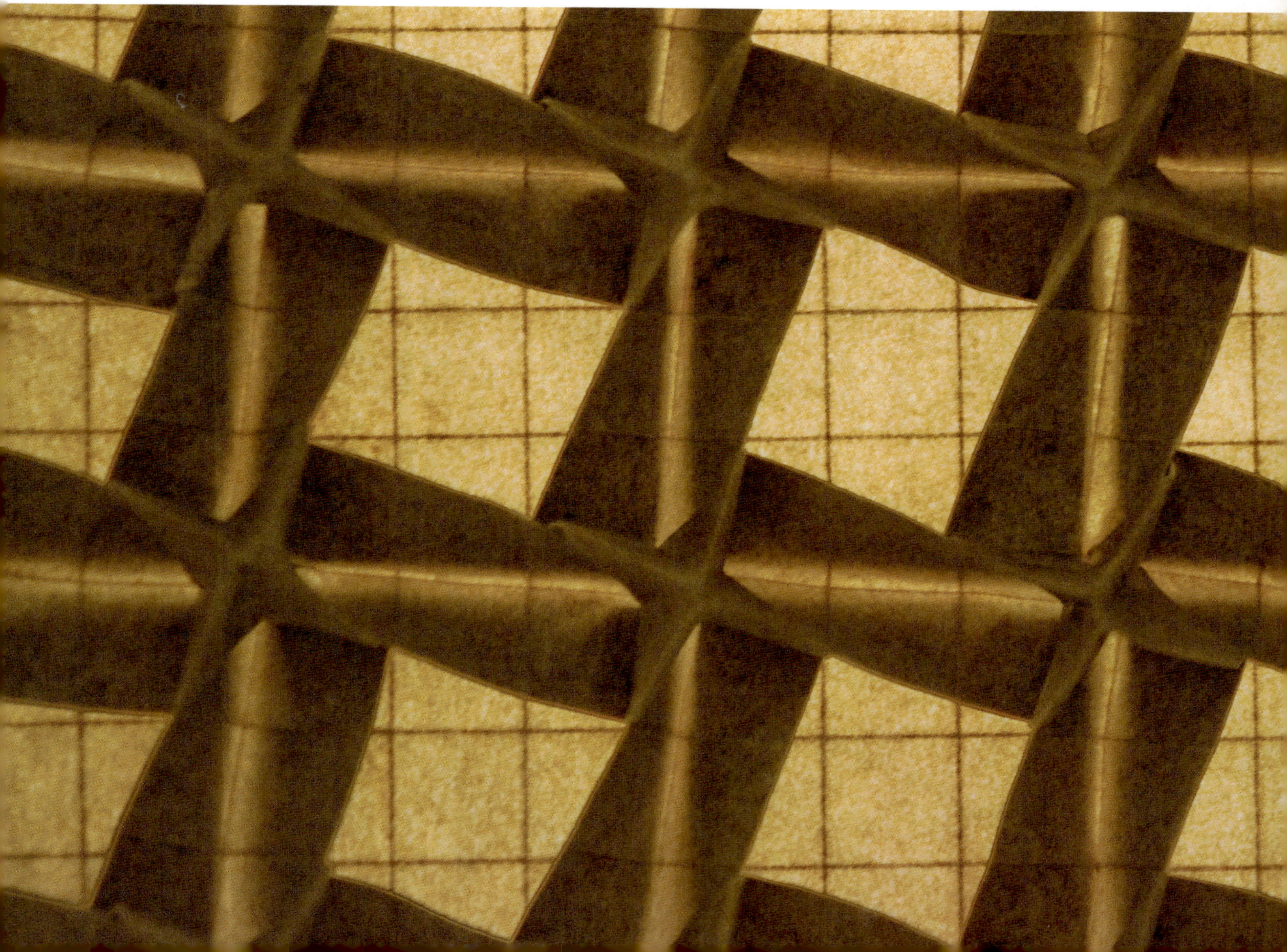

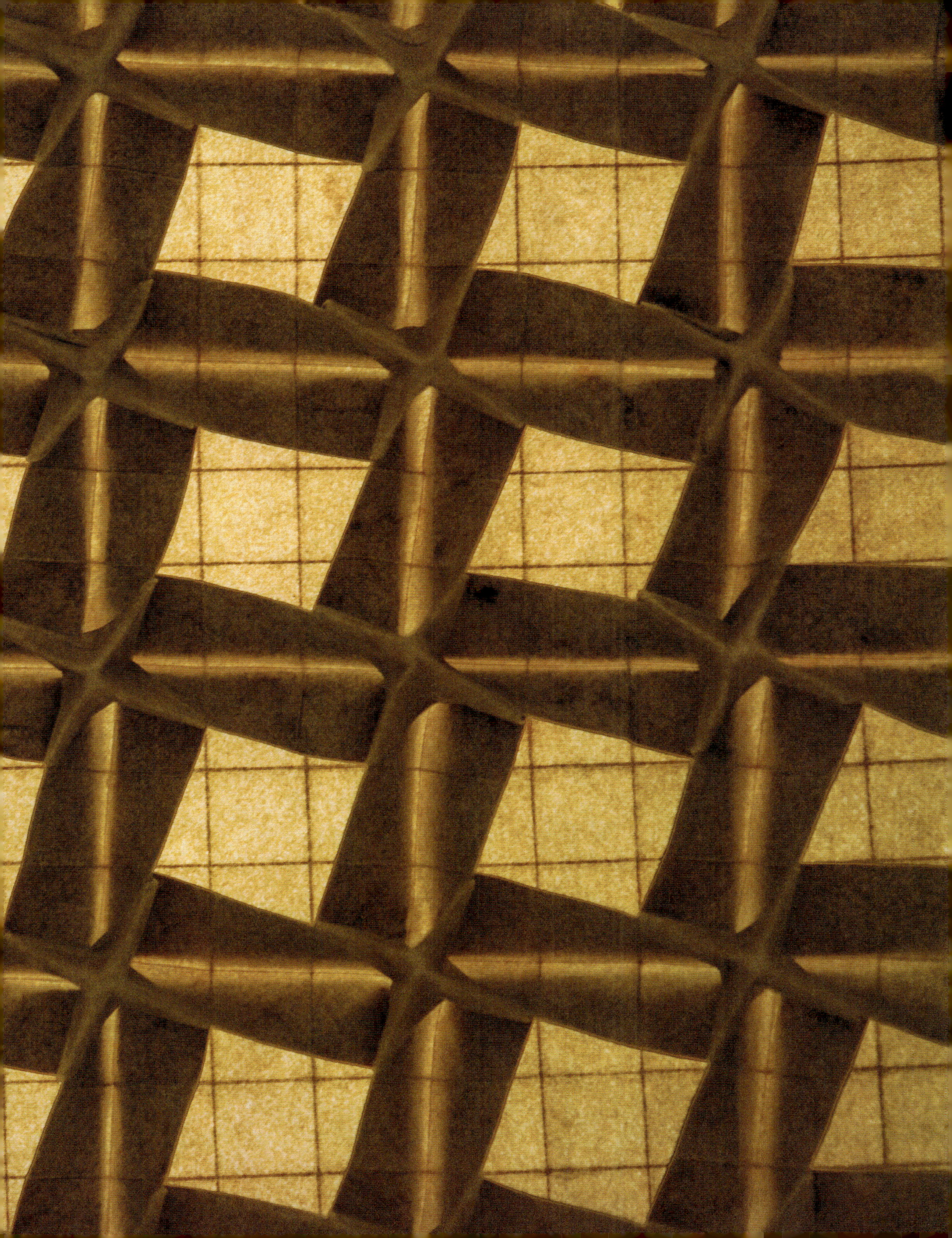

Introduction

This is the group of all the solitary models. Each has its own uniqueness and was born based on independent findings. All are made from a square grid, like most of my work.

The fact that each presents a stand-alone idea can make them fit into a family, in a way.

7 1 Mystery

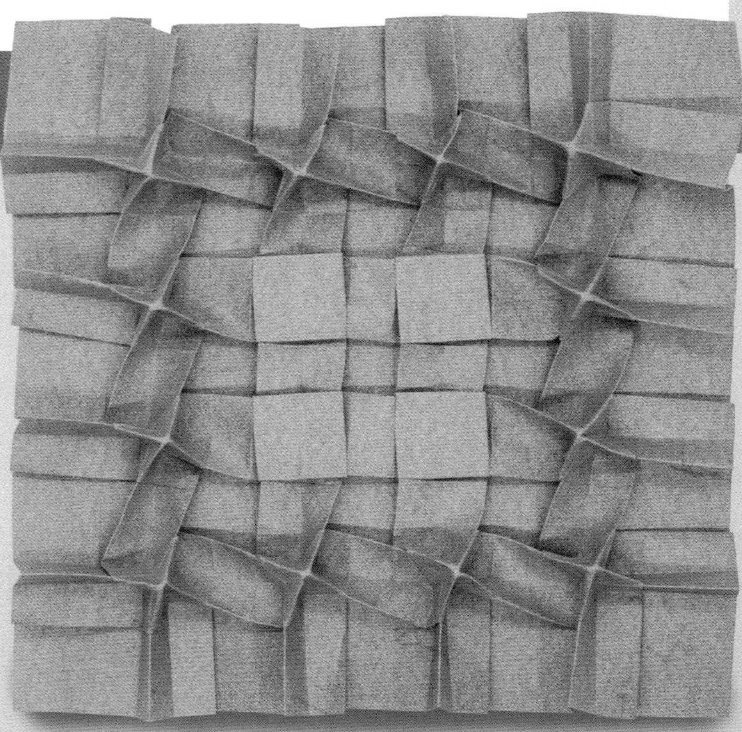

This model has no pre-creases. All it needs is a grid, and the molecule emerges only by reordering the layers.

The name came from the contrast between the simplicity of the CP and the final result. I found this a mystery!

I did try to follow the same concept with a hexagon grid, but it didn't work at all, so this model stayed in solitude.

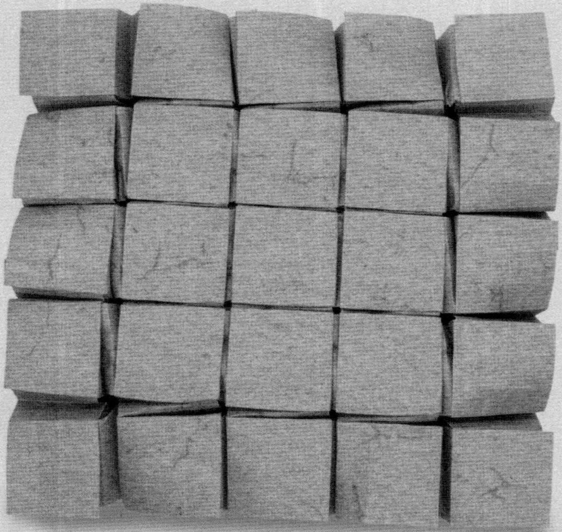

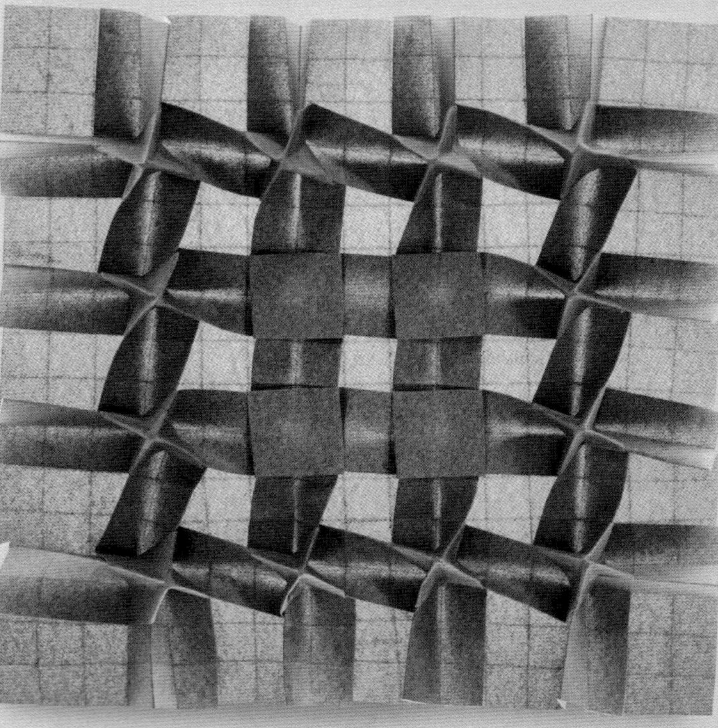

Top right: recto view of a 4 by 4–molecule Mystery tessellation.

Left: verso view of a 4 by 4–molecule Mystery tessellation.

Bottom right: recto view with back-light.

The Single Molecule

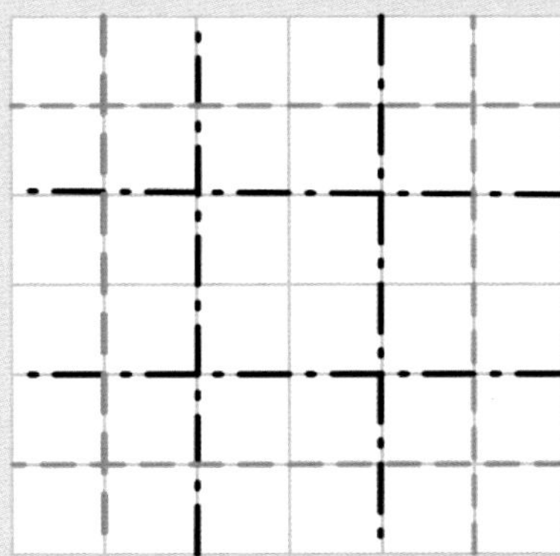

The molecule size is 6 by 6 but do not try to fold it at that size! The lack of extra paper makes this very hard to fold. This is why I do not show a version without spacing between the molecules.

The shrinkage ratio is 2:1.

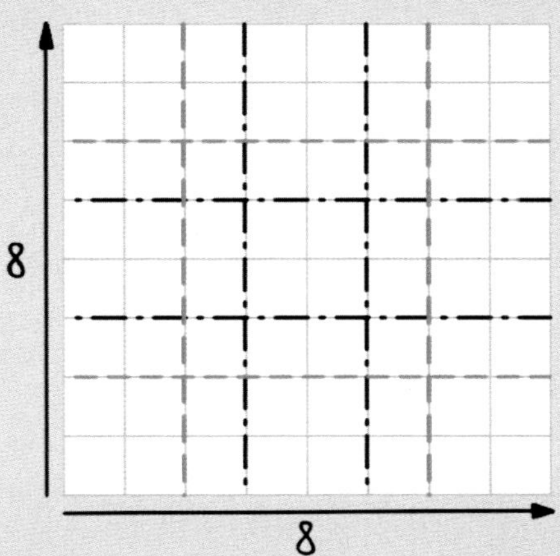

Start with a grid of 8 by 8, to allow extra rows and columns on all four sides.

Force with valleys the marked lines.

Add the mountains as shown.

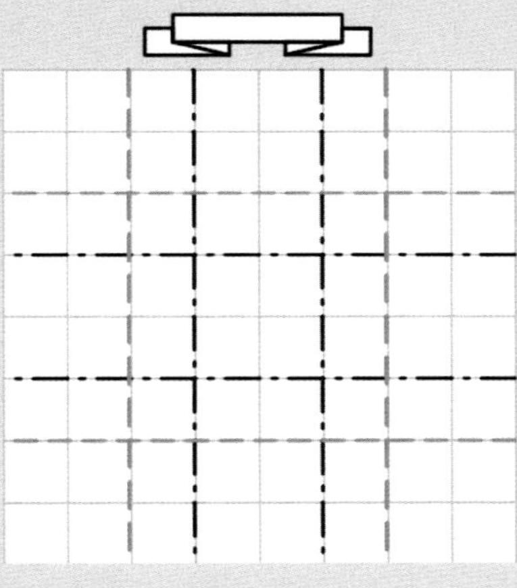

Pleat the vertical lines. See the stacking of the layers above!

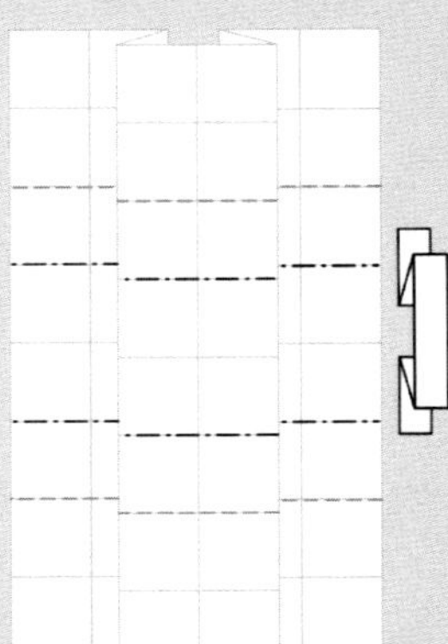

Repeat the pleating horizontally.

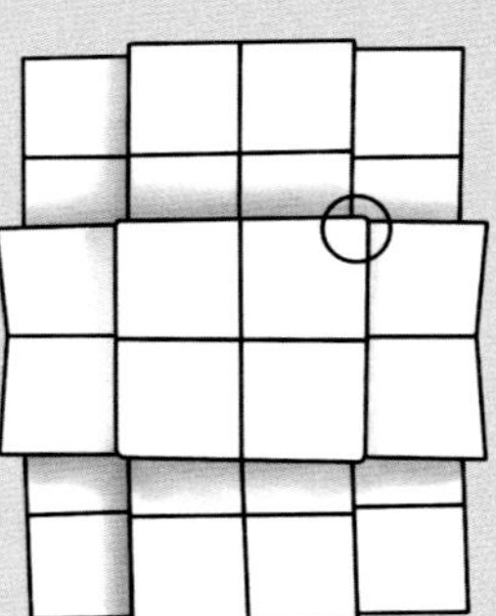

This corner is already with the correct layering.
To allow the relayering of the left corner, we need to unfold this corner but do remember the correct order here.

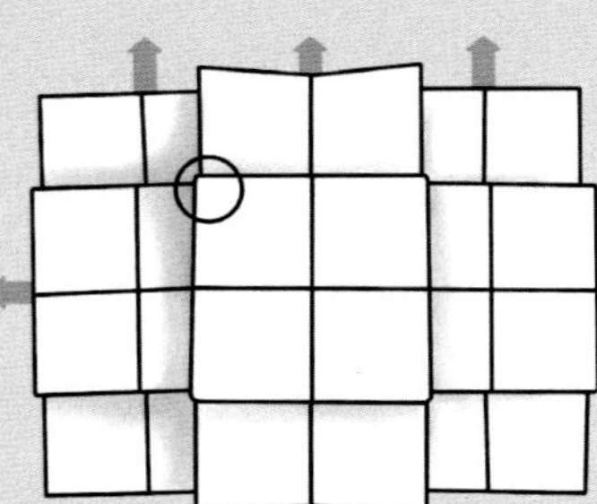

Now we will reorder the layers on the left corner.

Unfold.

Note the marked intersection.

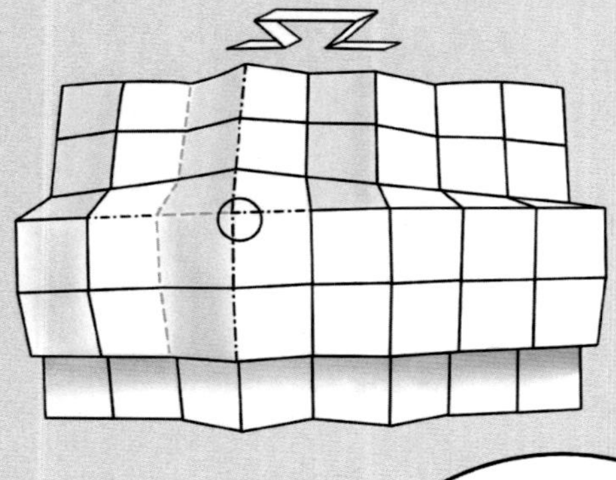

In process.

The horizontal mountain that goes through the marked corner is straight, while the vertical mountain is "broken" with a valley.

We are going to change that now!

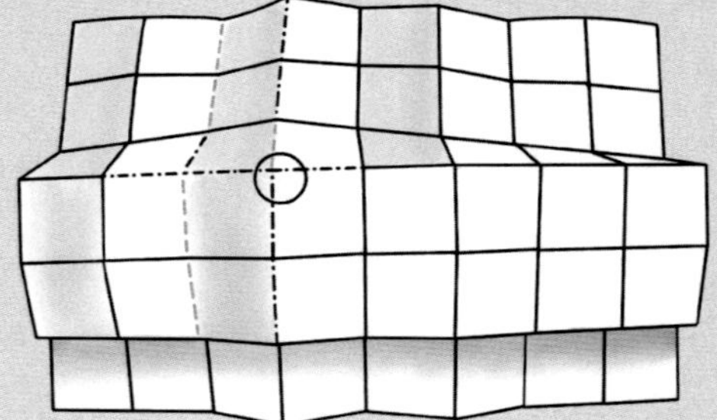

The horizontal crease will be broken now, and the vertical is all a mountain. Pleat it according to the symbol above.

Make the model flat.

The orientation of the layers changed!

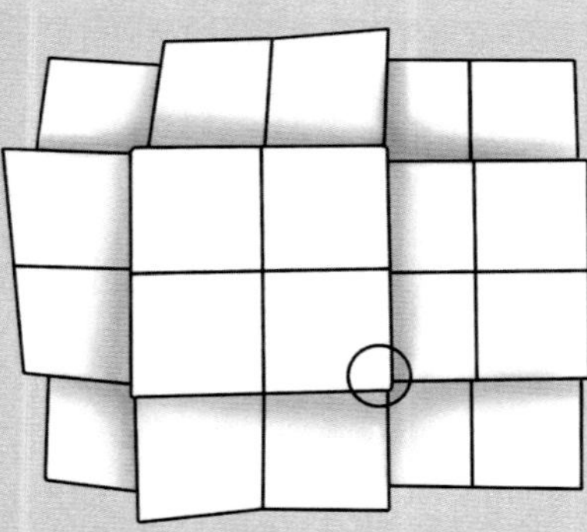

The bottom-left corner is layered correctly, nothing to do there. So we work now on the right corner (marked). Repeat the same process here.

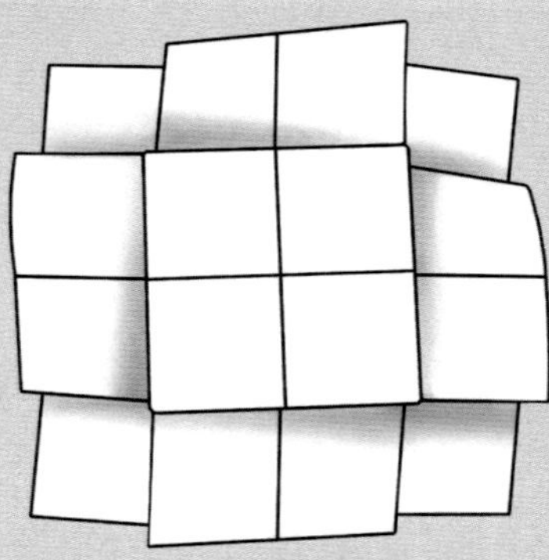

All the layers are correct now.

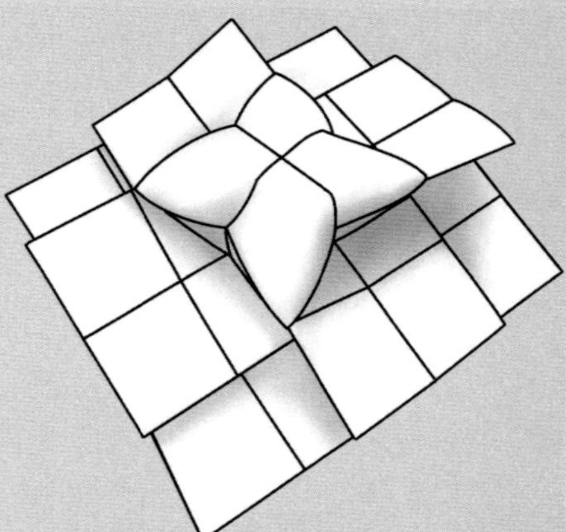

You can reshape the center square at will, by pushing in the four edges.

2 by 2 Molecules

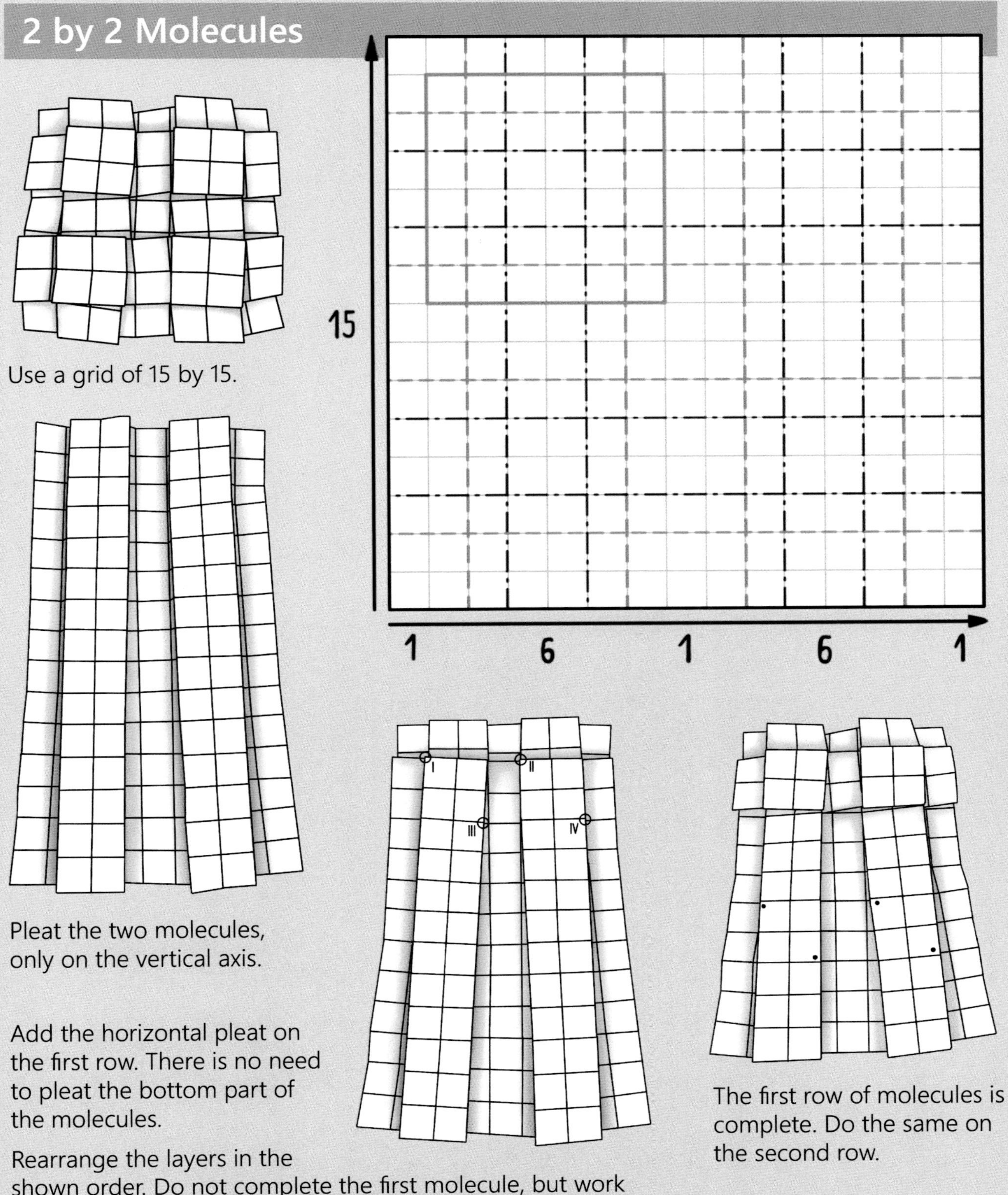

Use a grid of 15 by 15.

Pleat the two molecules, only on the vertical axis.

Add the horizontal pleat on the first row. There is no need to pleat the bottom part of the molecules.

Rearrange the layers in the shown order. Do not complete the first molecule, but work on all the corners on the highest row first.

To complete the first row of molecules (by folding the bottom part of the molecules in this row), pleat now the bottom and repeat the process (corners III and IV).

The first row of molecules is complete. Do the same on the second row.

4 by 4 Molecules

Make a grid of 31 by 31. A single-square width of a frame is enough and helpful.

The formula for the grid is 1 + 3 × 1 + 4 × 6 + 1 = 31.

The final result will be 13-square wide.

This is, by far, the most confusing collapse. Once you are beyond the first row of molecules, it becomes highly difficult to know which layer goes where.

My best tip is to be strict about the process, not to look for any shortcuts, and work corner by corner. Moreover, do not try the 2 by 2 project before you fold the single molecule a few times, and do not try this project before you do the 2 by 2 project several times!

Once it's all done, you can pinch the center of the molecule, forcing a Waterbomb base, to have the 3D version.

Above and Beyond—An 8 by 8 Project

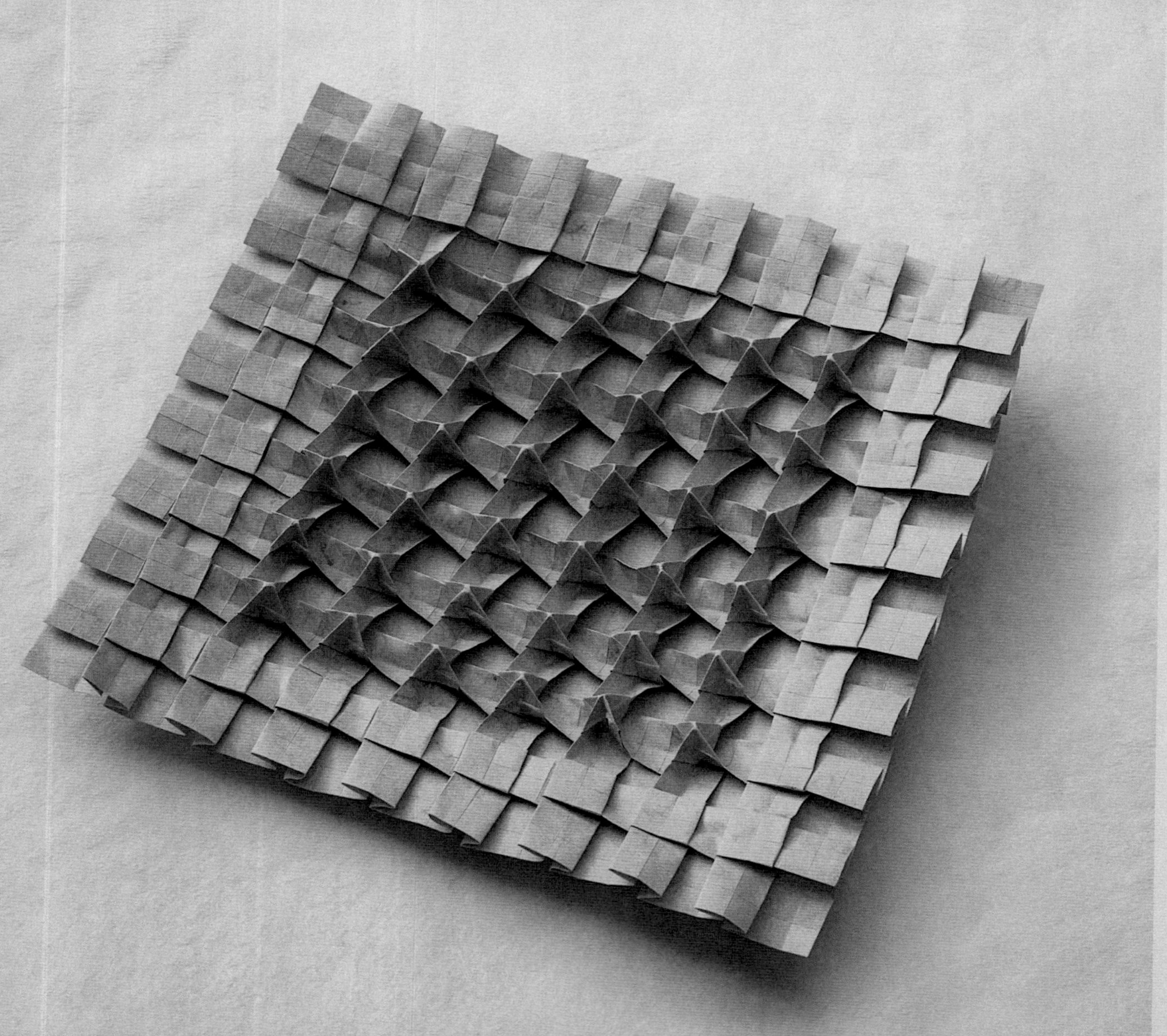

7 2 Mexico

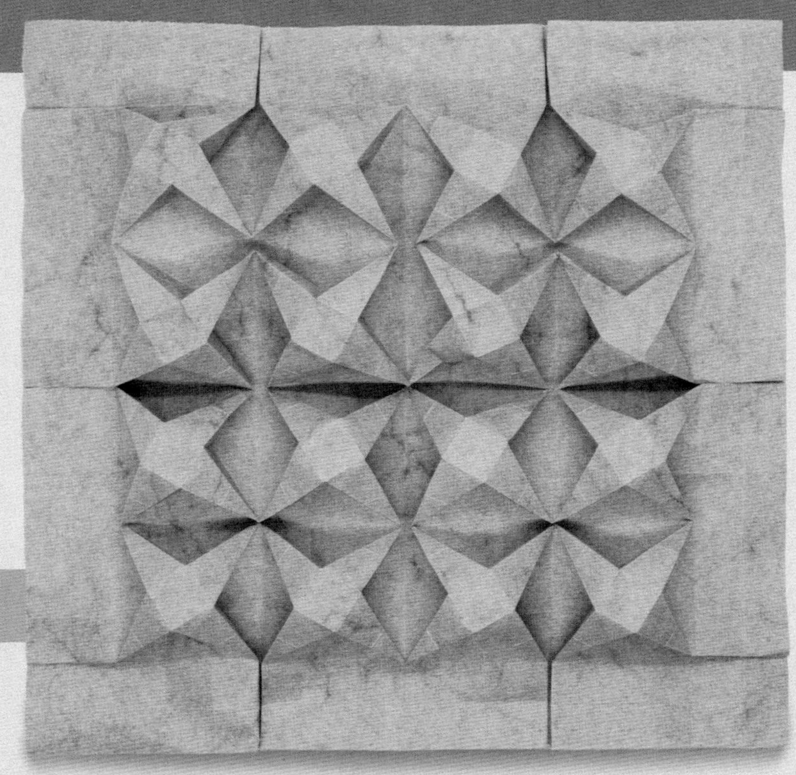

I designed this molecule for the Mexican convection, 2018. Having a square in the center may cause you to think it's another member of the cube family, but since it rotates just a little, and the mechanism is more like a twist, it does not belong there.

The Single Molecule

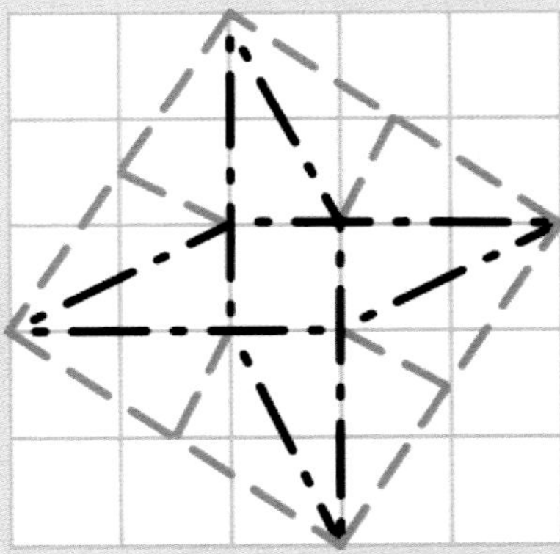

The molecule size is 5 by 5.

It is based on a twist fold and using the extra paper it gives you to create the truncated pyramid-like construction.

The shrinkage ratio is 5:3.

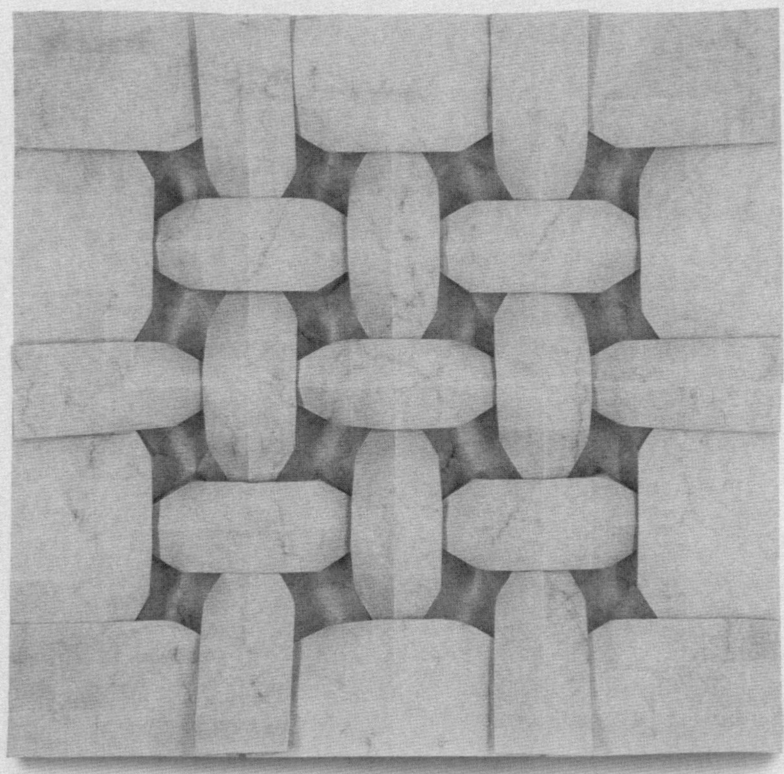

Top: recto view of a 4 by 4–molecule Mexico tessellation.

Bottom: verso view of a 4 by 4–molecule Mexico tessellation.

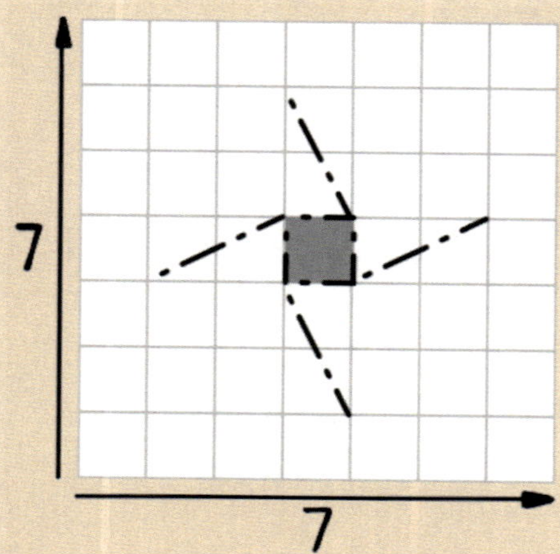

Start with a grid of 7 by 7.

Mountain-fold 2-unit diagonals out of the center square.

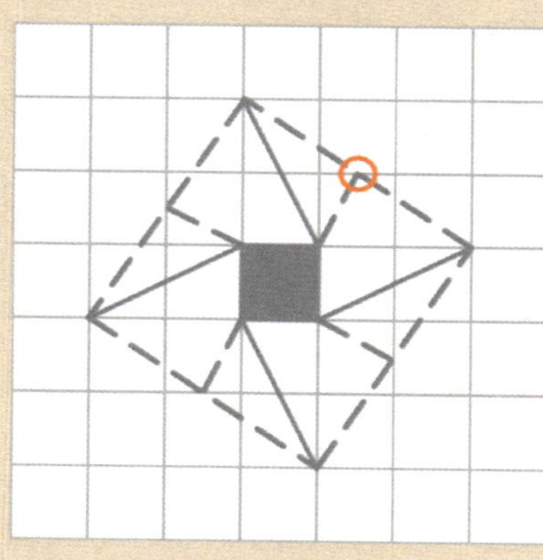

Add a tilted square as valleys.

Add four valley folds from the corners of the center square to the marked intersection! Please notice this is the middle of the outer square's edge! Do not be tempted to go more to the right or to the left (there are more intersections on this valley fold, and it **will** confuse you!)

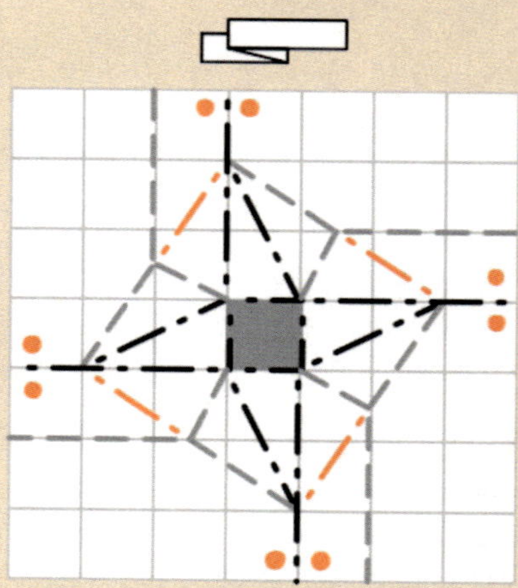

The complete CP.

Reverse the orange portion of the outer square to mountain folds.

Start the collapse by pinching the mountains reaching the edges of the paper, and pleat them as shown.

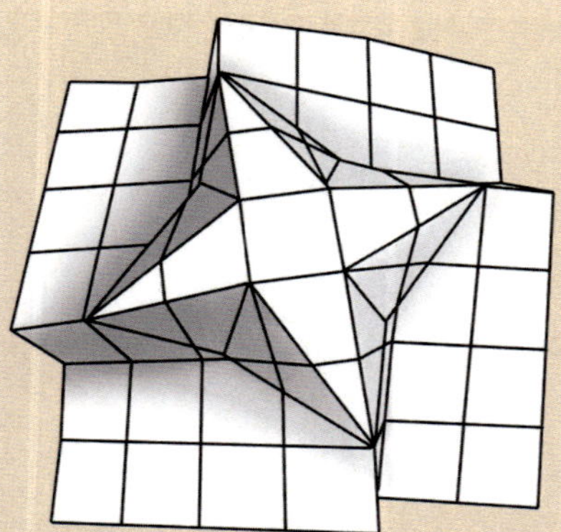

In process.

Make sure the center square is rising, while you rotate it counterclockwise.

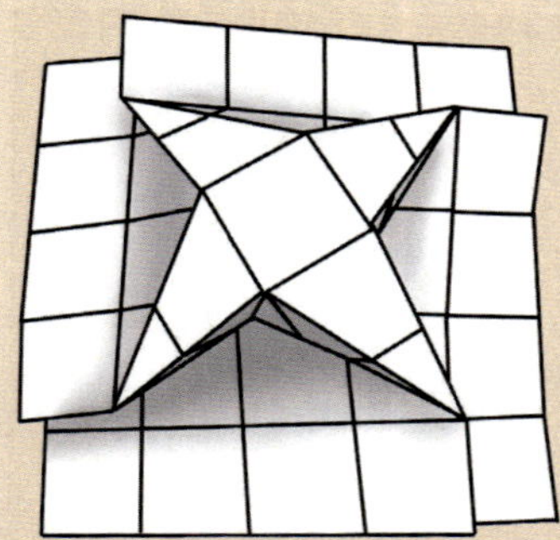

Fully collapsed.

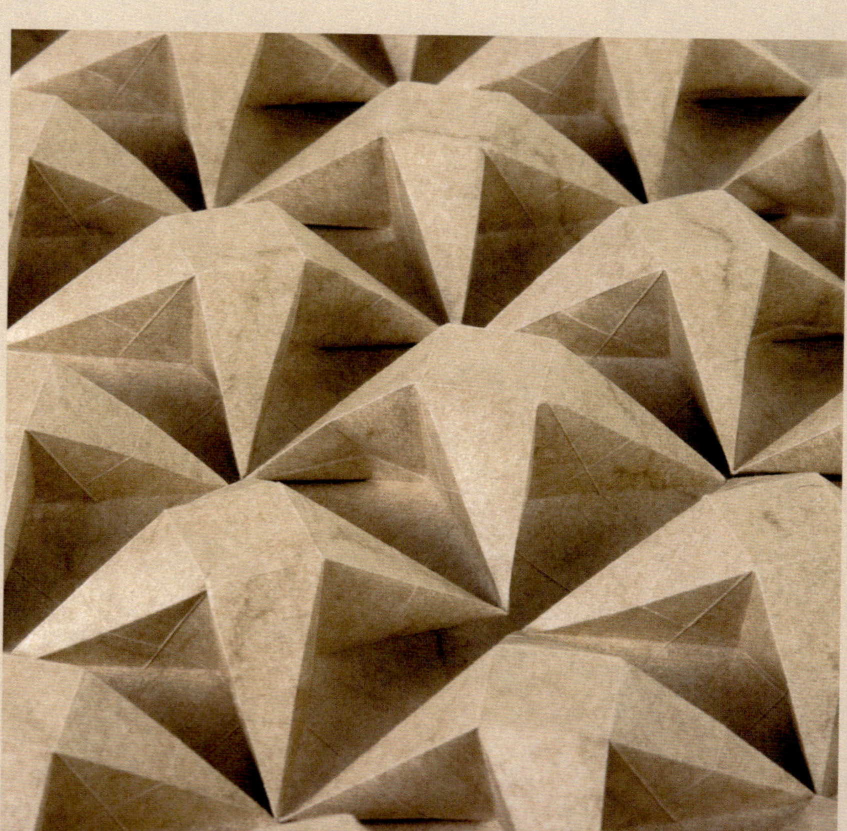

2 by 2 Molecules

Use a grid of 12 by 12.

Focus on the corners of the tilted square. Make sure to keep the center square high when you rotate the paper, and work on two molecules at once. It is easier to work on all the pleats on the edges and then to complete the inner ones.

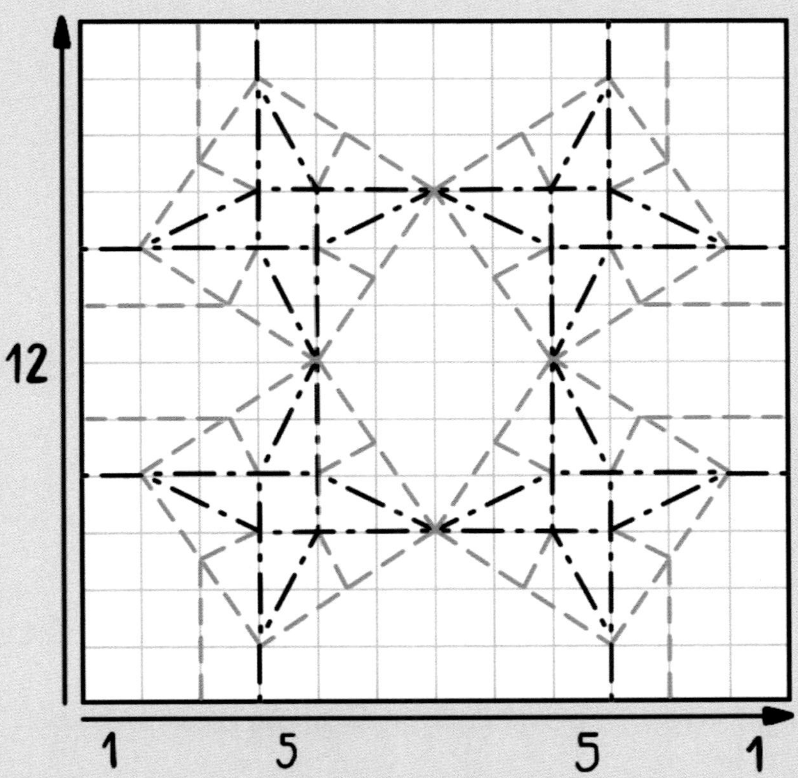

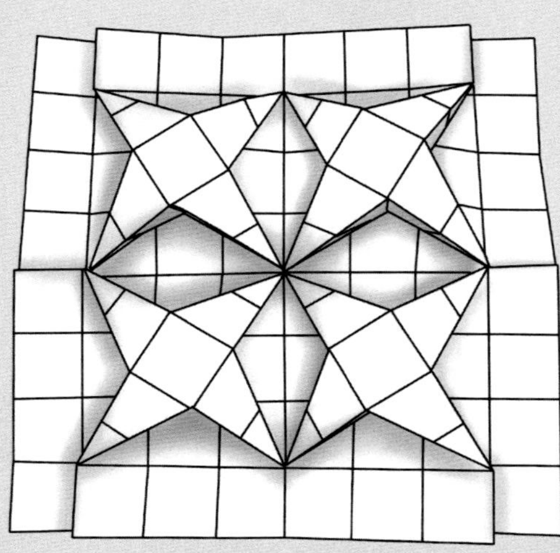

4 by 4 Molecules

Make a grid of 24 by 24, which will allow for a two-unit frame.

The formula for the grid is 2 + 4 × 5 + 2 = 24.

The final result will be 16 squares wide.

Mark the orange diagonals first. When you have all of them, turn the paper and mark the tilted squares, making sure you get the blue diamonds.

Only then add the short valleys. Make sure you meet the center of the tilted-square edges and not any other crease intersection.

Collapse row by row, working on pairs of molecules. You can also try to work on all the edges first, and then complete the inner molecules.

Keep the center squares up, by pushing them from behind with your fingers.

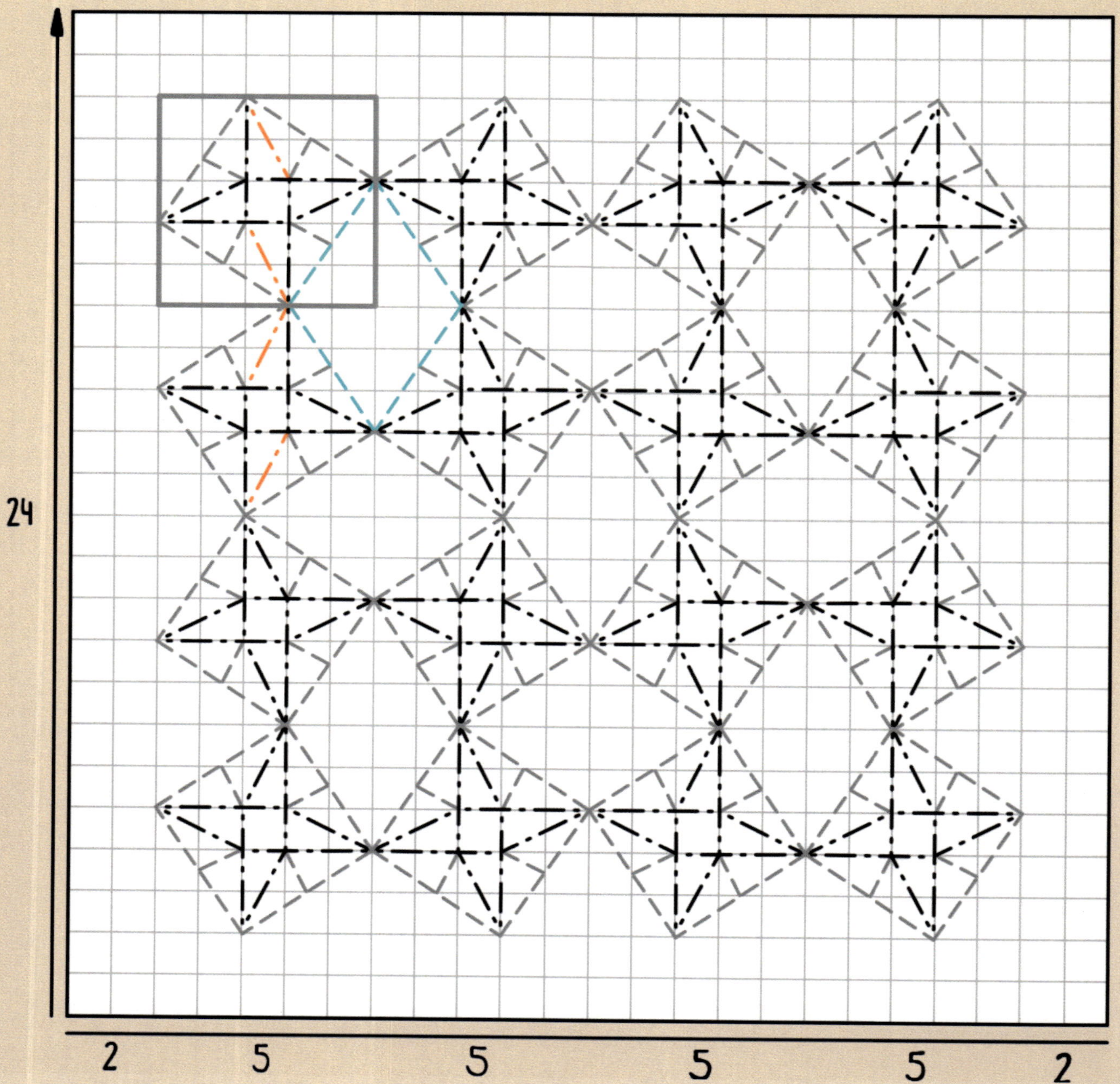
24
2
5
5
5
5
2

7 3 Hidden Garden

This design has a secret beauty, discovered only on one side. The backside is all messy and ugly, but once you turn it over, you find the hidden flowers.

There are two versions of this design. The original has curvy lines and is more natural. In the second, all the curves are creased, and the result is more structured.

The original version is hard to collapse, and the backside is too ugly to be presented. Nevertheless, the front side will flourish, so do not worry too much about how well-defined is the backside. See another angle on page 153.

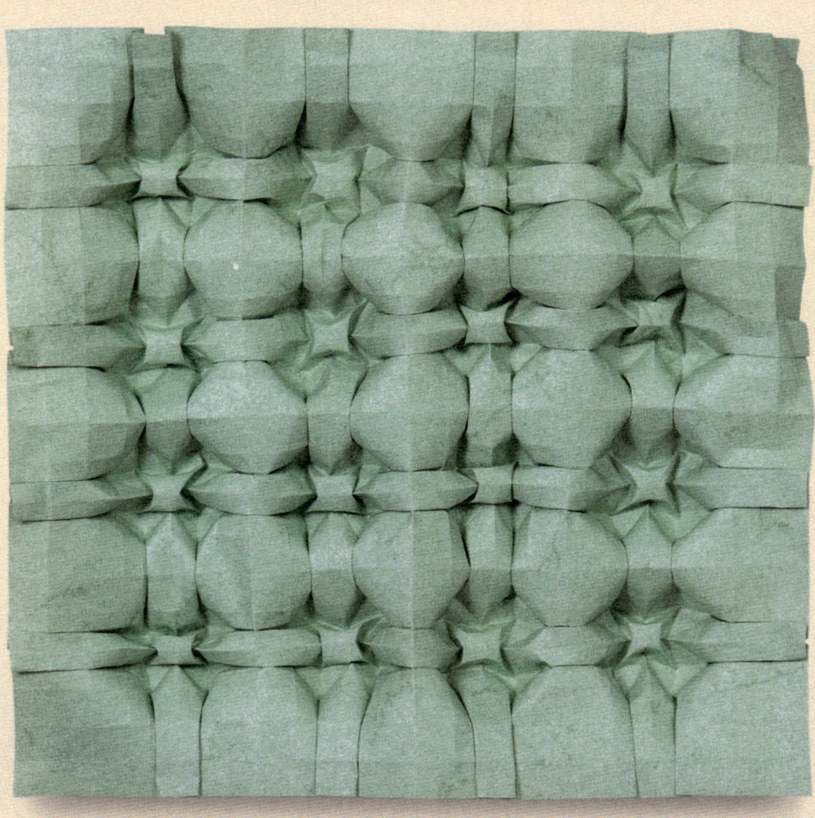

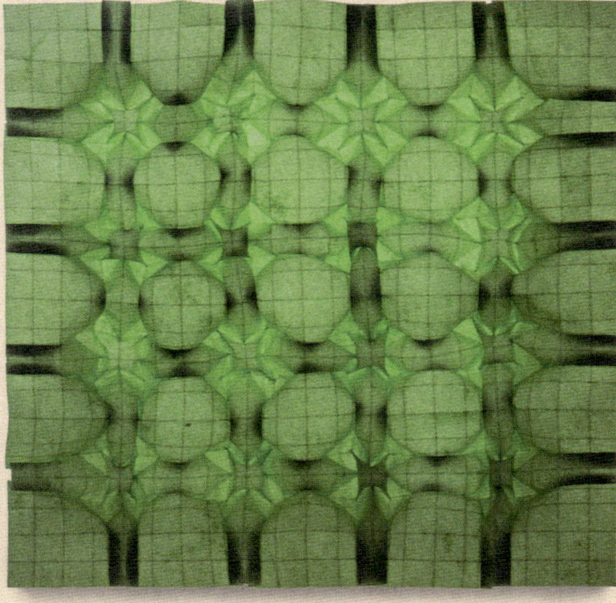

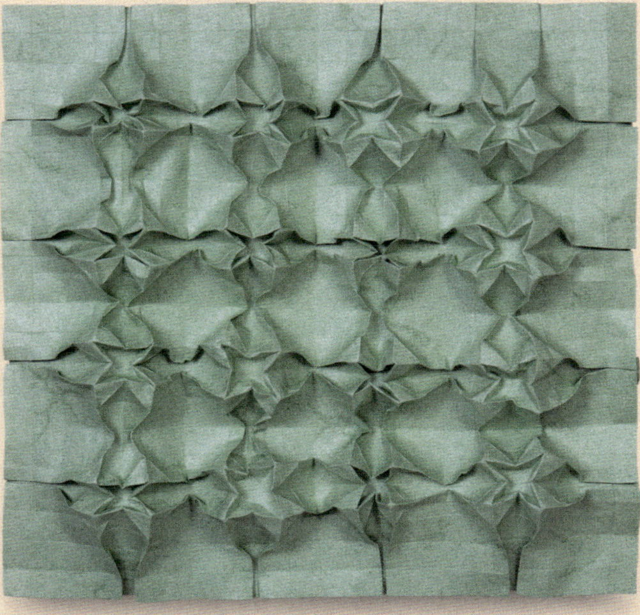

Top right: recto view of a 4 by 4–molecule Hidden Garden tessellation.
Bottom right: verso view of a 4 by 4–molecule Hidden Garden tessellation.
Left: recto view with back-light.

The Single Molecule

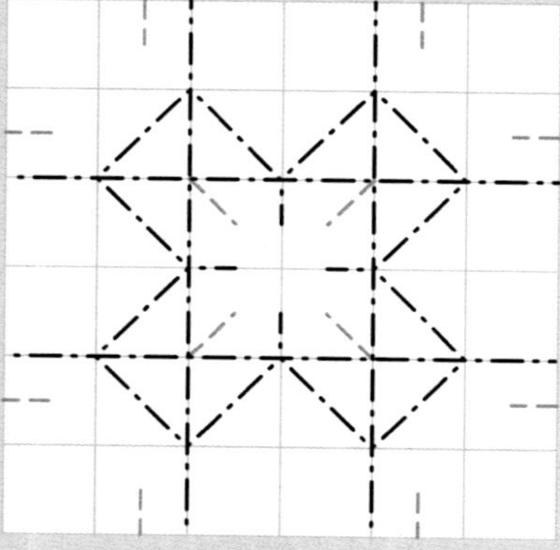

The molecule size is 6 by 6. It is based on a tilted cross made by mountains.

The CP shows the back side of the molecule. This molecule is unique. Some reference points are located in the center of a unit, and not on the grid. Of course, you can add those lines to be more accurate, but to complete the natural version this accuracy is not needed.

The shrinkage ratio is 3:2.

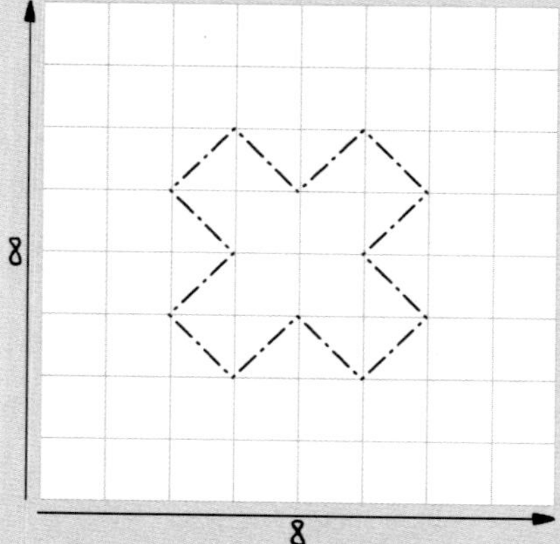

Start with a grid of 8 by 8, to allow extra rows and columns on all four sides.

Mark with mountains the cross shape.

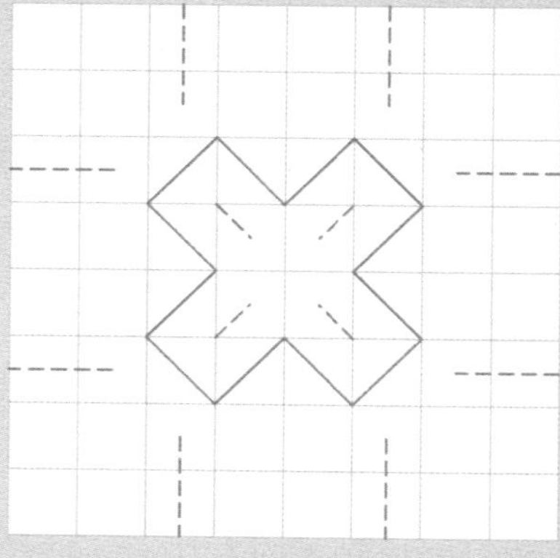

Add four valleys inside the cross. Note they do not reach the center, but stop halfway. These creases will form the flower.

Add more valleys on the outer rims of the molecule. Having those creases is not enough to go for a 16-grid, so you have no reference to ending them. Yet, you don't have to be highly accurate, just try to reach the center of a unit.

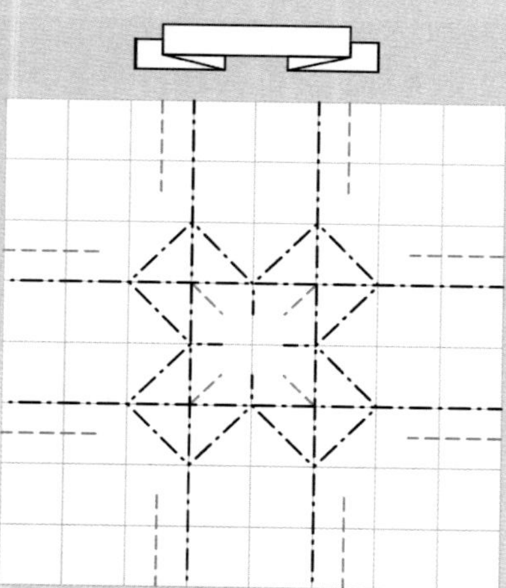

All the needed creases.

Start the collapse by following the zig-zag pattern on the four sides. While doing so, bring up the four sides of the cross to create four pyramids, using the valleys as well.

Sink the center.

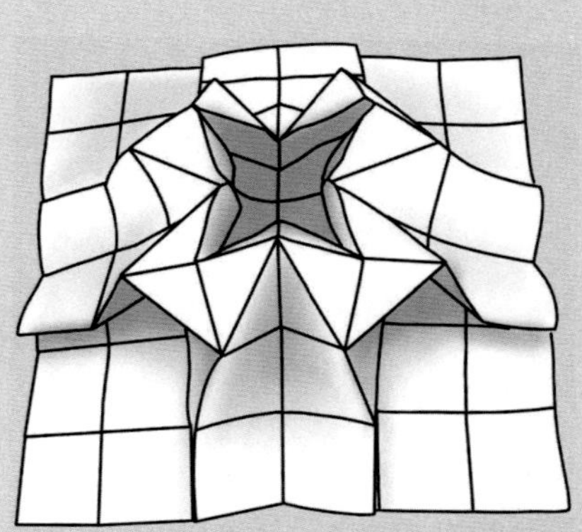

Fully collapsed.
Turn over.

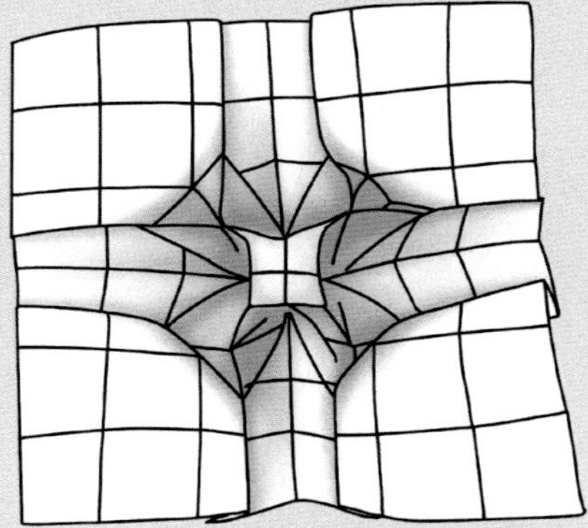

A flower is revealed. Note that the flower is a squashed waterbomb base. The squash is made by stretching the paper, without any pre-creases, so you will not get even results in the next molecule.

Alternative Molecule

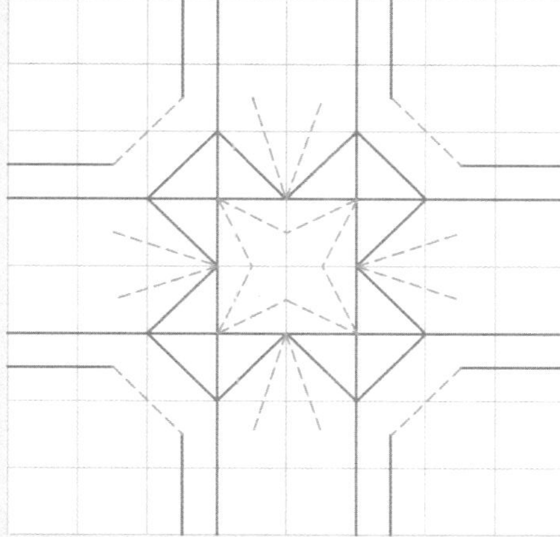

If you prefer sharp edges, or you find the original one as too hard to collapse, start with this version! All that is curved in the original molecule is firmly creased here. Again, the valleys have no marked endpoints, so try to guesstimate the unit's centers.

2 by 2 Molecules

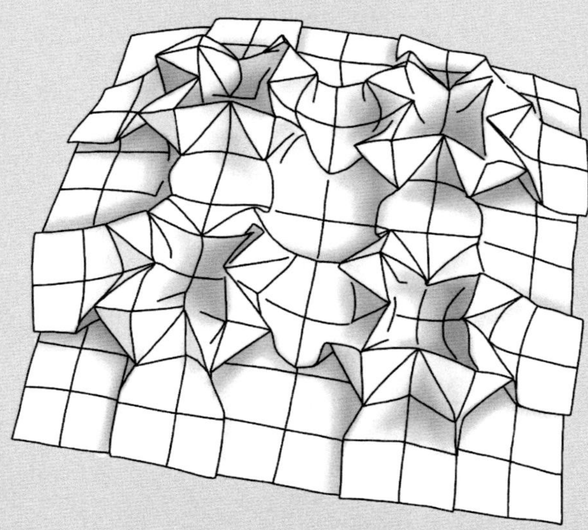

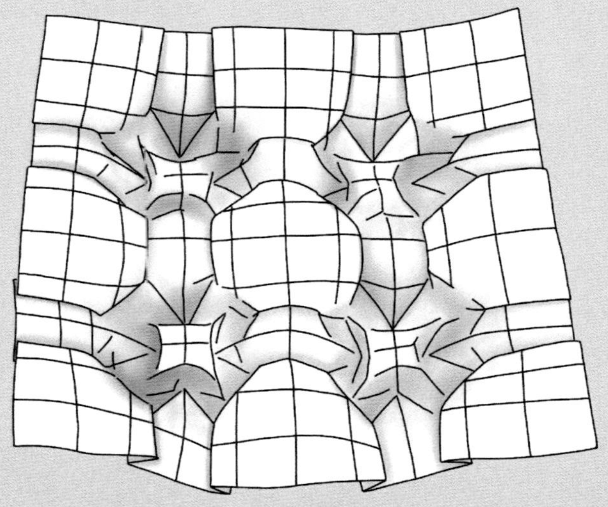

Use a grid of 14 by 14.

Start with the edges, and arrange all the layers accordingly. Form the little pyramids of each molecule, and sink the centers.

Focus your efforts on the valleys between the molecules. This will force the model to be flat.

Try not to mark sharp creases to maintain the curves that create the flowers.

Once you are done with the collapse, consider flipping all the pleats between the molecules, so they face each other. This can help keep the structure firm.

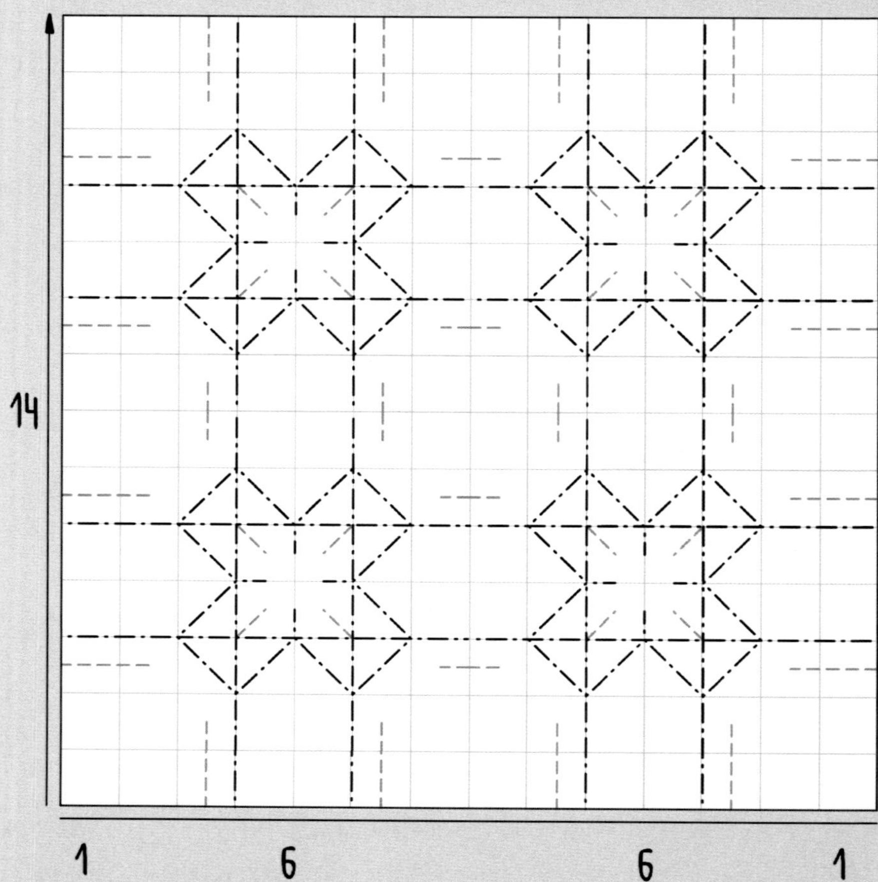

4 by 4 Molecules

Make a grid of 28 by 28, allowing for a two-unit width of a frame.

The formula for the grid is 2 + 4 × 6 + 2 = 28.

The final result will be 20-square wide.

Start the pre-creases with the crosses. You can do them in two swipes, creasing all the parallel orange lines in each direction at once, and then rotate the paper and complete the rest.

Next, add the valleys, in light blue. They go in between the crosses.

Last, add the short valleys inside each molecule.

Start the collapse at the corner and complete row by row. Hold the edges with pins, since you do not crease some of the folds, and this creates tension in the paper. The secret to success is to control the inner pleats, between the molecules. It is hard to pleat, but it is doable! This pleat brings up the four corners of the cross.

The corners of the cross tend to break and fall. This is natural, you will be able to fix it in the end.

Once you are done with the collapse, consider flipping all the pleats between the molecules, so they face each other. This can help keep the structure firm.

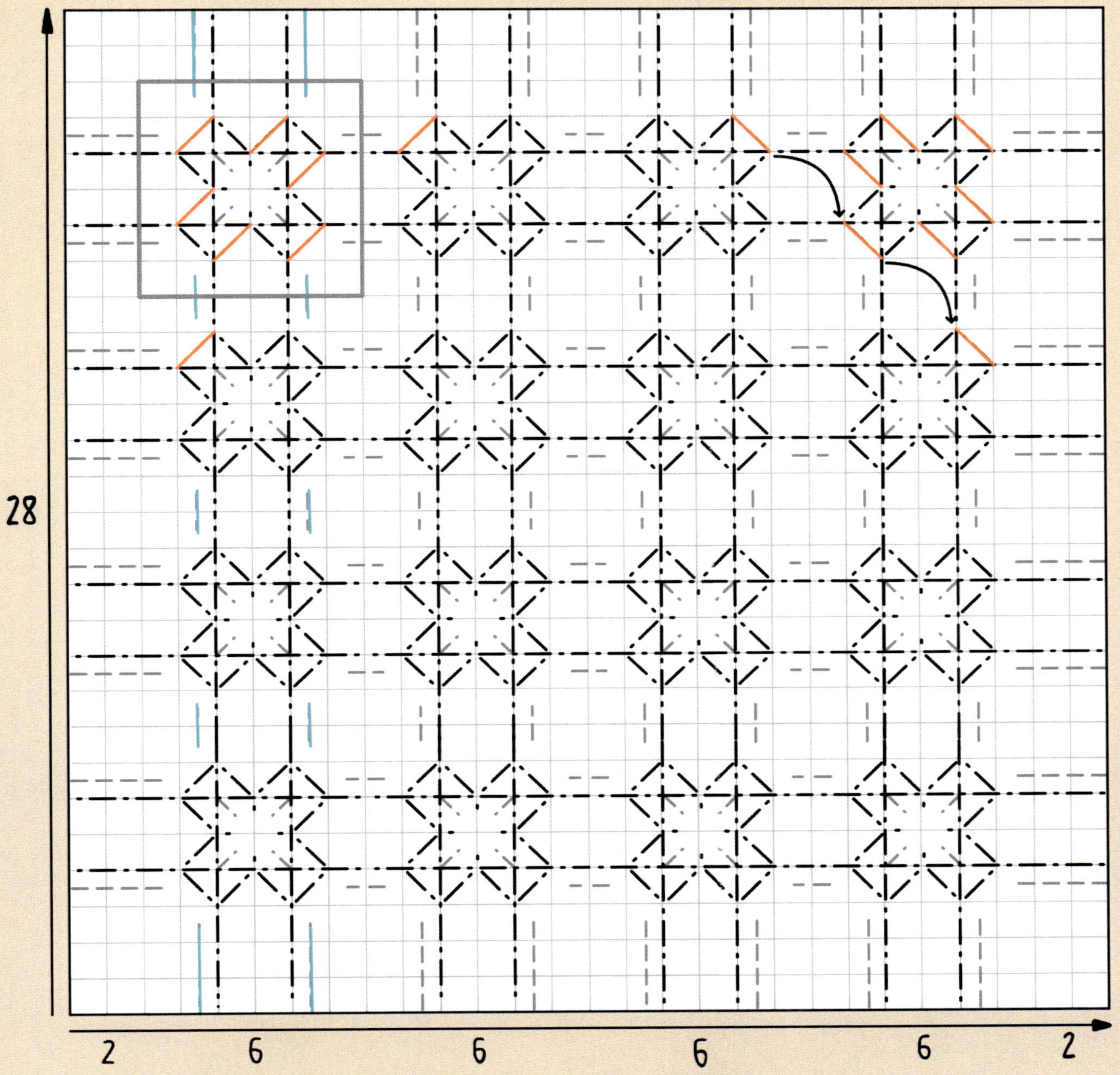

28

2 6 6 6 6 2

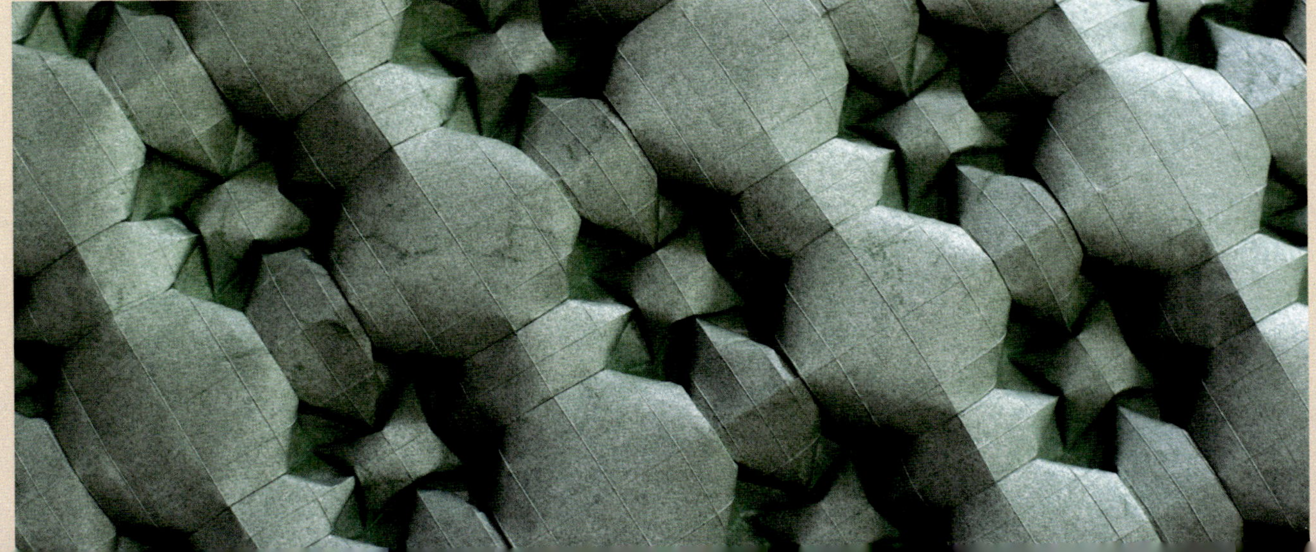

7 4 Bow-Tie

Not until I wrote this book
I realized two of my models have the same molecule!
I even named them differently.

The molecule is simple, based on two tilted squares, one inside the other. The models can stay flat, but I think the volume does bring an extra edge to the design. It really looks like intersected tubes.

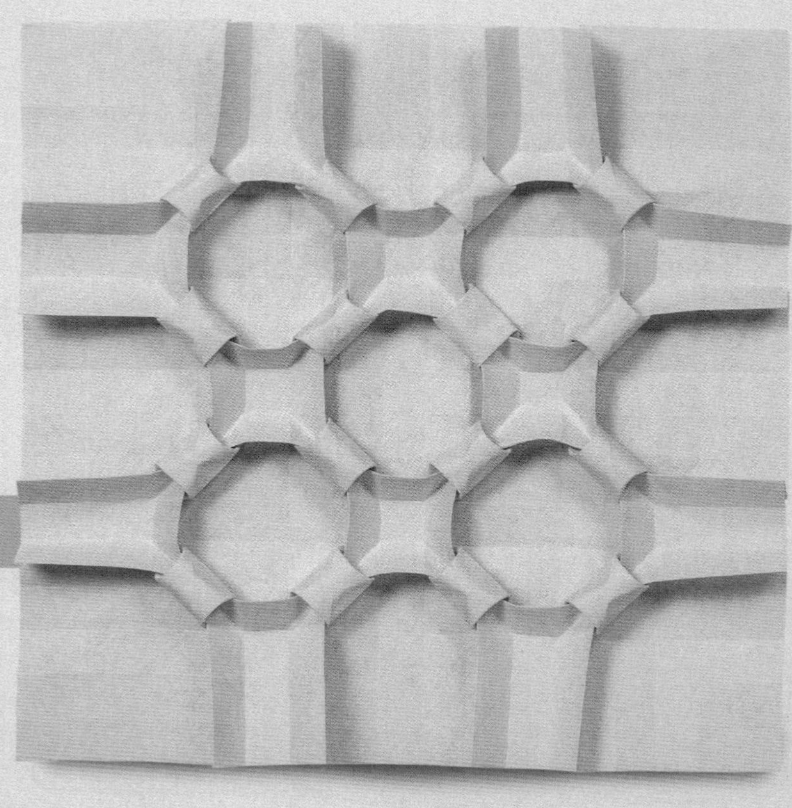

The Single Molecule

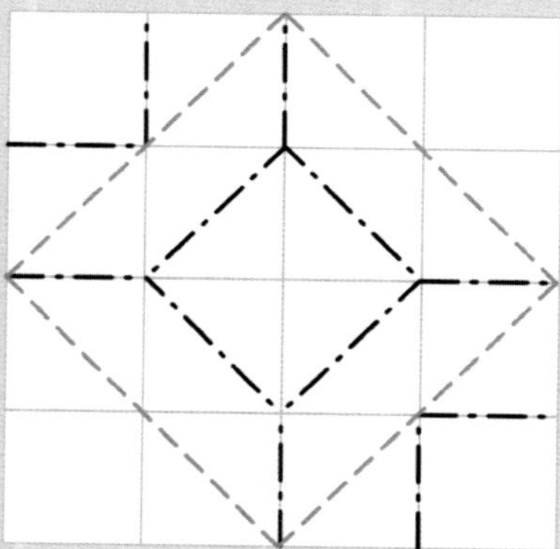

The molecule size is 4 by 4.

The molecule is the opposite of the **Red Flower** tessellation (see my first book, *Origami Tessellations for Everyone*).
It is made of two tilted squares, the outer is a valley, and the inner is a mountain. Since it is not symmetric on all four sides, the result is a diagonal pattern, which means every two adjacent molecules must be mirrored to connect.

The shrinkage ratio is 2:1.

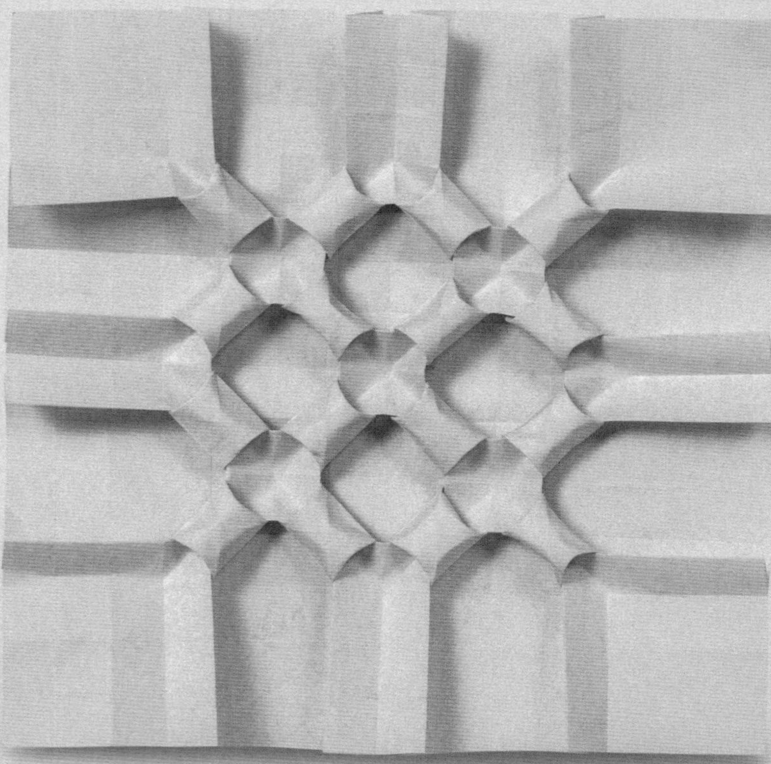

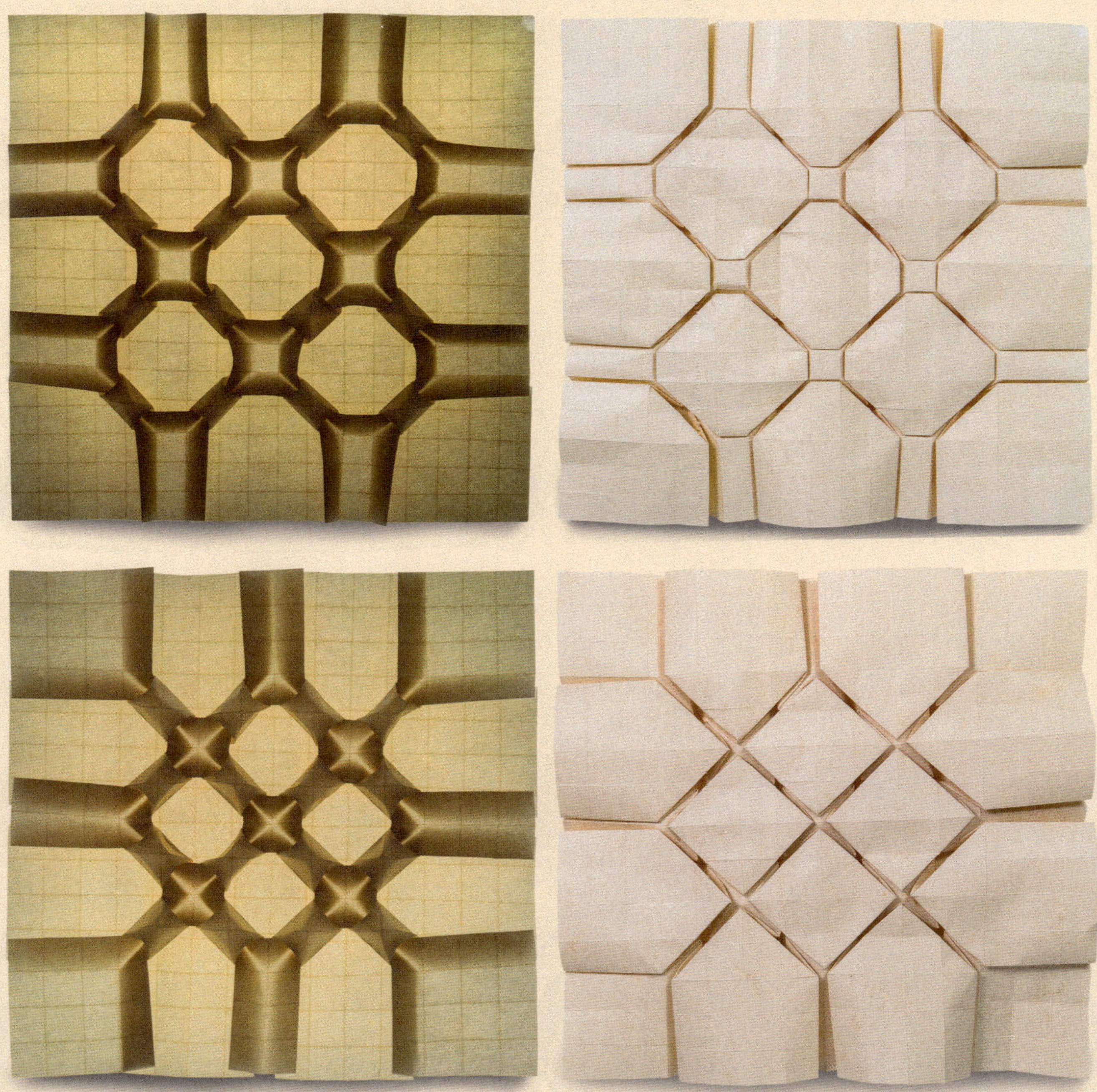

Top left: recto view of a 4 by 4–molecule Circle the Square tessellation.

Bottom left: recto view of a 4 by 4–molecule Bow-Tie tessellation.

Top center: back-light view of a 4 by 4–molecule Circle the Square tessellation.

Bottom center: back-light view of a 4 by 4–molecule Bow-Tie tessellation.

Top right: verso view of a 4 by 4–molecule Circle the Square tessellation.

Bottom right: verso view of a 4 by 4–molecule Bow-Tie tessellation.

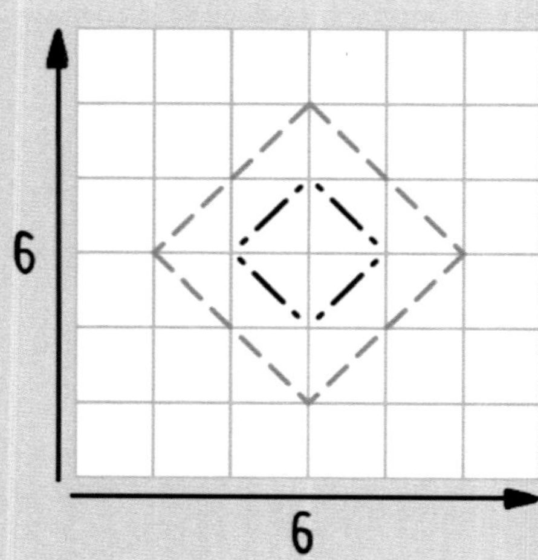

Start with a grid of 6 by 6.
Mark the inner square as a mountain.
Add the valleys around this inner square.

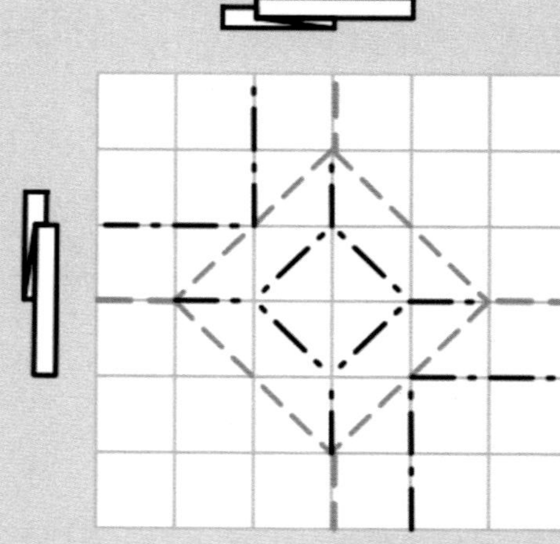

This is the complete set of creases needed. Force them all and start the collapse by pleating as shown on two opposite corners.

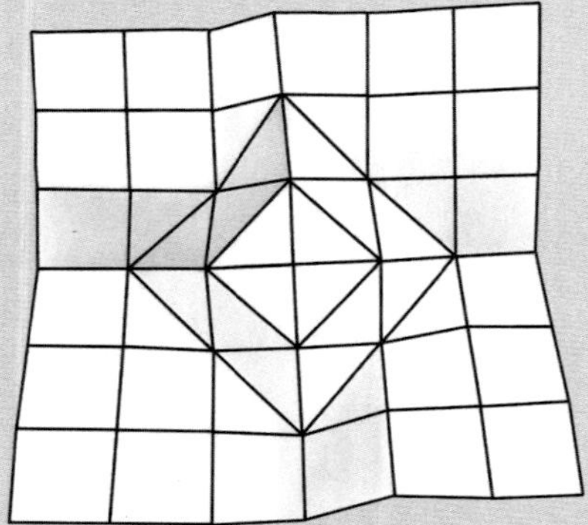

In process. Make sure every two mountains create a corner that will go **under** the inner square during the collapse.

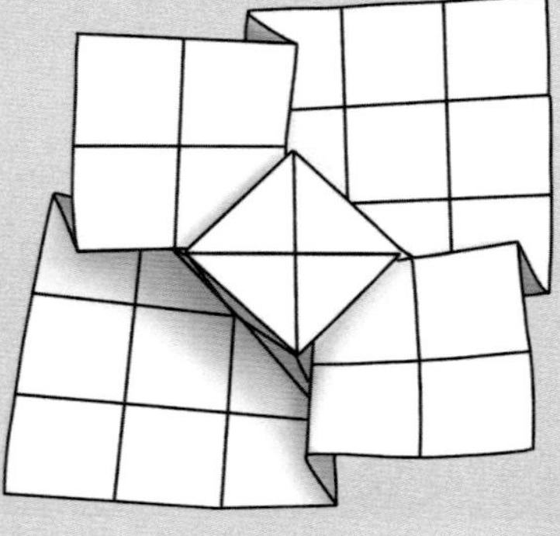

Almost there.

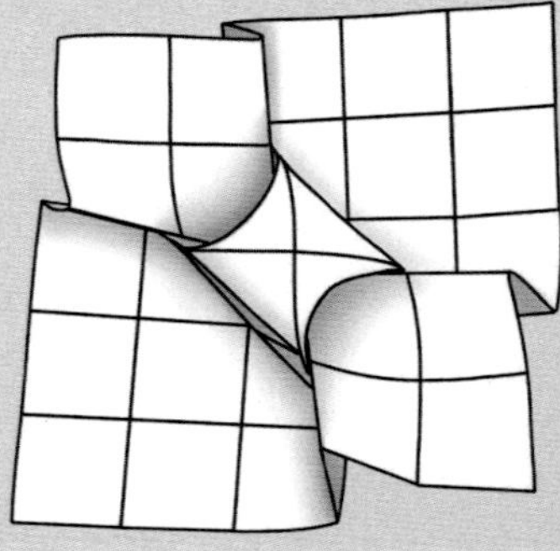

Fully collapsed. The center can stay flat, or be rounded, as shown here.

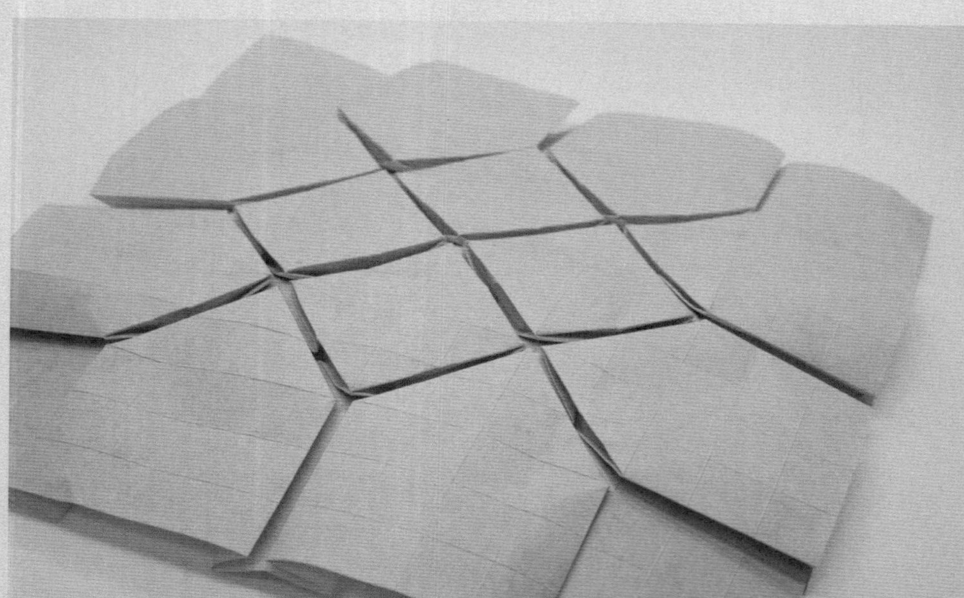

The back-side image can help you understnad the way to collapse the molecule.

2 by 2 Molecules

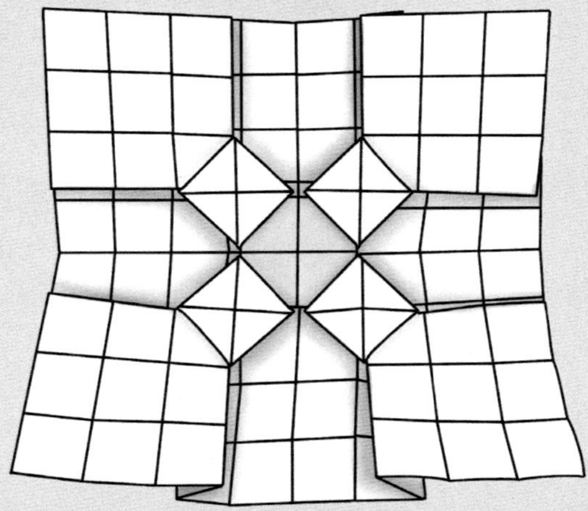

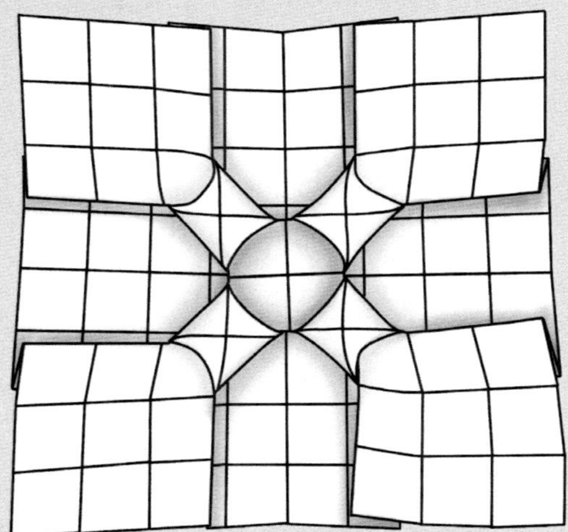

Use a grid of 12 by 12. Start by pleating the top edge. Now form the first row of molecules, starting with the top left corner.

Continue with the second row, again, by forcing the pleats on the edges. Turn over the model and make sure there are four corners pointing to the center. This will ensure the right layering of the molecules and allow the puffing part.

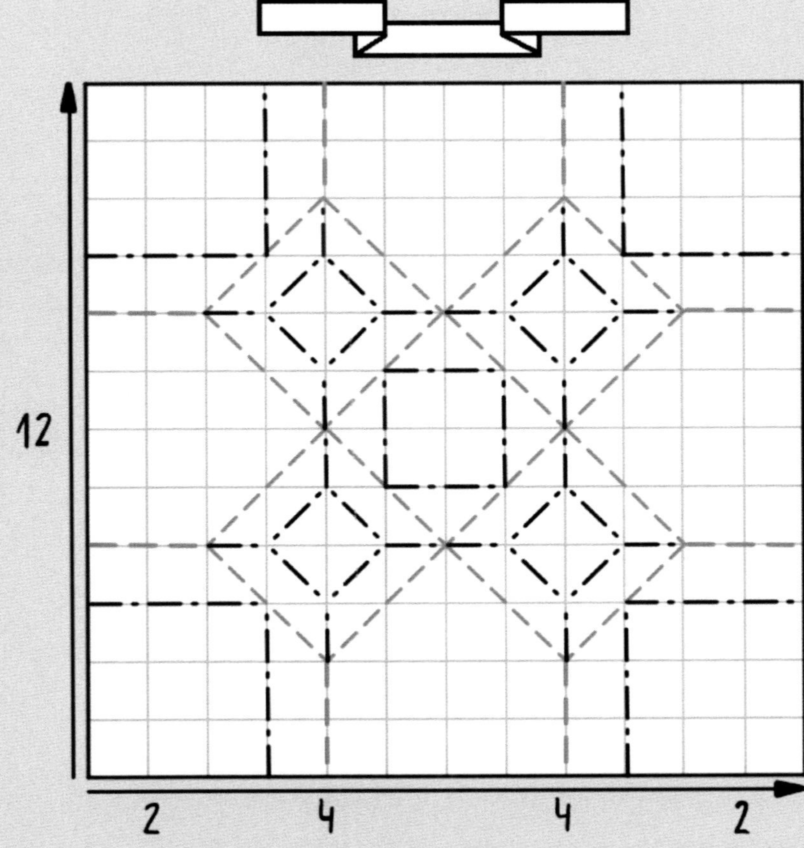

4 by 4 Molecules

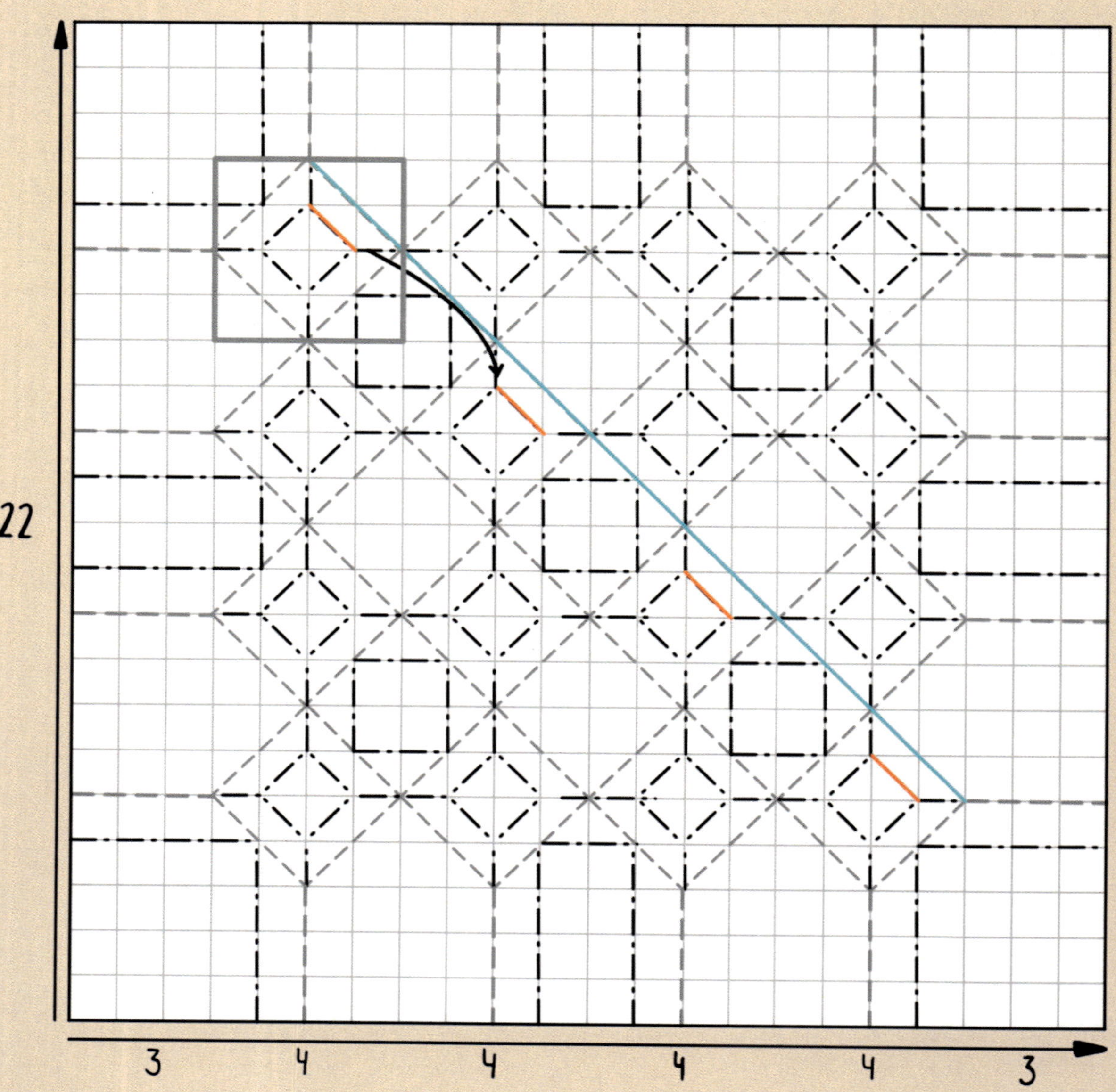

Make a grid of 22 by 22. A two-square width of a frame is nice for this model.

The formula for the grid is 3 + 4 × 4 + 3 = 22.

The final result will be 12 squares wide.

Mark the outer tilted squares first. They all align, see the light-blue line as an example.

Now add the inner square, in opposite orientation to the outer ones. The rhythm here is fold a square diagonal, and skip 3.

Collapse is done row by row. Make sure the pleats on the edges are correct.

Every four molecules (around the 2 by 2 square marked with mountains) have on the other side four corners meeting in the center. Check that during the collapse.

Once the collapse is done, puff all the flat squares into tubes.

Circling the Square Variation

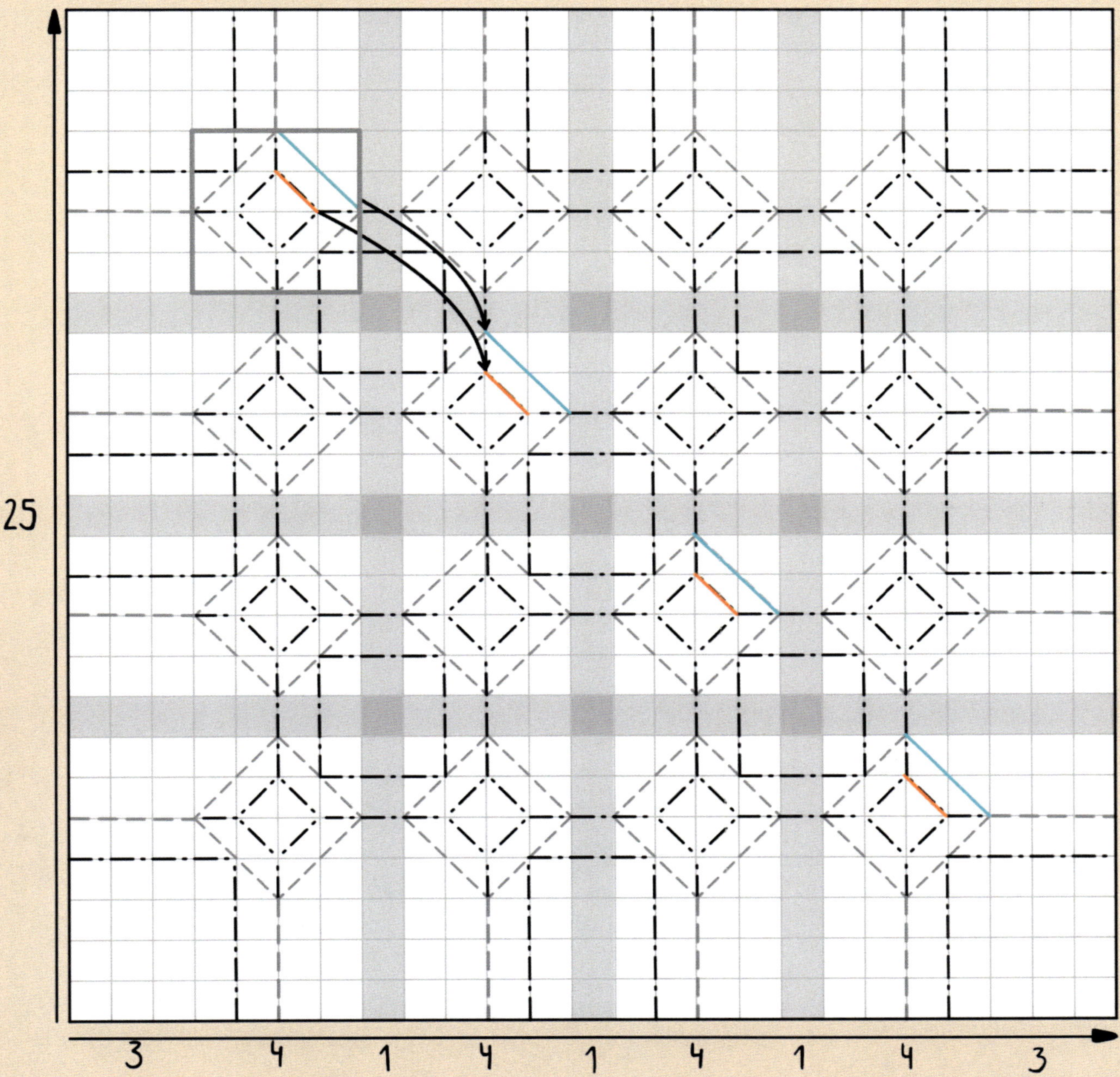

By adding a gap between every two molecules, the pattern looks like circles emerging out of the square grid!

The grid now is bigger by three squares.

Note that the light-blue lines are not aligned anymore. Now the pattern for them is fold 2, skip 3.

The collapse is easier than the original variation.

7 5 Saigon

This tessellation was found while I was in Vietnam, traveling. It is based on a hidden twist. I never tried this pattern without a space between every two molecules, but I am sure it's doable!

The Single Molecule

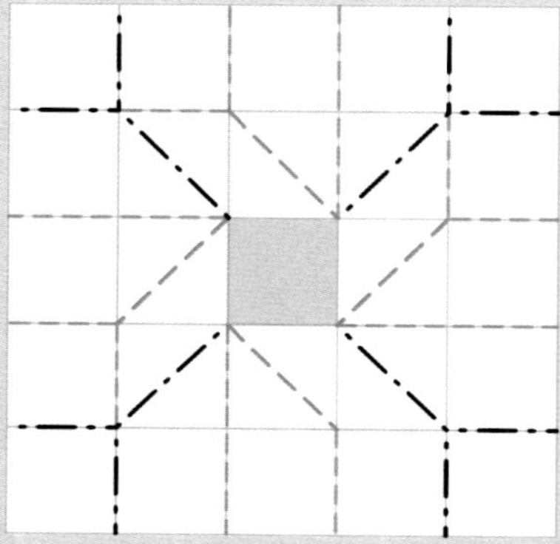

The molecule size is 5 by 5.

It is based on a twist fold on the backside of the paper!

The four valleys around the center square are the trademark of the **Cube** tessellation, but we are going to use it differently here!

The shrinkage ratio is 5:3.

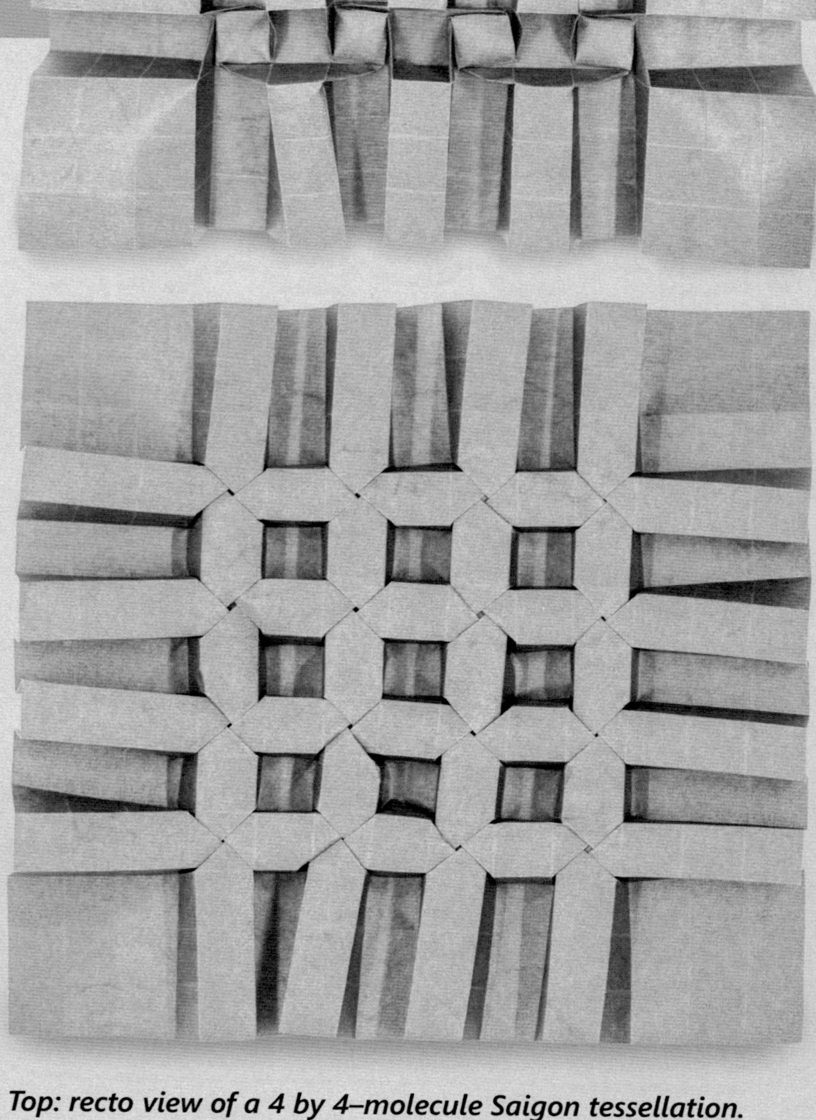

Top: recto view of a 4 by 4–molecule Saigon tessellation.

Bottom: verso view of a 4 by 4–molecule Saigon tessellation.

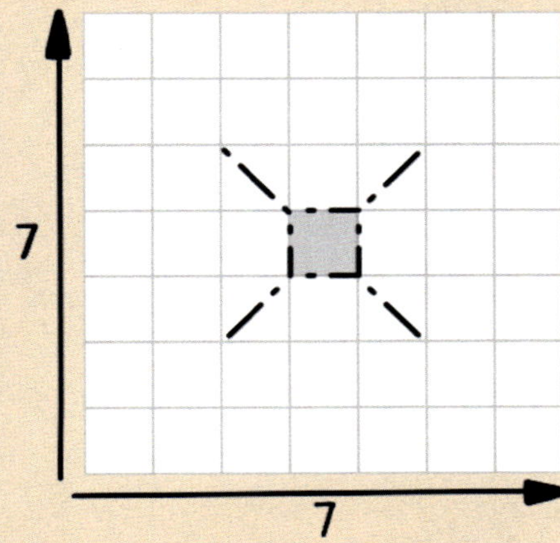

Start with a grid of 7 by 7.

Mountain-fold the diagonals out of the center square.

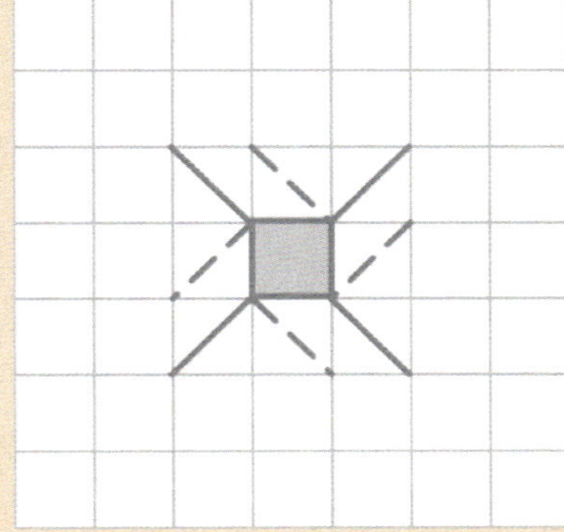

Add four valleys around the square.

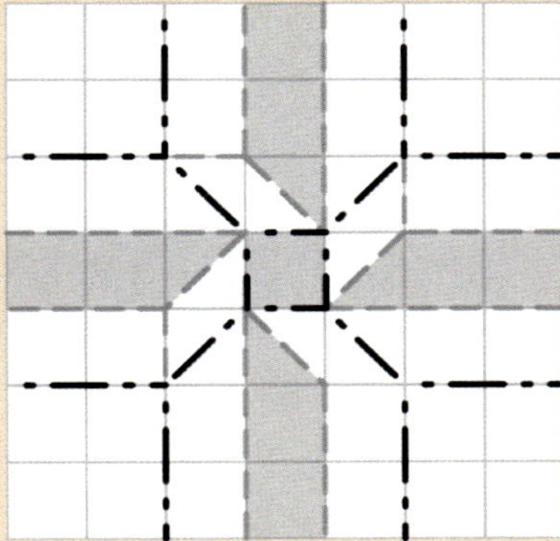

The complete set of folds you need to collapse. This is the backside of the molecule!

The light grey areas will stay at the table level, while the corners will be a square high.

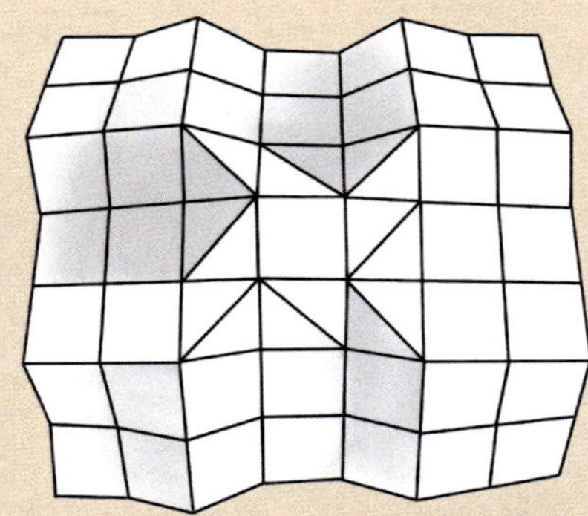

Start the collapse by forcing the four mountain **diagonal** folds. Try to raise the inner square, as a preparation for the twist to come.

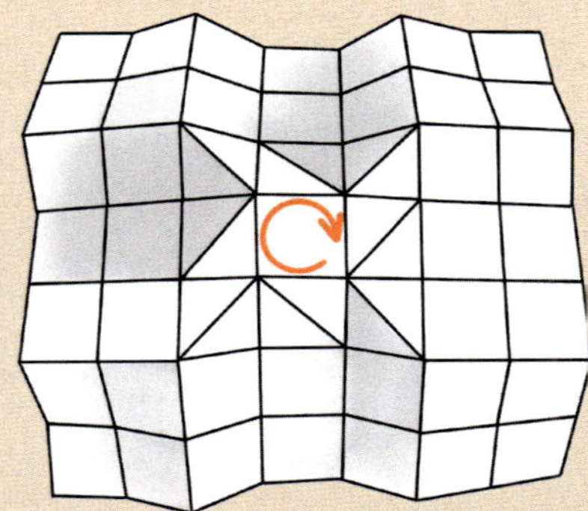

Now twist the center square clockwise. Everything falls into place now! The square drops down to the table level.

Arrange the corners.

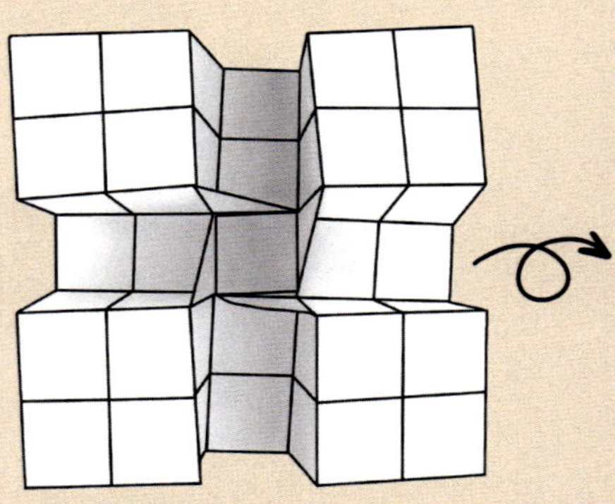

The result. Turn over.

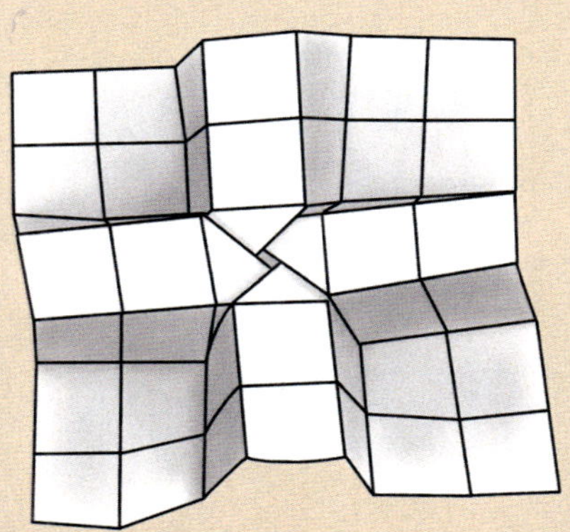

The finished molecule.

2 by 2 Molecules

Use a grid of 11 by 11.

The key point for easy collapse is the twist. In order to make it easier to collapse, make sure you prepare all the diagonals around each square. Do not forget to change the twist direction on the adjacent molecule!

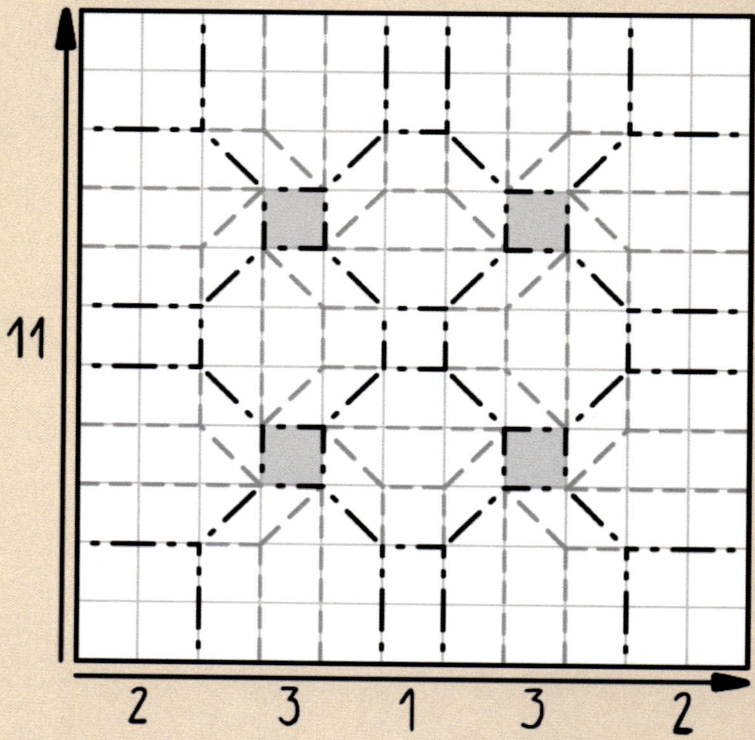

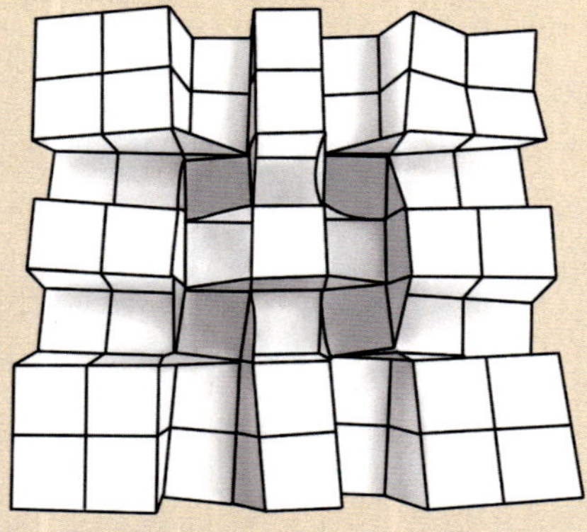

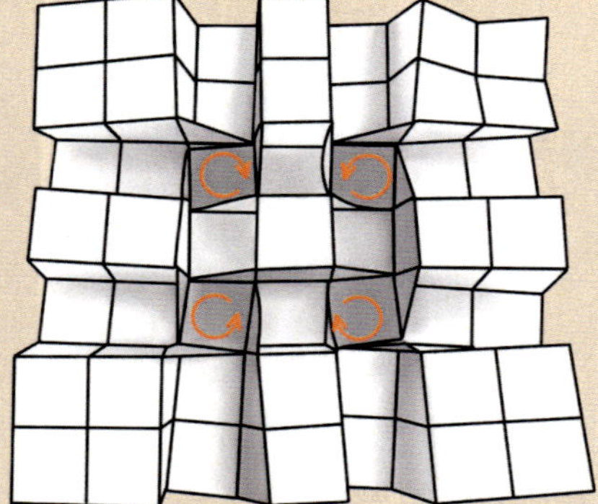

Note that every two adjacent molecules rotate in an opposite direction.

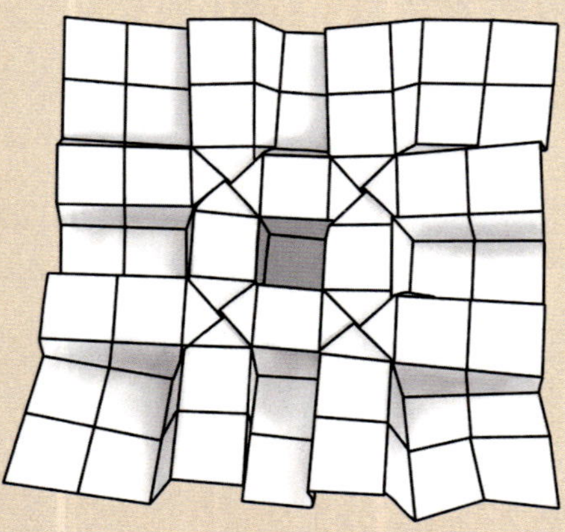

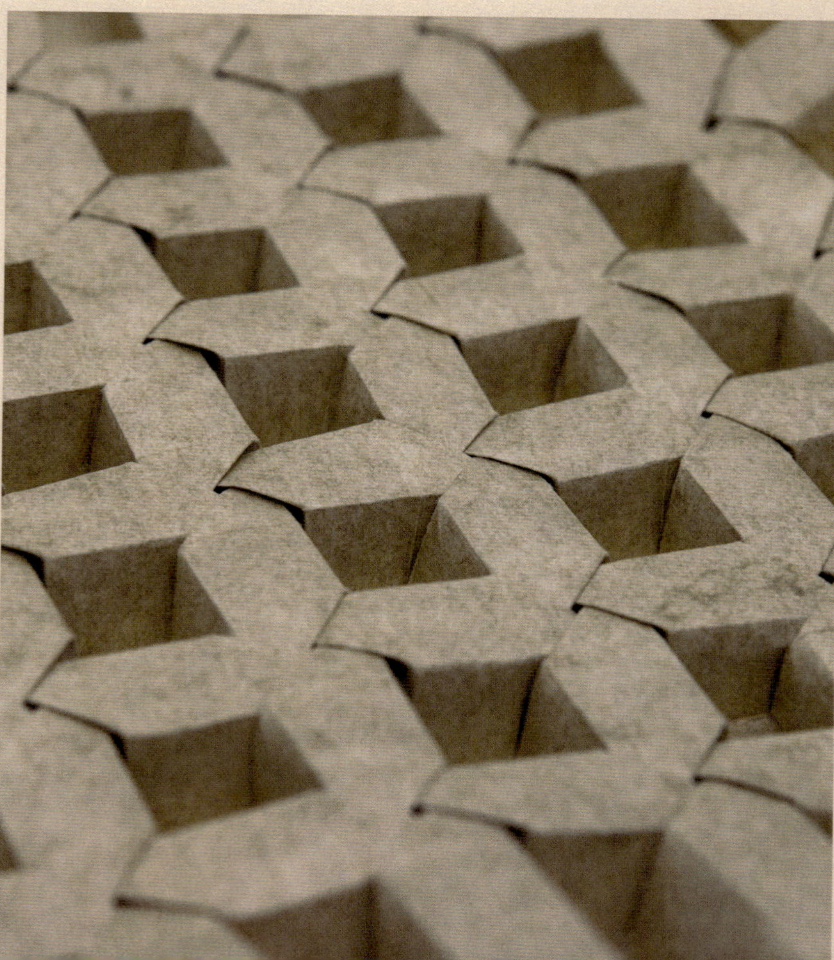

4 by 4 Molecules

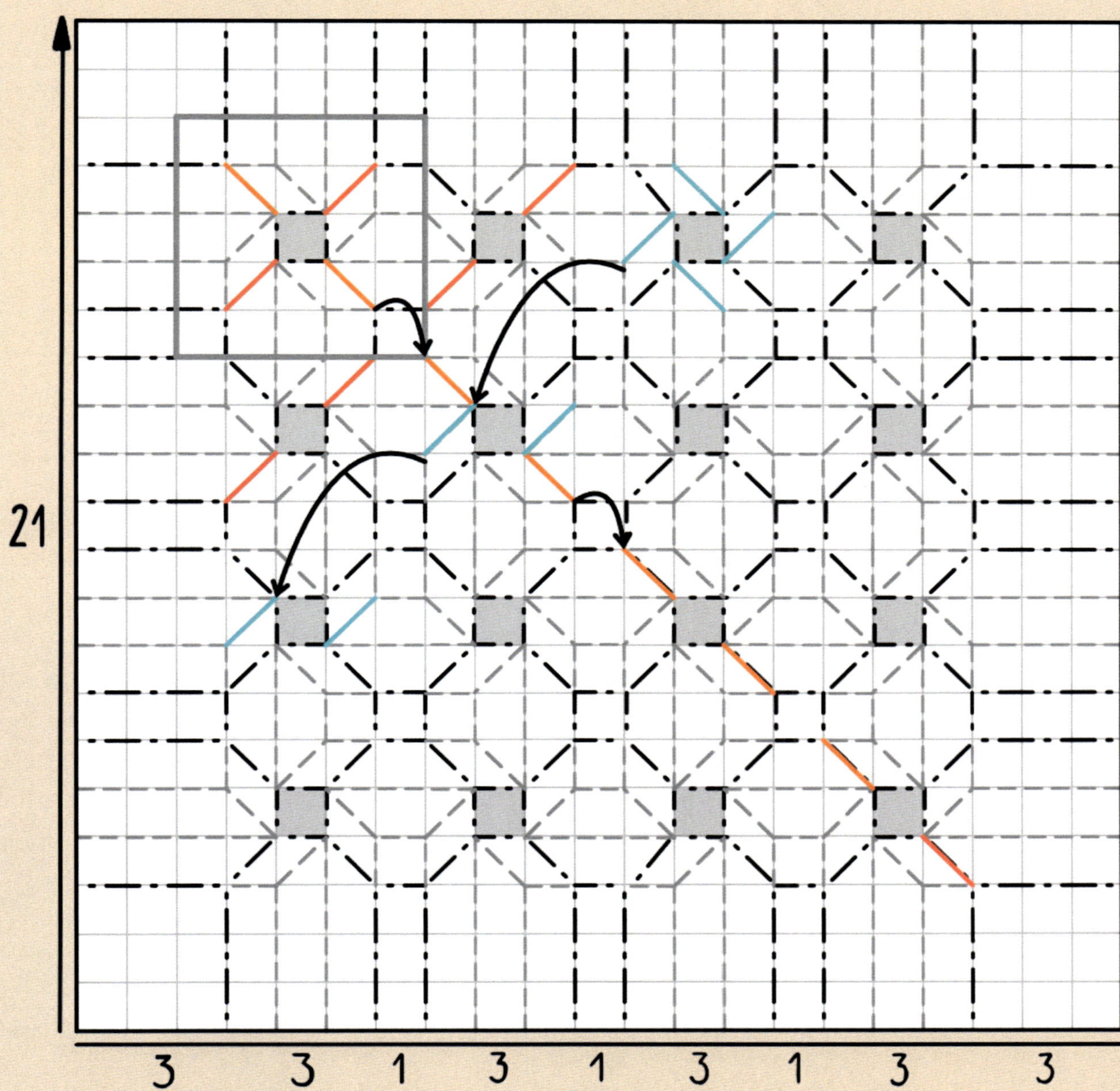

Make a grid of 21 by 21, which will allow for a **three-unit** frame.

The formula for the grid is 3 + 4 × 3 + 3 × 1 + 3 = 21.

The final result will be 13 squares wide.

Note that the outer rim of each molecule overlaps with the adjacent one. Although the single molecule is 5 by 5, I changed the formula to suit the overlapping units.

Mark the orange diagonals first. The pattern is simple, fold one, skip one.

Rotate the paper to complete the diagonals in the other direction.

Now you can make the light blue valleys. Follow the fold-one-skip-three pattern (as with the **Cube** tessellation).

Collapse is done by rows. Remember to change the twist direction as you move to the next molecule.

7 6 Ninja Star

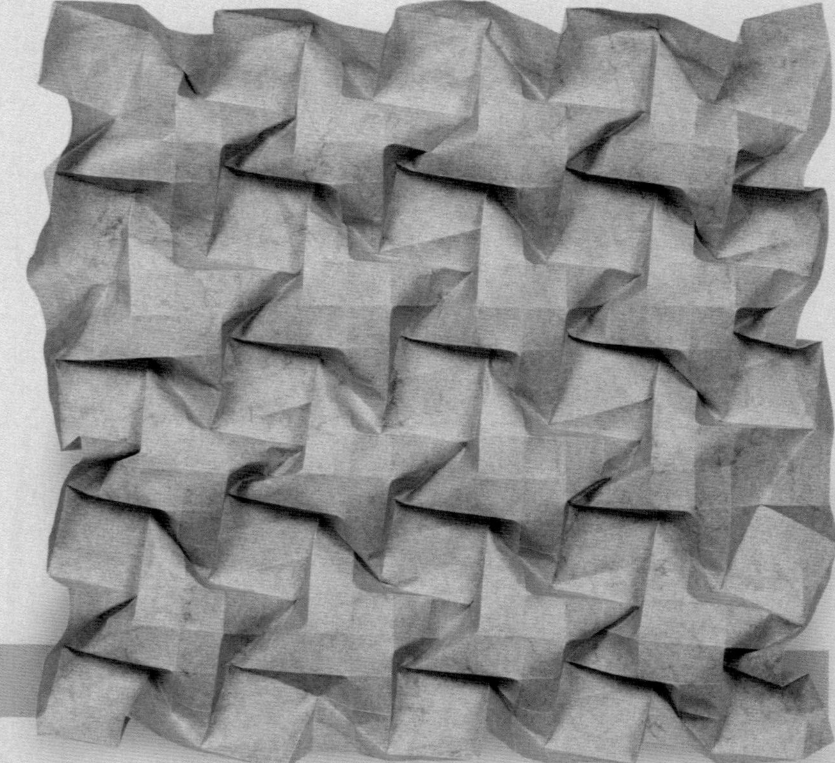

This tessellation was the result of a test: what would happen if I combine a diagonal grid on top of a square one? The new grid had to be other than 45°, which is overused.

I can't remember how I collapsed it, because it is not a natural step, but the result was mesmerizing! This design was chosen to be on the cover of a book about Japanese economy! I was so proud!

The Single Molecule

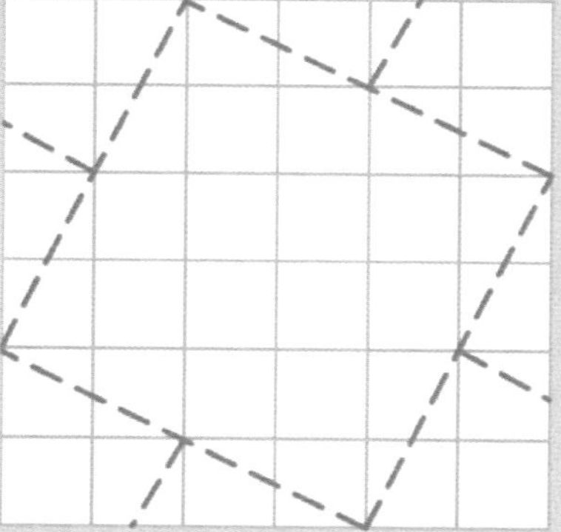

The molecule size is 6 by 6.

It is based on a diagonal grid, using 2:1 rectangles.

The shrinkage ratio is about 5:4.

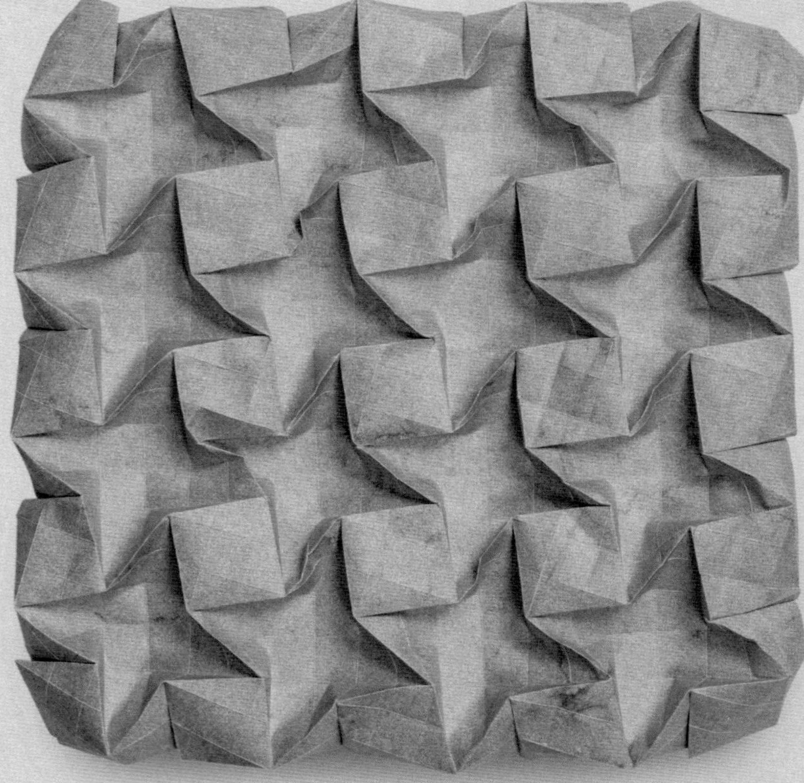

Top: recto view of a 4 by 4–molecule Ninja Star tessellation.

Bottom: verso view of a 4 by 4–molecule Ninja Star tessellation.

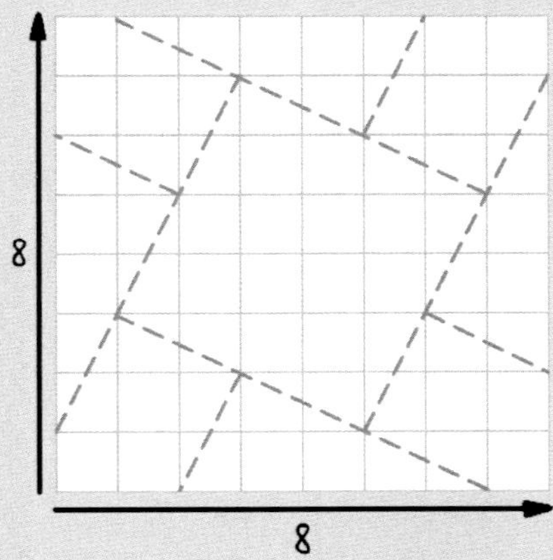

Start with a grid of 8 by 8.

Valley-fold the tilted square, notice that the lines are diagonals of 1:2 rectangles. Continue each line to reach the edge.

Add the valleys, at the same angle, going out from the middle of the square edges. Those lines will form another tilted square when you make more molecules.

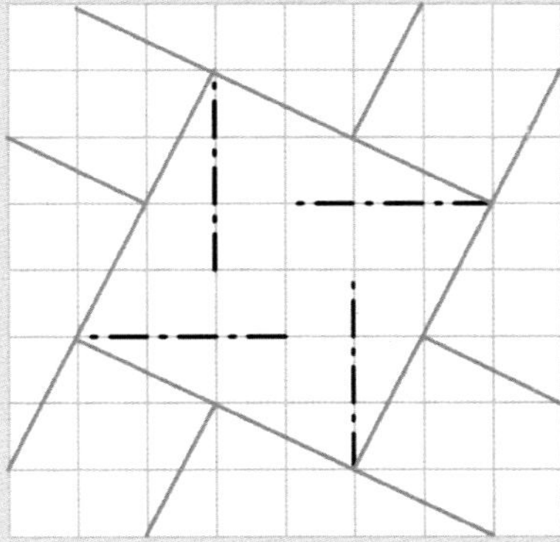

Force the mountains on the grid.

You can stop here if you want the four corners of the star to have curved surfaces.

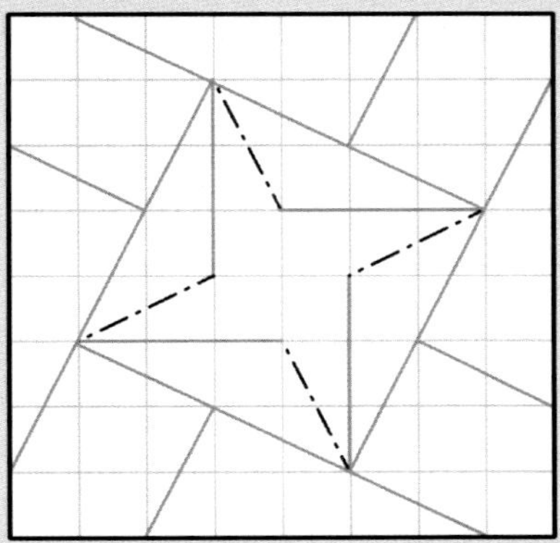

If you do not like curved lines on your molecules, you can add these lines. This will create a sharper molecule and enhance the similarity to **Mexico** (page 145). They are not the same, especially in the way they overlap each other.

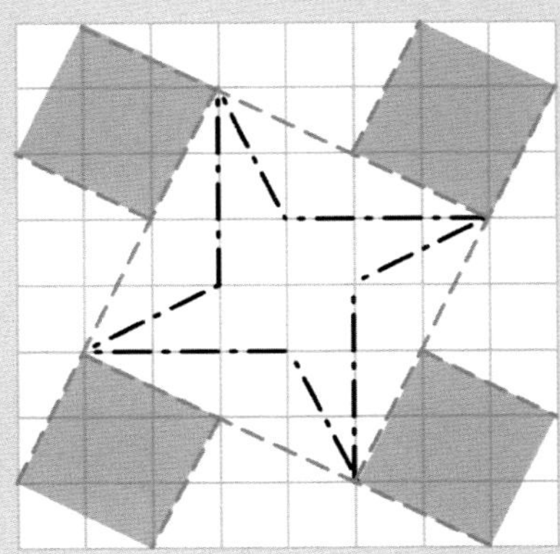

This is the complete set of folds needed for the collapse.

The dark areas are going to stay flat on the table during the collapse.

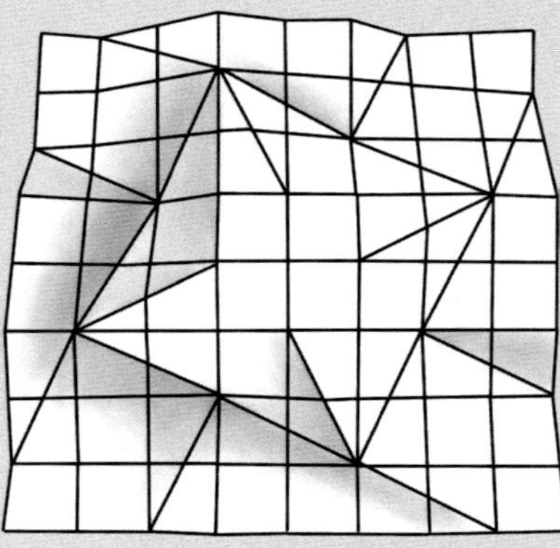

The collapse is fun and unique. All you need to do is to put four fingers, one on each corner, and bring them together, toward the center.

Let the inner part rise.

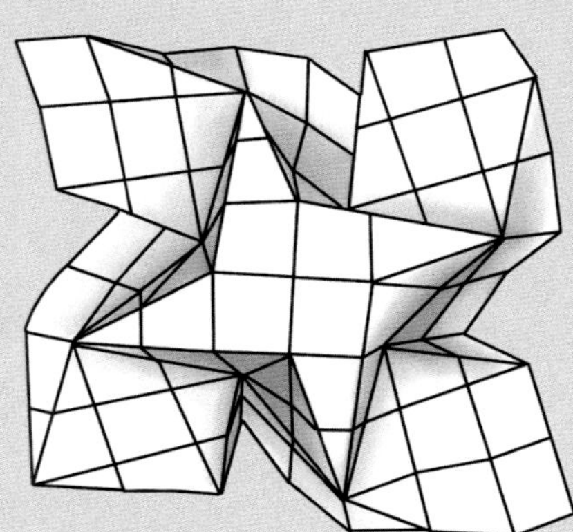

Fully Collapsed!

Note that parts of the four adjacent molecules are raised as well!

2 by 2 Molecules

Use a grid of 14 by 14.

Try to use the method to collapse the single molecule here as well! The paper will deform and won't be easy to handle, so consider using Blu Tack to hold the folded molecules to a surface below.

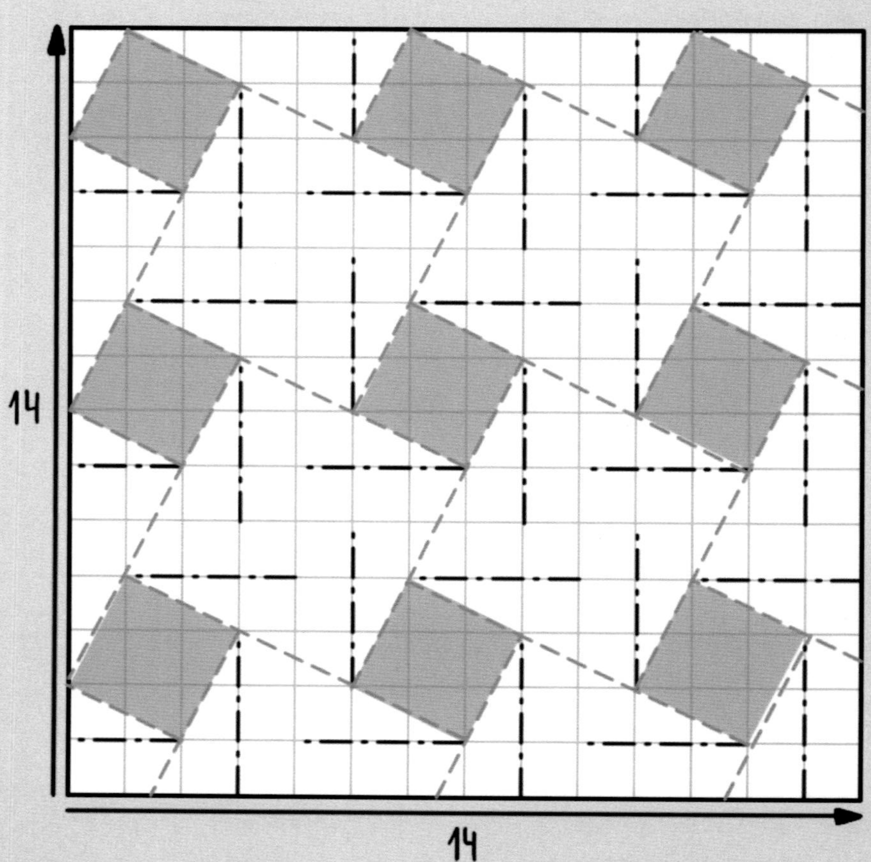

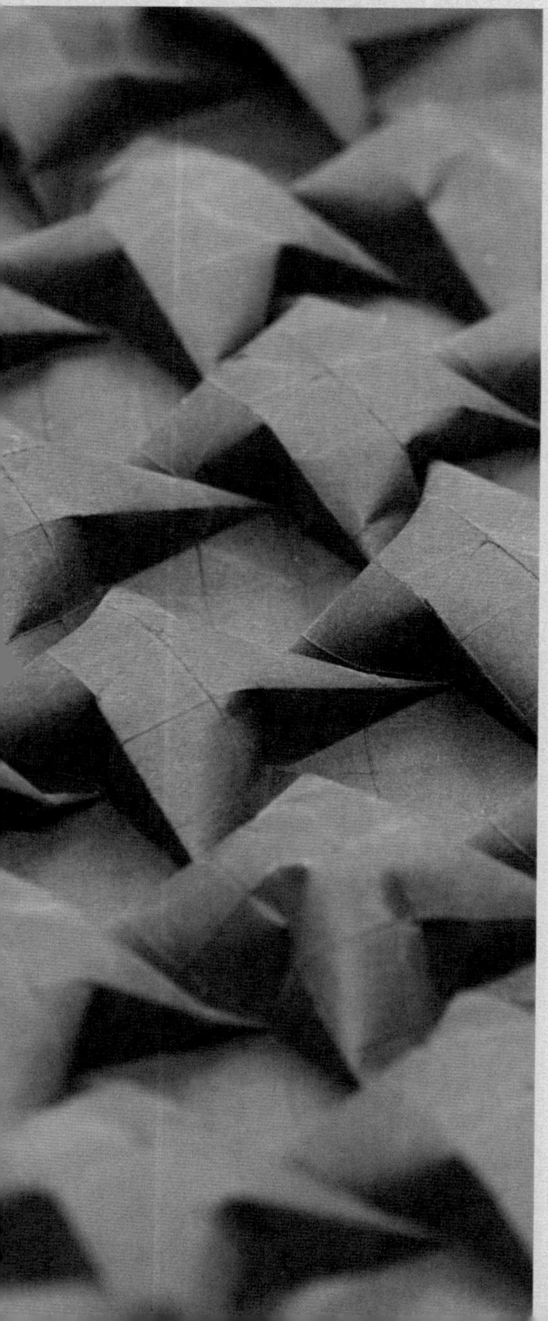

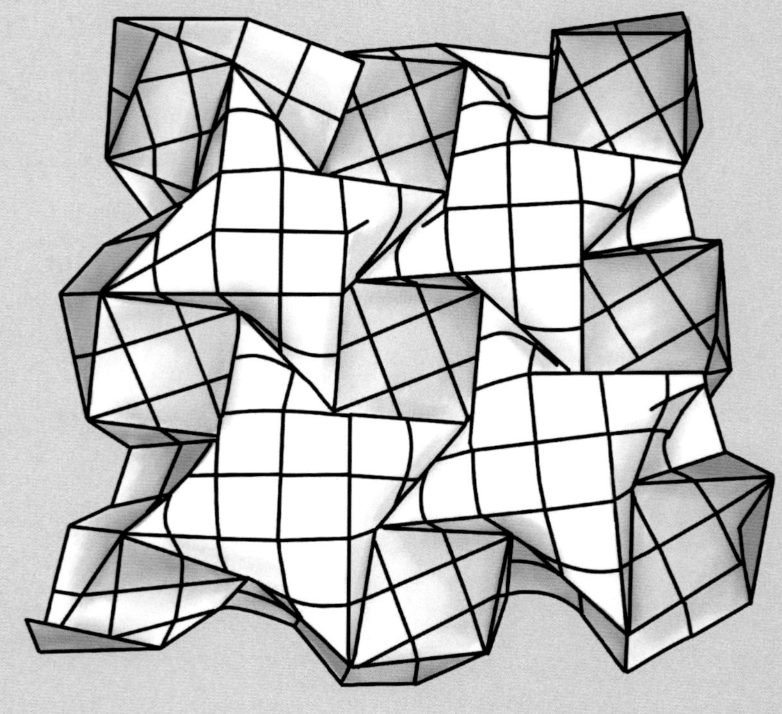

4 by 4 Molecules

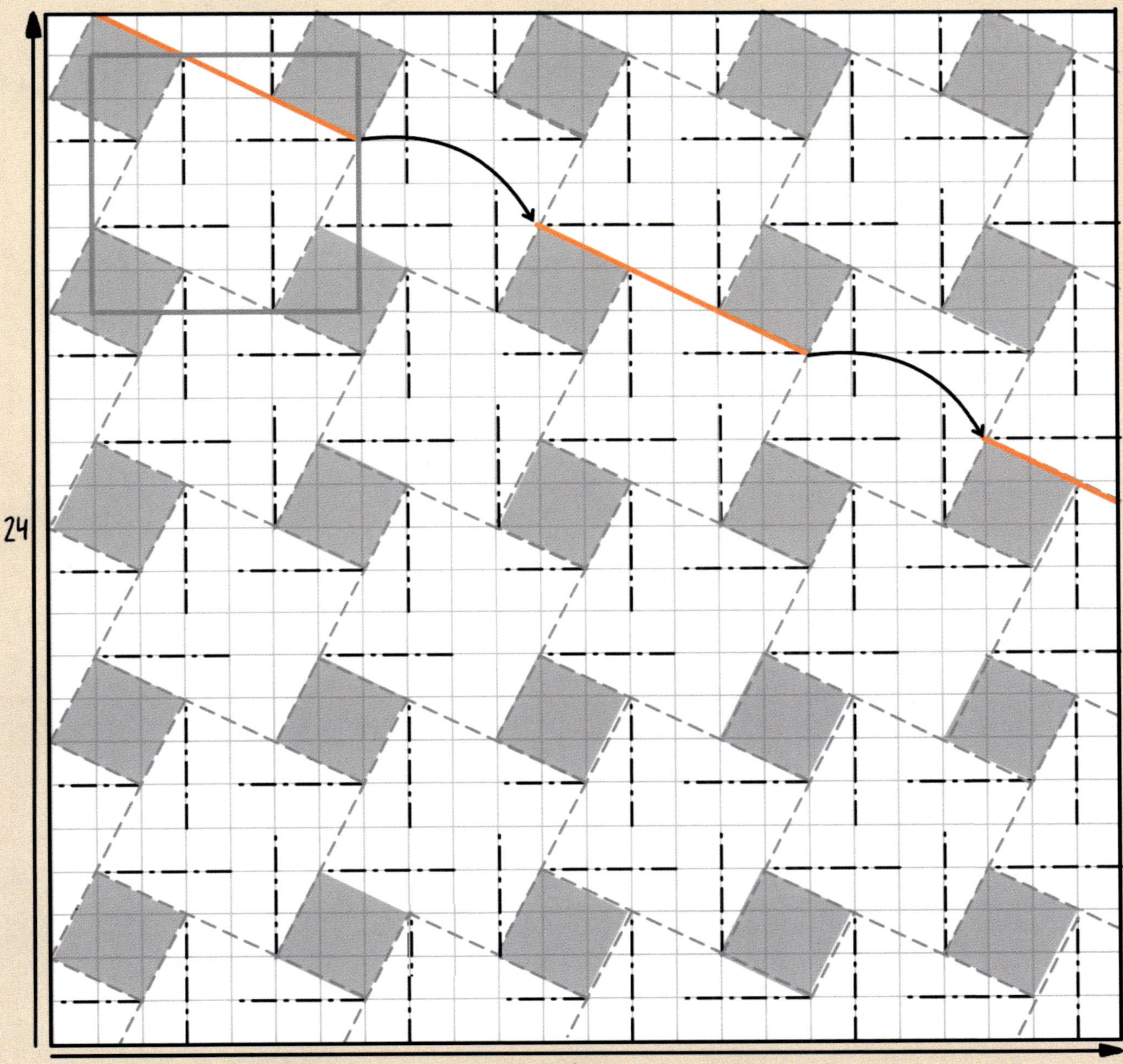

Make a grid of 24 by 24. There is no frame to this type of molecule.

The formula for the grid is 4 × 6 = 24. Since there is no natural border to this molecule, you can choose where to cut the edges of the full project you want to make.

The final result will be about 20 squares wide.

The pattern for the creases is fold 6, skip 4.

Start with the orange lines. If you count five units to the right, you will find the next set of lines to fold.

Collapse in rows, like always.

When you finish, take a look at the backside. Isn't it the pattern of the **Waterbomb** tessellation (page 29), with an extra space between the molecules?

7 7 Roses

I found this model on the way to the first Convention for Creators, I organized in Lyon, 2017.

Looking at the crease pattern it is hard to imagine what will be the outcome, and I was highly surprised by it, and happy, as I do think it is one of my best! Of course, beauty has its price! The collapse is one of the most demanding in the book, especially if you do not add spaces between the molecules.

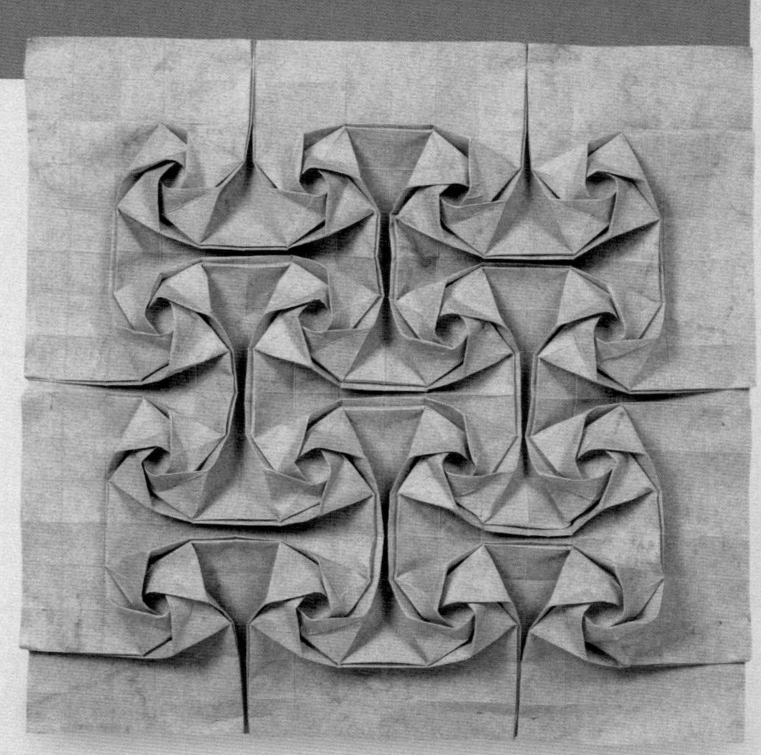

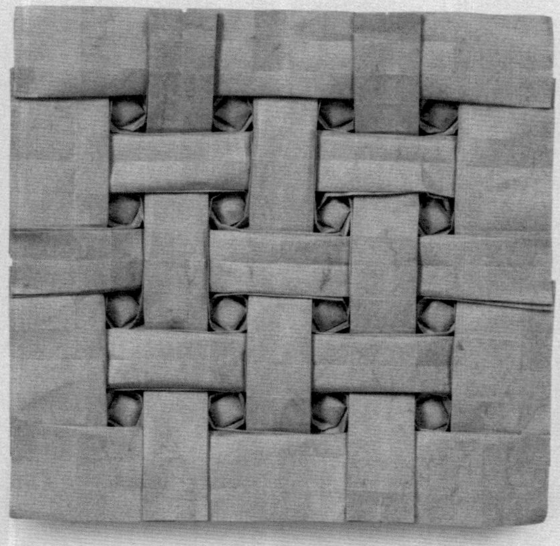

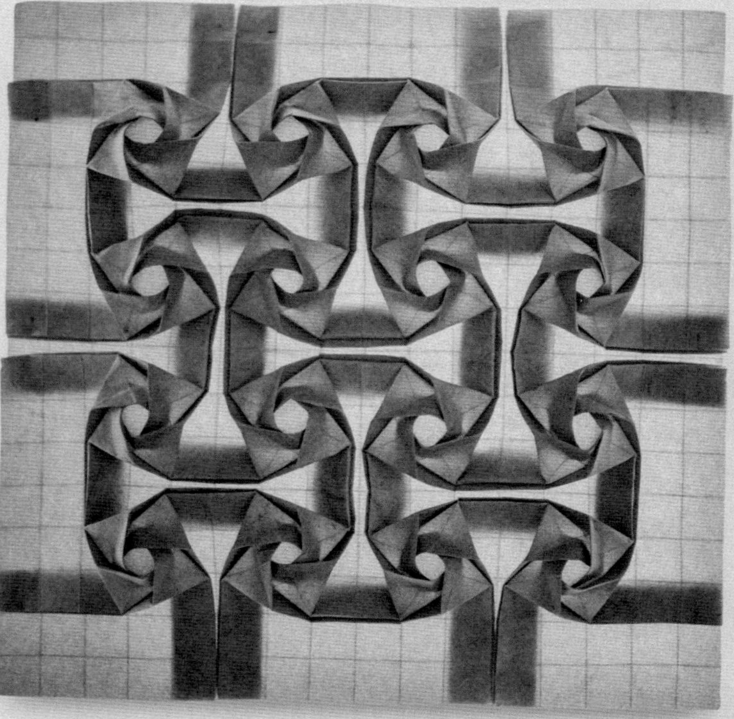

Top right: recto view of a 4 by 4–molecule Roses tessellation.

Left: verso view of a 4 by 4–molecule Roses tessellation.

Bottom right: recto view with back-light.

The Single Molecule

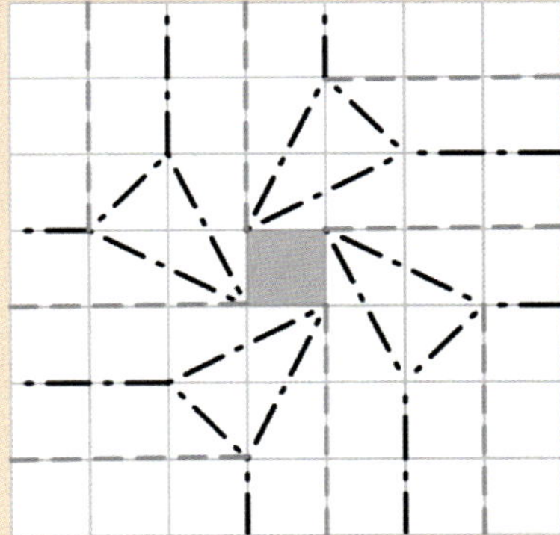

The molecule size is 7 by 7.

There is a double pleat on the edges.

The shrinkage ratio is 7:3.

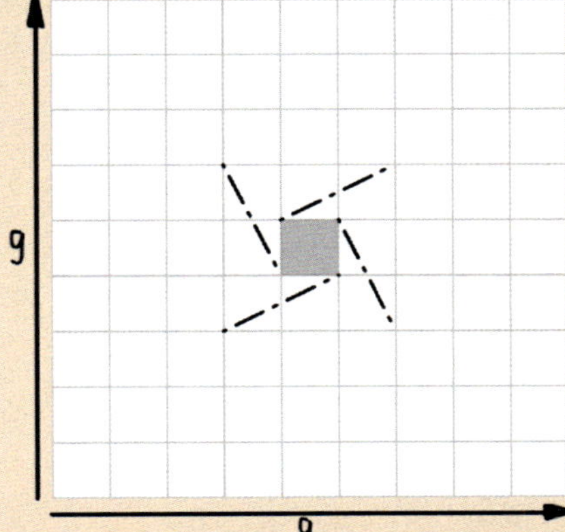

Start with a grid of 9 by 9, to allow extra rows and columns on all four sides.

Force the four mountains. This is just like the **Quadilic** molecule (see *Origami Tessellations for Everyone*).

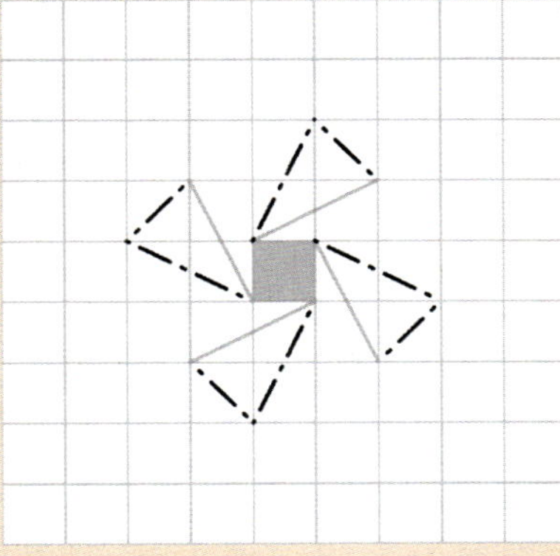

Complete the pre-creases by turning each mountain into a triangle of folds.

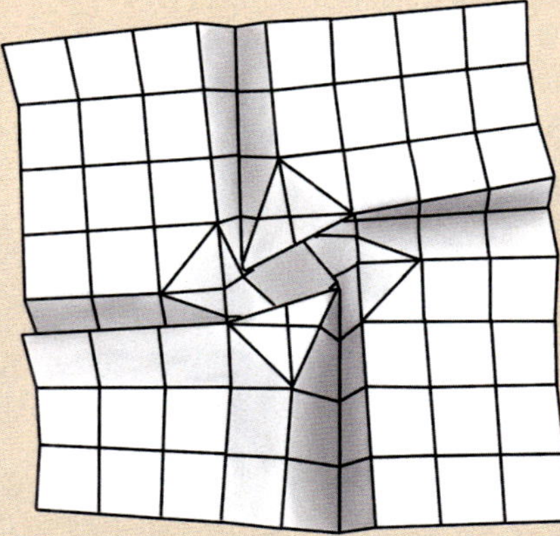

Almost there!

Rotate the mountains anticlockwise, so the shorter mountain (two-unit length) is on top of the long one (three-unit length).

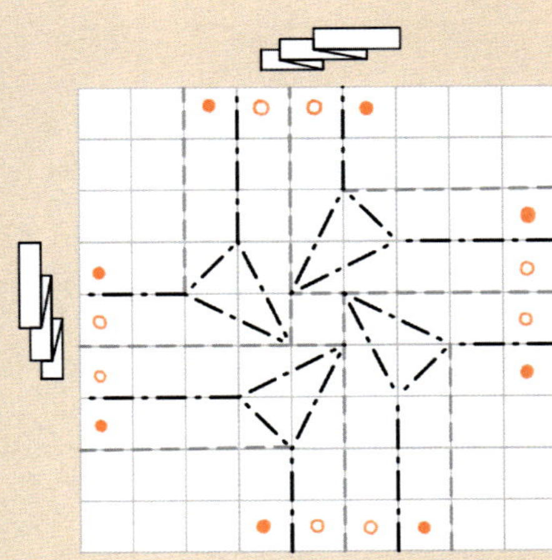

All the needed creases.

Start the collapse by following the zig-zag pattern of the pleats. Try and pinch all the orange circles together. While doing so, bring up the four triangles, but make sure the center square remains on the table.

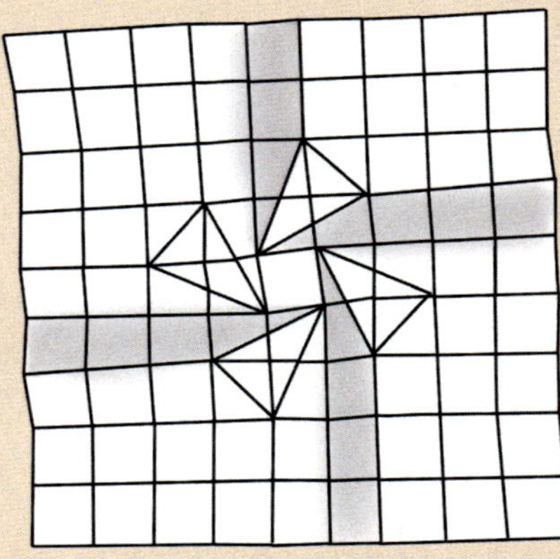

In process.

Bring the pairs of mountains to meet each other.

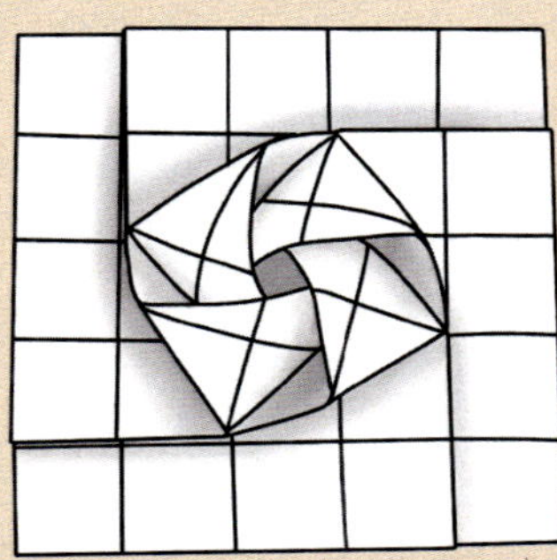

Fully collapsed!

2 by 2 Molecules

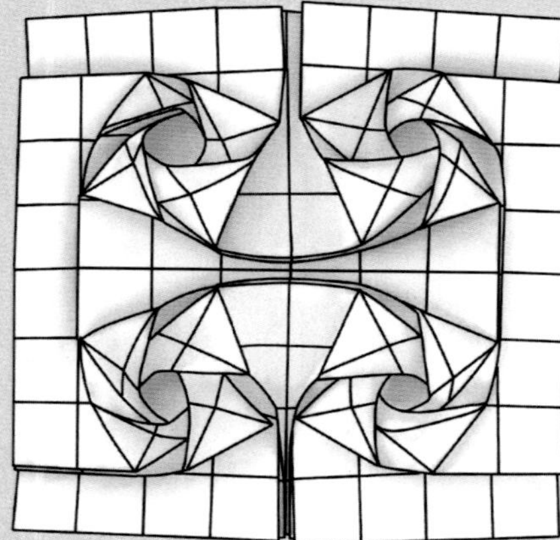

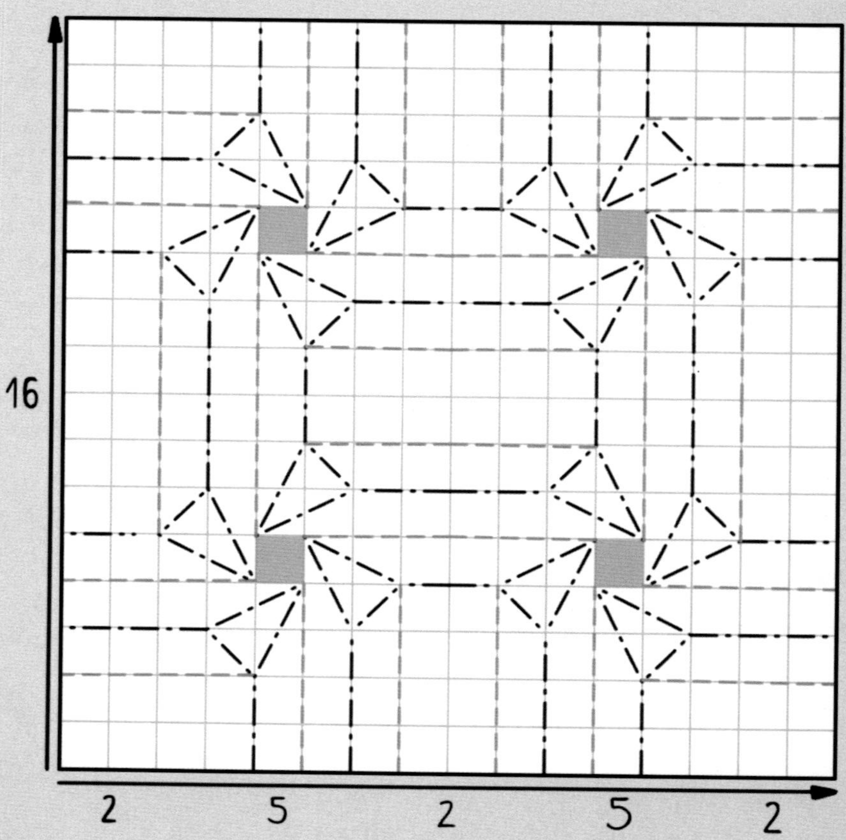

Use a grid of 16 by 16.

Start with the edges, and arrange all the layers accordingly. Form the triangles of each molecule, and sink the centers. You must put in order the adjacent molecules for every molecule you try to collapse. Otherwise, it will be impossible to arrange the layers on the inner sides of the molecule.

4 by 4 Molecules

Make a grid of 32 by 32, allowing for a two-unit width of a frame.

The formula for the grid is 2 + 4 × 7 + 2 = 32.

The final result will be 16-square wide.

Start the pre-creases with the orange mountains. That will help you mark all the molecules on the grid. Now add to it all the light blue ones. You can also complete the triangles with the mountain lines at the same swipe, but it may be too confusing.

There are no shortcuts to this phase.

Start the collapse at the corner and complete row by row. Do not force the edges with pins to allow some freedom to the paper when you try to work on the inner molecules. Always prepare at least the adjacent molecules before you try to collapse the one you work on.

Be patient, as this is a difficult collapse! You may want to try the same pattern with a single space between every two molecules.

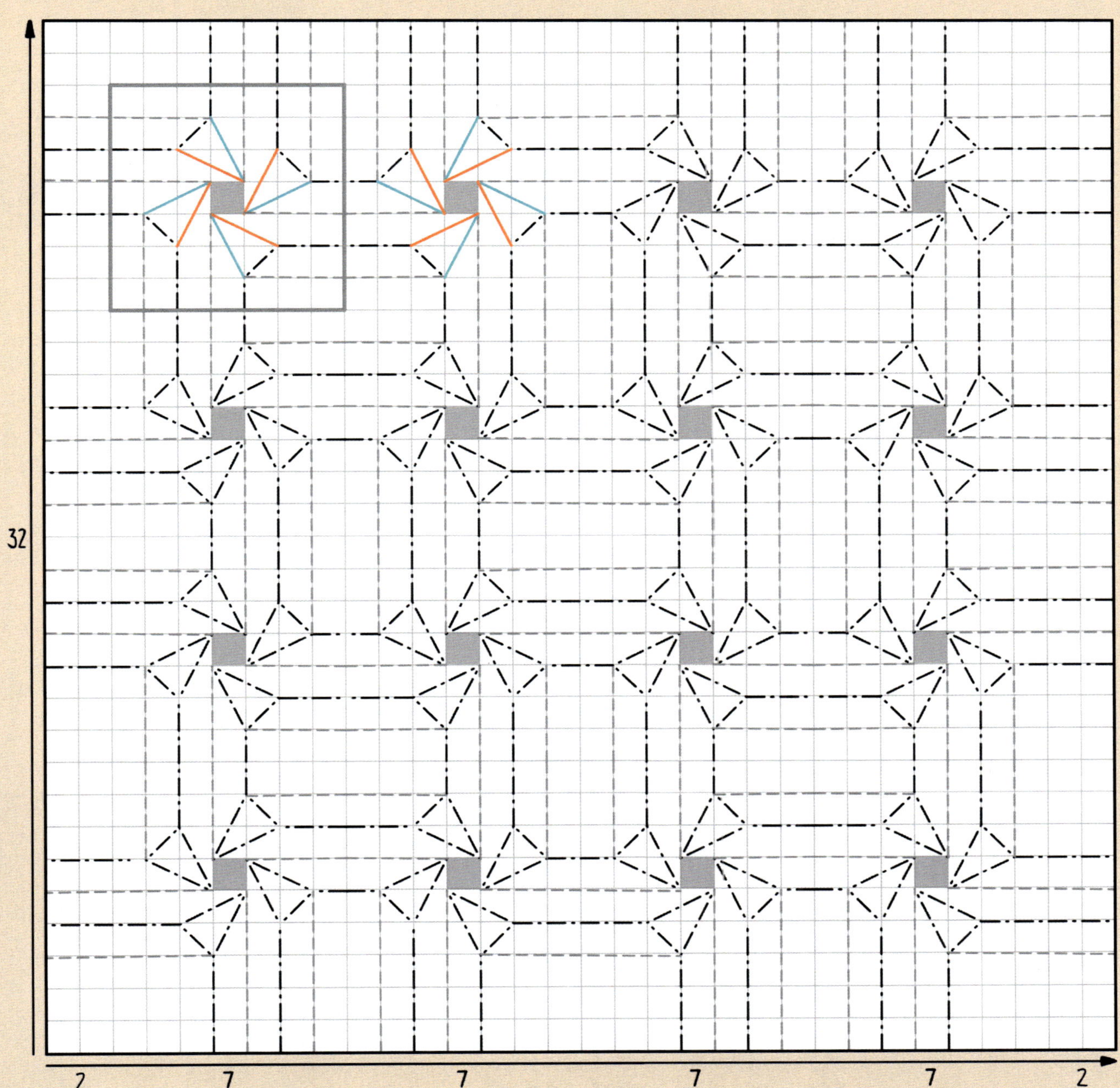
32
2
7
7
7
7
2

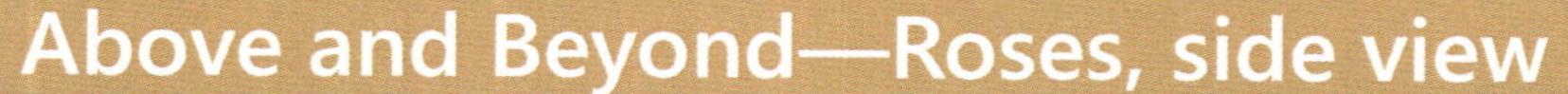

Above and Beyond—Roses, side view

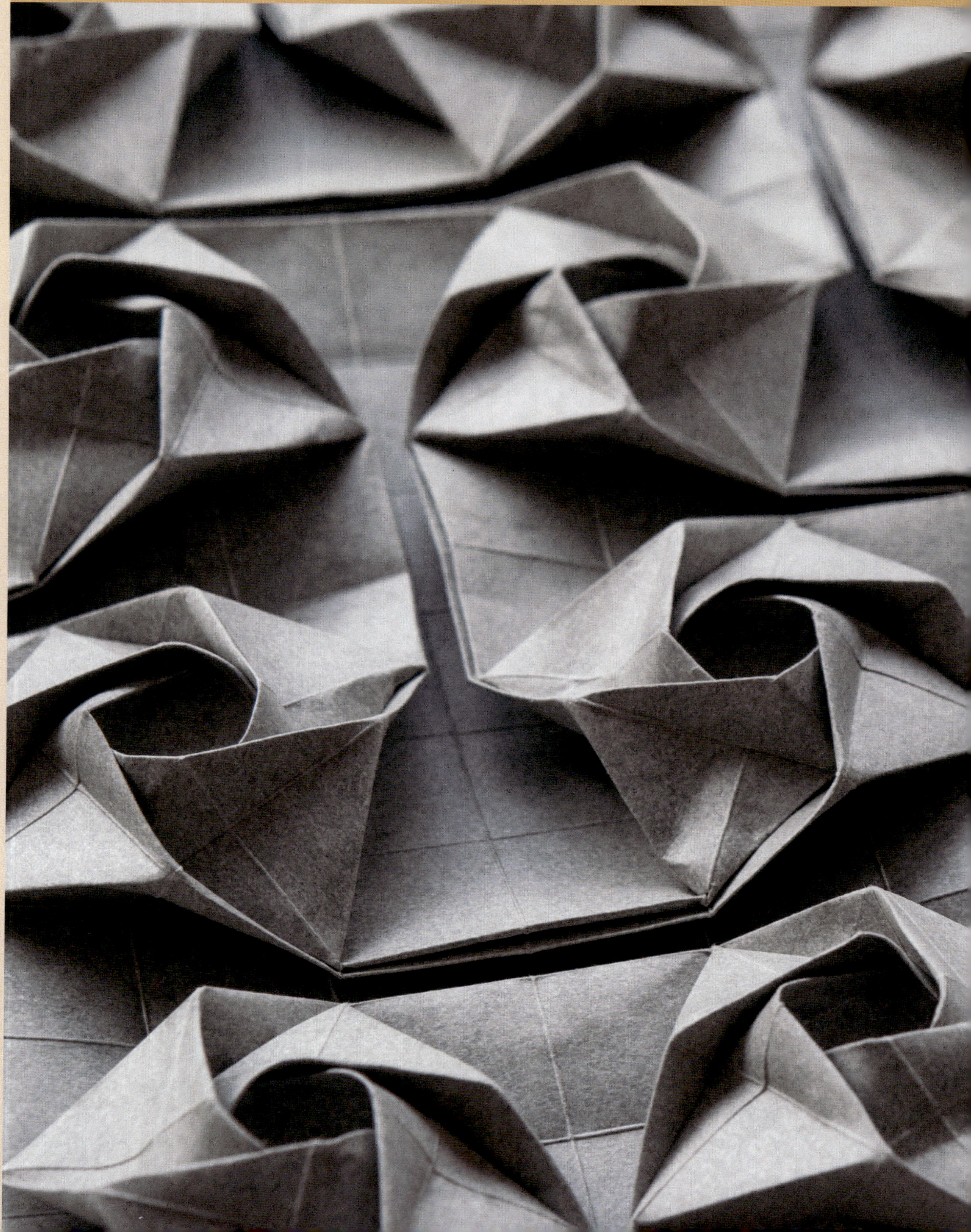

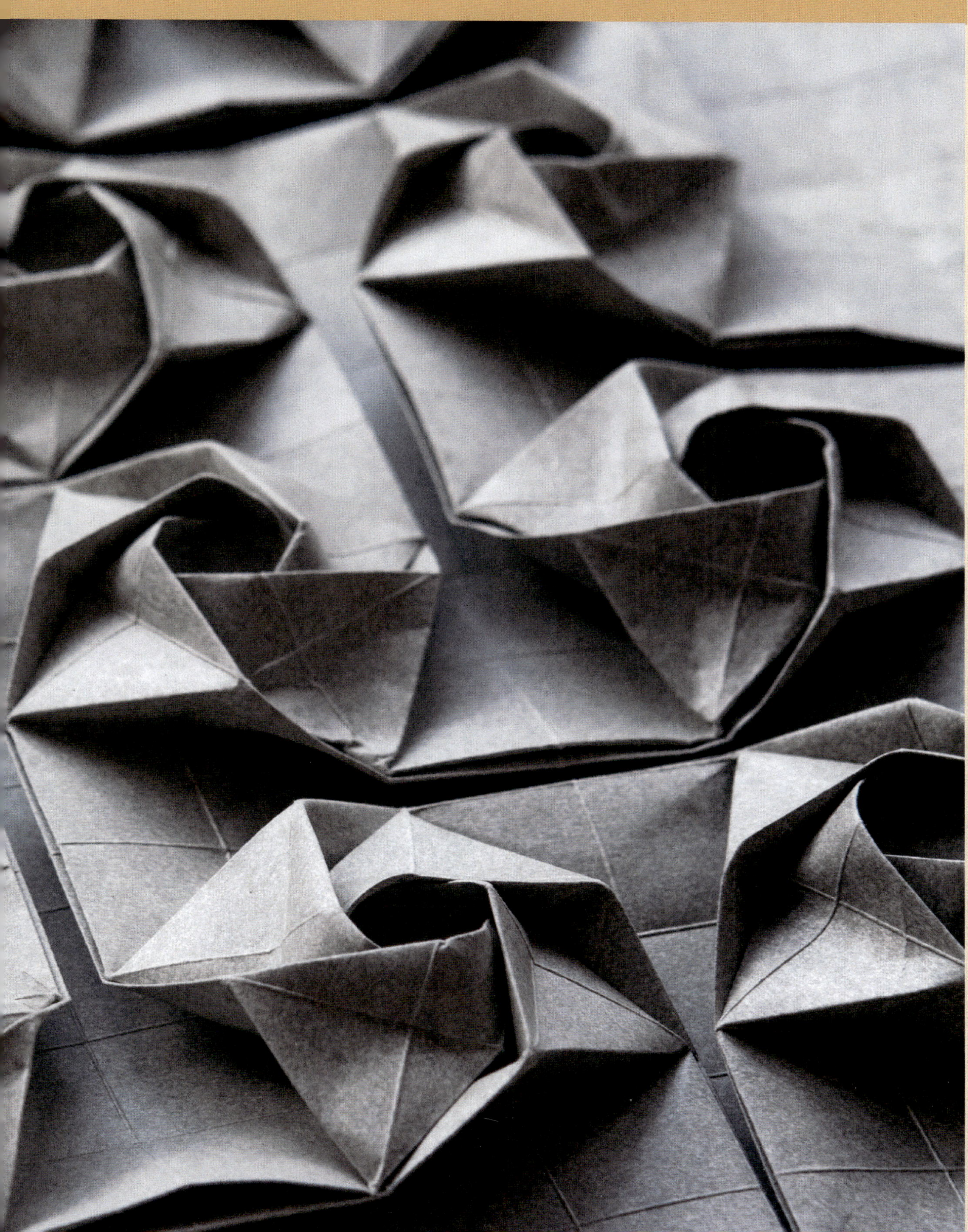

More from Ilan Garibi:

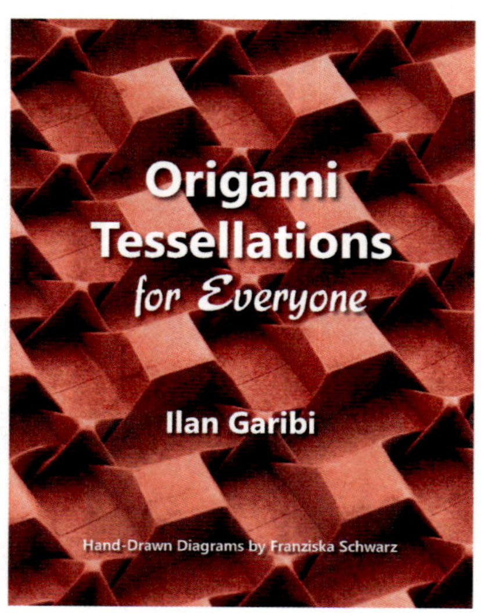

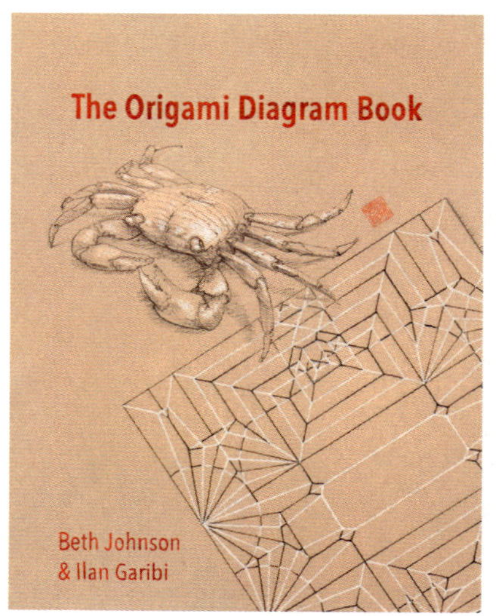

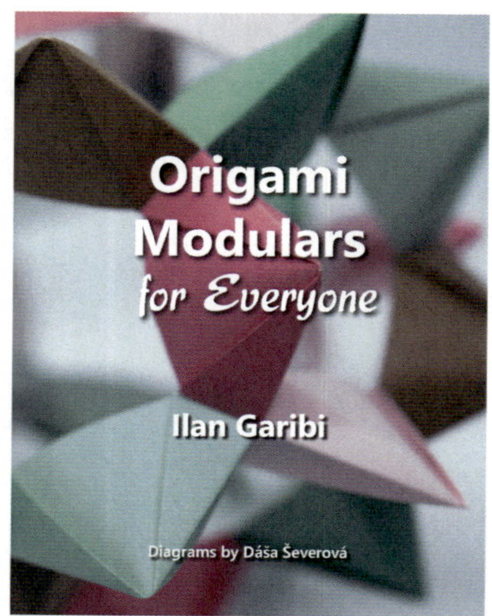

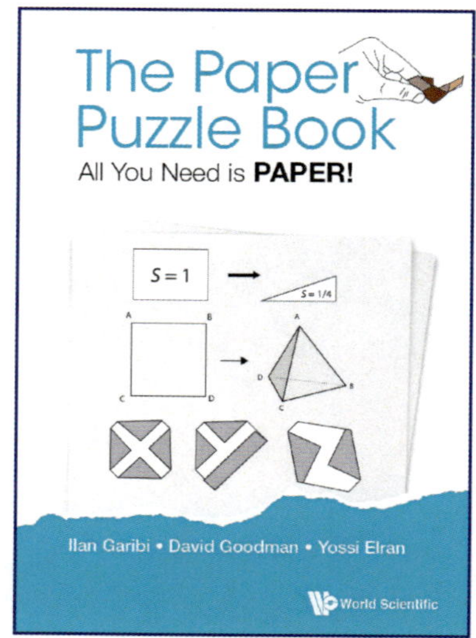

Made in the USA
Las Vegas, NV
05 July 2022

51144330R00105